DĀNA

Dāna

RECIPROCITY AND PATRONAGE IN BUDDHISM

edited by

ANAND SINGH

PRIMUS BOOKS

PRIMUS BOOKS
An imprint of Ratna Sagar P. Ltd.
Virat Bhavan
Mukherjee Nagar Commercial Complex
Delhi 110 009

Offices at

CHENNAI LUCKNOW
AGRA AHMEDABAD BANGALORE COIMBATORE
DEHRADUN GUWAHATI HYDERABAD JAIPUR JALANDHAR
KANPUR KOCHI KOLKATA MADURAI MUMBAI
PATNA RANCHI VARANASI

First published 2017

SBN: 978-93-84092-32-0 (hardback)
ISBN: 978-93-86552-39-6 (POD)

Published by Primus Books

Laser typeset in Times New Roman
by Guru Typograph Technology
Crossings Republic, Ghaziabad 201 009

Printed and bound in India by Replika Press Pvt. Ltd.

Contents

Editor and Contributors

ANAND SINGH, Associate Professor, School of Buddhist Studies and Civilization, Gautam Buddha University, Greater Noida

R.M. BHARADWAJ, Associate Professor, Department of History, Deen Dayal College, University of Delhi, Delhi

UMA CHAKRAVARTI, Professor, Miranda House, University of Delhi, Delhi

NEEKEE CHATURVEDI, Assistant Professor, Department of History, University of Rajasthan, Jaipur

PADMASIRI DE SILVA, Professor, Monash University, Australia

ARUNA K. GAMAGE, Lecturer, University of Kelaniya, Sri Lanka

SAIYID ZAHEER HUSAIN JAFRI, Professor, Department of History, University of Delhi, Delhi

VIDULA JAYASWAL, Professor, Department of AIH and Archaeology, Banaras Hindu University, Varanasi

MOTIUR RAHMAN KHAN, Assistant Professor, University of Delhi, Delhi

SARITA KHETTRY, Associate Professor, Department of Ancient Indian History, Vishwa-Bharati, Shantiniketan

KRISHNA KUMAR MANDAL, Associate Professor, Department of History, Tilka Manjhi University, Bhagalpur

K.T.S. SARAO, Professor, Department of Buddhist Studies, University of Delhi, Delhi

PRASHANT SRIVASTAVA, Professor, Department of AIH and Archaeology, University of Lucknow, Lucknow

KIRAN KUMAR THAPLYAL, Professor, Department of AIH and Archaeology, University of Lucknow, Lucknow

SUSHMA TRIVEDI, Associate Professor, University of Lucknow, Lucknow

Preface

THIS VOLUME ON *dāna* would not have been possible without genius and scholarly contribution of scholars who took immense pain to give their papers. The book is structured in such a way that it has covered nearly all dimensions on *dāna* in Buddhism. I am grateful that some of the most imminent scholars from India and abroad have contributed their papers in this book. The book is edited with the objective to explore and analyse the various dimensions of *dāna* in Buddhism through an integral approach to include a vast corpus of resources comprising both literary and archaeological ones. The book encompasses previous works on *dāna*, especially in Buddhism, given the fact that studies on *dāna* have not been given due attention in the past because scholars working on Buddhism prioritize their work on studies of monasteries, sects and philosophical tenets. Sometimes it has even been argued that *dāna* cannot be studied as a distinct phenomenon because its various threads are virtually tied to monastic and philosophical studies. In fact, the precise way in which the various domains of *dāna* are placed encourage us to explore various kinds of norms and traditions that *dāna* tradition has in Buddhism. The papers included in the book present more concise and up-to-date information on reciprocity and patronages in different Buddhist institutions, focussing on various traditions and practices that have emerged since the origin of Buddhism till its downfall in the Indian subcontinent.

The chapters are concerned with the study of *dāna* tradition in Buddhism with a special focus on the Indian subcontinent and trace the evolution and maturity of its different rules and practices. They cover conventional tradition as well as modern ethical approaches to learn the various forms as well as the historical development of *dāna* in Buddhism. The term *dāna* is used here as a generic reference, as it is traditionally used in Buddhism. The practice of giving is universally identified as one of the most basic human virtues, a quality that explores the core of one's humanity and one's capacity for self-transcendence. In the teaching of the Buddha, too, the practice of *dāna* earns a place of eminence, one which put it as being in a sense the foundation and seed of spiritual attainment. The character and nature of *dāna* changed when settled monasticism developed at the expense of the process of *dāna*, with the earliest form of monasticization of Buddhism that was not sedentary.

When the Buddha renounced home to become a wanderer, an overwhelming transformation occurred in his life. When he became the Buddha, he laid the foundation of *saṃgha* which was based on the *dāna* tradition. The nature of *dāna* changed from time to time from door-to-door personal begging, to patronages and grants by kings and merchants. Due to such large grants, the Mahāvihāra tradition took organizational shape in the Gupta age when the constellation of monasteries came under one single umbrella in Nālandā. It introduced new values in monastic life as a prelude to the transformation of the conventional character of monasteries, changing the orientation of Buddhist learning from 'study for faith' to 'study for knowledge'. Some of the chapters in this volume examine such traditions in Nālandā and Vikramśila Mahāvihāra.

I wish to express my sincere gratitude to all who have contributed their valuable papers in this book. Professor Uma Chakravarti has contributed a paper on my request, I am truly thankful to her for such a kind gesture. I must express my sincere thanks to Professor S.Z.H. Jafri and Professor Prashant Srivastava who have helped me in many ways to publish this book. Professor Padmasiri de Silva not only contributed a paper but also advised me on some of the topics; I would like to express my gratitude to him. Professor Siddharth Singh is always generous to me with all academic help; I thank him for his support. Dr K.K. Mandal, Dr Gurmet Dorjey, and Dr R.P.K. Singh have advised me on a number of issues and I would like to thank them as well. I would also like to thank the Archaeological Survey of India, New Delhi, which has granted permission to use the photograph that has been used on the jacket of the book.

Finally, I must express sincere thanks to my mother, brothers, and colleagues in the university for their immense support.

Gautam Budh Nagar
Greater Noida

ANAND SINGH

1

Introduction

ANAND SINGH

DĀNA IS AN unfailing source of study and knowledge of Buddhism in the broadest sense. In spite of the fact that *dāna* was the core of Buddhism throughout its development, it finds less attention in studies done in the field of Indian Buddhism. Rather, its study has been put to the background of the canvas on which the history of Buddhism unfolded. Often researchers in the Buddhist studies focus on doctrinal expositions, classification of conventions, construction of models, and theories on nature and characteristics of Buddhist sects and canonical literature. It is significant to put studies on *dāna* at the centre stage because it embodies virtues, regulations, and procedures in which the cradle of Buddhism evolved.

It is a fact that studies on *dāna* have not been given much attention in the past because the scholars working on Buddhism consider it non-specific. It may be argued that *dāna* cannot be studied as a distinct phenomenon because its various dimensions are virtually tied at every level and strand of Buddhist history. But, in the web of Indian Buddhism in which they have been embedded, is far from seamless. In fact, the precise way in which the various domains of *dāna* are placed within the various kinds of norms and traditions, almost always invite reflections of its characteristics. These are often tension, opposition, coordination, competition, and conciliation with or without an obvious solution or explanation. In the study of *dāna*, an exploration of such anomalies and reverberations could provide considerable insight into the formative process. The examination and analysis should be integrative and coherent with the phenomenon under consideration. The present work takes up some of the fundamental questions which have played an important role in shaping and defining the different dimensions of *dāna* throughout the long history of Buddhism. It helps us to understand the rational, ethical, and philosophical ideology behind the system of *dāna*. The interpretation of *dāna* as a 'give and take' or pure economic exchange only emphasizes its mythic, cultic, and non-religious dimensions. *Dāna* occupies the centre stage in Buddhism because it does continue and remain important in setting the parameters for origin, development, continuity, and decline of *saṃgha*. The study also raises related questions of the kind of study and evidences that have been used in attempting to understand the significance of the different threads of *dāna*. The type of evidences one chooses to examine significance could affect the conclusions. The *Vinaya* of the age of the Buddha could not satisfactorily explain the *dāna* and patronage, where the *Mūlasarvāstivāda Vinaya* is the main source. The topographical conditions, geographical barriers, nature of economy vary from region to region and when Buddhism expanded along the time, the rules and regulations were being transformed and modified to adjust such precarious situations. The Pāli *Nikāyas* have different interpretation from their Tibetan translations. So, it is pertinent here to emphasize that such anomalies should be kept in mind while developing the hypothesis on *dāna* with an attempt to put together the various dimensions into a coherent picture. It requires an understanding of the significance of the rules framed by the Buddha and to pay special attention to questions, occupying from appearance of discrepancies and contradictions, both within one text and across the line of the whole tradition.

The practice of *dāna* has been found within the whole corpus of Buddhist teachings in the Pāli scriptures. It seeks to understand the socio-economic as well as religio-spiritual functions underlying the Buddhist understanding of *dāna.* Primarily, through Pāli texts and some epigraphic evidences, aspects of the relationship of the laity and the *saṃgha* within the framework of *dāna* have also been dealt with. It has been argued that through *dānadhamma*, the society took care of the material needs of the spiritual community of Buddhist monks and the nuns and the practice was sustained by forging a socio-economic relationship between the two. The monks and the nuns were expected to bear dignified demeanour to strengthen social esteem associated with the giving of alms. Besides social and economic premises, *dānadhamma* also had spiritual dimensions. It helped the giver in attaining loftiness of character. According to the Buddhist scriptures, *dāna* helps to overcome the first root of greed—*jayet kadaryaṁ dānena.*[1] There is another Pāli term, *cāga,* an ethical quality rooted in the wholesome root (*kuśalakamma*) of non-greed (*alobha*). It leads to a disposition for making gifts in accordance with one's ability[2] and elevates its possessor to a higher spiritual level.[3] In describing the various types of virtues in the *Majjhima Nikāya*, the gift, the donor and the recipient are imbued with ethical connotations and one should strive to practise this *dhamma* accordingly. *Dāna* manifests that practising generosity led one to spiritual growth and was to be pursued conscientiously by the members of the laity as well as the *saṃgha*; the latter practised it mainly in the form of *dhammadāna.*

Buddhist *dāna* is different from other traditions as its socio-economic implications are as important as its spiritual significance. It cannot be simply explained as giving or getting, but is a thorough psychosomatic act, involving both mind and body at the same level. It further demands certain qualities to be cultivated by both the donor and the donee to become deserving for the act. One of the cardinal beliefs of Buddhism is that *dāna* is always an unhindered source of merit, even if a person throws the rinse of his bowl into the village pond with the thought that whatever animal living in there may feed on this, he incurs merit.[4] But the highest benefits are to be reaped by the pairing of an immaculate donor and a working donee. This requires mental and physical purification of both the participants. On the part of donor, the first step is preparation where he needs to get rid of ill will, should have no rush of passion and should develop a mind filled with loving kindness.[5] The second stage relates to the performance of the act itself and five right ways are suggested to do this, i.e. to give with confidence, to give carefully, to give quickly, to give firmly and to give, not pertaining to injury to oneself or the donee.[6] The outcome and impact of the practice of *dāna* in the prescribed manner is noticed in the third stage. As an outcome, the donor becomes an *ariya* disciple and as impact, permanent signs of change and consequent characteristics are visible in the donor's persona. It is elaborated in the *Aṅguttara Nikāya* that a noble disciple gives up the taking of life, gives up the taking of what is not given, gives up sexual misconduct, gives up intoxicating drinks and drugs and abstains from all of these.[7] The donor thus emanates as a person free from all sorts of defilements and evils. One issue that Buddhist texts are particular about is the practice of *dāna* as a regular habit for lay worshippers as well as householders. In the process, the state of mind and body evoked for the performance of *dāna*, becomes the permanent state of mind and body of the donor. This sort of training brings in positive orientation in the thoughts of the donor and his resultant actions generally conform to the right conduct and Buddhist ethics in specific. The psychological aspect of the *kamma* or deed is held as the most important paradigm in the evaluation of an act.

The recipient is likewise important in the conduct of donation. It is firmly believed that worthier the recipient, greater the merit accrued by the donor. Sometimes, it is felt that attaching too much importance to the role of the recipient in determining the fruits of *dāna*, reduces the value of ethical intention of *dāna*. Again the recipient's responsibility is contradicted because the donor chooses the donee, therefore, the onus solely lies with the donor to fructify his donation. If this aspect is examined in a broader horizon, the recipient emerges as a conditioning factor for the progression of *dāna*. The emphasis on worthiness of the donee is not 'counterintuitive' but it complements the donor's intention. The first and foremost requisite for the donor is that he should have confidence, and one of the sources of his confidence is the recipient whose response, attainments, and spiritual stature encourage him to follow the path. There is a correlational equation between the two hinging on the crux of 'worthiness'. The worthy donee strengthens the resolve and the inclination of the donor, thereby producing more religious merit for the donor and more *dāna* for the monk or the *saṃgha*.

Dāna in Buddhism has not been enlisted as an element for the realization of *nibbāna* but its role to tread along the way to *nibbāna* unbounded. It is one of the three meritorious deeds (*punnakiriyavatthu*), among the four types of benevolence (*sanghavatthu*), and the first of ten *pāramitas* (*dāna-pāramita*) and is identified with generosity (*cāga*).[8] Buddhist literature mentions the category of donees such as *samanas*, brāhmaṇas, *kapana* (destitute), *vanibbaka* (forest dweller), *yācaka* (beggar), etc.[9] The *Aṅguttara Nikāya* mentions that the *ahuneyyaggi* (parents), *gahapataggi* (family) and *dakkineyyaggi* (mendicants) must be cared for.[10] The *Saṁyutta Nikāya* says that *dāna* should be given to the monks who get rid of the five mental hindrances (*nivarana*) and cultivate *śila*, *samādhi*, *paňňa*, *vimuttī*, and *vimuttinanadassana*.[11] The *saṃgha* is considered to be the best field for *dāna* (*annuttaram punnakkhettam lokaśa*) because it comprises worthy monks.[12] With the emergence of Mahāyāna, the field of *dāna* was widened and the *Bodhisattva* was expected to give food, silver, gold, elephants, his family members, his body organs, and even his whole body as an altruism and generosity. The best gifts were the ones that came from the people holding meagre amount, as the rich could afford to donate some part of their earning but the poor could not. So, a small gift from the economically deprived was highly commendable rather than high rewards from the affluent.[13]

This whole procedure of *dāna* contributes not only in shaping up of a perfect donor but also a good citizen of the society. This behavioural transformation of an individual as the donor assisted in maintaining the social order. In this sense, Buddhist *dāna* seems to be very close to the ideal of the civil society in present days, where individuals care for each other and care for the interest of each other. The original concept of civil society referred to the ways through which rules were imposed to avert social conflict by means of voluntary agencies that restricted citizens from harming each other. This is the very outcome of perpetual practise of *dāna* and as such Buddhist *dāna* with all its paraphernalia has all potential to assume the same function which the non-governmental agencies play in the modern societies. This reflection of Buddhist *dāna* has not been hitherto paid much attention. Such an attempt would be relevant for the present where peace-building and conflict resolution are the most deliberate issues.

In the economic sphere, *dāna* is seen as an instrument of redistribution of wealth. This is supported by a synchronized growth of economy and influx of donations received by the *saṃgha*, especially in the Gangetic plains and western India. How the wealth was channelized is seen in a very early example. The Buddha allows monks to wear robes given by the laities,[14] as there were reverberations that people were eager to make donations to the *saṃgha* but could not find the ways as the monks wore *paṅsukūla* rags collected from dust heaps or funeral grounds. As the follow up of this provision, it is narrated that within no time, thousands of robes were donated by the lay people. Buddhist *dāna* presents a cyclic model of economy which is a very carefully devised composition of corporeality and spirituality. Herein, the outflow of wealth assured the inflow of wealth in its multiples, along with other benefits. In an exposition to avoid conflicting situations, the Buddha says that, as long as the Vajjiputtas make sure that monks are provided amply and they live in ease and comfort, there is no chance of their decline but their prosperity may increase further and further.[15] Consequently, the accumulation of wealth in a few hands was prevented and this was well evident in the professions and class distribution of the donors at early Buddhist sites. The most redeeming feature of *dāna*, in economic context was that the wealth received by the monastic institutions was neither blocked nor pulled out of economy. Rather, making use of it as per monastic laws, mostly the surplus was put to some productive use and was circulated back into the economy. This is an established fact that the monasteries took active part in trade. The trans-Asiatic Silk route thrived in the reflected glory of Buddhism and moneylending was used for regular activities of *saṃgha*. This is often severely criticized and treated as morally deviational behaviour of monks. If this situation is viewed the other way round, it may be realized that the *saṃgha* actually followed the dictum of '*Bahujana hitaya, Bahujana sukhaya*'. A positive approach and methodology is needed to harness the real impact of the utilization of *dāna*-wealth, on the economic affairs of the society.

Dāna studies often miss the dynamism of doctrine which is too obvious in the linear movement of *dāna*, in terms of acceptances, from *nissaya* to *parikhara* and from *parikhara* to *vihāra*. Even in the earliest phase of the coagulation of the idea, the pace of evolution was too swift and galloping changes were brought about. This dynamism and constant evolutionary process is inherent in the procedural way of Buddhism. He believed that rules should be formulated as and when the need arose. The Buddha, at first, did not prescribe any rules for the monks at the time of the inception of the *saṃgha*. When a perplexed Sāriputta, an esteemed disciple of the Buddha brought this to his notice, the Buddha replied that no rules will be laid down until and unless the monks committed offence. The first set of rules came into existence after twenty years of the foundation of the order of the *bhikkhus*. Even while framing laws, the contextual premises always added to the narration. Without referring to the contextual premises, the real content and purpose of the *dāna* could not be properly considered. This element of dynamism lends Buddhism an edge over other religious systems as it makes it flexible, open to augmentations and moderations, at the same time without compromising with the fundamental values. This dynamism is best reflected in votive tradition. *Dāna* remained a meritorious deed throughout, the list of objects to be received became more and more prolific, newer classes got incorporated among the donors, apparently due to the rising stature of *saṃgha*, and wider acceptance and enhanced social engagements of the monks. One of the basic rules to be followed by a monk was not to touch gold or silver or money and thus, such donations were interpreted as the monks were not allowed to accept these items as donations. Under certain circumstances, they were allowed to accept money as a devotion, still they were not to touch it, and neither use it personally nor hoard it as a personal belonging. This examined that such changes do not appear as contradiction but may be dealt as a notion of positive progression.

The *Aṅguttara Nikāya* mentions five right ways of *dāna*, viz., give with *saddha*, to give carefully, to give quickly, to give firmly and to give not pertaining to any injury to oneself or to the donee.[16] In early Buddhist donations, all strata of societies contributed, right from the king to the commoner, though the kings and *gahapatis* had overwhelming contribution. The contemporaries of the Buddha such as Bimbisāra, Ajātaśatru, Pasenadi, and Udyana patronized Buddhism generously. Aśoka built thousands of *stūpas* and raised pillars to commemorate the Buddha. It is also suggested that he faced some opposition for his large-scale munificence.[17] Such large-scale donations were also granted by the Kushāṇas, the Guptas, Harshavardhana and the Pālas. The *setthis* were one of the most important group of donors. Anāthapindika contributed many dwelling houses, including the famous *vihāra* of Jetavana.[18] The *shrenis* also patronized Buddhism on a large scale. The *gandhikas* were generous donors. The ironsmith, goldsmith, carpenters, and garland makers were also an important group of donors.[19] The guild ivory carvers ornamented the *toranadvāras* of the Sānchī *stūpa*.[20] The reference of donation by ploughman (*halakiya*) has been found. Bhāja cave inscription mentions gift of Bādha, wife of *halakiya*.[21] Śailawārdi Buddhist cave inscription records gift of a *lēna* by Siagutanikā, wife of *halakiya* and householder (*Kudubika*) Usabhanaka, residing at Dhēnukākada, together with her son and *gahapati* Nanda.[22] The *Milindapanho* says that a daughter of peasant sold her hair to feed a Buddhist monk.[23] Women were an important category of donors in Buddhism. Vishakha, mother of *setthi* Migara built *vihāra* for the Buddha and donated her ornaments.[24] Ambapalī gifted her property to *saṃgha*.[25] Sumana gifted her girdle to *saṃgha*.[26] Kuda cave inscription informs donation of *caityagraha* by a brāhmaṇa woman.[27] Out of one hundred and thirty-three post-Mauryan votive records from Mathurā, forty-five donations have been recorded in the name of women.[28] The donations by monks, nuns have also been reported by Sārnāth, Sānchī, Bharhut, Amarāvatī, Kauśambī, Śravastī and Nālandā. The *Cullavagga* informs that large quantities of gifts were accumulated in the *vihāras*.[29] In early medieval age, it is informed that large landholdings and untold wealth had been accumulated in the monasteries of Bengal and Bihar.[30]

The Buddha always talked about good *dāna* (*sappursadāna*). The *Aṅguttara Nikāya*[31] mentions various characteristics of a donor, viz., the donee does not feel humiliated by the motives of *dāna* (*sakkaccam dānam deti*), with all respect (*cittikatva dānam deti*), should be given by own hand (*sahattha deti*), not to give what is perished (*na apaviddham deti*), not to give in a manner that desists the donee not to come again (*na anagam anaditthiko deti*), give with faith (*saddhaya deti*), always give in dire need (*kalian deti*), give in difficulty (*anuggahacitti dānam deti*), give not to injure oneself or the other (*attanan ca paran ca anupahacca dānam deti*), with understanding and discretion (*viceyyadānam sugatappasattham*).

In all Indian religions, *dāna* is a cardinal virtue and voluminous literature has been produced referring to the conditions, procedures, and the nature of *dāna*. In recent researches, few references of donations and patronage have been made but comprehensive researches are only few. P.V. Kane[32] tried to explain various merits of *dāna* mentioned in brahmanical literature. K.V.R. Aiyanger describes the aspects of *dāna* mentioned in the *Dānakanda* of the *Krityakalpataru*.[33] Vijay Nath[34] was one of the first scholars in India who tried to examine the various dimensions of *dāna*, especially from the brahmanical and Buddhist point of view. Though he emphasized on the socio-economic dimensions, other attributes of *dāna* were also discussed by him. James Hasting also discussed the aspects of charity in ancient religions, especially Judaism, Christianity, Hinduism, and Buddhism but his study was only peripheral.[35] Jan Gonda has written about the economic exchanges in Indian religions.[36] Romila Thapar also examines *dāna*, patronage and economic exchanges in her articles '*Dāna* and *Dakṣina* as Form of Exchange', and 'Patronage and Community'.[37]

Ellison Banks Findly's work *Dāna: Giving and Getting in Pāli Buddhism* with Pāli sources is supposed to be the first major work in the field of Buddhist studies. It comprehensively examines *nissaya* requirements and other needs of *dāna*. She analyses important aspects of *dāna* dealing with the relationship between monks, donors, and *saṃgha*.[38] Findly examines major areas of *dāna* only in the early phase of Buddhism. With the emergence of Mahāyāna and Vajrayāna, various new dimensions of *dāna* were added in Buddhism. The nature of gift and patronage were also changed during this age. With the traditional *nissaya* requirements, the donation of image and votive offerings such as *stūpas* became a part of the donations. Now *dāna* was not restricted between *saṃgha* and laity, but the monks and the nuns also participated in donations. With proliferation of such tendencies, questions were also raised about the possession of property in *saṃgha*. Reiko Ohnuma[39] studies the special dimension of *dāna* related to body sacrifice by the *Bodhisattva*. She has given special attention to the Mahāyāna doctrines and *dāna-pāramita* which eulogized the gift of body organs, eyes, even the whole body, for sake of generosity and altruism. She has mentioned two types of plots, first in which the motive of the *Bodhisattva* was tested by deity Sakka who restored the body, eyes, and head of the *Bodhisattva* after a successful test. Second, the *Bodhisattva* performs the act of altruism on his own and dies. She also categorises such *dāna* into two categories—evil and pitiful. In pitiful situations, the *Bodhisattva* sacrificed himself for the welfare of public and the demand of sacrifice was genuine. But, in case of evil, the person who demands has no good intention but his selfish motive encourages him to demand the head or life of the *Bodhisattva*. Bhikkhu Bodhi[40] edited a book *Dāna: The Practice of Giving*. Lily de Siva, Susan Elbaum Jootla and M O'C Walshe have contributed their articles, emphasizing the various dimensions of *dāna*. Phyllis Granoff[41] has written a paper on Manicuda's sacrifice and traced the efficacy of the *Bodhisattva's* action for *dāna-pāramita*. Gregory Schopen[42] has produced a number of articles based on the epigraphic records to examine the different aspects of *dāna* in Buddhism. He tried to explain the idea of possession, hereditary connections about property for the monks and the nuns, *bhikkhu's* role in donation, etc. With the epigraphic records, he used the *Mūlasarvāstivāda-Vinaya* as his main source. The rules and practices of *nissaya* requisites have been evolved in thousands of years and it could not be explained in singular strand, based on a particular era, literature, or sect. The geographical and local factors, tradition and economy play an important role in the formation and accommodation rules governing the existing society. So, the rules regarding *dāna* was not only geocentric but also time-centric. The pattern of *dāna* in alluvial flood plain Ganga Valley with its agricultural wealth and fresh underground water, stored in porous and coarser strata, accessible by ordinary means were the highest economic asset of the region which could not match the *dāna* tradition of the north-west region, where the climatic conditions were hostile because of hilly and arid climate.

With the introduction of 'Functional' and 'Structure-Functional' models to study the social structure by Emile Durkheim, 'gift' as an exchange and a social action was studied by Functionalism, Structure-Functionalism, Structuralisms, etc. Bronislaw Malinowski,[43] in his path-breaking study on the Trobriand islanders in Melanesia describes inter-tribal trading relations among the natives of New Guinea. His study was focussed on *kula* ring of gift exchange among the Trobriand islanders. He identified seven types of economic exchanges among them, ranging from 'pure gift' to simple trade. He calls it 'social act' that did not result in economic transaction. Claude Levi Strauss[44] expanded the horizon of studies in 'gift' by exploring the role, status, and kinship relationship in such economic exchanges. Marshall Sahlin[45] further elaborated this concept on the basis of their nature and characteristics and called it Generalized Reciprocity, Balanced Reciprocity, and Negative Reciprocity. Marshal Mauss[46] says that gift exchange was totally a social action, comprising all types of institutions—social, religious, political, economic, and cultural. All find simultaneous expressions in any primitive economic exchange. Under the influence of these social models, studies were conducted to explain the pattern of gift exchanges among the religions and Buddhism was not left untouched. Jonathan Parry argues that the reciprocated gift between the priest and the lay worshipper belonged to the profane world and the unreciprocated gift, often supposed to signify the sacred, *nibbānic* or the soteriological requirements.[47] Richard F. Gombrich says that the unreciprocated gift in Buddhism is the ritual offering made to the Buddha. He is not present and unattainable to the laities but he is capable of receiving the ritual offerings. It is a basic contrast one finds between the reciprocal gift one makes with the gods and unreciprocal exchange one makes with the Buddha.[48] Reiko Ohnuma says that:

> The gods in Theravada Buddhism are understood to be in charge of worldly goods and benefits. One gives offering to the gods in exchange of their assistance and protection; one haggles and bargain with the gods, just as one haggles and bargain in the market place. The Buddha on the other hand does not deal in worldly benefits. Therefore offerings to the Buddha point beyond the present world and should properly be renunciating in flavour. In the language of Theravada Buddhism, the gods are laukika 'worldly' in nature, whereas the Buddha is lokottara-beyond the world or transcendent.[49]

Melford Spiro examines the monk-laity reciprocity and says that, in order to retain the fruits of the *upāsakas's dāna* and convert them to transcendent *karmic* fruits, the *bhikkhu* should not reciprocate in any explicit manner, not even by an expression of gratitude.[50]

The identification and description of *dāna* in Buddhism as an anthropological object has been done by many other prominent scholars. However, *dāna* in Buddhism has been viewed as a single religious tradition and not as composition of separate stratum to be analysed in continuum. Most of these studies exhibit an idealized Functionalist view. This kind of conventional, essentialized, theoretical conceptualization in order to further the study of *dāna* has been questionable. Such theoretical formulations cannot explain the true intentions and the nature on which the structure and characteristics of *dāna* evolved in Buddhism. The need to compensate for everything was part of the importance of wealth in primitive tribal societies. Giving as a means for people to establish their status through the exact reciprocation was not enforced in Buddhism. The reciprocity in the form of *dhamma* talk or blessing for future could be granted but such notions were not mandatory or enforced, nor was it related to the status of the monk and the laity. In the famous *kula* rings, by which gifts were exchanged by canoe over the vast distances in Melanesia, lifelong partnership was desired, that could be transferred to the next generation by mortuary rights, symbolizing the stability of the relationship. The individual did not join *kula* but was co-opted by fellow members. In Buddhism, no such regulations or norms were prescribed. The laities were encouraged for *dāna*, but on their own will, without any hereditary obligations. Even one *upāsaka* donating to Buddhism, could gift to other religions. So, there was no ascribed status of the laity in Buddhism. It was his achieved status that depended upon his willingness and virtue. There should be cautious optimism while constructing any theory or model to study *dāna* aspects in Buddhism to avoid dichotomies in theoretical formulation. It would be interesting to consider *dāna* as socio-ethical action into which long historical tradition of Buddhism got mobilized. *Dāna* in Buddhism had a long history with fluid boundaries and indigenous strands. The tribal economy, based on subsistence farming and domestication could not be equated with flourishing agrarian economy of the Ganga Valley. The nature of livelihood, socio-economic structure, mode of communication and religious traits were totally different in the primitive societies of Australia, Africa, and America. Their parameters and social construction approach could not be fully utilized to examine and analyse the *dāna* tradition of Buddhism. The cradle of Buddhism flourished in the full civilization strand.

Dāna in Buddhism has been a continuous and evolutionary process. Though reciprocation is between the monk and the laity, but factors such as geography, nature of economy, political patronage, Buddhist sects, and literature (canonical and non-canonical) have always influenced the process of *dāna*. It is not necessary that what is prohibited in canonical literature is also banned in non-canonical literature. The body sacrifice was highly condemned by the Buddha but praised in Mahāyāna. The modalities of *dāna* that culminated in agrarian field of Ganga Valley could not be implemented in the same form and nature in the hilly, hazardous region of the north-west part of the Indian subcontinent. Probably, it was a conscious policy of *saṃgha* to absorb some of the local traditions that could be fruitful for the growth and penetration of Buddhism in the tribal belts and the floating population of Afghanistan and Mongolian deserts. Similarly, *dāna* practices evolved during the age of the Buddha and mentioned in canonical literature could not be the same, as mentioned in the *Mūlasarvāstivāda Vinaya* or other Mahāyāna-Vajrayāna sources because the socio-economic and the political scenario of India was totally transformed since the sixth century BCE to the early medieval age and consequently, the *Vinaya* rules were also transformed, redefined, and accommodated.

This work on *dāna* takes up several of the fundamental questions that have played an important role in defining and structuring rules and traditions throughout its long history. The interpretation that explores *dāna* as primarily rational and ethical, emphasizes its superimposing, mythic and cultic dimensions, all of which are fully attainable only to the eye of faith. There has been an attempt to argue *dāna* in Buddhism either with contemporary religious traditions or without any bias or prejudice. The idea is not to discredit the established hypothesis but to remove occasional extremes to which they are credited and prone to carry exaggerations.

Uma Chakravarti, in her paper, discusses *dāna* as human ethics. Her paper has three important domains. In the first, she examines *yajnas* and *dāna* and deliberates that how *dāna* became central to Buddhism by replacing *yañña* at the periphery. Second, she argues *dāna* on basis of the *Vessantara Jātaka* who gifted his miraculous elephant and his children to fulfil the vow of *dāna pāramita*. Last, she has given the example of the *Manimegalai* by explaining the meaning of communitas and *dāna* in the *Manimegalai*. She says that the early concern for community and sharing, and values of compassion taught by the Buddha are carried forward in the *Manimegalai*.

Vidula Jayaswal studies the donors of Sārnāth with ethno-archaeological perspective. She deals with the archaeological evidences for the identification of *Rishipatana* of Sārnāth as a Buddhist pilgrimage and the contribution of donors on account of the archaeological findings of Sārnāth-Vārānasī and Chunar region. She also explores stone carving practices in Vārānasī region and the archaeological discoveries at the periphery of Sārnāth that have brought to light the chain of craft villages where carvings were produced. Most of the icons and carved stones were donated to Sārnāth. She notices a clear relationship between the chronology and density of their carving centres, and the fluctuating quantum of lithic offerings at Sārnāth. Additional factors which helped fulfil the large demand of images at Sārnāth, growth of carving craft in Vārānasī, availability of good quality of sandstone in Vārānasī from neighbourhood hills of Chunar, extraction of desirable block of stone, and transportation through navigation to the workshop site were the significant deductions of her field studies.

Saiyid Zaheer Husain Jafri and Md. Motiur Rahman Khan explore endowments, grants and charities in medieval India with a special reference to Mahābodhi temple of Bodhgayā. Their case study attributes grants given to Mahābodhi temple of Bodhgayā during the medieval age. They cite that how the identity of the temple was transformed from Mahābodhi temple to a Śaiva *matha* and Mughal grants were given to Śaiva *mahanthas* and *matha*. They also seek continuum of the grant that began in the Mughal age and continued in the colonial government. The paper also describes the dispute occurred between Śavaite *mahanthas* and Buddhist monks over the possession of the temple.

Prashant Srivastava studies the Buddhist donations recorded in Kharoṣṭhī inscriptions in north-west India. A majority of these inscriptions are concerned with Buddhism. In certain inscriptions, it is not clearly mentioned but has to be referred. The large number of inscriptions record the donation of water bodies like ponds, wells, etc. It is surprising that despite the abundance of coins in the area and at time of the inscriptions, reference to cash donations is quite rare. Although, in other areas like Maharashtra, there are abundant references to cash donations usually made with guild. This shows that in north-west India, the tradition of cash donation was not very popular.

My paper traces the history of *dāna* tradition in Buddhism since its inception to early medieval age. It starts with *nissaya* tradition and explores changes in the nature of *dāna*. With four basic requirements of robes, food, medicine and shelter, how images, votive monuments became the subject of *dāna* is also a part of study. It also introspects body sacrifices by the *Bodhisattva*, which was quite popular in Mahāyāna tradition. The Mahāvihāra tradition, where the village grants became the main source of *dāna* to fulfil the *nissaya* requisites has been also examined.

K.K. Thaplyal's paper deals with the Nasik inscription of the time of Nahapāna which records donations made by the son-in-law Ushavadāta in favour of some monks of the Bhadaniya sect of Buddhism, residing in a cave on Tiranhu hill. These donations were not made directly to the monks, rather the amount was deposited with the weaver's guild to arrange light meal and *civara* for the monk from out of the interest accruing on the sum deposited. This was a method of making donations quite popular at that time and the inscription throws light on the involvement of guilds in such charitable works.

Sushma Trivedi examines the ascetic donations at the early Buddhist sites with the idea of transgression of monastic codes. She says that a large number of ascetic donations are noted at Buddhist sites which have been the most enigmatic issue related to the Buddhist monastic order. It emphasizes that donations made by the monks and the nuns have to be approached in contextual manner because of their different nature, not being a simple case of gift-giving or reciprocity which could be evaluated in modern thematic framework. She probes legitimate source of their donations and realizes more upon the internal evidences facilitated by the first-hand account of the donors.

K.K. Mandal, in his essay, has tried to locate and interpret the growth of Vikramśilā Mahāvihāra and its popularity on the basis of patronage as gleaned from the inscriptional and sculptural data discovered at Antichak. He suggests that Vikramśilā Mahāvihāra may be interpreted in the context of emerging power structure and the nature of polity. The nature of patronage was multidimensional. On the one hand, patronage extended by the local kings and power elite for their legitimacy, individual or group patronage emanated from the desire to acquire upward mobility in the making and gain accepted for the assured status. Patronage of Vikramśilā Mahāvihāra, thus, provided a major channel for the status enhancement to those who wanted to move up within the hierarchal caste society. At the same time, patronage extended to the local autochthonous deities indicates the beginning of regional/local formation. The social invisibility of women in the patronage system at Antichak manifests the acceptability of an entrenched brahmanical society premised on varna/caste ideology.

Padmasiri de Silva explores the ethics of *dāna* and generosity and how actions are evolved in the terms of motivation, nature of gift, etc. He looks at different models in ethics for explaining *dāna* and describes personality types, mentioned in Buddhism as the greed type (*rāga carita*), deluded by ego (*moha carita*), the generous *type* (*cāga carita*), and the aggressive type (*dosa carita*). He looks at different models in the ethics which are emerging in the West and compares it with the Buddhist ideas and practices.

Sarita Khettry, in her essay '*Dāna-Deya* Dharma: Donation in the Buddhist Records of the North-West (*c.* Second Century BCE– Third Century CE)' states that *dāna* was pre-Buddhist in date and has been defined and interpreted differently in brahmanical and non-brahmanical religions. The emergence of Buddhism in the sixth century BCE produced a large number of renouncers and wandering monks who lived exclusively on alms. Reference to terms such as *dānapati* (munificent giver of alms), *dānavato bhikkhu*, *dānagga* (a house where alms or donations are given), *dānādhikar* (supervision on charge of alms distribution), *dānavatthu* (object for a gift), and *dānaraho* (worthy for a gift) were understood more in the sense of alms and charity, rather than ritual gift. In the context of archaeological sources, the concept of *dāna* is found in the Aśokan inscriptions dating back to the third century BCE and are mainly written in Prakrit language and Brāhmī script. The term in this inscription is used in the sense of gift. A large number of inscriptions are discovered from different sites of north-western part of the Indian subcontinent (which includes the territory now politically in Pakistan [Pak-Punjab, North-West Frontier Province, Sind, and Baluchistan, Jammu & Kashmir (partly occupied by Pakistan), the Punjab and parts of Haryana and Himachal Pradesh and also Eastern Afghanistan]. These inscriptions are Buddhist and donative in nature.

Aruna K. Gamage cites references of almsgiving mentioned in the Buddha's utterances. He emphasizes upon food offering mentioned in Pāli *Nikāyas* and discusses two types of *dāna* mentioned in Pāli *Nikāyas*. He also points out the brahmanical view of *dāna* and offers explanation of the secular and supra-mundane propensity to the donor and its penultimate spiritual attainment which removes unwholesome mental bondage to get rid of rebirth and the attainment of bliss.

Neekee Chaturvedi's chapter informs that *dhammadāna* or giving, in the form of spiritual instruction, is considered to be the most superior gift. To combine the charitable disposition of the laity with reverence, the renunciates should confer upon them a unique gift, something that the householders cannot beget from elsewhere. With this socio-economic understanding, the Buddhist tradition of generosity tapped into its spiritual reservoir. The essay postulates that the teachings and consequent merit and blessings could only be conferred by a spiritually trained renunciate, making him worthy of receiving, through the practice of *dhammadāna.* The laity was limited to the role of recipient of teachings and the giver of material objects, while the monks and nuns practised the giving of spiritual as well as material gifts, as recorded in many votive inscriptions. The interrelationship of *dhammadāna* with the larger corpus *dānadhamma* and canonical teachings manifests that the symbiotic relationship of the material and the spiritual aspects was a strong factor in the historical growth of Buddhism, in general and spiritual evolution of Buddhists, in particular.

K.T.S. Sarao relates *dāna* doctrine with *karma* and rebirth. His source of study is Pāli *Nikāyas.* He discusses it with sociological ideas of reciprocated and unreciprocated gift. He enumerates the influence of *dāna* on the ethical and social life of an individual, by examining one's preoccupation about giving, moral disciplines, and motivation. He says that the merit earned through *dāna* was an important activity in early Buddhism. Since the transfer took place through a formal ritual, the monks and the nuns acted as channels of transference and they received *dāna* for their role in the ritual.

R.M. Bharadwaj mentions gifts and grants in the name of the *Buddha Bhattaraka* in the *vrata* tradition. During the early medieval age, despite several instances of bitterness between the heterodox sects, particularly Buddhism and Brahmanism, it has been noticed that several *vrata* grants were given on the occasion of the celebrations of Buddhist festivals.

Notes

1. *Dhammapada*, V.223.
2. *Vśuddhimagga*, p. 184.
3. *Saṁyutta Nikāya*, V.369–70.
4. *Aṅguttara Nikāya*, III.57.
5. *Suttanipāta*, VV.506–7.
6. *Aṅguttara Nikāya*, III.172.
7. Ibid., VIII.39.
8. Har Dayal, *The Bodhisattva Doctrine in Buddhist Sanskrit Literature,* Delhi: MLBD, 1970, p. 172.
9. *Dīgha-Nikāya,* I.137, II.354.
10. *Aṅguttara Nikāya*, IV.44.
11. *Saṁyutta Nikāya*, I.233.
12. *Majjhima Nikāya*, I.447.
13. *Saṁyutta Nikāya*, I.20–2.
14. Richard Gombrich, 'The Ethic of Intention', in *Buddhist Ethics: A Cross-cultural Approach*, Charles S. Prebish, Dubuque Iowa: Kendall/Hunt Publishing Company, 1992.
15. *Mahāvagga*, VIII.35.
16. *Aṅguttara Nikāya*, III.172.
17. John S. Strong, *The Legend of King Aśoka: A Study of Tradition of Aśokavadāna*, Delhi: Motilal Banarsidass, 2008, p. 97.
18. *Cullavagga*, VI.4.10.
19. Vijay Nath, *Dāna: Gift System in Ancient India: A Socio Economic Perspective*, Delhi: Munshiram Manoharlal, 1987, p. 61.
20. A. Foucher, *The Beginning of Buddhist Art and Other Essays in India and Central Asian Archaeology*, Delhi: Asian Educational Services, 1994, pp. 67–8.
21. H. Luder, no. 1084, *A List of Brahmi Inscriptions: From Earliest Time to About* AD *400 with the Exception of Those of Aśoka*, Calcutta: Superintendent Government Printing, 1912.

22. Ibid., no. 1121.
23. *Milindapanho*, IV, p. 68.
24. *Sutta Vibhanga*, VI.I.
25. *Mahāvagga*, VI.30–5.
26. Motichandra, *The World of Courtesan*, Delhi: Vikas Publishing House, 1973, p. 48.
27. Luders, no. 1050.
28. Ibid., nos. 16–149.
29. *Cullavagga*, V.37.
30. Pushpa Niyogi, 'Organization of Buddhist Monasteries in Ancient Bengal and Bihar', *JIH*, II, p. 534.
31. *Aṅguttara Nikāya*, III.172 (The *Aṅguttara Nikāya* also mentions the eight types of motives of dāna—*assaja dānam deti* (with insult), *bhaya dānam deti* (with fear), *adasi me ti dānam deti* (reciprocation), *sadhu dānam ti dānam deti* (in good faith), *aham pacami ime ni pacanti, na arhami pacanto apacantanam adatuni ti dānam deti* (If one does not cook, one should be given), *imam me dānam dadato kalyano kittisaddo abbuggacchati ti dānam deti* (to earn good reputation), *cittalankara cittaparikkaratham dānam deti* (to earn peace and sublime mind), *Aṅguttara Nikāya*, IV.236.
32. P.V. Kane, *History of Dharmasastra*, vols. I–V, Poona, 1930–74.
33. K.V.R. Aiyanger, *Aspects of Ancient Indian Economic Thought*, Vārānasī, 1965.
34. Vijaya Nath, *Dāna: Gift System in Ancient India: A Socio Economic Perspective*, Delhi: Munshiram Manoharlal, 1987.
35. James Hasting, *Encyclopaedia of Religion and Ethics*, Edinburg: T and T Clark, 1908–27.
36. Jan Gonda, 'Gift', in *Change and Continuity in Indian Religion*, The Hague: Mouton, 1965, pp. 198–228.
37. Romila Thapar, *Cultural Pasts: Essays in Early Indian History*, Delhi: Oxford University Press, 2000, pp. 531–6, 589–611.
38. E.B. Findly, *Dāna: Giving and Getting in Pali Buddhism*, Delhi: Motilal Banarsidass, 2003, pp. 7–8.
39. Reiko Ohnuma, *Bodily Self-Sacrifice in Indian Buddhist Literature*, Delhi: Motilal Banarsidass, 2009.
40. Bhikkhu Bodhi, *Dāna: The Practice of Giving*, Kandy: BPS, 1990.
41. Phyllis Granoff, 'The Sacrifice of Manicuda: The Context of Narrative Action as a Guide to Introspection', in *Kalyanmitra*, ed. V.N. Jha, Poona: Poona University, 1990, pp. 225–39.
42. Gregory Schopen, *Indian Monastic Buddhism: Collected Papers on Textual, Inscriptional and Archaeological Evidence*, Delhi: MLBD, 2010, also see, *Bones, Stones and Buddhist Monks: Collected Papers on the Archaeology, Epigraphy, and Text of Monastic Buddhism in India*, Hawaii: University of Hawaii Press, 1997.
43. Bronislaw Malinoswki, *Argonauts of The Western Pacific: An Account of Native Enterprises and Adventure in the Archipelago of Melanesian New Guinea*, London: George Routledge and Sons, 1932, pp. 175–7.
44. Claude Levi Strauss, *The Elementary Structure of Kinship*, London: Eyre and Spottis Woode, 1989.
45. Marshal Sahlin, *Stone Age Economics*, Chicago: Aldine Atherton, 1972.
46. Marshal Mauss, 'A Category of Human Mind: The Notion of Person: The Notion of Self', in *The Category of the Person: Anthropology, Philosophy, History*, tr. W.D. Halls, ed. Michael Carsithars et. al., Cambridge: Cambridge University Press, 1985,

pp. 1–45, also see, *The Gift: The Form and Reason for Exchange in Archaic Societies*, New York: Norton.

47. Jonathan Parry, 'The Gift, The Indian Gift and the "Indian Gift"', *Man*, vol. XXI, 1986, pp. 453–73, see p. 462.
48. Richard F. Gombrich, *Precept and Practice: Traditional Buddhism in the Rural Highlands of Ceylon*, Oxford: Clarendon Press, 1971, pp. 117–18, 150–3, also see, *The Perfect Generosity of Prince Vessantara*, Oxford, 1977.
49. Reiko Ohnuma, op. cit., pp. 146–7.
50. Melford Spiro, *Buddhism and Society: A Great Tradition and Its Burmese Vicissitudes*, Berkeley: University of California Press, 1970.

2

Of Communitas and Sharing

The Place of *Dāna* in the Humanist Ethics of Buddhism

UMA CHAKRAVARTI

IT HAS BEEN ARGUED that the context for the Buddha's own spiritual quest was the increasing individualism that accompanied the rise of cities and monarchies, of individual private property, and the breakdown of forms of community and sharing that were part of the earlier kin-clan units that occupied tracts of land in the first millennium BCE.[1] Individualism placed limits on the affective relations creating notions of insiders and outsiders, confining love and sharing to those with whom one had affective links, thereby excluding others from its purview. One way of dealing with the disease of individualism was to create alternative communities that approximated the communities of the past but were built on new principles that sought to contain individualism as well as the inequalities that accrued from the idea of private gain. The new community of the *saṃgha*, the community of *bhikkhus* and later, the *bhikkhunis* forged new bonds based on non-possessive affective links, caring and sharing, leaving each to pursue salvation at one's own pace. The Buddhist world view thus, represented a distinct set of values that were advocated to its adherents in consonance with a new mode of thinking about the individual and the community, and the links between the two. While the *bhikkhu* as the renunciate, and the *upāsaka* as a lay follower and a 'man' in the world, followed different paths they were linked together through the institution of *dāna*: as truthfinders who abstained from the world of production and reproduction. The *bhikkhu* and the *bhikkhuni* had no means to sustain their bodily needs of hunger and shelter. Being the producers of food and the acquirers of goods, the *upāsakas* were in a position to make a gift of alms, clothing and shelters to the renouncer. The one object associated with the renouncer was the alms bowl: with this in their hands the *bhikkhunis* and the *bhikkhus* went forth once a day, accepting what was given, returning the generosity of the almsgiver by giving back to them the gift of the *dhamma*. They did this by teaching the householders the basic tenets of the *dhamma* so that they too could, at some point, reach the goal of salvation, which the renunciate was committed to pursuing with single-minded devotion.[2]

To bring this structure of reciprocity into place, the older modes of acquiring merit and control over the world through the performance of *yaňňas* (Pāli for *yagnya*) needed to be re-ordered. *Yaňňa* brought the individual mundane merit: worldly goods that the gods bestowed in return for the offerings provided by the *yajamāna* which led to individual gains for the performer and his family. Typically also, *yaňňa* was performed by those people who possessed 'worldly' goods: cattle, land, food grains, and material prosperity as well as good health to enjoy these possessions. What was offered to the Gods in the sacrifice brought abundant returns to the *yajamāna*. This was regarded by the Buddha as a lower form of acquiring merit. Instead, turning the focus away from *yaňňas* which spelt great cruelty to animals, the Buddha advocated a *yaňňa* of the mind. But, better still, was the gift of alms to those who renounced the world of obligations and set forth from home to homelessness, as the Buddha himself did in search of the truth. And as did countless other teachers in the Buddha's own day.

It may be noted that the Buddha did not completely replace the performance of sacrifices by *dāna*, but rather moved *dāna* to a central position for the layman and edged *yaňňa* to the periphery. A stock passage in the Pāli canon indicates this very clearly: those who did not believe in *dāna* or *yaňňa*, nor the results of action, were criticized for their barren and perverse philosophy. Sacrifice was not completely eliminated, only animal sacrifice was rejected, but *yaňňa* was now to take a secondary place in the Buddhist scheme of things. *Yaňňa* for the welfare of the family was redefined as a perpetual *dāna*. The *Kūṭadanta Sutta* makes this very explicit. When the Brāhmaṇa Kūṭadanta wished to perform a large *yaňňa* he consulted the Buddha on the subject. The Buddha told him the story of King Mahāvijita who had wished to perform a great animal sacrifice but was persuaded by his wise *purohita* to distribute gifts instead. Interestingly, the gifts were used as a means to end harassment and bring peace to a realm that was suffering from the pillage of dacoits. The usual method of fines and punishment did not help to eradicate the unrest. The wise *purohita* suggested other means to bring peace: giving those who wish to work a means to do so—seed to those who will farm, to others wages and food. Gifts from the king here were part of good governance. When everyone was happy a sacrifice in which all the people can participate but no slaughter or force is to be used could be performed. The sacrifice must be entirely voluntary with only those who wished to work helping in its organization. The Buddha identified himself with the wise *purohita* of the past and tells Kūṭadanta that better than performing sacrifices was the giving of perpetual gifts to the virtuous recluses. Even better was to put up *vihāras* for the *saṃgha*, and at the top of the scale came the observance of *pañcaśilas* (five rules), which of course, related to the cultivation of the mind and therefore to the moral uplift of the individual rather than a means of gaining merit.[3]

Dāna, or sharing through the giving of alms, has been regarded as a total institution encompassing the socio-economic, juridical, religious, moral, and mythical values. The exchange of gifts was a moral transaction bringing about and maintaining harmony in social relationships through equitable relationships between individuals and groups belonging to the same society. *Dāna* was also a system of redistributive justice and came to be regarded as the highest form of acquiring merit. In sum, charity in the form of *dāna* became a substitute for the imperative of justice.[4]

While the principle of *dāna* was exhorted in general the Buddhists also made it clear that the maximum merit would accrue when the donor made a gift to a worthwhile donee. The Buddha did not advocate the termination of gifts to other religious sects even though he was unfairly accused of this occasionally. Nevertheless, he did indicate that his own *saṃgha* was the best recipient of *dāna* and often described the Buddhist *saṃgha* as the 'peerless field of merit'. The description of Siha's acceptance of Buddhism is a good example of the Buddha's position on *dāna*. Siha, a Lichchhavi, was originally a follower of the Jainism but, on expressing his desire to switch allegiance to Buddhism he was asked to continue giving alms to the Jains too. This might have been a result of the Buddha's recognition of the general need for support through alms, in the *samana* way of life. Given this, it might have seemed unethical to advocate a complete severance of all relations with other religious sects, merely because the teachings of one particular sect were more appealing to a lay follower.[5] That gifts of food should be given respectfully and not merely to gain merit is also outlined in the *suttas*: there was to be no hierarchy of food eaten or clothing worn and given: what one would not eat oneself should not be given away as alms: the principle was sharing not giving what one would not use oneself: 'Give ye your gifts with thoroughness, with your own hands, with due thought and give not as if you were discarding something.'[6]

In the *Sigalovāda Sutta*, which is regarded as the text par excellence outlining the *upāsaka's* social ethics a householder is given instruction on how to perform his duties towards close kin: these are to be informed by the spirit of *anukampanti*, the protective tenderness of the strong towards those placed under the protection of the householder. It is an emotional force even stronger than *karuṇā* or compassion. Two categories of people are outside his kin or affective unit: these are the *dāsa karmakāras*—servants and workers, and the brāhmaṇas and śramaṇas: the former helps him to generate his productive resources and the latter helps him to cultivate himself. Accordingly, his treatment of the *dāsa karmakāras* should be moderate: he should give them work according to their strength, and supply them with adequate food and wages. He must also tend them in sickness, and share with them the unusual delicacies at his home and ensure that they get time off to rest, recover, and entertain themselves. To those who have renounced the world, the householder must extend gifts of food and other basic necessities; in return they will gift him the knowledge of the *dhamma* and lead him on the path to his own ultimate salvation.[7] A number of persons are associated with *dāna* in the early Buddhist texts. These include Anāthapindika, the *setthi* who gifted the Jetavana to the *saṃgha*, paying an enormous price for it by covering the *vana* with gold coins; Ambapalī, who gifted a mango grove to the *saṃgha* after feeding the Buddha and the *bhikkhus* who accompanied him to the meal; Vishakha, the *upāsikā* who gifted robes to *bhikkhunis*, among many others too numerous to mention. All acquired merit, some like Ambapalī went on to renounce the world. Two figures are particularly marked out for special merit: one is Sujātā who fed the Buddha the *payas* just before he sat down to the meditation that led to his enlightenment; and Cunda who fed the Buddha his last meal that led to the illness that ended in his passing away. Ever mindful of the possible blame that might be apportioned to Cunda of feeding him with food that led to his end the Buddha sought to pre-empt such charges of wrongdoing. He told Ānanda:

> These two offerings of food are of equal fruit and much greater profit than any other . . . the offering of food which when a Tathagata has eaten, he attains to supreme and perfect insight and the offering of food, which when the Tathagata has eaten, he passes away by utter passing away in which nothing remains behind. . . . There has been laid by Chunda the smith, kamma redounding to good fortune . . . and sovereign power. . . . To him who gives shall virtue be increased. . . .[8]

It might be of some significance to point out that the *yañña* appears to have been specially associated with the brāhmaṇas and the kings in the Pāli canon. It is only they who are depicted as making arrangements for the performance of the *yaññas*. According to the Brāhmaṇa Sundarika Bharadwaja the categories of people who made oblations to the Gods were *isis*, brāhmaṇas, and kṣatriyas. The absence of the *gahapati* is striking since in every way he should have been an ideal sacrificer—he was eminent, wealthy and learned. In this context it might also be useful to point out that according to Pāli canon, the system of sacrifice, especially the large animal sacrifice, did not have the support of the common people. The *dāsa kammakāras* who were required to help in making the preparations are described as being forced into doing so. They are pushed around, with tears on their faces, and 'hectored' about by blows in the process. The importance given to *dāna* on the other hand brought the large majority of the people into the orbit of religious experience. Everyone from the king and the *gahapati* downwards, including the more humble sections, could make a small gift to the *saṃgha* by feeding a few of the *bhikkhus*. *Dāna* thereby replaced *dakkhina* (*dakṣina*) as the major link between the religious categories on the one hand and the people on the other.[9]

II

In this section we will examine the central place of *dāna* in the popular Buddhist narrative tradition: the most well known *Jātaka* story describing the great acts of *dāna* by the prince Vessantara. As the story begins Vessantara was given a lineage of well-born pious parents but he was born on a street named Vessa; so taking neither his mother nor his father's name he was called Vessantara. But the day is unusual because on the same day a miraculous female flying elephant brought a young elephant and left it in the royal stable.

This elephant was linked to the destiny of Vessantara as we shall see as the narrative unfolds. When Vessantara was just four or five years old, he began his acts of giving—he gave away all the gold given to him to his nurses and refused to take it back. The king gave him more precious things, but the boy Vessantara gave these away too, nine times over. When he was eight, he thought that all that he had given up until then was from without—he should instead give from within and thought of giving away parts of his own body, but miraculous happenings stopped any untoward happening. At sixteen, he was married and went on to have a son and then a daughter. During these years, his gift giving increased as he went mounted upon his special elephant to the great alms hall to distribute gifts every month.

But then Vessantara's troubles started. In a section titled *dāna khandam* the story unfolds, as does the disaster; in the kingdom of Kalinga there was a terrible famine. Tormented by want, the people gathered in front of the king and upbraided him for not doing anything to bring in the rains. The king then fasted and kept many holy vows yet the rain did not come. Then he was told about Vessantara's glorious white elephant and that wherever the elephant it started raining. The king of Kalinga then sent eight brāhmaṇas to ask for a gift of the elephant from Vessantara on an auspicious day when he was giving alms by the southern gate of the city. Vessantara then thought to himself: 'I am willing to give anything that is my own from my head onwards and what they ask is something without me; I will fulfil their wish.'[10]

And so he gave away the elephant along with jewels, money and many precious things. But then the portents became ominous; there was a terrible earthquake. The town trembled as the brāhmaṇas took the elephant away. The people of the kingdom were angry with Vessantara for ruining the kingdom and the king, Vessantara's father, fearing Vessantara's safety banished him from the kingdom. Vessantara's dutiful wife insisted on accompanying him and their children too who were very young went along with the parents.

Vessantara and his family journeyed through difficult terrain; always the gift giver, he gave his chariot and horses away to brāhmaṇas who had missed the great gift-giving earlier. With no vehicle, the family walked, the father carrying the boy and the mother carrying the little girl, towards the mountains. On the way, the trees bent down with their fruit so that the children could reach them and so assuage their hunger; the *yakkhas* shortened the road they traversed so moved were they by the children's weariness. At times they received warm hospitality along the way—at other times it was hard. Finally, they reached the mountain and found a pleasant spot which became their hermitage abode. Adopting the life of a celibate sage, Vessantara and his family lived on fruits and roots which Maddi, Vessantara's wife insisted she would collect. In a pleasant role reversal she went out during the day and Vessantara looked after the children; and so they lived happily in their little pleasures.

In a parallel story, an old Brāhmaṇa Jujaka, collected a sum of money through alms—not a way of life endorsed by the Buddha—and left it with another brāhmaṇa while he went off to collect some more. Meanwhile the brāhmaṇa family, in whose custody the money had been deposited, spent the money. Unable to repay the money when Jujaka returned the brāhmaṇa family gave their daughter in marriage to the old Brāhmaṇa Jujaka. We see here, the negative associations that are often alluded to the brāhmaṇas in the early Buddhist *suttas*: the brāhmaṇas entered the world of economic transactions, began to hoard goods, and then also entered the world of sexual relations and reproduction. This is not the way the brāhmaṇas of 'old' had lived so obviously there might be a degeneration of the original values. The narrative proceeds to recount the growing dissatisfaction of the young wife with the old brāhmaṇa who was reviled by people for the misalliance whenever she goes out. Finally, she refuses to go out to fetch water and do other chores and demanded the services of a maid. The old brāhmaṇas offered to do the chores himself but the young and petulant wife insisted on a slave, or else she will leave him. The brāhmaṇa then pleads: 'How can I buy a slave? I have no craft, no corn; come, be not angry, I will do your work.'[11]

The brāhmaṇa's wife refused once more and suggested him to go to Vessantara to ask him for a slave and even threatened to leave him and went to another man if Jujaka does not bring in a slave. And so Jujaka prepares for a journey meeting many people along the way. Maddi sensed danger and had a nightmare portending danger. Frightened she knocked at Vessantara's door and is upbraided by him for seeking him out as that endangers his vow of celibacy. Maddi explained her situation and is consoled by Vessantara who urges her to put her fears aside. But he also understands the meaning of the dream: 'The perfection of my giving is to be fulfilled; this day comes a suitor to ask for my children.'[12]

That very day Jujaka arrived at the mountain hermitage in the day time when Maddi was away collecting food. He asks for the children to take home as his slaves. Vessantara pleaded for him to wait till Maddi returns but Jujaka said: 'Women no generous givers are, to thwart they always try. They know all sorts of cunning spells. . . . Let him who gives a gift in faith not see his mother's face or she will find impediments!'[13]

The children were given away and though fearful of what was to come did not resist, at least initially. The brāhmaṇa binded then with ropes and beating them all the while he took them away (recalling the binding of animals in a brāhmaṇa sacrifice). The boy then broke away and returned to his father begging not to be sent off when the mother is away. As the narrative tells us Vessantara was not unaware of the machinations and the cruelty of the brāhmaṇa. But then he thought to himself that it was not right to give a gift and then regret it. Just as the gift of the miraculous elephant had led to the trembling of the earth so too did the earth resound when the children were given away. When Maddi returned she was heartbroken and faints. The gods understand that she too can be given away so they assumed the shape of a brāhmaṇa and asked for Maddi, but also returned her to Vessantara. Sakka then offers Vessantara eight boons. Vessantara chooses to be reconciled to his father and to return to his kingdom, continue to be able to give gifts and so reach his earthly existence.

While Vessantara and Maddi continued to stay at the hermitage the children undergo many travails. Fortunately, they were aided by the gods who look after them in the night, feeding them and keeping them secure till daybreak. Ultimately the king, Vessantara's father heared of the children and what has happened to them. He bought their freedom from Jujaka who died soon after being unable to digest the largesse he is given. Vessantara returned to Sivi, continues to give gifts through his lifetime, and came to an end of his earthly sojourn. The *Jātaka* then tells us that the Buddha himself was Vessantara in his former birth as a *Bodhisattva*. In telling this story, the Buddhist ethic of giving, albeit of the past, was both expanded and contrasted to the brahmanical degeneration and lack of ethic: far from giving up on animal sacrifice they are including human beings among the objects that good people must give up to their cruel demands for gain. The kingly duty of gift-giving is severely tested but upheld. Communitas, though is disrupted, and sharing does not seem to be valued especially in the brahmanical world view.

III

This section deals with the real meaning of communitas in special reference to the *Manimegalai*. The *Manimegalai* is narratively a sequel to the famous Tamil classic *Śilappadikaram*, the story of Kovalan, a merchant, his wife Kannagi, and a beautiful *devadasi* Madhavi with whom Kovalan fell in love and therefore neglected his dutiful wife. He also squandered away all his wealth and then returned to his wife with whom he plans to start life anew. The couple went away to another city hoping to start a livelihood once more but fate determines otherwise: there is a miscarriage of justice and Kovalan was killed as a thief; Kannagi was angered and cursed the king and the city to burn and herself ascended to heaven as a goddess. Manimegalai, the heroine of the text named after her, was the daughter of Kovalan and Madhavi. The story picks up on the themes of love, betrayal, and justice in the *Śilappadikaram* which it explores within a Buddhist ethos, of which we get a glimpse even in the earlier text, since we are told that Madhavi renounces her profession and becomes a *bhikkhuni*.

When the story of Manimegalai opened she was on the threshold of womanhood. Born to a beautiful dancer and into a *devadasi* household she was exhorted by her maternal grandmother to become a courtesan. The prince of the kingdom fell in love with her but Manimegalai, though drawn to him and to the path of beauty and *śriṅgāra*, was also moved by compassion for her fellow citizens and by Buddhism. Before she can decide which way to go, she is charged with killing the prince—a miraculous being has assumed her form and created that mirage, and so she is cast in prison. Released from prison, she teaches the Buddhadharma to the queen. At the same time Manimegalai was gifted a magical alms bowl of the Buddha himself by the gods: it can produce food endlessly and so feeds anyone who is hungry. With this miracle bowl Manimegalai feeds the famine-stricken populace and also prisoners, who too seem to be starved as part of their punishment.

A woman/deity imbued with the spirit of charity teaches Manimegalai the power and goodness of true charity. She tells Manimegalai, to whom she will give the miraculous alms bowl, the importance of feeding those who are hungry and the merit that accrues from it: 'Hunger destroys good birth, kills nobility, cuts the learning of the learned, deprives people of shame, spoils qualities that are beautiful, and makes people stand in front of the houses of others with their wives. Such indeed is the sinful nature of craving.'[14] Thus, poverty is not merely a lack of the basics of life: it is a social relationship of injustice. The goddess then describes what is true charity: 'Food provided to allay the hunger of those who cannot otherwise satisfy it, is true charity. Among those that live in this world those that give food are those that give life. Therefore go forward and give to those that are hungry that which will destroy hunger.'[15]

Manimegalai, whose good deeds have been rewarded with the gift of the miraculous alms bowl says this to invoke limitless food: 'I believe that this hunger relieving bowl has come into my hands. Like a mother's breast that which at the sight of her hungry child begins yielding milk, I wish to see this bowl in my hand provide food inexhaustible at the sight of those oppressed with hunger.'[16]

Manimegalai does not stop at feeding only the hungry who are poor; in the course of her wanderings she went to the chief prison in the city and began to feed with great kindness and pleasant words, those who were suffering from hunger while undergoing punishment.[17] The king was impressed by Manimegalai's goodness and asked her what she thought he could do to help her in her work. Manimegalai said: 'Only destroy the prison house and erect there, in its stead, with kindness of heart tenements useful for those who follow the path of dhamma.'[18]

The 'cruel house' was then turned into a house of charity; the state prison became a shrine for the teaching of truth. Ultimately as an ascetic Tapasi having heard the excellent *dhamma*, devoted herself to self cultivation and sought to reach the end of the bondage of earthly existence. How do we understand the intent and inner meaning of the Manimegalai narrative? It seems to me that the early concern for communnity and sharing and values of compassion taught by the Buddha are carried forward, both the *Vessantara Jātaka* (even as the Vessantara plays out other themes like greed, passion and degeneration of the higher values associated with the brāhmaṇas of old) and in the *Manimegalai* but are vastly enhanced in the latter. What is significant to me is that Manimegalai inverts the *bhikkhu* and *bhikkhunis* renunciate existence where those who have joined the *saṃgha* receive alms from the people and give them the *dhamma* teachings in return. She uses the alms bowl to receive food for herself but then transforms the food into an inexhaustible supply by which she feeds the hungry—here the renunciate does not take food as much as give it to those who really need it—the poorest and the humblest, the famine-stricken destitute and the imprisoned. These are categories of people who would normally work for others as they have no productive resources themselves, or those who are barred from the productive process as they are confined in state institutions. The experience of social suffering is the immediate trigger for Manimegalai's transformation from an alms receiver to a giver of food. She, as a woman, nurtures in the best traditions of *karuṇā* and *anukampanti* and that leads her to the path of salvation. Instead of becoming a recipient of common wealth she miraculously produces food for those who cannot themselves produce anything or give to others. Thus, she fully repudiates the individualism of the new society with its emphasis on private property, hoarding, rising inequalities and the violence that follows from these new arrangements (it is not without thought that the author of the *Manimegalai* tells us that she is specially concerned with the prison, which she has experienced herself). Through an expansion of the values of the Buddha, she creates a new sense of community going far beyond the individual material quest pursued by most human beings or even spiritual quest which we see as the renunciate ideal in the early Buddhist texts. She links the *bhikkhuni* with the rest of society in a uniquely compassionate way, breaking down the binaries of givers and recepients as stable and unchangeable categories of people. There are many lessons to learn from the Buddhist values of community and sharing, of *karuṇā* and *anukampanti* given the increasing levels of inequality that we are witnessing today.

Notes

1. Trevor Ling, *The Buddha: Buddhist Civilization in India and Ceylon*, London: Penguin, 1976, pp. 16–35.
2. Uma Chakravarti, *The Social Dimensions of Early Buddhism*, New Delhi: Oxford University Press, 1987; Romila Thapar, *Ancient Indian Social History: Some Interpretations*, New Delhi: Orient Longman, 1978.
3. T.W. Rhys Davids, *The Dialogues of the Buddha*, London: Pali Text Society, 1973, vol. II, pp. 160–85.
4. Nalin Swaris, *The Buddha's Way to Human Liberation: A Socio Historical Approach*, New Delhi: Navayana, 2011, pp. 50–5.
5. Chakravarti, *The Social Dimensions of Early Buddhism*, p. 61.
6. Rhys Davids, *Dialogues of the Buddha*, pt. II, p. 374.
7. Ibid., pt. III, pp. 163–84.
8. *Mahāparinibbāna Sutta: Dialogues of the Buddha*, pt. II, p. 148.
9. In the shift of focus away from *yañña*, *dāna* never came to occupy the central role of *yañña* in the brahmanical system. *Yañña* had been the core of the brahmanical religion, so vital in its potency that almost everything including, the seasons, creation, and the world itself were founded on the sacrifice. *Dāna* on the other hand despite its tremendous significance for the layman, was only a means of gaining merit available to people leading a lay life. Anānthapindika, who was famous for his generous *dāna* to the *saṃgha*, was once asked not to be satisfied with *dāna* alone but to undertake further training. By itself *dāna* would not achieve even as much as the observance of the five *śīlas*, by the *upāsaka*, and it was certainly not a means to the ultimate goal of *nibbāna*.
10. *Vessantara Jātaka: The Jātaka,* tr. E.B. Cowell, vol. VI, Delhi: Motilal Banarsidass, 2005, pp. 243, 246–306.
11. Ibid., p. 271.
12. Ibid., p. 279.
13. Ibid., p. 281.
14. S. Krishnaswami Aiyangar, *Manimegalai and its Historical Setting*, London: Luzac, 1927, p. 139.
15. Ibid., p. 140.
16. Ibid., pp. 140–1.
17. Ibid., p. 158.
18. Ibid., p. 160.

3

Donors and Growth of Buddhist Pilgrimage at Sārnāth

An Ethno-archaeological Perspective

VIDULA JAYASWAL

Among the four important places—Lumbinī, Bodhgayā, Sārnāth, and Kuśīnagar—related to the Buddha's life, Sārnāth may be accepted as the most significant one, as it was the place where Buddhism originated. The place of the first Sermon of the lord after attaining enlightenment, had caused Sārnāth to become a flourishing Buddhist pilgrimage, as soon as Buddhism got deep-rooted in the society. Donation of icons and structures for more than 1,500 years, between the Mauryan and early medieval times, by devotees, helped Sārnāth achieve the reputation of a world-famous storage of stone-carving masterpieces, and an enriched pilgrimage. But, its glory was buried beneath the thick earth cover during medieval times. The past glory of Sārnāth was retrieved by archaeologists in early twentieth century CE. The first archaeologists' spade which scientifically unearthed the buried remains of Sārnāth (Longitude 83° 2′ E and Latitude 25° 23′ N) was in the year 1905.[1] This was followed by subsequent excavations of early twentieth century,[2] as a result of which, nature and grandeur of this religious establishment was brought to light. The chronology of the material remains of this site was ascertained between the time of the Mauryan King Aśoka (*c.*273–236 BCE)[3] and Kumāradevī, one of the queens of the Gahadvala King Govindchandra (1114–1154 CE).[4] After about a century of the initial discovery of Sārnāth, archaeological investigations were again carried out in the years 1994–8, with the aim of identifying supporting settlements of this religious establishment. It was also directed towards locating deposits contemporary to Gautam Buddha, which are not reported by the earlier excavators. Also the question that why did the Buddha choose Sārnāth for his First Sermon, remained unanswered. Answer to this appeared to be imbedded in the pre-Buddha archaeological horizons, which were required to be studied in detail.

The periphery of the Buddhist settlement at Sārnāth was, therefore, subjected to probe. Two areas—Varunā valley and banks of Rajapur-nālā were selected for archaeological investigations by the author, in the year 1994.[5] Varunā with its tributaries and Rajapur-nālā encircle Sārnāth at south and south-west and east and south-east. Channels of both these systems were dotted with small sites. The northern periphery of Sārnāth marked by the shore of Sārang-tāl, too was explored.[6] But, this area was devoid of ancient deposits. The most promising water channel around Sārnāth is the river Varunā. Its tributary stream Aktha-nālā, connects river Varunā with Sārang-tāl, on the southern shore of which is located the monuments of the pilgrimage. Located on the confluence of Aktha-nālā and Narkhoh-nālā, a small tributary water channel of the former, Aktha is a small village about 1 km. south-west of Sārnāth.[7] Excavation at Aktha brought to light archaeological horizons contemporary to the Buddha, and also evidence for identification of *Rishipatana* of the Buddhist text. The chrono-cultural sequence unearthed through 18 habitation layers at Aktha is divisible within five periods—the Later Vedic, the *Janpada*, the Maurya-Śunga, Kushāṇa and Late Kushāṇa. On account of the C_{14} dates obtained from the middle floor of the Period I at Aktha, the earliest occupation of the site is datable between *c.*1800 and 1200 BCE.[8] This date bracket corroborates the reference to '*Kasis*', a tribe mentioned as the residents of Vārānasī region in the Later Vedic *Saṁhita.*[9] An ancient channel, which was connecting river Ganga to Sārnāth was traced during our field survey. This dried-up rivulet, Rajapur-nālā, was dotted with a chain of small rural settlements, where icons and stone blocks were carved. The stream was utilized for transportation of large blocks of sandstone, the carving medium during early historical times. The carvings were prepared at sites like Kotwa, Rajapur, and Asapur and were utilized to adorn monuments of Sārnāth. The modern village of Kotwa (Longitude 83°03′ 15″ E and Latitude 25°20′ 20″ N) is a small settlement situated on the left bank of Rajapur-nālā.[10] Except for a small part (to the west), which is under cultivation, the mound at Kotwa (with an extension of 250 m. × 75 m.), is extensively inhabited. Kotwa was a small ancient craftsmen village, a little away from the confluence of the Rajapur-nālā and the main course of the river Ganga. Excavations at Kotwa revealed four floors, on and around which rested huge accumulation of stone debris, indicating large scale chiselling of sandstone. The rural bias with predominance of chiselling refuge was distinct at this site. Associated with these were potsherds and broken pieces of carvings. On account of the typology of the pots and style and subject of the carvings, a date bracket between *c.* first/second century BCE and eleventh/twelfth century CE, could be ascertained for this site.[11]

Archaeological findings of all the three sites discussed above—Sārnāth, Aktha and Kotwa unveiled a number of factors related to the origin of Buddhism, makeup of Sārnāth pilgrimage and the stone carving art of ancient Sārnāth-Vārānasī, which are discussed below.

Aktha: The ***Rishipatana***

Sārnāth is referred as *Isipatana-Migadāya* (Sanskrit *Rishipatana-Migadāya*) in the *Mahāvastu*, which describes it as . . . 'an open space near Benāras where was situated the famous *Migadāya* or Deer Park'.[12] The Buddhist texts, further clarify that, 'Isipatana was so called because sages on their way through the air (from the Himalayas), alight here or start from here on their aerial flight'.[13] The following deductions are obvious from these references:

1. That the *Isipatana* was located away, but near the city of Vārānasī.
2. That the *Isipatana* was the abode of *Rishis* who were moving from one place to the other, particularly between the Himalayas and the Ganga plains.
3. This abode of the *Rishis*' would logically be a hermitage-based settlement.
4. *Migadāya*, the Deer Park, was adjacent to the abode of the *Rishis*, *Isipatana*.

The ancient city of Vārānasī, which is identified with the archaeological remains of Kāśī-Rājghāt[14] is a little away (about 5 km. south-east), from Aktha. In the modern administrative records of today, Aktha village is a part of Paharia locality which is known as a port for imported fruits and vegetables brought in from distant places for consumption of the city. As this place is well connected with metal roads with most of the important cities of the Middle Ganga plain, all modern land routes (highways) connecting north and south Bihar and various parts of Uttar Pradesh—Buxar, Vaiśālī, Sonapur, Patna, Allahabad, Gorakhpur, Ayodhyā, Lucknow, etc., pass through Aktha-Paharia. The geographical location of Aktha, indicates that this place was situated at the junction of such major routes, which were connecting various regions in ancient times also. There was 'the old Grand Trunk Road from Rājagaha through Vārānasī, Sāketa, and Śravastī towards Takshaśilā and frontiers, linking India with Central and Western Asia'.[15] The genesis of Grand Trunk Road may be pushed back to the later Vedic times, when movement of people from west to east had intensified. The later establishment of major trade route, the *Uttarapatha* (northern route) during the historical times was perhaps the follow up of the same. It may be significant to note that in Aktha, a resort settlement at the junction of these routes, dates between later Vedic and Kushāṇa periods.

Besides good connectivity, Aktha had other few geographical advantages. It was very well drained by perennial streams like Narkhoh-nālā, Aktha-nālā and the river Varunā, along with a number of ponds. These water bodies were not only a source of sweet water, an imperative to support a settlement, but also did not swell up to such levels as to threaten habitation. The fertile land of the neighbourhood with access pools was another added advantage. The long stretch of grasslands, along with patches of jungle, which was the presumed ecology of the second millennium BCE of the region was suitable for the quadric-pedal fauna like deer. Deer park/parks, therefore were part of natural habitat of Varunā valley in second/first millennium BCE. It may be held that Sārnāth, the '*Migadāya*', and Aktha, *Rishipatana* close to each other were results of natural makeup. Akthians, were adapted in the above-mentioned ecology for about 2,000 years, the first thousand years or little more (1,200 years) of which was pre-Buddha. Testified by the thickness of the earliest horizon (about 3 m. thick), the Period I at Aktha suggests hermitage-habitat marked by simplicity in artifacts. For example, though ceramic traditions were quite a few and good quality of pots were in use, yet the other remains were marked by simplicity. Both black and red pottery along with the combination of Black-and-Red ware evidence advanced potting technology. Use of fast wheel and thin and well baked pots, particularly, variety of bowls is noteworthy. But, the tendency to use these pots without painting was a typical feature of Aktha. The daily utility items made of bone, iron, copper were perhaps associated with wooden articles also. The shelters were also made of perishable material like mats, grass, wood, bamboo, and earth. The nature of the findings not only corresponds with the descriptions found in the Late Vedic texts, but the simplicity and long unchanged techno-typological characteristics of the artifacts may suggest that this settlement had a strong hermitage bias for considerable length of time. Even though the area of excavation was limited, exposure of two extensive rammed floors with post-holes, was significant.[16]

As the nature of shelter of Period I at Aktha, corresponds with the description of the Later Vedic *Saṁhita* which mentions that the dwelling houses, *grihas*, were made of wooden posts and beams. Wooden posts or *upamitas* were the upright pillars over which *parimits* were placed. The latter was to provide support to super structure of split bamboo and thatch of the roof.[17] The *Śāla-sukta* of the *Atharva Veda* mentions use of *chatai* (mat) and *phusa* (hay) for the construction of the superstructure of *śālas*. *Śāla* provides shelter for rest to the world and wears or is wrapped in *chatai*, and covered by *phusa*.[18] Reminiscent of such a structure which is composed of mats, thatch, and wooden posts, in archaeological context would be the post-holes attached with rammed floors, like the ones which were encountered in the deposits of Period I of Aktha. Another significant category of artifact found in Period I at Aktha was the geometric pot-shreds or the *kapala*[19] which occurred in high proportion. It has been shown elsewhere that, pottery-discs bear close similarities with the *kapala*, an important ritual object of the Vedic *yajna*. Literal meaning of *kapala* is the broken piece of clay pot or a pot-shred.[20] Used for baking sacrificial cakes for obligation during the time of *yajna*, *kapala*, the circular pot-shred containers are mentioned in various contexts while describing rituals in the Vedic *Saṁhitas*. Their occurrence in archaeological context in the Middle Ganga Plain goes back to around third millennium BCE. Pottery-discs along with the floors with use of fire at Aktha, thus, testify dwelling of followers of the Vedic rituals. Main reason for the establishment of Aktha in the later Vedic period appears to be movements of saints from north to south-east on the northern land route, or the route of migration of communities from the west (Sarswati Valley) to the east (banks of Sadanira in north Bihar). Located by the side of this route, this small settlement appears to take form of a resort for *Rishi*s and sages who were frequently going up and down from Himalayan region to various parts of the Middle Ganga Plain. Soon it might have earned fame as the port of the sages, or *Rishipatana*. That these visitors were followers of Vedic religion is testified by the nature of exposed habitation floors and associated antiquities. The floors, with the use of fire and *kapalas* (the containers of the Vedic sacrifice), are indicative of performance of Vedic ritual at large scale at Aktha. The hermitage format appears to continue throughout its lifespan (between eighteenth century BCE and third/fourth century CE) of this settlement.[21] It may be held that the visit and stay of the sages and the learned ones helped Aktha, to gain reputation of being a centre of wisdom. To the Buddha, who was eager to preach his wisdom and learning to the mankind, such a place of reputation would certainly have been attracted. Also, since Aktha was located en route a major connective system of Indian subcontinent, it was also suitable for the spread of his teaching to distant places. *Rishipatana* and *Migadāya* were two separate entities. For, according to the *Divyāvadāna*, Aśoka gives a list of the places to be visited where he wished to construct *stūpas*. In this list *Isipatana* and *Migadāya* are mentioned separately supporting the above hypothesis.[22]

The possibility for identification of *Isipatana*, with the present-day religious establishment of Sārnāth is remote. Since this date, there is no indication for pre-Mauryan remains at Sārnāth. Contrary to this, Sārnāth is invariably referred in the texts and the epigraphs as '*Migadāya*'. Similarly, the archaeological findings of Aktha testify that this settlement was *Rishipatana* of the Buddhist text. If this is accepted then it can logically be assumed that the initial format of Sārnāth, the *Migadāya*, at the time of the First Sermon by the Lord was adjacent to *Rishipatana*, a moderate but a reputed hermitage-based settlement, Aktha. Both of these locales were situated amongst forest patches and grassland of the Varunā valley, south of the river Ganga. In spite of its location on the main land routes, Aktha did not develop as a trade centre, and continued as a hermitage based settlement. This was also the situation at the time of the arrival of the Buddha to Vārānasī-Sārnāth region, and even many centuries later. Remains of Period II at Aktha, which is of the Northern Black Polished Ware (NBPW) complex was of the time when the Lord came to the *Rishipatana-Migadāya*.

Advent of the Buddha to *Rishipatana-Migadāya*

The archaeological horizons of the Middle Ganga Plain, which could be identified being contemporary to the Buddha is the NBPW. This period is a well ascertained archaeological horizon of the Ganga Plain in general and the Middle Ganga Plain in particular. Characterized by the *deluxe* ceramic NBPW, the chrono-cultural position of this phase is well established. The date bracket of this period, for quite some time is accepted to be *c*.600–200 BCE.[23] But, the recently acquired early dates, including that of Ramnagar pushes back the beginning of NBPW horizons to at least 600 years. The date under consideration is countable to 1190 BCE (1405 BCE) on the basis of the charcoal sample from Period II of Ramnagar, which was processed for carbon dating by the Birbal Sahani Institute of Palaeobotony, Lucknow. Similar dates are also reported from Ayodhyā.[24] The other noteworthy point is that the later end of the bracket remains almost unaltered (third/second century BCE). And also, not all the dates of the recently excavated sites fall within the early bracket. For example the samples from NBPW period of Jhusi, are dated by the C_{14} method, between seventh and second centuries BCE.[25]As the evidence stands today, the total time span now for NBPW is countable to about 1,000 years, between *c*.1200 and third/second centuries BCE, which makes it contemporary to the date bracket assigned to the *Janpada* and the *Mahājanpada* period, by the traditional sources. According to the Buddhist sources, the listed states of the *Śoḍāsha-Mahājanpadas* flourished around 550 BCE. This is very close to the calculated time of the Buddha (date of *Mahāparinibbāna* 487/88 + total lifespan 80 = 567/568 BCE).[26] The archaeological horizons contemporary to the Lord therefore would be the later-half of the revised time-bracket of the NBPW period.

The territorial recognition of *Kāśī-Janpada* in the list of *Śoḍāsha-Mahājanpadas*, leaves no doubt that when the Buddha came to *Rishipatana-Migadāya* to deliver his First Sermon, near Vārānasī, it was the capital of Kāśī kingdom. Incidentally, excavation of Kāśī-Rājghāt, the identified capital of *Kāśī-Janpada*, was occupied only about a couple of centuries prior to the arrival of the Buddha at *Rishipatana-Migadāya*. For, the first inhabitants, known from the lowest deposit of Period IA, seem to clear the swampy land, on the left bank of the river Ganga, on its confluence with Varunā in around 800 BCE. The total of 2.87 m. thick deposit of their habitation was completely devoid of structural remains.[27] But, material remains show a combination of advanced technological knowledge, and simplicity in the daily utility items. As, 'They used iron implements, tools of bones and large number of terracotta objects like pottery discs (both unperforated and with single perforation), wheels, balls, ear ornaments, skin-rubber and stoppers. Among stone objects, main category was, 'balls of different sizes'. Beads of terracotta, paste and bone were the other reported forms.[28] Typical pottery of the time was Black-Slipped Ware (both plain and painted), Black-and-Red Ware (both plain and painted) and Red Ware (slipped and unslipped). The deposit of this period is said to be devoid of the NBPW. This village continued to exist for about 200 years (*c*.800–600 BCE). In the succeeding Period IB, NBPW, at Kāśī-Rājghāt though the earlier culture traits continued, advancement in pottery production and richness in other utility items is glaring. Terracotta objects like pottery discs, beads, etc., continued, in addition to some new forms, like double perforated pottery disc, etc. Similarly, in stone, increased number of beads, bowl, weight and pestle were reported.[29] Prevalence of clay modelling was another trait, which is represented by the handmade animal figures—elephant and bull—in grey and red fabric and one human head. The culmination of the grey ware ceramic technology in this period is marked by the prevalence of the NBPW, which not only forms a good percentage but appears in various kinds of surface treatments. A range of colours from shining black to golden and also some painted shards reveal the *deluxe* character of this ceramic. The other wares, of the earlier phase, like Black-Slipped and Black-and-Red Wares, continued. Though remains of dwelling structures of the period could not be unearthed, their existence in the form of reed walled huts with mud plastering has been assumed.[30] That perishable material was being used at the time for major structural activities, was also attested by the traces of a large wooden platform (34 m. long and 5 cm. thick) along the bank of the river. But the most significant structural activity of this period is a collective effort to construct a flood protective device in the form of a clay embankment. It was about 5.10 m. high with basal width of 10.80 m. After some time, this embankment was raised further by 1.10 m. There appears a strong need or compulsion to live by the side of the river Ganga, even though the settlement was threatened on and off by periodical floods. The date for Period IB on account of the C_{14} date of 490 ± 100 BCE is countable to *c.* sixth/fifth to fourth centuries BCE, which makes it contemporary to the Buddha.[31]

It may also be important to note that the Buddhist literature is silent about the Buddha's visit to this capital city. But, Vārānasī occurs numerous times in the texts, as '*Rishipatana-Migadāya* was said to be located near Benāras'.[32] Suggesting the Lord went directly to *Rishipatana-Migadāya*, Aktha-Sārnāth, the area not only close to the capital city, but was also located within its boundaries. Remains of Period II of Aktha, testifies that it was a well established settlement when the Lord came here. Further, its earlier format, marked by simplicity of the artifacts and structures and strong hermitage-bias, continued.[33] Nature of Sārnāth between the First Sermon (sixth century BCE) and the Mauryan king Aśoka (third century BCE) is not known through the archaeological remains. One is not sure whether the place continued as *Migadāya*/Deer Park, or had developed into a settlement as pre-Aśokan period has not been identified in the archaeological records of Sārnāth. Moreover, it might be significant to recall that in the list of the 8 *stūpas* (8 + 2 if Piplivan, and Drona are included), constructed on the ashes of the Lord just after his *Mahāparinibbāna*, *Isipatana*/Sārnāth does not fair in the Buddhist texts. In spite of the paucity of the material remains, it may be held that donation at Sārnāth might have started right from the time of the First Sermon of the Buddha. Life of a Buddhist follower, monk/nun depends primarily on the offerings by the devotees. Be it food, clothes or shelters (when constructed), every necessity of life is provided to them in the form of offerings or donations. It is therefore hard to comprehend that offerings by devotees were not made at *Migadāya*, the place where the First Sermon was delivered by the Lord, and *saṃgha* was formed immediately thereafter. In the *Vinaya Pitaka* it is said that a merchant, Yaśa, went to the Deer Park *Rishipatana*, and was accepted as a lay disciple by the Lord. At the time *saṃgha* was already formed by the induction of the 5 disciples to whom the First Sermon was delivered by the Lord.[34] Glimpse of offering by lay devotees to the monks too can be had from the Buddhists texts. According to the *Vimānavatthu*, for instance, a resident near Fisherman Gate of Vārānasī, when saw monks passing through the gate, took them to her house and offered them food, etc. She also constructed a pavilion to place them and listen to *dhamma*.[35] Suggesting that even common citizens of Vārānasī city, were making offerings to the monks. Indications of structure building too are found in such literary descriptions. These instances are suggestive of donation of structures at the pilgrimage from sixth century BCE. The paucity of material remains of pre-Mauryan period at Sārnāth, may be due to the use of perishable material for the construction of buildings, as was the case during the NBPW period in the Middle Ganga Plain. That remains of such constructions are difficult to survive, is also demonstrated from the findings of Period IB of Kāśī-Rājghāt. The possibility of religious and dwelling structures in the form of donations in pre-Buddha period at Sārnāth, therefore is strong.

Donations and Growth of *Migadāya*

Migadāya, the place of the First Sermon of the Lord, has been identified by the clusters of ruins on the southern shore of Sarang-tāl at Sārnāth. The land mark of which is Dhāmeka *stūpa,* standing over ground, and the low lying structures in its southern and northern vicinity. Discovery of Sārnāth was made by a savaging operation of 1794, by Jagat Singh, a contractor building a locality of Vārānasī city, Chetaganj. A *stūpa* named after the contractor, Jagat Singh was dismantled up to its foundation. The area lying north of this structure, in the form of a high mound was excavated by Oertel in 1904–5 which brought to light remains of a large temple complex, known as Main Shrine, and the pillar of Aśoka.[36] He also examined Chaukhandī mound and unearthed 476 pieces of sculptures and 41 inscriptions.[37] Subsequent excavations by Marshall and his team in the years 1907 and 1908, covered the northern and southern part of the mound. From northern half he unearthed three monastic buildings of the Late Kushāṇa period while from the southern area, particularly around the Dharmarājikā *stūpa* and on the north side of the Dhāmeka *stūpa,* he brought to light numerous small *stūpas* and shrines.[38] In the discoveries inscribed statue of the Buddha, part of inscribed umbrella and stone inscriptions of eleventh century CE and that of Kumāradevī are noteworthy. Excavation at Sārnāth was resumed again in the year 1914–15 to the north, east, and west of the Main Shrine, by Hargreaves.[39] Recovery of inscriptions of Kumārgupta II, and Buddhagupta, along with a number of carved pieces ranging from the Mauryan to the medieval periods were significant additions to Sārnāth collection. Later, Sahani conducted intensive excavations in the covered area lying between Dhāmeka *stūpa* and the Main Shrine, and the monastery lying in the north-western corner of the site.[40] Among the remains of structures exposed by him, the passage/*suranga* for meditation of monks, was significant. As a result of these field investigations, and later cleaning operations by the Archaeological Survey of India, this Buddhist complex is strewed with structures and icons dating between Mauryan and early medieval times. These remains are material expression of the faith of the devotees in the *dhamma*, and were donations at the place of the First Sermon. On account of the style of carvings, epigraphs, and context of findings the material remains of Sārnāth are divisible within—Maurya, Śunga, Kushāṇa, Gupta, and post-Gupta. Nature of donation of each period is discussed with the help of important archaeological findings. Contribution of the Mauryan period at Sārnāth is identified in the form of three monuments—The Dharmarājikā/Jagat Singh *stūpa*, the apsidal temple/monastery and the inscribed pillar with Lion Capital.

The Dharmarājikā *stūpa*, as is known after the inscription of tenth century giving name to the monument, and was constructed at the instance of King Aśoka. It is referred in the texts that after dividing the ashes of the Lord obtained from reopening 7 of the earlier *stūpas*. Aśoka constructed many *stūpas* at Buddhist sites with the same name.[41] He is also recorded to have desired to visit *Isipatana* and *Migadāya*, where he wanted to construct *stūpas*.[42] On account of which it can logically be deduced that the dismantled *stūpa*, Jagat Singh of the site too was constructed in the Mauryan times. However, Marshall's investigations of 1907–8, confirmed this assumption, as the earliest format of this *stūpa* is composition of Mauryan bricks (measuring 19½″ × 14½″ × 2½″ and 16½″ × 12½″ × 3½″). It was of 44′3″ diameter[43] and was crowned by a stone *harmika*, which was found inset in the southern chapel of the Main Shrine. The *harmika*, a plain square monolithic railing (measuring 8′4″ in length and 1′9″ in height) of sandstone bears characteristic Mauryan polish.[44] Parts of this railing retain donative records of the later period, which has been discussed a little later. Excavation of the western side of the Main Shrine area first by Oertel and then by Marshall, brought to light fragments and *in situ* base of the Aśokan column. This pillar with Lion Capital, as per engravings on it was erected at the instance of emperor Aśoka. The content of inscription sheds light on the date of apsidal monastery in front of which was this pillar erected. It has also been recorded, by the excavators, for instance that: 'Due west to the Aśokan column and at a distance of 54′4″ were discovered the foundations of an apsidal building 82′ 6″ in length, 38′10″ in width, the apse towards the west the entrance presumably facing the Aśokan column.'[45]

Dated to the late Mauryan times by the excavators, this structure appears to be earlier than the time of Aśoka. The king in the epigraph shows concern about laying norms to be followed by the monks and the nuns in order to maintain discipline in the *saṃgha*. The translated version of the epigraph as per Sahani reads as: 'His sacred Majesty King Piyadasi. . . . The Church is [not] by anyone to be divided. But whosoever, monk or nun break up the Church, shall be made to don white robes and made to dwell in another dwelling.'[46]

This would mean that a good number of the monks and the nuns were already residing here when Aśoka was addressing them, suggesting the monastery to be of pre-Aśoka in date with the possibility that a pre-Mauryan structure made of perishable material is strong. That it was the same which was renovated in brick during the time of Aśoka, though is difficult to establish, due to fragmentary nature of the Aśokan epigraph and lack of proper exposure and recording of the basal deposits of the monastery, its likelihood is strong, that all the architectural marvels, discovered at *Migadāya* were donations by the Mauryan emperor Aśoka will go unquestioned. Being royal in nature, these donations are confined to large building constructions complying imperial dictate. It may be significant to note that the structural offerings at the Buddhist sites initiated by king Aśoka laid foundation for the construction of large worship monuments, which was subsequently, Śunga to medieval, followed at large scale. Taking into account the significance of *Migadāya* to Buddhism, the remains of Śunga period are very restricted at Sārnāth in comparison to the sites like Sānchī, Bharhut, etc. Contribution to the period is represented by a group of 53 railing posts, coping stones and cross-bars about a dozen of which were unearthed by Marshall and Konow not *in situ*, but inset in a mud-brick floor (rectangle in shape and later in date), located in the north-east of the Main Shrine area.[47] On account of palaeography and the style of the carvings of the posts, a date bracket of second first centuries BCE could be assigned to this group. The epigraphs mention name of the donors in Brāhmī script, a practice popular during Śunga times. All the Śunga remains were part of a railing. Whether a railing was attached to the Mauryan *stūpa*, Dharmarājikā during Śunga period as part of offering to this sacred place is an open question. For, it was a common practice of the Śunga period to enlarge the earlier *stūpas* and provide them an ornamented enclosure, which is attested by the remains at Sānchī and Bharhut. There could be another possibility that the construction was made independently during Śunga period, at this site. In the present state of our knowledge these questions are difficult to answer. But, it is certain that the pillars of the Śunga railing had such reputation that these were reused in the Main Shrine complex, in later centuries. This has been noted by Sahani, who records that some of the pillars were reused as base pillar for lamps in Gupta times with contemporary donors' name.[48]

Donation of Buddhists icons at the pilgrimages was the practice initiated during Kushāṇa period. The *Bodhisattva* images from Śravastī, Mathurā and Sārnāth are illustrated examples. The *Bodhisattva* image of Sārnāth is significant for more than one reason. One that it is inscribed and two that its medium and style is not indigenous. Cut in red sandstone of Sikari, this colossal image (8′ 1½″ high and 2′ 10″ wide) with tenon base was attached with a large umbrella. Carved in Mathurā style, this image was inscribed, both in front and at the back of the pedestal. Besides, the octagonal shaft of the umbrella also retains a 10 line inscription of almost the same content as of the main statue. The epigraph records donation of this image at Vārānasī, where the Lord walked . . . by Bala Bhikkhu (Pushyavudhi), who was the master of *Tipitikas* . . . 'together with the *kshatrapas* Vanaspara and Kharapallana, and together with four classes'. The date given for this donation is 'third year of Maharaja Kanishka'.[49] Incidentally, this is the earliest known Buddha image at Sārnāth. The content of this epigraph is particularly important for the history of Buddhist icon-making in general and Vārānasī-Sārnāth school of sculptures in particular. As the date 81 CE (third year of Kanishka = 78 + 3 CE) , specifies the beginning of donation and export of the *Bodhisattva* images from Mathurā, the sculpture-centre of Kushāṇa to main Buddhist pilgrimages; the style of carving and the medium of the Bala Bhikkhu donational image of Sārnāth, subscribe the fact that the roots of Vārānasī-Sārnāth school of sculptures, which flourished in the subsequent centuries, was in the Kushāṇa images of Mathurā. The content of the epigraph under consideration is also noteworthy for determining involvement of sections of society in causing the installation of donational images during Kushāṇa times. The group of donors mentioned on the *Bodhisattva* image of Sārnāth, are a learned monk, two *kshatrapas* and four classes. The 'Four Classes', are inferred to be the 'monks, nuns, laymen, and laywomen'.[50] It appears to be a courtesy in which credit is extended to all, or the blessing to be procured by the pious deed of donation is to be shared by all. Two names of *kshatrapas*—Vanaspara and Kharapallana—are of the persons belonging to affluent administrative class of the society, who might have financed the making and installation of the image.

The learned monk, Bala, is said to have supervised the making of the image. Another noteworthy feature is that the learned monk is given priority in the order of the donors in the epigraph. The mention of Bala, the supervisor of the image making/donor as master of *Tipitikas*, was perhaps to assign authenticity to the icon. It may be recalled that the practice of carving Buddha images had begun in Kushāṇa times. In a situation like this it is logical to assume that for the acceptance of an icon (produced as earliest samples) by the devotees, it is necessary that its iconography is testified by a reliable religious person, who is well versed with the relevant texts. Bala Bhikkhu appears to be one such authority who was master of *Tipitikas*, to authenticate the *Bodhisattva* images being produced at Mathurā. Since he was a monk, monetary support for acquisition of medium, payment to the sculptor and transportation of the image from Mathurā to Sārnāth was acclaimed from the *kshatrapas*—Vanaspara and Kharapallana. If this is accepted then it may be held that donation of the icon at the Buddhist pilgrimage during Kushāṇa times was a joint venture of affluent persons and the learned monks.

The practice of offering of images at *Migadāya* intensified during the Gupta period. This tendency is glimpsed in the catalogue of Sārnāth collection.[51] A cluster of images of fourth/fifth century CE was recovered from the vicinity of the Main Shrine. But, a good proportion of the collection received severe damage, particularly the ones with epigraphs. For almost all inscribed images recovered from Sārnāth up to 1914, are partly preserved.[52] In these name of the donors like 'Skandvarnna', 'Dhandeva', 'Buddha-priya', 'Bandhugupta' and 'Kumārgupta' may be mentioned. The list includes lay devotees, monks, and the king. Though inscriptions of Gupta period are known for their accurate recording of the time of the events, these donational epigraphs are dated on paleographic account, which is suggested to be of fourth/fifth and sixth/seventh centuries CE. However, a group of the Buddha images which were recovered from the east of the Main Shrine in the course of excavation of 1914–15 are dated in Gupta era 154 and 157. All the three images were gifts by monk Abhayamitra between 473/4 and 476/7 CE.[53] Practice of donating statues at *Migadāya*, picked up such a momentum during Gupta times, that earlier carvings and architectural members were re-donated at this pilgrimage. Two inscriptions engraved on Mauryan railing, for instance, claim donation of this composition by the Sarvāstivādin sect in third/fourth century CE over-engraving an earlier inscription, which was written four centuries before.[54] This would mean that the composition in consideration was donated three times—Mauryan, Śunga/Kushāṇa, and Gupta. Similarly, one of the railing pillars of the Śunga period retains inscription of Gupta period, which reads: 'This is a pious gift of the devoted worshipper Kirtti, a lamp put up in the Principal Shrine'.[55] Buildings were also constructed as part of offering to the pious place of the First Sermon of the Lord during the Gupta period. Monastery II, north-west of the Main Shrine at Sārnāth has been identified as an early Gupta structure.[56] All the above examples suggest that donation of icons and carvings at Sārnāth had increased greatly during Gupta times.

The post-Gupta period witnessed similar tendency, when icons, as well as structures were profusely donated at Sārnāth. Among the devotees who contributed to Sārnāth there were also the followers of brahmanical pantheon. For example, the inscription on pedestal of preaching the Buddha of eleventh century CE, mentions that the donors Sthirapala and his brother Vasantapala (of Bengal), who had also established in Kāśī the temple of Iśān/Śiva and Chitraghanta /Durga, built the shrine of *gandhakutī*, at Sārnāth. The inscription also records restoration of two principal monuments of *Migadāya*.[57] A well documented construction of Monastery I, by Kumāradevī, the Buddhist queen of Govindchandra (1114–1154), is example of monumental donation at the site by followers of *dhamma*.[58] Offering of the 'pious gift', the idol of the Buddha at *Migadāya* in its history had a rising curve with regard to the quantum, from Kushāṇa to the Medieval times. The import of image had to change into the local production, in accordance with the successive increasing demands. Archaeological findings of Vārānasī-Sārnāth region of last decade suggest that there was cause-effect relationship between the sculpturing centres and the quantitative demand of icons to be offered at Sārnāth.

Sārnāth School of Sculpture: Origin and Development

The narration of the *Babbu-Jātaka* for instance, elaborates that the *Bodhisattva* was born a stone cutter in Kāśī, who used to quarry and shape stones in a rural set up.[59] It suggests that, stone carving was an established craft in Kāśī, in the ancient times. It would also suggest that the primary theme of stone carving was Buddhists. Date of the *Jātakas* is a matter of debate. However, the time bracket assigned to this group of literature is between Śunga and Gupta Periods.[60] Corroboration and details of the referred to incident are reflected in the archaeological remains of chiselling workshops and image collections of Sārnāth and Vārānasī. A chain of stone carvers' villages were identified and a few also excavated on one of the paleo-channels Rajapur-nālā a tributary stream of the river Ganga, near Sārnāth. Kotwa, which was excavated extensively, was a small village-cum-stone-carving-workshop which was active between *c.* first and twelfth centuries CE.[61] The three periods identified at this site were—Kushāṇa, Gupta and post-Gupta/early medieval. It is not without significance that this time span by and large corresponds with the history of stone images which have been obtained from the Buddhist pilgrimage of Sārnāth. It may be clarified, that the earlier stone sculpture, the Lion Capital and some other specimens stored in Sārnāth Museum, date back to Mauryan times, third century BCE.[62] Though these examples are also chiselled on Chunar sandstone, the medium used mostly for the production of ancient carvings in Vārānasī, these cannot be accepted as products of local craftsmanship. I have shown that these examples were modelled under the direction of royal dictate, and may not be accepted as the workmanship of local stone cutting tradition.[63] There is also no impact or continuity of these carvings, in the succeeding stage, Śunga period (first/second century BCE), which also appears to yield only a couple of stone sculptures—Aktha Yaksha and parts of railing, stored now in Sārnāth Museum.[64] Not only the number of specimens is very restricted but, there is no archaeological finding to support that sculpture making was an indigenous practice in Vārānasī, at this point of time. Beginning of Common Era witnessed the dawn of stone-carving craft in Vārānasī. It is interesting to note that the images of this time (Kushāṇa period, between first and third centuries CE), which are stored in Sārnāth Museum, comprise both local produce and the imported ones. For example, out of nine Kushāṇa images described by Sahani, three are carved of *Sikari* sandstone, the medium used at Mathurā centre of lithic carving. While the remaining six have been carved from Chunar sandstone.[65] Sahani, also concludes that the later images were modelled by local sculptor, who copied the *Bodhisattva* image made at Mathurā centre, particularly the one which was donated by Bala Bhikkhu. It is also testified from the chiselling *debris* of workshop sites, as the one at Kotwa, that chiselling operation had started during first occupation—Period I, dated to Kushāṇa times. The demand of icons for religious monuments and rituals in this period appears to be confined primarily to Buddhism, and also limited in amount, in Vārānasī-Sārnāth region. Another noteworthy aspect is that as large block of stone was required for carving of colossal independent figures of the *Bodhisattva*, quarry and transportation of the medium from Chunar hills to the workshops in Vārānasī, was special in nature.

The succeeding period, coeval with the dynastic rule of the Guptas, is a stage of excellence in the history of sculpturing art of Vārānasī. The culmination of carving art of the time is marked by impressive proportion of figurative forms, mastery of composition of the theme, and divine expression of the images, which is characteristic of the classical Indian art. Numerous masterpieces donated to the Buddhist establishment at Sārnāth are illustrative examples of the fine execution of the Vārānasī school of sculptures.[66] The earlier style, (Kushāṇa) though had initiated sculpture-making in this region, the local craftsmanship took this craftsmanship to far-reaching heights. Because, they could combine their own chiselling mastery and artistic amplitude with that of classical Indian expressions and idioms. The style of Kushāṇa times was modified and perfected considerably. Archaeological findings suggest, that the earlier workshops continued. Period II of Kotwa, which is of Gupta period, testifies this. For at this site, Gupta chiselling debris rests just above a Kushāṇa chiselling floor.[67] But besides continuation of the earlier carving workshops, many new settlements were at work. Survey of Rajapur-nālā has brought to light sites like Rajapur, Asapur, etc., which form part of new workshop sites of Gupta times. The large quantum of the images appears to have been produced at the workshops due to considerable increase in the demand of icons. It may be recalled that the increase in the demand of icon was because the practice of offerings images at Sārnāth had intensified during Gupta period. The mushroom growth of stone sculpturing workshops in the vicinity of Sārnāth, is also indicative of migration of a number of artisans in the region. The increase in the demand of products, and fulfilment of it by masters with high artistic amplitude of carvings might have helped the workshops earn high reputation. This reputation might have prompted export of images to other pilgrimages, resulting in further increase in demand and production of masterpiece compositions for both local and export consumptions. Besides, icons carvings were also utilized for adorning structures. The carved slabs on the Dhāmeka *stūpa* are characterized by classical Gupta floral panels and are examples of skilled carving of the time. The post-Gupta period also experienced large-scale stone-cutting for both image-making and decorative architectural panels, by master craftsmen of the region. This is evident from very a large collection of carvings at Sārnāth. Continuation of the earlier workshops, and perhaps becoming of some others, were catering the needs of the early medieval demands of Sārnāth. The remains of Period III at Kotwa are dated to the same period. One of the major factors for the growth of sculpturing centres, besides the demand, was the availability of the suitable quality and quantity of medium in the neighbourhood. In Vārānasī-Sārnāth region, the choice of the medium throughout the historical period was fine quality sandstone. Chunar hills, which are composed of Vindhyan formations, retain fine quality sandstone, and are the nearest resource. Archaeological findings suggest that large quantities of sandstone blocks, in a number of hue, was being quarried from these hills, between third century BCE and the twelfth century CE.[68] Though Chunar hills are located at a distance from Vārānasī-Sārnāth region, this resource area is upstream from the consumer centre. Also, the sandstone formation lies close to the river Ganga, which facilitated navigation of blocks of stone to Vārānasī, without much surface transportation.

The small streams, like Rajapur-nālā, connected main course of the river Ganga with the workshop sites. These sites were located on the banks of this palaeo-channel, and away from the main channel of the river Ganga. I have demonstrated elsewhere, that an effective mechanism of transportation of large sandstone blocks was already devised and was in practice between Chunar hills and settlement of ancient Vārānasī from the time of emperor Aśoka. It is thus, logical to conclude that this system had continued in the Kushāṇa and later times also, as even today many times Chunar slabs are transported to the city of Vārānasī through navigation. It may not be a mere coincidence that the workshop sites, in the form of small village settlements were located on Rajapur-nālā. A smooth route of transportation of huge blocks of stones was formed by this stream and the connecting river Ganga (main route of transportation) on the side of which is located Chunar hills. Desertion of Buddhist establishment of Sārnāth, sometime around twelfth/thirteenth century CE, appears to uproot the long flourishing sculpturing tradition of Vārānasī. There appears to be desertion of sculptors' settlements in the region, and sudden lowering proportion of ornate monuments. My ethnographical study indicates that after a long gap of about seven to eight centuries, stone sculpturing in this region was initiated afresh. With a view to understanding the sculpturing craft, icon-making workshops of Vārānasī city were studied. The modern carving centres are of two categories—one where portraits of important persons are modelled, at others images of divinities are produced.

It is the latter which have relevance to the present theme, as their format represent traditional carving. In modern times, Jaipur has a reputation for icon carving. Following Jaipur style of sculpturing the present-day workshops of Vārānasī city cater to the local needs, as well as those of neighbouring small townships, like Mirzapur, Jaunpur, Ghazipur, Chunar, etc.[69] Ethnographic information was gathered from one of the most famous and active centres of icon-making—Lallapura, by visiting and interviewing the craftsmen in the year 1993.

Jaipur Murty Kendra is located in Lallapura Mohalla, a densely populated area of Vārānasī city. The main produce of this workshop is the images of gods and goddesses carved primarily on white or grey marbles, the medium popular for such icon in modern times in north India. But sandstone and other soft stones are also used, at times. The choice of medium depends mostly on the demand of the customers, while the images are made following the Jaipur style, a modern tradition of sculpturing which has in recent years gained popularity in north India. It has been observed that most of the idols installed in modern Hindu temples of northern India, are carved in Jaipur style. The name of the centre under consideration appears to claim direct rapport with the earned reputation of Jaipur region famous for making images of divinities. We were informed that at the initial stage, a couple of sculptors were actually brought to Vārānasī from Jaipur, who established Jaipur style at this workshop. The workshop under study is an enclosed open space, where raw material and carved sculptures are accumulated in heaps at the periphery, while carving activities are performed in the centre, which is kept more or less spacious and empty. Owned by Ram Sewak Prasad, who himself supervised the entire chiselling operation, a team of 25 to 30 craftsmen works here from dawn to dusk. Each craftsman specialized in one type of work, e.g. primary dressing, chiselling of the physiognomic details, rubbing the surface, and colouring, etc. Three to five persons are engaged in each category of work. But, there was only one master craftsman named Bachau, who is actually responsible for the formulation of the composition and execution of the finer details. It was his artistic amplitude and skill which is mirrored through the entire produce of this icon-making workshop. Our study revealed that sculpturing processes at Lallapura workshop were initiated by the chief sculptor, Bachau. He first used to draw the composition over the select suitable block of stone. The entire carving theme is sketched along a vertical line. The figurative form in this case, thereafter, used to be drawn in accordance with the traditional way of relative measurement units, which are also recommended in ancient texts.[70] For instance, the entire length of a standing figure is divided into four equal parts or *bhaga*s. At Lallapura centre, each of these measuring units from top to bottom, are—crown to neck, neck to nave, nave to knee and knee to the bottom of the feet, respectively. Similarly, width of different parts of the body is determined by using various combinations of this unit. The centre of the forehead, tip of the nose, middle of the chin, nave of the central figure fall invariably on this centrally drawn main line of the composition.

Chiselling of an image is done in two to three stages. The first stage of chiselling is confined to the primary dressing of the select block of stone. Using *takani* and *tipani* (local names for broad edged chisels), the stone-cutter, not the master sculptor, knocks out the extra mass of stone from the drawn composition. The primary dressing operation is carried out by a select few chisellers. In the second stage, general shape of various parts of the composition is brought out. Rough form of parts of the body like hand, crown, ornaments, etc., are carved out in this process. The same group of chisellers who perform primary dressing, execute chiselling in the second stage. In the third stage, when details of human anatomy, hair dress, ornaments, dress, etc., are carved, the task is performed invariably by the chief craftsman. Various types of fine edged chisels are used for careful carving at this stage. For example, round-edged chisel, *takuli*, pencil-pointed chisel, *kaudena*, etc., are used for executing minute details like pupil of eyes, brows, nostrils and details of ornaments, hairstyle, etc. It is this stage which is responsible for denoting the stylistic features to the sculpted figures. The final stage of finishing of the image under process of carving includes rubbing and at times even colouring. In order to remove the chisel marks and smoothen the surface of the carving, a laborious task is performed. The carved surface is rubbed by *kurum* stone (a type of porous hardstone) by sprinkling water over the surface from time to time. Unskilled persons, the boys of the stone-cutters and chief sculptors' family are usually engaged in this task. In case of painted images, oil colours are applied over the rubbed and finished surface by the painters of this workshop.

The historical evidence indicates that during the Kushāṇa period, there were important icon producing centres in north India, like Takshaśilā, Mathurā, etc., but, Sārnāth had yet to rise up to the status of image-making centre of repute. The donation demand of Sārnāth was fulfilled by importing images from the famous and nearby centre Mathurā. Import of the *Bodhisattva* icons from Mathurā to Sārnāth is attested by the epigraphical records which were discussed above. When the demand for icons increased, there was need to produce images locally. This need was fulfilled by making copies of the Mathurā style of compositions at Vārānasī in the same period. This is apparent from the other contemporary *Bodhisattva* images made of Chunar sandstone, at Sārnāth. There is no doubt that such an initiation marked the beginning of icon production in the area of this study. But, the question is whether the copies made in Vārānasī were products of local artisans or were creations of a workshop headed by the master craftsman from Mathurā? Clues for answer to this lie in the ethnographic instance. It was shown above, for instance, that image-making in modern Vārānasī was initiated by bringing master craftsmen from Jaipur, which is the main icon-producing centre of north India. This was after Vārānasī had lost the past glory of sculpture chiselling in the last century. A speedy growth of the craft is possible in this situation. And also a team of local persons receive training in this process. It may be held that a similar process had taken place during Kushāṇa times also, which established stone carving as one of the main crafts of Vārānasī. Because, in the following centuries, this craft could reach the status of world-famous carving tradition under the banner of 'Sārnāth School of Sculptures'. Moreover, it may not be an overstatement that the main reason for the growth of Sārnāth style was the continuous and successive increase in the demand by the donors.

Conclusion

Origin of Buddhism at Vārānasī with the First Sermon of the Lord enriched the culture milieu of the region, which already appears to have gained high reputation of being the place of wisdom. Growth of Buddhist pilgrimage at Sārnāth provided impetus for quantitative and qualitative development of arts and crafts in Vārānasī region. The statement that, 'Sārnāth could attain status of one of the most significant and well established pilgrimage of Buddhism of the ancient times, because of the generous patronage of the donors', would not look an overstatement if one glances through the structures and sculptures of Sārnāth. The earliest group of structures and sculptures—monastery, Dharmarājikā *stūpa* and the Lion pillar of the time of Mauryan emperor Aśoka, for instance—to the *vihāra* of the medieval period which was constructed by Queen Kumāradevī, are donations to this Buddhist establishment. The offerings of independent icons at this site during Kushāṇa times was very significant. It initiated practice of donating images. This practice in turn became one of the major factors for the origin and development of stone sculpturing craft in and around Sārnāth. As a result of which, by the Gupta period Sārnāth had earned the reputation of one of the most productive and artistic centres of icon-carving.

Gupta stage was the stage when not only the nucleus of the sacred place was enlarged, but also the landscape of Sārnāth expanded towards the southern axis, up to the river Ganga (about 5 km.). This was due to the reason that the demand of stone carvings at Sārnāth gave impetus for the growth of craft centres on Rajapur-nālā, which was well connected with resource area, Chunar hills. Besides, the large demand of icons at Sārnāth from donors, there were other supporting factors which helped this region to become one of the world-famous centres of sculpture production in ancient India. Easy availability of good quality sandstone in the neighbourhood, the hills of Chunar, and natural facility for the transportation of the medium through navigation were the other added advantages. The archaeological findings of Chunar and Vārānasī-Sārnāth regions throw significant light on the entire mechanism of sandstone carving and also reveal inter se relationship of the main consumer centre, the

Buddhist establishment of Sārnāth, with the craft villages/workshops (Kotwa) and the resource area (Chunar). The entire mechanism of lithic craft developed and continued on the grounds of the nature and quantum of demand of donors of the idols and the monuments.

Notes

1. F.O. Oertel, *Annual Report of Archaeological Survey of India*, 1904–5, Delhi: Swati Publications (repr.), 1990, pp. 59–104.
2. John Marshall, 'Excavations at Sārnāth', *Archaeological Survey of India Annual Report, 1904–5*, Delhi: Swati Publications, 1990; Marshall J. and S. Know, 'Sārnāth', *Archaeological Survey of India*, Delhi: Swati Publications, repr. 1990.
3. R.K. Mookerji, *Aśoka*, New Delhi: Motilal Banarsidass, 1968, p. 89.
4. D.C. Ganguly, 'The North India During the Eleventh and Twelfth Centuries', in *The Struggle for Empire*, Bombay: Bharatiya Vidya Bhavan's History and Culture of Indian People, 1957, ch. II, pp. 52–4.
5. Vidula Jayaswal, *From Stone Quarry to Sculpturing Workshop: A Report on the Archaeological Investigations around Chunar, Vārānasī and Sārnāth*, New Delhi: Agam Kala Prakashan, 1998, p. 110.
6. Ibid., p. 112.
7. Ibid., pp. 110–11.
8. Vidula Jayaswal, 'Antiquity for Vārānasī as Revealed by the Excavation at Aktha (2008–9)', *Puratattva*, Bulletin of Indian Archaeological Society, 2009, vol. 39, pp. 141–6.
9. E.B. Havell, *Benares: The Sacred City*, Vārānasī: Vishvidaylaya Prakashan, 2002, repr., p. 2.
10. Vidula Jayaswal, *From Stone Quarry to Sculpturing Workshop: A Report on the Archaeological Investigations around Chunar, Vārānasī and Sārnāth*, New Delhi: Agam Kala Prakashan, 1998, pp. 114–15.
11. Ibid., pp. 184–210.
12. I.B. Horner, *The Collection of the Middle Length Sayings* (*Majjhima Nikāya*), Oxford: Pali Text Society, 1995 (repr.), vol. I, p. 214.
13. J.J. Jones, *The Mahāvastu*, translated from the Buddhist Sanskrit (first published 1949), London, 1987, repr., vol. I, p. 37.
14. A.K. Narain and P. Singh, *Excavations at Rajghat*, Vārānasī: Banaras Hindu University, 1977, pt. III, p. 19.
15. R.K. Mookerji, *Ancient Indian Education*, New Delhi: Motilal Banarsidass, 1980, p. 606.
16. Vidula Jayaswal, *Ancient Vārānasī: An Archaeological Perspectives* (*Excavations at Aktha*), New Delhi: Aryan Books International, 2009, p. 60.
17. G.C. Pande, *Vedic Samskriti* (in Hindi), Allahabad: Lokbharati, 2001, p. 268.
18. Ibid., pp. 268–9.
19. Vidula Jayaswal, 'Aktha: A Satellite Settlement of Sārnāth, Vārānasī (Report of Excavations Conducted in the Year 2002)', p. 57, *Bharati*. Bulletin of the Department of Ancient Indian History, Culture and Archaeology, Banaras Hindu University, vol. 26, 2003, pp. 61–180.
20. T.N. Dharmadhikari, *Yajnayudhani* (*An Album of Sacrificial Utensils with Descriptive Notes*), Poona: Vaidika Samsodhana Mandala, 1989, p. 20.

21. Vidula Jayaswal, 'Antiquity for Vārānasī as Revealed by the Excavation at Aktha (2008–9)', *Puratattva*, Bulletin of Indian Archaeological Society, 2009, vol. 39, pp. 141–6.
22. G.P. Malalasekera, *Dictionary of Pali Proper Names*, New Delhi: Munshiram Manoharlal, 1995, repr., vol. I, p. 325.
23. A.K. Narain and T.N. Roy, *Excavations at Rajghat*, Vārānasī: Banaras Hindu University, 1976, pt. I, p. 23.
24. B.R. Mani and Sureshwar D. Sinha, *Origins of Civilization: New Light and Fresh Perspectives on Ancient History*, New Delhi: Bharatiya Kala Prakashan, 2011, p. 234.
25. V.D. Misra, J.N. Pal, M.C. Gupta and P.P. Joglekar, *Excavations at Jhusi (Pratishthanapur)—A fresh light on the Archaeological Profile of the Middle Gangatic Plain*, New Delhi: Indian Archaeological Society, 2009. Special Report no. 3, p. 42.
26. V.S. Pathak, 'Date of Buddha's Mahaparinibbana and Inscriptions of Aśoka', *Bharati.* The Bulletin of the Depdrtment of Anceint Indian History, Culture and Archaeology, ed. V. Jayaswal, vol. 26, 2000, pp. 5–28.
27. A.K. Narain and T.N. Roy, *Excavations at Rajghat*, p. 22.
28. Ibid., pp. 22–3.
29. Ibid., pp. 23–4.
30. Ibid., p. 24.
31. Ibid.
32. F.L. Woodword, The Book of the Kindred Sayings (*Saṁyutta Nikāya*) or Grouped Sutta, Oxford: The Pali Text Society, 1996, repr., pt. IV, pp. 101, 111–12.
33. Vidula Jayaswal, *Ancient Vārānasī: An Archaeological Perspectives* (*Excavations at Aktha*), New Delhi: Aryan Books International, 2009, p. 9.
34. I.B. Horner, *The Book of the Discipline* (*Vinaya-Pitaka*) (*Mahāvagga*), London: The Pali Text Society, 1951, repr. 1982, vol. IV, pp. 23–4.
35. I.B. Horner, *The Collection of the Middle Length Sayings* (*Majjhima-nikāya*), Oxford: Pali Text Society, 1954, repr. 1993, vol. I, p. 43.
36. *Annual Report of the Archaeological Survey of India, 1904–5*, pp. 59–104.
37. B. Majumdar, *A Guide to Sārnāth*, New Delhi: The Manager Government of India, 1947, p. 24.
38. Ibid., pp. 24–5.
39. Ibid., p. 25.
40. Ibid., pp. 25–6.
41. J. Ph. Vogel, 'Buddhist Sculpture from Benares', *Annual Report 1902–4*, New Delhi: Archaeological Survey of India, 1906, pp. 212–26.
42. *Divyāvadāna*, pp. 389–94.
43. B. Majumdar, *A Guide to Sārnāth*, p. 26.
44. Ibid., p. 30.
45. *Archaeological Survey of India Annual Report*, 1914–15, p. 109.
46. D.R. Sahani, *Catalogue of the Museum of Archaeology at Sārnāth*, Calcutta: Superintendent Government Printing, 1914, p. 30.
47. Ibid., pp. 208–16.
48. Ibid., p. 211.
49. Ibid., p. 35.
50. Ibid., pp. 35–6.
51. Ibid., pp. 40–86.
52. Ibid.

53. Marshall, 'Excavations at Sārnāth', p. 98.
54. B. Majumdar, *A Guide to Sārnāth*, p. 30.
55. D.R. Sahani, *Catalogue*, p. 211.
56. B. Majumdar, *A Guide to Sārnāth*, p. 38.
57. D.R. Sahani, *Catalogue*, pp. 88–9.
58. B. Majumdar, *A Guide to Sārnāth*, pp. 36–7.
59. *Jātaka*, no. 137.
60. M. Winternitz, *A History of Indian Literature*, New Delhi: Munshiram Manoharlal, 1987, repr., vol. II, pp. 115–16.
61. Vidula Jayaswal, *From Stone Quarry to Sculpturing Workshop: A Report on the Archaeological Investigations around Chunar, Vārānasī and Sārnāth*, pp. 208–10.
62. D.R. Sahani, *Catalogue*, pp. 28–31.
63. Jayaswal, *From Stone Quarry*, p. 208.
64. C.G. Lin-Bodien, 'An Early Yaksha from Aktha near Sārnāth (Vārānasī, UP), *Chahavi (Rai Krishnadas Felicitation Volume)*, vol. 2, ed. Anand Krishan, Vārānasī: Bharat Kala Bhavan, 1981, pp. 294–7; D.R. Sahani, *Catalogue*, p. 32.
65. Ibid., pp. 37–41.
66. Ibid., pp. 37–8.
67. Vidula Jayaswal, *From Stone Quarry*, p. 208
68. Ibid., pp. 208–12.
69. Vidula Jayaswal and I. Singh, 'Sculpturing Process: A Study of Past and Present', in *From Stone Quarry to Sculpturing Workshop: A Report on the Archaeological Investigations around Chunar, Vārānasī and Sārnāth*, New Delhi: Agam Kala Prakashan, 1998, pp. 232–7.
70. T.A. Gopinath Rao, *Elements of Hindu Iconography*, New Delhi: Motilal Banarsidass, 1968, repr., vol. I, pt. II, p. 3.

4

Endowments, Grants, and Charities in Medieval India

A Case Study of Mahābodhi Temple

SAIYID ZAHEER HUSAIN JAFRI and
MOTIUR RAHMAN KHAN

The Nature of Grants, Endowments and Charities

THERE HAD BEEN attempts by numerous scholars to study the series of documents coming from institutions and families of custodians of the institutions to study the rising fortunes of various establishments with the help of public/archival records. Such studies mainly examined the state policies under various rulers vis-à-vis the institutions which are the subject of study. It also examined the issues of succession in matters of management, division of property among various categories of claimants, and subsequent growth of the landed properties of the institutions which had a modest beginning at the initial stages. Sometimes, it had also been possible to examine the issues of the use of customary law in preference to various canonical/personal laws. The competent and pioneering works on Parsees by J.J. Modi and H.H. Hodivala, and on the Mughals and Jogis of Jhakbar by J.S. Grewal and B.N. Goswami are some of the leading works on the field. Numerous articles based on the Vrindavan collection of documents by Late Tarapada Mukherjee and Professor Irfan Habib are the fresh attempts to use the family collections of Mughal documents related to religious institutions with much more sophistication. The main concern of these studies had been to examine the institutional growth chiefly based on the official records, which provided us the data related mainly to the property aspects of the establishment. What appeared missing in such studies is the other side of the picture: the institutions were established to carry on a cause and to promote some philosophy and not to acquire the property and amass wealth. Perhaps, the latter was a consequence of the earlier aspects rather than the other way round. The elite came forward in support of the institutions only when they realized that the institutions were really promoting their religious and cultural duties, and attributes.

Perhaps one can study the nature of revenue grants, endowments, and charities as it operated during the medieval times. These grants were made by the rulers, who basically alienated the right to collect land revenue and other taxes from a given area for the lifetime of the grantee or in perpetuity. Such grants were known as *milk* (pl. *imlak*), *inam, syurghal*, and finally as *madad-i-m'ash* (aid for subsistence). The grantees came to be known as *aimmadars* and during the later period as *m'aufidars.* These grants did not invest the grantees with any rights not claimed previously by the administration. They could not demand a larger amount of land revenue. The rights of the peasants and the village headmen were somehow protected. The grants so made were defined as something held on loan, 'ariyat, hence the grantee could never claim full-fledged property right over his possessions and held it only according the pleasure of the emperor. The non-propriety nature of these grants is shown by the fact that its possession could neither be sold nor transferred as an ordinary article of property. The matters of inheritance and succession were governed by imperial order and not by the laws of *shariat.* An order by Emperor Aurangzeb in 1690 CE thus, allowed a direct share in such property, to a grandson if his father has predeceased his grandfather; it deprived a daughter of her share if she was married or otherwise provided for; and it laid down that a widow might keep her husband's grant before its passing to her husband's heirs.

Theoretically speaking, these grants were an act of charity for the maintenance of the poor and indigent creatures of God. Thus, those who were engaged in service (*naukar*) or in any trade (*qasib*) and had other means of livelihood could not be entitled to these grants. The land originally assigned in the grant had to be marked out, half in cultivable waste and half in cultivated land. In the cultivated land, one could do nothing except to collect the land revenue while in the other half he was free to make his own arrangements except to sell or transfer it to somebody else. The grantees were predominately Muslims but the grants were open to Hindus, Jains and Parsees as well. Hence, we find Emperor Akbar making grants to the priests of Virandavan temple as early as in 1565 CE, similarly the *jogis* of Jakhbar (modern Punjab) of Jangam Math (mod. Vārānasī) and the *purohitas* of Allahabad were given these grants.

The women of respectable families were also recipients of the land grants. Their number was substantial enough to require the appointment of a women of high standing at the court under Emperor Jahangir to supervise the processing of such grants. Employees and officers old enough to perform no duties were also given land grants. Sometimes, these grants were made to the physicians who were to treat 'poor and indigent' patients free of cost.

The grants were open to various categories of people as well as the institutions. It is difficult to work out its magnitude in terms of the total percentage of the land revenue alienated through these grants during the medieval period. We come to know about the sporadic nature of these assignments through the private collections maintained by the families of the grantees or their references in chronicles or through the judicial and revenue files in the various courts of law during the colonial period. However, the *Ain-i-Akbari*, the gazetteer of the Mughal Empire at the close of the sixteenth century provides statistical figures through which one can have the idea of the percentage of the total income of the empire spent on the land grants, charities, and endowments. In Table 4.1 the percentage of the revenue alienated in grants as percentage of the total revenue is given for the six Mughal provinces in the upper Gangetic valley.

The figures in Table 4.1 serve only as rough indicators of the size of grants in relation to the total income at the close of sixteenth century. The modest percentage indicates that the state patronage to the individuals, ideologues, institutions of learning, and of mystic predilections was in no way substantial, however the patronage of the state was a major means of support for a particular class of the people and type of the institutions, the local potentates. The zamindars and the officials could also make these grants (land as well as cash) and in the course of time, these grants were recognized by the imperial officials. One can very well imagine that the size of the land grants must have increased proportionately in the subsequent centuries, for which, unfortunately we don't have any definite data. No particular bias has come to our notice in matters of revenue grants to any particular institutions or any group of individuals. It depended mainly on the importance of social roots and the general acceptability of the individuals, and institutions that made them entitled for the receipt of the imperial favours.

The 'Buddhist Past' and the Medieval Indian History

At the outset, it needs to be highlighted that much of India's past was perhaps, obliterated or was in the process of being forgotten from the popular

TABLE 4.1: Revenue Alienated in Grants as percentage of the Total Revenue

Province	*Total of pargana*	*Total of sarkar*	*Figure as stated for suba*
Bihar	1.024	1.024	1.024
Allahabad	4.750	5.256	5.256
Awadh	4.199	4.213	4.224
Agra	3.992	3.900	2.216
Delhi	5.497	4.811	5.498
Lahore	1.748	1.763	1.763
Average	3.535	3.497	3.330

memory as well as from the memory of the 'informed elite'. This can be shown by citing the well-known incident when Sultan Feroz Shah Tughlaq (r.1351–1388) sought to transport Aśoka's Shivalak pillar from its original site to Delhi and installed it at Feroz Shah Kotla in 1367 CE. It appears that his motive was purely antiquarian and he wanted to preserve this pillar for posterity by fixing it at a more prominent place. At the same time, he wanted to know about its history as well. He approached the learned for any possible information but he was told only stories as none of his informants seems to have been aware of India's Mauryan past or remembered the great Mauryan Emperor Aśoka! Perhaps, his Buddhist antecedents might have been a reason for such neglect. It is not for nothing that there is complete silence about Buddhist religion and philosophy in the Sanskrit text of medieval times. It appears that the Sanskrit scholars/writers were more concerned about the 'exclusion of the others' in their writings. It will be interesting to understand their notions of 'otherness' which kept on adding more and more categories.

Another aspect which requires some thinking on our part is that adjacent to or in the close proximity of important religious Buddhist sites, grew centres of Muslim pilgrimage during the medieval period. The *dargah* of the legendary saint martyr namely, Saiyid Salar Masud Ghazi, came up in the city of Bahraich, very close to the Buddhist township of Srāvastī. Leaving all the discussion on the 'legendary' and 'historical' aspects of the debate, one would like to point out that by the close of the thirteenth century, his *dargah* has become popular enough to merit the comment by Amir Khusro in as early as 1287 CE that 'in the town of Bahraich, the fragrant tomb of *sipahsalar-ishaheed* scents entire Hindoostan with the perfume of odorous woods' (*Behraichazmazar-imuattarsipahsalar-ishaheedhaman Hindoostanbu e oudgriftaast*). Thereafter, Ibn Battuta, in 1341 CE, writes with regret that he could not pay his respects at the holy *mazar* due to the enormous crowds of people, in spite of the fact that he was in the royal entourage of Sultan Mohammad Bin Tughlaq.[1] This attests to the massive scale of popular participation in the annual celebrations even in the pre-Mughal period. By the close of the eighteenth century, his legend had become a part of the collective memory and captured the popular imagination throughout northern India. The folk singers (*dafalis*) and other storytellers have added a flavor of their own by incorporating elements of chivalry and romanticism to the legend. Perhaps, the holy nature of the Buddhist site around the township of Bahraich might have contributed to the growth of another holy site though belonging to a different tradition. The level of the participation and psychic of participants might not have undergone much alteration.

The holy Buddhist site of Sārnāth also saw the growth of 'Muslim Culture' in the nearby twin township of Benāras, where Sufic presence was quite noticeable during the pre-Mughal times. It is not for nothing that the famous

Shia divine namely Shaikh Ali Hazin decided to make Vārānasī his headquarter and had a very receptive audience in the township. We find the growth of the intellectual aspects of the Islamic culture side by side with a very strong Sanskrit tradition of learning. One could not miss the important angle that the development is taking place in the immediate vicinity of a Buddhist holy site at Sārnāth. It appears that the 'devotional spaces' vacated by the Buddhist pilgrims and the memory of their holy spots had many claimants.

In addition to the places of reverence with a religious 'halo', there were extensive ruins of the erstwhile Buddhist seminaries like Nālandā and Takshaśilā as well as the massive *stūpas* like the one at Sānchī which ought to have been noticed by medieval writers simply for antiquarian and architectural value. But surprisingly, no notice appears to have been taken of these remains, which were extensive enough at the physical landscape. In fact, there are enough references of the huge statues of Buddha at Bamiyan in Persian literature. Such apathy with the Buddhist remains is difficult to explain, however it appears that, by this period, Buddhism had totally disappeared from this region.

Bodhgayā was an important place connected with the Buddhist theology and history. It was a place greatly revered in the Buddhist tradition for the obvious reason that the Buddha had attained the ultimate enlightenment here itself. The place was obviously forgotten during the period under review. However it was during the sixteenth century, that its memory could be revived, interestingly, not as a Buddhist site but as a Śavaite seat under the custodianship of one Ghamandi Giri of Gir Gosain order of the *sanyasis*. The place gained prominence since then and received further patronage by the subsequent Mughal rulers and officials. The history of this shrine, on the basis of the legends, traditions and public record has been traced by Motiur Rahman Khan and it is included in this paper as a separate section. Perhaps, this is the only Buddhist site, whose documentations are available from sixteenth century onwards and one gets a chance to examine the fortunes of a Buddhist site during the medieval times. However, one looks for similar studies relating to other Buddhist sites of similar nature. When some more data is available, only then one can present a general picture and theorize about the Buddhist remains and ruins in medieval Indian history.

Mahābodhi Temple and the Bodhgayā Math: Donations, Management and Disputes up to 1980s

Legends, Traditions and History

Bodhgayā in Bihar is famous for being the place where Gautam Buddha is said to have got enlightenment under a *pipal* (*ficusreligiosa*) tree. The place, over a period, became the most venerable pilgrimage site for the Buddhists.

During the times of the Guptas, a monastery came into being and the great Mahābodhi temple was built. By this time, Buddhism had spread in other countries and the pilgrims started arriving at Bodhgayā from these countries. It seems Sri Lankans were the first among the foreign visitors of Mahābodhi Temple. Bodhirakshita of Tambparna (Sri Lanka) visited the temple in first century BCE who left an endowment inscription on rail bars of the Mahābodhi tree.[2] The Sri Lankans were not just enthusiastic about going to Bodhgayā on pilgrimages; they also did much to make it a vibrant and thriving centre of Buddhism. I-Ching (seventh century CE) met a monk who had come from what is now Kazakhstan. Vietnamese began coming to India on pilgrimage soon after the introduction of Buddhism into their country, in the sixth century CE. In about 402 CE, Chinese monk Faxian reached Bodhgayā journeying all the way from Central Asia. He left an account of his pilgrimage which, in later centuries, inspired hundreds of others to follow in his footsteps. The most famous of these was Xuanzang who stayed in India from 630 CE to 644 CE visiting Bodhgayā at least twice during that time. His account of the pilgrimage gives detailed information about Bodhgayā. In fact, we are able to identify many locations in and around the Mahābodhi temple and know their origin and evolution and the legends associated with them, because of Xuanzang's book. Another account by a Tibetan Dharmmasvamin is very useful for us to know about Bodhgayā's medieval past. He arrived in the spring of 1234 CE only to find that:

> the place was deserted and only four monks were staying there. One of them said: 'It is not good! All have fled from the Turushka soldiers'. The monks blocked up the door in front of the Mahābodhi image with bricks and plastered it. Near the image, they placed another image as a substitute. They also plastered up the outside door of the Temple. On its surface they drew an image of Maheśvara to protect the Image from the non-Buddhists. One of the monks said: 'We five dare not stay here and shall have to flee'. As the days were long and the heat stifling, they felt tired and as it became dark, they remained there and fell asleep. Had the *Turushkas* come they would not have known it.[3]

For seventeen days Dharmmasvamin could not see the main image of Mahābodhi temple. After some days a woman brought the news that the 'Turushka soldiery had gone far away'. Dharmmasvamin stayed there for three months, went to Rājgir and Nālandā and then returned to Tibet. His biography includes details of everything he saw and experienced in Bodhgayā. However after this episode, we do find some evidences of pilgrimage to this site but Bodhgayā now ceased to be the centre of 'active Buddhist cult'.[4] Abul Fazl discusses Buddhism at length in his work *Ain-i-Akbari*, but does not mention the place at all in this regard. Gayā, for him is Brahmā Gayā for it was a known land of the Brhamā.[5] It seems by the time Abul Fazl was writing, the place was completely forgotten, except the name of the *mauza* 'Mahābodh' where the actual shrine existed.

It seems the locale of Mahābodhi were dominantly Śavaites from the time of Pāla rulers of ninth century. In 850 CE, Dharampāla installed an image of Maheśwara for the 'benefit of inhabitants of Mahābodhi' (Mahābodhi *nivasinam*).[6] And as Dharmmasvamin notes, the image of Maheśwara was drawn to save the actual idol from not only the invading *Turushkas* but also from other non-Buddhists, who finding the monastery deserted might harm the image. Dharmmasvamin relates a legend about the 'self-creation' of the main image of the temple, where he clearly shows the conflict between the followers of Maheśwara and the Buddhists. In this story, Maheśwara himself says that he has everything to comfort this life but when asked about the life after this world, he ordered the three brothers to pay respect to the Buddhist monks.[7] It is not clear how and why Buddhism lost its social support during the medieval times but this created a space for the Śavaites who already enjoyed dominant devotional space.

The 'Revival' and the 'Memory' of the Shrine during the Mughal Era

In 1590 CE, one Gosain Ghamandi Giri, a Śaiva *nagasanyasi* came to choose this site for his monastery and took care of Mahābodhi temple and allowed the Buddhists to pray in the temple.[8] It is only during the Mahanthship of Mahadeva Giri (d. 1682 CE), who is said to have got a bowl from Annapurna Devi with a blessing that the *math* will never run out of wealth if it distributed grain to the poor from this bowl, the monastery became famous 'for feeding itinerant *fakirs* and providing shelter to the *gosains* and for the *Sadabrit*,[9] that it attracted royal patronage.[10] A village document dated 18th Ziqad Fasli 1118/1711 CE, issued by the order of Emperor Bahadur Shah, says that the *chak* Mastipur in *mauza* Mahābodh, *pargana* Maher was granted to the 'righteous Gosain Lal Gir as *madad-i-m'ash* by the former rulers' and it was further continued as '*khairat* in the name of God to Gosain Lal Gir'.[11] The Mughal Emperor Farrukh Siyar in his fourth year of reign, added two more villages 'Antaria, Tappa Nagbansi and the waste jungle therein' from *pargana* Chainpur, *sarkar* Rohtas for the maintenance of Gosain Keshav Gir of the *math*.[12] Similarly, Emperor Muhammad Shah in his ninth regnal year granted villages Bagula and Dharahra Khurd in *pargana* Sherghati and again by another *farman* villages Mastipur and Taradih in *pargana* Maher to Lal Gir for the maintenance of the *math* with the familiar condition of Mughal chancery, 'to pray for the everlasting empire'.[13] Later, confirmatory documents for the above grants were obtained from Mirza Muhammad Akbar Shah Bahadur, son of Emperor Shah Alam in 1791 CE.[14] Interestingly, no Mughal document mentions anything about Buddhism or the Buddhist temple. The *madad-i-m'ash* grant was given to the chief of the Śavaite *math* for their piety, their good work of distributing *sadabrit* and for maintaining their Śavaite institution.

It seems the Buddhist places of importance were completely appropriated by local cults in absence of 'higher tradition' of the Buddhist faith and the rulers did not notice their exclusive identity.

From Religious Endowment to Superior Fiscal Rights

At a time when the colonial masters were busy discovering the native written past, an infant science of archaeology was also growing, which was limited to the profiling of artefacts, so that 'an accurate description . . . of such remains as deserve notice' can be obtained.[15] Much of the attention of the colonial archaeologists was to smuggle the artefacts. When Cunningham returned to England in 1865, 'he carried on a profitable business in coin selling'. It is said that 'he had amassed a unique and unrivalled collection of coins, seals, stone implements, and other objects including smaller statues and relic caskets'.[16] In such a scenario, the Śavaite *math* of Bodhgayā escaped from their mind and the Buddhist temple again acquired the centre stage, after which Burmese mission arrived in 1874 for repairs and restoration of Mahābodhi temple. And from this time onwards 'Hindu-Buddhist conflict' revived afresh, now, for the control of the great temple. The Bodhgayā *math* is known among the academicians for this only.[17] The *math anagaakhara* (monastery of 'warrior *nagadashnamis*'), which was instrumental in shaping up the mid-eighteenth-century political history of the *doab* region,[18] was overshadowed by the grandeur of the Mahābodhi temple.

Subsequent histories of the *dashnaminagasanyasis* tell us that they were active players in chaotic environment of the mid-eighteenth century, yet the Bodhgayā *math*, it seems did not take any active part in any of these 'chaos' despite being located in the historically important place where Shah Alam II in 1761 CE fought a battle (Battle of Manpur) against the British.[19] From the sources available to us, it seems the *math* enjoyed good relations with the ruling authorities. They were favoured by the Mughals with *madad-i-m'ash* grants, *shivaprit* by the local zamindars and later the British also confirmed these grants. It seems the *math* had enough influence over the local population that it was given patronage by the ruling powers. Even at the time when the holders of the *l'akharaj* grants suffered at the hands of British, after their accession to the *diwani*, the *math* was successful in retaining its *madad-i-m'ash*. Alan Trevithick, while looking at the role of British in the temple possession case, has rightly observed that 'maintenance of peace' was achieved by favouring the *mahantha*.[20]

However the *math*, at times, had to face hardships from the British administration, perhaps, due to the compromises of local power and dilution in the British policies for the Mahābodhi temple. In 1840 CE, the *madad-i-m'ash* grants by the Mughal emperors, along with some other villages, were resumed by the British under Bengal Regulation II of 1819 and Regulation III of 1823 under which all the land which was not assessed at the time of first decennial settlement or passage of the Regulation XIX and XXXVII of 1793 were to be assessed and included within the limits of a nearby estate settled under decennial settlement or subsequent to that.[21] But after a thorough enquiry, the British issued *sanads* confirming the villages granted by the Mughal rulers in the name of the *mahantha* who was recognized as the custodian of the *math.*[22] The British *sanad* further says that the villages were to be released provided that the *mahantha* file an *ikrarnama* (agreement), in Persian and English, that the *mahantha* would claim all the sum equal to *mustajirijama* from the *mustajirs* or the holders of those villages and no claim would lie with the government.[23] Also the *mahantha* was asked, in the fashion of the Mughals to: 'appropriate as usual the produce of these tenures towards the performance of noble works, such as *sadabrit* alms, and to pour blessings on the Government.'[24]

All the grants, thus, resumed in July 1840 were released within one year, i.e. in October 1841. The delay of two decades after the passage of the said Regulation in resumption of the grant and the hurriedness in releasing the villages can be understood in terms of the local British official's conflict with the *math* and unwillingness of the superior officials of the British East India Company to disturb the *math* in any way. Such attitude can also be seen in the case of famous H. Dharampāla, where the Collector-Magistrate ordered conviction of the *mahantha* who was levied a fine for disturbing the worship and manhandling of the Ceylonese Buddhist.[25] The Calcutta High Court later set aside the order of the subordinate court.

The Establishment during the Uprising of 1857

At the time when the famous Gayawal brāhmaṇs, in spite of their assurances to the British did not provide any substantial helps during the Uprising, the *math* 'rendered services to the Company government' in the 'dark days of Sepoy Mutiny'. In fact, British attitude after the Great Uprising towards *m'aufidars*, especially those who did not help the colonial government during the rebellion of 1857 turned very harsh and either they wanted to resume the grant and where they could not do so—due to charitable nature of grant, they confirmed the grant as *waqf*, reserving the power of interference into their hands and such other terms and conditions of assisting the British government which, actually diverted the attention of the grantees from the original purpose of social welfare. Owing to the help and services rendered by the *mahantha*, the British did not harm the *math* after the Great Uprising of 1857.[26]

Moreover, the colonial government rewarded the *mahantha* with a 'Certificate of Honour' from the Queen Empress of India for the services he provided to the government during the famine of 1874. The *mahantha*, being 'one of the most influential and respectable zamindars of the district', was exempted from 'personal appearance in the civil courts'.[27] *Mahantha's* loyalty was also recognized by awarding him exemptions 'from going armed and possessing arms without licenses' under the qualification category of landholders.[28] The fortune of the *math* rose day by day, apart from *l'akharaj* tenures it also purchased proprietary rights of many villages. By 1892 CE, the *math* acquired land in 212 villages, having a gross rental of Rs.59,004 and 9 *ana* 10 *paisa* under several tenures.

> The assets of the estate are always in a very solvent state owing to good management. One peculiar feature in the management of the domestic and foreign affairs of the estate is that all the posts in and outside the monastery are reserved for the members of the order. All persons employed—from the grass-cut to the highest priest, or biggest village agent—are *girgosains* of Saivite school, disciples of His Holiness the *Mahanth* of Bodhgayā.[29]

The *mahantha*, time to time, helped the British government by 'repairing roads in his *zamindari*' and once Mahantha Krishna Dayal Gir showed 'good public spirit and liberality in the right direction by subscribing Rs.5,000 to the "Grierson Well and Public Gardens Fund".'[30] All the help provided to the British government did not go in vain, the *mahantha* was recognized as the sole proprietor of the *math* property and he managed all of it single handedly despite the passage of Bengal Charitable Endowment Act, 1810 and Religious Endowment Act, 1863 which provided for a committee of interested parties in the management of such properties, viz., *madad-i-m'ash, m'aufi* and *l'akharaj.*

Management and Succession Disputes in the Shrine

However, Mahantha Krishna Dayal Gir in his last days executed a deed of trust dated 13 February 1932 and divested himself from the management of the properties of the trust, known as Mahantha Krishna Dayal Gir Trust.[31] The same year Mahantha Krishna Dayal Gir died and a dispute of succession arose between two of his *chelas* namely, Narain Gir and Ram Lakhan Gir. Nevertheless, Narain Gir emerged successful and occupied the *gaddi* but a case against him was filed and from the district court they made a compromise on appointment of Arbitrators for resolution of the dispute. One of the named persons by the court did not agree to become arbitrator and in the meantime the *mahantha* went to Calcutta High Court for the revision of the decision of appointment of Arbitrator as he had agreed only on the two named persons. Mahantha Narain Gir also argued that the property was not of charitable nature. When the counsel for defendant referred a case related to the appointment of trustee of a *waqf* property, the Judge held thus:

In the present case the plaintiff merely admitted that the muth belonged to an order of Gir Sanyasis. There is nothing on the record to show the strength of this order and no indication whether the members of the order can be regarded as any large section of a community. Furthermore, there is nothing to suggest that the muth was of the nature of the public charity and that the income was to be spent on public purposes and was neither mere religious order nor confined for the benefit of a group of persons belonging to that order.[32]

After this episode, the *mahantha* by a registered deed dated 19 September 1935 cancelled the aforesaid deed of trust and the *mahantha* continued to manage the *math* as sole proprietor.[33] In 1953, *mahantha* Dansukh Giri filed a title suit claiming all the properties as his personal properties which the Patna High Court dismissed in 1955 saying the properties were of a public trust. Aggrieved by the judgement the *mahantha* filed a revision appeal in Supreme Court of India which ended up in a compromise in 1957, it was settled that some of the properties were of trust of which the *mahantha* was entrusted with the administration while some other were declared to be *mahantha's* personal properties.[34]

Land Reforms and the Math *after Independence*

Passage of Zamindari Abolition Act, 1953 did not affect the *math* in any way and it continued to enjoy all the previous rights. However, Bihar Land Reforms (Fixation of Ceiling Area and Acquisition of Surplus Land) Act, 1961 brought difficulty to the *math* and the *mahantha* could not remain quiet. However, it is a well known fact that the land reforms had never been implemented well in Bihar but the *mahantha* had to file returns and he did file it in 1970 CE. But before that the then *mahantha,* Shatanand Giri filed a petition seeking permission from the Board of Religious Trust to divide the property in the names of 17 deities. And after getting permission he accordingly prepared a deed of arrangement dated 20 January 1970 and the properties were carved out in seventeen schedules respectively allotted to the 17 deities. And with this provision each of the 17 deities being a juristic person could hold land within the ceiling area prescribed even though the properties were not divided between them.[35] Thus the total 2,000 acres of agricultural land was divided into 17 deities and only approximately 300 acres of surplus came into purview of Bihar Land Reforms (Fixation of Ceiling Area and Acquisition of Surplus Land) Act, 1961. Therefore, A.K. Banerjee the then additional collector passed the order on 3 August 1971 that the deities were not left with any surplus land and proceeded to make a recommendation to the government to grant exemption from the operation of section 5 of the Act. But the state government did not agree and ordered to the effect that the 'alleged deed of arrangement dated the 20th of January, 1970 being neither a gift nor a deed of transfer must be ignored and Shri Mahantha Krishna Dayal Giri's Trust' was considered to be the sole owner of the properties and was, therefore, 'entitled to only one unit under the ceiling law'.[36] And to this effect only 100 acres of land was allowed to retain and 1896.661/4 acres of agricultural land was declared surplus under the said Act. This action was challenged in an appeal to the district collector of Gayā, who rejected the appeal by his order dated 15 January 1976. Aggrieved by this order, the *mahantha* further filed an appeal with the commissioner, Patna who also rejected the same on 9 July 1976. Again the *mahantha* filed revision appeal before the Board of Revenue where the *mahantha* only got some more exemptions and an option to select the land to be retained in 12 January 1977. Against this order, the *math* moved to the Patna High Court.[37]

Sampurna Kranti/*J.P. Movement and the End of the Legacy of the* Math

The *math* was there fighting the legal battle; a political movement in the background was taking shape for abolishing the 'zamindari' of the *math.* Alongwith the J.P. Movement, Naxalites were very active in the region with a support base among the landless peasants. However, the *math* was aware of the voice against its zamindari from the time of Mahantha Shatanand Giri, who not only tried to make legal arrangements of dividing the properties among 17 deities but also tried to strengthen his political power by fielding his *darbari* (deputy) in assembly elections from Gurua and opened some schools and colleges for making hold on the populace. Shri Mahantha Shatanand Giri College, Sherghati and a Sanskrit College of Bodhgayā after his name are well established institutions in the present times. But these measures did not work for too long and Bodhgayā became the seat of 'Total Revolution' [*Sampurna Kranti*] of Jaya Prakash Narayan. In 1977–8, the Chatra Yuva Sangharsh Vahini formed by Jaya Prakash (in 1975) organized agricultural labourers in Bodhgayā and led a historic movement known as 'Bodhgayā Andolan' against the *math.*[38] Where the Chatra Yuva Sangharsh Vahini led the peaceful struggle for the purpose; the simultaneous Naxalite movement supported them by cutting down grains from the standing crops, popularly known as '*baalichhapayee*'. But it is interesting that, at a time when the *mahantha* was fighting legal battle with government to save its zamindari, administration was supporting the *mahantha* against the revolutionaries. However, the government was under pressure and had to give up. The *math* sensing the situation started 'donating' the land to landless peasants.[39] Nearly 300 acres of agricultural land was thus 'donated'. The *math* ultimately lost its case against ceiling in Patna High Court on 10 December 1984.[40] Now Mahābodhi temple was put under a trust comprising both the Hindu and the Buddhist priests and it is flourishing as a symbol of enlightenment.

Notes

1. Mahdi Husain, *The Rehla of Ibn Battuta*, Baroda, 1976, pp. 110–11, 'The Sultan crossed it (River Sarayu) with the object of paying his homage at the tomb of the virtuous hero Shaikh Masud who had conquered most of those parts. Many marvelous stories are told about him and some noble battles are attributed to him . . . we visited the tomb of the aforesaid pious personage which lay in a dome as we could not enter on account of the crowds', cf. *The Islamic Path: Sufism, Politics and Society in India*, ed. S.Z.H. Jafri and Helmut Reifeld, Delhi: Rainbow, 2006, see esp., pp. 30–3.
2. First century BC, inscription on rail bar of the Mahābodhi tree (ficusreligiousa) which reads, 'Gift of Bodhirakshita of Tambaparna (Ceylon)', see plate X, no. 3 in A. Cunningham, *Mahābodhi or the Great Buddhist Temple under the Bodhi Tree at Buddha Gayā*, London: W.H. Allen and Co. Publisher to India Office, 1892, p. 16.
3. Roerich George, *Biography of Dharmasavamin: A Tibetan Monk Pilgrim*, Patna: K.P. Jayaswal Institute, 1959, p. 64.
4. Alan Trevithick, *The Revival of Buddhist Pilgrimage at Bodhgayā: 1811–1949*, New Delhi: Motilal Banarsidass, 2006, pp. 2–3, also see, S. Dhammika, 'A History of Bodhgayā', http://www.buddhanet.net/e-learning/pilgrim/pg_histbg.htm, accessed on 6 January 2010.
5. Abul Fazl, *Ain-i-Akbari*, vol. 2, tr. H.S. Jarrett, Delhi: Low Price Publication, repr., 2011, p. 164.
6. Alexander Cunningham, *Mahabohi or the Great Buddhist Temple*, inscription no. 3 on plate XXVIII, also see p. 3.
7. Roerich, *Biography*, pp. 69–70.
8. Sir Jadunath Sarkar, *A History of Dashnami Naga Sanyasi*, Sri Panchayti Akhara Mahanirvani, Daraganj, Allahabad, 1959, p. 281. Sarkar's compilation of the history of *Dashnami Naga Sadhus* mainly deals with the Giri sect of the *dashnamis* who were very active as fighting mercenaries for different players of power in mid-eighteenth century in north India. The Giri sect and their *math* were also known for their money lending business, they were said to have financed the Nizams of Hyderabad in the days of crisis, see pp. 281–2. For their career as mercenary see, William R. Pinch, *Warrior Ascetic and Indian Empires*, Delhi: Cambridge University Press, 2006, also see, Mathew Clark, *The Dashnami-Samnyasis: The Integration of Ascetic Lineages into an Order*, Brill Leiden, Netherlands, 2006 for their belief and organization of *maths* and *akharas*; Legends say that the *sanyasi* was killed by a tiger and buried, according to the customs of *Giris* in a *samadhi* near the Mahābodhi temple. He was succeeded by his disciple Chaitanya Giri in 1022 *fasli* (1615 CE). Mahantha Chaitanya Giri was known for his learning and austere piety and spent his time in religious devotion. He was also buried within the great Mahābodhi temple and a small temple was made over his *Samadhi* which still exists.
9. According to Wilson's *Glossary, Sadavrat* or *Sadabrit* is 'distribution of provisions daily to passers by, mendicants, and paupers: in Kamaon, a grant of land to provide for the distribution of food at certain fixed spots to pilgrims, see, H.H. Wilson's *Glossary of Judicial and Revenue Terms*, W.H. Allen and Co., London.
10. It is said that the third *mahantha* of Bodhgayā, Mahadeva Gir (1642 CE–1682 CE) was a worshipper of '*Anna Purna*, the Goddess of Plenty', who pleased by his devotion and presented him a cup (*katora*) for distribution of grain, the virtue of which was such that so long as alms were distributed by the *mahanthas* from it, the monastery

would never lack'. Moreover, its contents were always sufficient to exactly satisfy the appetite of the recipient of the alms dealt with it'. Grierson, District Magistrate and Collector of Gayā in 1892 further writes, 'this cup is still in existence, and is used daily for the distribution of alms to the numerous pilgrims who pass by the monastery,' see, Grierson George A., I.C.S., *Notes on the District of Gayā*, Bengal Secretariat Press, Calcutta, 1893. p. 17.

11. Attested copy of *chaknama* dated 18th Ziqad, 1118 Fasli (1711 CE) corresponding to fourth year of Bahadur Shah's accession to the throne, English translation reproduced in Rai Ram Anugarah Narayan Singh Bahadur, *A Brief History of Bodhgayā Math*, Bengal Secretariat Press, Calcutta, 1892, p. 5, also see confirmatory *sanad* of Deewan Sahib for the same grant in the same date see ibid., pp. 6–7.
12. *Farman* of Emperor Muhammad Farrukh Siyar, dated 15th day of Ziqad 5th regnal year, ibid., pp. 4–5.
13. *Farmans* of Emperor Muhammad Shah also bearing seal of Nasrat Jang Itmadudaulah *Wazir-ul-Mamalik* Qamruddin Khan Khan Bahadur dated 1st and 11th day of Rabi I, respectively, in the ninth year of his accession to the throne, i.e. AD 1728, ibid., p. 4.
14. *Nishan* of Mirza Akbar Shah Bahadur bin Hazrat Shah Alam Badshah Ghazi dated 3rd day of Shawal 30th RY, says that *mauza* Mastipur and others in *pargana* Maher, *sarkar* and *suba* Bihar were 'conferred upon the Mahantha Rahmit Gir under Royal *farman* as *madad-i-m'ash*, and that the said *farman* has been lost'. The *mahantha* pleaded for 'a *parwanaazdaftarkhassharif* prohibiting every person from interfering with the said property', ibid., p. 5, it is interesting to note that the document was issued 25 years after the grant of *diwani* to the Company and was actually considered valid by the Colonial government even after passage of the Bengal Revenue-free Lands (Badshahi Grants) Regulation, 1793 by which only the '*altamgha, jagir, aima, madad-i-m'ash* or other *badshahi* grants made previous to the 12 August 1765, the date of the Company's accession to the *Diwani*' were deemed valid, see, Bengal Regulation XXXVII of 1793 dated 1 May 1793 in *Bengal Code*, fifth edn., vol. 1, Bengal Government Press, Alipore, 1939.
15. Alexander Cunningham, *Archaeological Survey of India Report*, vol. I, Delhi: Indological Book House, 1972, pp. ii–iii.
16. Sir Imam Abu, *Alexander Cunningham and the Beginning of Indian Archaeology*, Dacca: Asiatic Society of Pakistan, 1966, p. 232 cf. Alan Trevithick, 'British Archaeologists, Hindu Abbots, and Burmese Buddhists: The Mahābodhi Temple at Bodhgayā, 1811–77', *Modern Asian Studies*, 1999, 33: 635–56, Cambridge University Press, p. 647.
17. For discussion on Hindu-Buddhist conflict see, Alan Trevithick, 'British Archaeologists, Hindu Abbots, and Burmese Buddhists: The Mahābodhi Temple at Bodhgayā, 1811–77', *Modern Asian Studies* (1999), 33: 635–56, Cambridge University Press.
18. For their carrier as mercenary in the army of Awadh Nawabs against Afghans and Raja of Benaras see, Sir Jadunath Sarkar, *A History of Dashnami Naga Sanyasi*, Sri Panchayti Akhara Mahanirvani, Daraganj, Allahabad, 1959.
19. See *District Gazetteer of Gayā*, 1957, p. 41.
20. Alan Trevithick, *The Revival of Buddhist Pilgrimage at Bodhgayā* (*1811–1949*), New Delhi: Motilal Banarsidass, 2006, p. 26.
21. See, British *sanad*, dated 10 May 1841 of Court of Khas Mahal, Zila Bihar in Rai Ram Anugarah Narayan Singh Bahadur, *A Brief History of Bodhgayā Math*, Calcutta: Bengal Secretariat Press, 1892, pp. 7–8, also see The Bengal Land-revenue Assessment

(Resumed Lands) Regulation no. II of 1819 and The Bengal Land-Revenue Assessment (Resumed Lands) Regulation no. III of 1823 in *Bengal Code*, 1939, for the provisions of the said Regulations.

22. Ibid.
23. Ibid.
24. See, British *sanad*, 11 October 1841 in Rai Ram Anugarah Narayan Singh Bahadur, *A Brief History of Bodhgayā Math*, p. 8.
25. *The Bodhgayā Temple Case: H. Dharampala vs. Jaipal Gir and Others* (Proceedings of the Gayā District Court), Calcutta: W. Newman and Co. Caxton Press, 1895, Judgement of the High Court, pp. 1–11.
26. See, Prof. S.Z.H. Jafri, 'Madrasa and Khanqah, or Madrasa in Khanqah? Education and Sufi Establishments in Northern India', in *Islamic Education, Diversity, and National Identity: Dini Madaris in India Post 9/11*, ed. Jan-Peter Hartung and Helmut Reifeld, Sage Publications, 2006, pp. 88–92; the British government after the Uprising noticed that the particular grantee (*sajjadanashin* of the *khanqah-karimiya,* Salon) did not help the British and hence 'cannot be considered to have any just claim on our government'. And on condition of payment of Rs. 28,000 *nazrana,* to get the grant confirmed with government's right to interfere in expenditure since it was a trust, hence the Financial Commission did not agree on this suggestion and waved the amount of Rs. 28,000 (see, p. 90).
27. Rai Ram Anugarah Narayan Singh Bahadur, *A Brief History of Bodhgayā Math*, Bengal Secretariat Press, Calcutta, 1892, p. 2.
28. See Police Notification, 19 July 1880 in ibid., p. 15.
29. Ibid., p. 3.
30. Ibid.
31. The deed is still kept with Deen Dyalu Giri, present *Darbari* of the *math*; also see, Judgement dated 10 December 1984 of Patna High Court in the matter of Mahantha Dhansukh Giri And Ors. *v.* State Of Bihar And Ors., www.indiankanoon.org.
32. See, Judgement of Calcutta High Court dated 11 December 1933 in the matter of (Mahantha) Narain Gir *v.* Ram Lakhan Gir and Anr, www.indiankanoon.org.
33. See, Judgment dated 10 December 1984 of Patna High Court in the matter of Mahantha Dhansukh Giri and Ors. *v.* State Of Bihar And Ors., www.indiankanoon.org.
34. Ibid.
35. Ibid.
36. Ibid.
37. Ibid.
38. Jose J. Nedumpara, *Political Economy and Class Contradictions*, Delhi: Anmol Publications, 2004, p. 110.
39. One important aspect of the Bodhgayā Andolan was that the women who participated in the Andolan were successful, though lately, in getting '*pattas*' in their name contrary to the old Land Tenancy Act which did not allow women to own agricultural land see, ShafiqurRahman Khan, 'Women and Land Rights', http://www.charkha.org/newsletter/datamay09/engfeaturemay01.html accessed on 27 August 2009 also see his 'Bhumi Adhikar Evam Mahilayei', http://diarybysrk.blogspot.com/2009/04/blog-post_01.html accessed on 27 August 2009.
40. See, Judgement dated 10 December 1984 of Patna High Court in the matter of Mahantha Dhansukh Giri and Ors. *v.* State of Bihar and Ors., www.indiankanoon.org.

5

Aspects of Buddhist Donations in some Kharoshṭhī Inscriptions from North-Western India

PRASHANT SRIVASTAVA

In India, Kharoshṭhī inscriptions are known mostly from the north-western parts and their neighbourhood, with a few exceptions, like the Mathurā Lion Capital inscription of Rañjuvula and Śoḍāsha. Though fewer in number, in comparison to the inscriptions in Brāhmī, they form an important source of the political, social, religious, and economic aspects of ancient Indian history. A majority of these Kharoshṭhī inscriptions record donations of various articles—coins, wells, water halls, tanks, ponds, trees, vessels, etc., to religious institutions, generally Buddhist establishments, made by royalty as well as commoners. Certain aspects of these donations are interesting. First, it is necessary to produce a list of some significant Kharoshṭhī inscriptions, from north-western India and its neighbourhood, recording such donations. While doing so, I shall touch upon, very briefly, only those aspects of these inscriptions, which might have a direct bearing on the subject of the essay. Often, the inscriptions are engraved on the article donated itself.

I

Donation of Gold

1. The major rock edict VIII of Aśoka is engraved as a part of a set of the fourteen major rock edicts of Aśoka, and is found at several places. Two copies of the set of edicts are engraved in the Kharoshṭhī script. One of these copies is located near the village of Shahbazgarhi, on the banks of the river Makām, nine miles from Mardan, in the Yusufzai region of Pakistan.[1] The other copy is located to the north of Mansehra, near Hazara in Pakistan.[2] At one place in the Shahbazgarhi version, we have the words

vudhanaṁ daśana hirañapraṭividhane,[3] which has been translated by E. Hultzsch as 'visiting the aged and supporting (them) with gold'.[4] The Mansehra version has *vudhrana draśana cha hiñapaṭividhane*.[5] Aśoka is here describing his *dhammayātrās*, that is tours of righteousness, in the course of which he interacted with the aged, and donated gold to make provisions for their support. But this gold could not very well have been coins. It is well known that during the Mauryan period, only punch marked coins circulated in India, and authentic gold punch marked coins are not yet known.

Donations of Coins

2. The Shahdaur inscription of Śivarakshita is engraved on a boulder, found at Shahdaur in the Agror valley near Hazara, and is damaged at many places. It records the donation of 10,000 *kārshāpaṇas* by Śivarakshita, who is described as a rich man. The mention of Gotama towards the end of the inscription shows that the record has Buddhist affiliation. The inscription is dated in the Azes era, which is believed to be the same as the Vikrama *saṁvat*, commencing 58/57 BCE, but the portion mentioning the year is damaged. Attempts have been made to read the date as year 102 (= 44 CE) or 80 (= 22 CE).[6]
3. The Takshaśilā rectangular silver plate inscription is engraved on the back of the rectangular silver plate from Sirkap (Takshaśilā). It records the donation of 20 *staters* and 1 *drachm* by Muṁjukrita.[7] According to Konow, the coins mentioned in the inscription represent the value of the silver plate, on which it is engraved and which is being donated.[8] However, this does not seem to be acceptable, as a silver plate, 8.8 inches long, 6.12 inches broad, and weighing 5,378 grains,[9] even with its legs,[10] could not possibly have cost 20 *staters* and 1 *drachm* (below). It is, thus, possible that the coins (20 *staters* and 1 *drachm*) were kept on the plate, and the plate together with the coins, represented the gift of Muṁjukrita. The religious affiliation of the record is not certain.
4. The Takshaśilā circular silver plate inscription is engraved on the outside of a circular silver plate, measuring 8¾ inches in diameter, and weighing 7,505.3 grains,[11] found during the excavations at Takshaśilā. It records the donation of 30 *staters* and 2 *drachms* by Muṁjukrita.[12] This donor seems to be the same as Muṁjukrita of the Takshaśilā three-legged silver plate inscription, above. The religious affiliation of the record, too, is not certain. According to John H. Marshall, this vessel is a stylized version of the Greek *phiale mesomphalos*, popular in the third-second centuries BC.[13] This, incidentally, would give us an idea about the date of the present vessel and inscription engraved on it.
5. The Takshaśilā silver saucer inscription of Aśpavarman, engraved on a silver saucer, with everted rim, measuring 6.12 inches in diameter, and weighing 2,603.7 grains, was found during the excavations at Takshaśilā.

It records the donation of 11 *staters*, 2 *drachms*, and 1 *obol* by *Strategos* Aśpavarman of the Apracharaja family.[14]

Donations of Wells

6. The Fatehganj inscription of the year 68 is engraved on a stone, found at Mahjia in Fatehganj, near Attock, and presently in the Punjab Museum, Lahore. It records a donation made by the Vadhitira 'companions'.[15] The term *sahayaṇa*, in the inscription, has been rendered by Konow as *sahaya* (Sanskrit, *sahāya*), and translated as 'companions', and regards these 'companions' as forming some sort of brotherhood. But he expresses his inability to make any suggestions regarding the nature of these brotherhoods.[16] However, the Peshawar Museum inscription, No. 20, of the year 168 mentions 'companions' in connection with the Khudacha *vihāra*.[17] This would seem to hint at the Buddhist affiliation of these brotherhoods. All the donations made by 'companions' would, then, seem to be Buddhist. The donation is not specified in the inscription. Konow is, however, of the view that the inscription records the donation of a well, as gifts of well are similarly mentioned in four other similar inscriptions—the Muchai inscription of the year 81, the Mārgūz inscription, the Kala Sang inscription of the year 100(?), and the Peshawar Museum inscription, No. 20.[18] However, Boyer proposes to read *vadhitira* as *[De]vadhitira*, which he regards as the name of the donor. Further, he regards *hayana* in *sahayaśa* (the reading of Konow, meaning 'companions'), as a variant for *śayana*, which, on the authority of the *Amarakośa*,[19] he translates it as a covered carriage or palanquin, which, he believes, is the gift of a person named [De]vadhitira.[20] N.G. Majumdar, who accepts Boyer's reading *[De]vadhitira* and Konow's reading *sayahaśa*, suggests that the inscription records the 'gift of Sahaya, daughter (*dhitira*) of Deva', but he does not specify the gift.[21] The inscription states that the donation was made on the sixteenth day of Prashṭhapada, in the year 68, which, if referred to the Vikrama *saṁvat*, would correspond to 10 CE.
7. The Muchai inscription of the year 81 is engraved on a slab of sandstone, found in a cell in Muchai in the Yusufzai region. It records the donation of a well by the Vashiśu 'companions'.[22] R.D. Banerji dates it to the later Śaka or the Kushāṇa period.[23] The characters of the inscription are quite close to those of the Takshasīlā copperplate inscription of Patika, and, on this basis, Konow dates it to the period of that Śaka ruler, that is the first quarter of the first century CE.[24] The inscription itself gives the date of the donation as year 81, which, if referred to the Vikrama *saṁvat*, would correspond to 23 CE.
8. The Kala Sang inscription of the year 100(?) is engraved on a stone, found lying on the hill side of Kala Sang near Cherorao on the border of Yusufzai, and presently housed in the Punjab Museum, Lahore. It records the donation of a well by the Pipalakhaä 'companions'.[25] The

name, Pipalakhaä, might have Vedic overtones as Pippalāda, the famous Atharvavedic school, is very near to it. But Konow finds it difficult to explain the dropping of intervocalic *da* of Pippalāda in Pipalakhaä.[26] Besides, the donation recorded in the inscription has been made by the Pipalakhaä 'companions', and, as seen above, these brotherhoods seem to have Buddhist affiliation. The inscription seems to give the date of the donation as the year 100(?), which, if referred to the Vikrama *saṁvat*, would correspond to 42 CE.

9. The Mount Banj inscription of the year 102 is engraved on a stone slab, perhaps from an ancient well, found by M. Aurel Stein near Banj,[27] and presently housed in the Punjab Museum, Lahore. It records the donation of a well, in the *vajrastūpa*, by the Makadaka scion.[28] The inscription states that the donation was made in the year 102, which, if referred to the Vikrama *saṁvat*, would correspond to 44 CE.
10. The Pāja inscription of the year 111 is engraved on a stone from Pājā, situated between Jamalgarhi and Takht-i-Bahi, in the Yusufzai region, and presently housed in the Punjab Museum, Lahore. It records the digging of a well by Saṁghamitra, the son of Ānanda. The inscription states that the donation was made on the fifteenth day of Śrāvaṇa, in the year 111, which, if referred to the Vikrama *saṁvat*, would correspond to 53 CE.[29] The religious affiliation of the donation is not specified in the inscription. However, Saṁghamitra, the name of the donor, and Ānanda, the name of the donor's father, would seem to hint at their Buddhist inclinations.
11. The Mārgūz inscription of the year 117 is engraved on a marble slab, found near a village named Mārgūz, near Peshawar. It records the donation of a well by some 'companions', the initial part of whose name is obliterated in the inscription; only the latter part can be made out as . . . *dara*.[30] The inscription seems to give the date of the donation as the year 117 (?), which, if referred to the Vikrama *saṁvat*, would correspond to 59 CE.
12. The Peshawar Museum inscription (no. 20) of the year 168 is engraved on a stone, the provenance of which is not known for certain. It records the donation of a well, in the Khudacha Vihāra, by the Travaśakura 'companions'. The inscription states that the donation was made on the fifteenth day of Jyeshtha, in the year 168, which, if referred to the Vikrama *saṁvat*, would correspond to 110 CE.[31] As stated above, the mention of 'companions' in connection with the Khudacha *vihāra* in this inscription would seem to hint at the Buddhist affiliation of these brotherhoods.
13. The Zeda inscription of the time of Kanishka I, year 11 is engraved on a rock, near the entrance of the village of Zeda, near Und,[32] presently housed in the Punjab Museum, Lahore. It records the donation of a well by Hipeä Dhiä, during the reign of the Kushāṇa king, Kanishka I, and in honour of the *kshatrapa*, Liäka, for the increase of the Sarvāstivāda sect of Buddhism.[33] The well was donated, together with a 'water-giver' (below).

The inscription states that the donation was made on the twentieth day of Āshāḍha, in the year 11, which, when referred to the Śaka *saṁvat*, would correspond to 89 CE.

14. The Peshawar Museum inscription (no. 21) is engraved on a stone, presently housed in the Peshawar Museum. It records the donation of a well by the Brāhmaṇa Vāsudeva, the son of Indradeva, a resident of Obhara. The date of the donation was mentioned in the inscription, but is obliterated.[34] The donation, being made by a brāhmaṇa, should be regarded as brahmanical. However, what has been read by Konow as *brāhmaṇeṇa* in line 3 of the inscription, was read as *Kshemadeveṇa* by N.G. Majumdar.[35] Hence, the brahmanical affiliation of the donation is not certain by any means. Konow himself seems to associate the inscription with Buddhism, particularly the Sarvāstivādin sect.[36]
15. The Shakardarra inscription of the year 40 is engraved in an old well at Shakardarra, near Campbellpore in the erstwhile North-West Frontier Province, and presently housed in the Punjab Museum, Lahore. It records the donation of a well, dug at the Śāla ferry, by the Droṇīpadra 'companions'.[37] The inscription states that the donation was made on the twentieth day of Prashṭhapada, in the year 40, which, when referred to the Śaka *saṁvat*, would correspond to 118 CE.
16. The Ara stone inscription of the time of Kanishka II, year 41 is engraved on a stone, found at Ara, about 12 miles south-west of Attock, and presently housed in the Punjab Museum, Lahore. It records the donation of a well by Dashavhara, the Poshapura (Purushapura) scion, during the reign of the Kushāṇa king, Kanishka II. The inscription states that the donation was made on the twenty-fifth day of Jyeshṭha, in the year 41, which, when referred to the Śaka *saṁvat*, would correspond to 119 CE.[38] The religious affiliation of the donation is not specifically stated in the inscription. However, the dedication formula would seem to associate with Buddhist donations.
17. The Und inscription of the year 61 is engraved on a stone, found in the village of Und, about 15 miles from Attock; at present, its whereabouts are not known. It records the donation of a well by the Saviras. The inscription states that the donation was made on the eighth day of Chaitra, in the Pūrvāshāḍha asterism, in the year 61, which, when referred to the Śaka *saṁvat*, would correspond to 139 CE.[39] According to Konow, the Saviras might be some sort of an association. If the nature of this association was similar to that of the 'companions', above, the donation might have Buddhist affiliations.

Donations of 'Water-giver'/Water Hall

18. The Dewai inscription of the year 200 is engraved on a stone, reportedly from the fort of Dewai, on the eastern slope of Mahaban,[40] and presently housed in the Punjab Museum, Lahore. It records the donation of a

'water-giver' by a person named Hima. The inscription states that the donation was made on the eighth day of Vaiśākha, in the year 200, which, if referred to the Vikrama *saṁvat*, would correspond to 142.[41] The actual word in line 3 of the inscription is *toyaṁda*, which, according to Konow, means 'some contrivance or place for drawing or serving water'.[42] The religious affiliation of the donation is not certain.

19. The Zeda inscription of the time of Kanishka I, year 11, engraved on a rock, near the entrance of the village of Zeda, near Und,[43] presently housed in the Punjab Museum, Lahore. It records the donation of a 'water-giver' by Hipeä Dhiä, during the reign of the Kushāṇa king, Kanishka I, and in honour of the *Kshatrapa*, Liäka, for the increase of the Sarvāstivāda sect of Buddhism.[44] The 'water-giver' was donated, together with a well (above). The inscription states that the donation was made on the twentieth day of Āshāḍha, in the year 11, which, when referred to the Śaka *saṁvat*, would correspond to 89 CE.
20. The Tor Dherai inscriptions are engraved on some pot-sherds, discovered by M. Aurel Stein during the excavations of a Buddhist site at Tor Dherai, near Dabarkot in Baluchistan. They record the donation of a *prapā* (water hall), for the order of the four quarters, by Shāhi Yola Mira, described as master of the *vihāra*, for the Sarvāstivādin monks.[45] According to Konow, the characters of the inscriptions resemble those of the Wardak inscription, the Kharoshṭhī *Dhammapada*, and the Niya Kharoshṭhī documents, and may be dated to *c*.200 CE.[46]

Donations of Tanks/Ponds

21. The Kaldarra inscription of the year 113 is engraved on a stone, found in the Kaldarra Nadī, near Dargai, to the south of the Malakand pass, in the Swat region, and is presently housed in the Punjab Museum, Lahore. It records the donation of a tank by Thaïdora,[47] the Datia scion, in honour of all beings. The inscription states that the donation was made on the twentieth day of Śrāvaṇa, in the year 113, which, if referred to the Vikrama *saṁvat*, would correspond to 55 CE.[48] The religious affiliation of the donation is not specifically mentioned in the inscription. However, the dedication, 'in honour of all beings', in the record is met with in several Buddhist dedicatory records.
22. The Pathyar inscription is engraved on a rock, found at Pathyar, 9 miles south of Kanhiara, in the Kangra region. The three word epigraph names the pond as Rathitara Vayula's *pushkariṇī*.[49] According to Konow, the characters of the inscription resemble those of the edicts of Aśoka, and the record may be dated to the second or early first century BCE.[50] The pond is not specified as a donation, nor is there any indication of the religious leanings of Vayula.

23. The Karnal inscription is engraved on a stone, reportedly from Karnal in Haryana, and presently housed in the Punjab Museum, Lahore. It records the donation of a pond by Kriśakavi, the names of whose grandfather and father, though mentioned in the epigraph, can no longer read.[51] The religious affiliation of the donation is not specified in the inscription.

Donations of Trees

24. The Panjtar inscription of the year 122 is engraved on a stone from Panjtar, near the banks of the river Indus; the inscription is no longer traceable. It records the donation of two trees by Moïka, the Urumuja scion, during the reign of *Maharaya* Gushaṇa. The inscription states that the donation was made on the first day of Śrāvaṇa, in the year 122, which, if referred to the Vikrama *saṁvat*, would correspond to 64 CE.[52] Towards the end of the inscription occurs the word *Śivathala* (Sanskrit, *Śivasthala*). If it means 'a Śaiva sanctuary', the donation has Śaiva affiliation. *Śiva*, however, means 'auspicious', and Konow prefers to translate *śivathala/śivasthala* as 'an auspicious ground'.[53] If one follows Konow in this regard, the religious affiliation of the donation is not specified in the inscription, and it may be associated with Buddhism.

Donations of Vessels

25. The two almost identical Bimran vase inscriptions are engraved on a steatite vase, discovered in one of the several small *stūpas* at Bimran, 7 miles north-west of Jalalabad in Pakistan,[54] and presently housed in the British Museum, London. They record that the vase is the gift of Śivarakshita, the Mūjavata scion, for consecrating the relics of the Buddha. Four copper coins, all belonging to Azes, found in the vase, help in dating the inscription to the end of the first century BCE.[55]
26. The Takshaśilā gold plate inscription is engraved on a thin gold plate, 2¾ inches long and 1 inch broad, found from a mound in the Babarkhana suburb of Sirkap at Takshaśilā; as per the testimony of Alexander Cunningham, it is no longer traceable.[56] It records the donation of the gold plate by a woman named Śira, who is consecrating the relics of the Buddha.[57]
27. The Manikiala silver disc inscription is engraved on a silver disc, 0.9 inch in diameter, found by Ventura in a small chamber during the excavation of the great *stūpa* at Manikiala in 1830,[58] and presently housed in the British Museum, London. It records the donation of the silver disc by Gomaṇa, the architect.[59] A gold coin of the Kushāṇa ruler, Huvishka, has been found with the disc, giving us some inkling of the date of the inscription. As the disc has been found inside the great *stūpa* at Manikiala, there can be no doubt regarding the Buddhist affiliation of the donation.

28. The Takshaśilā silver cup inscriptions are two identical inscriptions, engraved one each of two silver cups, and found during the excavations at Sirkap, Takshaśilā in 1926–7. They record the donation of the silver cups by Theüdora (Greek, Theodoros), the son of Thavara.[60] Persons named Theodoros are also known from the Swat relic casket inscription and the Kaldarra inscription (above), but it is not certain whether Theodoros, the donor of the present silver cups, was related to the Theodori of the two inscriptions from the Swat region. The religious affiliation of the donation is not specified in the inscription.
29. The Takshaśilā silver sieve inscription is engraved on a round, conical silver sieve, having two handles and an upper diameter of 8 inches, found in the course of the excavations at Sirkap, Takshaśilā, in 1926–7. It records the donation of the sieve by Jhaṇdanama, the son of Gomanada.[61] The religious affiliation of the donation is not specified in the inscription.
30. The three Pālāṭu Dheri Jar inscriptions are engraved, one each on a jar, found in a row in the south-eastern part of the mound at Pālāṭu Dheri,[62] and presently housed in the Peshawar Museum. The three jars have been labelled A, B, and C, respectively. The inscription engraved on Jar A records the donation of the jar by Gadaka(?), to the order of the four quarters. The name of the sect of the monks, to whom the donation was made, too, was mentioned in the inscription, but it is no longer legible. The inscription engraved on Jar B records the donation of the jar, to the order of the four quarters, in the acceptance of the monks of the Bahuśrutiya and Kāśyapīya sects. The name of the donor, too, was mentioned in the inscription, but it is no longer legible. The inscription on Jar C records the donation of the jar by the *Śrāvaka* Dharma, 'to the congregation of his relatives'.[63] There can be no doubt regarding the Buddhist affiliation of these donations.
31. The two identical Takshaśilā copper ladle inscriptions are found engraved, one each on a copper ladle, unearthed during the excavations at Mahal, near Sirkap (Takshaśilā),[64] and are presently housed in the Takshaśilā Museum. They record the donation of the copper ladles, on which they are engraved, by Īśvaraka, to the order of the four quarters, in the Uattarārāma of Takshaśilā, for the monks of the Kāśyapīya sect.[65]
32. The Bedadi copper ladle inscription is engraved on a copper ladle, reportedly from Bedadi, about 12 miles north-west of Mansehra in Pakistan. It records the donation of the copper ladle by Saṅgharakshita, to the order of the four quarters, in the Uraśā region, for the monks of the Kāśyapīya sect.[66] The inscription is believed to belong to the pre-Kanishka period.
33. The Dharmarājikā (Takshaśilā) lamp inscription is engraved on a lamp found during the excavations of the Chir *stūpa* (Dharmarājikā *stūpa*) at Takshaśilā, by John H. Marshall.[67] It records the donation of the lamp,

in the Dharmarājikā compound of Takshaśilā, by the monk named Dharmadāsa.[68] Konow dates the inscription to the first century CE, or slightly later.[69]

II

The first thing to strike one, as one goes through this above list of inscriptions recording Buddhist donations, is the near absence in it of any edict of Aśoka. It is not that that Mauryan ruler was averse to making donations. On the contrary, he enumerates *dāna* as one of the virtues of his *dhamma*, when he defines that *dhamma* in his major pillar edict II,[70] and, at places, he exhorts people to practice seemly behaviour and liberality towards friends, acquaintances, and kinsmen, and towards brāhmaṇa and *śramaṇa* ascetics.[71] Literary tradition also represents him as a great donor, who gave lavish gifts to the Buddhist *saṃgha*. The *Divyāvadāna* informs us that, on the occasion of his visit to each of the various Buddhist places of pilgrimage, he gave away one lakh gold pieces.[72] According to a legend, he even donated his empire (Jambudvīpa) to the Buddhist order thrice, and, each time, bought it back.[73] Such extravagance was not much appreciated by Samprati, the heir-apparent, and Rādhagupta, the minister, who are reported to have almost divested the king of his royal powers.[74] In his various edicts, we find him planting trees along roadsides,[75] digging wells,[76] constructing watering places[77] and rest houses for travellers,[78] making provisions for the medical treatment of human beings and animals,[79] and planting medicinal plants within his own dominions and those of his neighbours and Hellenistic rulers.[80] These philanthropic acts have, however, rightly been labelled as 'public works of utility' by scholars like R.K. Mookerji.[81] Nowhere in his edicts, which are believed to be Aśoka's own words,[82] is the emperor found making any donations to the Buddhist *saṃgha* or any other religious establishment. Of course, in his major rock edict VIII, we find *vudhanaṁ daśana hirañapraṭividhane*, that is 'gift of gold to the aged'.[83] But this liberality is towards the aged in general, and not specifically towards the Buddhists or towards followers of any other religious sect. As seen above, only at one place, that is in major rock edict VIII,[84] he speaks of giving *dāna* to the brāhmaṇas and *śramaṇas*, while he was on *dhammayātrā*. But here, too, he refrains from specifying the religious denomination of the *śramaṇa* ascetics.

What could possibly be the reason for this strange phenomenon? One possibility is that Aśoka, who believed in showing equal respect to all religious sects,[85] did not want to record the donations he lavished upon the Buddhist *saṃgha*, in any of his edicts, which are believed to represent Aśoka's own words, as it might alienate followers of other sects. An alternative suggestion might be that the Mauryan emperor gave greater importance to the ethical side of religion, and did not regard the doctrinal aspect of religion, comprising theology and rituals, as significant, because of its 'dubious efficacy'.[86] He extolled *dāna* as a virtue, but, at the same time, regarded *dhaṁmadāna*, that is 'gift of *dhamma*', as the greatest gift.[87] And he was liberally giving the gift of *dhamma* to people, that is preaching the qualities of *dhamma* to them, in most of his edicts.[88]

Donations of wells, tanks, and ponds (inscription nos. 6 to 17, and 21 to 23) seem to be very popular in Kharoshṭhī inscriptions of north-western India. Making provisions for the thirsty was deemed a meritorious work, and, even today, *pyāūs* (watering places) are a common sight, particularly during the harsh summer months. Two inscriptions (nos. 18 and 19) refer to donations of *toyaṁda*, which has been taken by Konow to mean 'some contrivance or place for drawing or serving water' (above). Is it possible that *toyaṁda* is not an object at all, but is some person, appointed and paid by the donor, and entrusted with the task of providing water to the thirsty, or oversee the maintenance of the well or tank or pond donated?

Other objects donated to religious institutions, mainly Buddhist, range from jars and copper ladles, through silver cups, plates, and sieves, to gold plates (inscription nos. 25 to 32). One inscription (no. 24) refers to the donation of two trees, apparently for the enjoyment of either their fruits or their shade. Another inscription refers to the donation of a lamp (no. 33). Donations of lamps to temples and other places of worship, and making provisions for the lighting of lamps there, were quite common, and referred to in Brāhmī inscriptions also.[89]

Only four inscriptions (nos. 2, 3, 4 and 5), out of a total of 33 Kharoshṭhī inscriptions selected for study here, that is a little over 10 per cent of these inscriptions, record donations of coins. This would lead to the inference that cash donations were quite rare in the area and period of the Kharoshṭhī inscriptions. This is surprising, in view of the fact that coins were quite abundant in the area and the period concerned. Some of these Kharoshṭhī inscriptions are as late as the second century CE.[90] In the first half of that century, elsewhere, that is in Maharashtra, too, we have evidence for donations made in cash, as, for instance, the ones recorded in the Nasik cave inscriptions of the time of Nahapāna, years 41, 42, 45.[91] But in that case, the cash was deposited as *akshaya nīvi* with weavers' guilds, and the interest accruing on these deposits was to be spent on providing light meals and clothes to some Buddhist monks. Hence, the donations in cash were not given directly to the beneficiaries.

It may, further, be observed that, as regards the Kharoshṭhī inscriptions engraved on the rectangular silver plate (no. 3) and circular silver plate (no. 4) from Takshaśilā, John H. Marshall regards the two inscriptions as recording the fact that the plates were the property of Muṁjukrita, in case of inscription no. 3,[92] and of Muṁjukrita in case of inscription no. 4.[93] But this interpretation of the inscriptions would not explain the relevance of the mention of coins in the inscriptions. As mentioned above, Konow regards the number of coins mentioned in the two inscriptions as the value of the respective silver plates, on which the inscriptions are engraved. The silver plate on which inscription no. 3 is engraved weighs 5,378 grains.[94] The inscription mentions 20 *staters* and 1 *drachm*. A *stater* is a gold coin weighing 134.4 grains. Hence, 20 *staters* would represent (20 × 134.4 =) 2,688 grains of gold. Taking the ratio of gold to silver as approximately 1 : 10,[95] 2,688 grains of gold would be equal to (2,688 × 10 =) 26,880 grains of silver. A *drachm* is a silver coin weighing 67.2 grains. Twenty *staters* and one *drachm*, therefore, represent (26,880 + 67.2 =) 26,947.2 grains of silver. It would be absurd to agree with Konow that 20 *staters* and 1 *drachm*, that is 26.947.2 grains of silver, was the value of a silver plate weighing 5,378 grains. Similar arguments can be given against accepting the view of Konow, that the coins mentioned in inscription no. 4, that is 30 *staters* and 2 *drachms*, represent the value of the circular silver plate, which weighs 7,505.3 grains, as well.

We get the earliest epigraphic evidence for land grant, in the *dakṣināpatha*, from a Sātavāhana record dating from the first century BCE.[96] As mentioned above, some of the Kharoshṭhī records, from north-western India, date as late as the second century CE till, in all the Kharoshṭhī inscriptions selected for study here, rather, in all the inscriptions published by Sten Konow in his corpus, there is not a single instance of donation of land. This would seem to indicate that, although the practice of granting land, as per the epigraphic evidence, had started as early as the first century BCE, the people of north-western India had not picked up the practice till the second century CE.

Notes

1. E. Hultzsch, *Corpus Inscriptionum Indicarum* 1, Inscriptions of Aśoka, New Delhi: Indological Press, 1969, p. xii.
2. Ibid.
3. Ibid., p. 59.
4. Ibid., p. 60.
5. Ibid., p. 77.
6. Sten Konow, *Corpus Inscriptionum Indicarum* 2(1), Kharoshṭhī Inscriptions with the Exception of those of Aśoka, Calcutta: Government of India Press, 1929, no. 10, pp. 16–17.
7. Ibid., no. 37, p. 98.
8. Ibid.
9. John H. Marshall, *Taxila*, New Delhi: Motilal Banarsidass, 1975, repr., vol. 2, p. 613.
10. According to Sten Konow (*Corpus Inscriptionum Indicarum* 2(1), Kharoshṭhī Inscriptions with the Exception of those of Aśoka, Calcutta, 1929, p. 98), the number of legs, on which the plate rests, is three. John H. Marshall, *Taxila*, vol. 2, repr., Delhi, 1975, p. 613, however, gives the number of legs as four.
11. Marshall, *Taxila*, vol. 2, p. 612.

12. Konow, *Corpus Inscriptionum*, no. 37, p. 99.
13. Marshall, *Taxila*, vol. 2, p. 612.
14. Ibid., p. 613. Also Prashant Srivastava, *The Apracharajas: A History based on Coins and Inscriptions*, New Delhi: Agam Kala Prakashan, 2007, pp. 122–3.
15. Konow, *Corpus Inscriptionum*, no. 12, pp. 21–2.
16. Ibid., p. 22.
17. Ibid., no. 28, pp. 77–9.
18. All four of these inscriptions have been discussed below.
19. *Amarakośa*, II.8, 52.
20. *Journal Asiatique*, 10 (3), 1904, p. 465.
21. N.G. Majumdar, A List of Kharoshṭhī Inscriptions, *Journal and Proceedings of the Asiatic Society of Bengal*, vol. 20, no. 10, 1924.
22. Konow, *Corpus Inscriptionum*, no. 14, pp. 29–30.
23. R.D. Banerji, *Indian Antiquary*, 1908, vol. 37, p. 64.
24. Konow, *Corpus Inscriptionum*, p. 29.
25. Ibid., no. 18, pp. 52–4.
26. Ibid., p. 53.
27. *Archaeological Survey of India: Frontier Circle*, 1904–5, pp. 33ff.
28. Konow, *Corpus Inscriptionum*, no. 19, pp. 55–7.
29. Ibid., no. 23, pp. 63–5.
30. Ibid., no. 25, pp. 66–7.
31. Ibid., no, 28, pp. 77–9.
32. I. Loewenthal, *Journal of the Asiatic Society of Bengal*, vol. 32, 1863, p. 5.
33. Konow, *Corpus Inscriptionum*, no. 75, pp. 142–5.
34. Ibid., no. 81, pp. 155–7.
35. N.G. Majumdar, A List of Kharoshṭhī Inscriptions, *Journal and Proceedings of the Asiatic Society of Bengal*, vol. 20, no. 55, 1924.
36. Konow, *Corpus Inscriptionum*, p. 156.
37. Ibid., no. 83, pp. 159–60.
38. Ibid., no. 85, pp. 162–5.
39. Ibid., no. 87, pp. 170–1.
40. E. Senart, *Journal Asiatique*, 9(4), pp. 510ff, and pl. V., 34, 1894.
41. Konow, *Corpus Inscriptionum*, no. 39, pp. 104–6.
42. Ibid., p. 105. He, however, admits that 'we cannot say what is exactly meant'. Cf. ibid., p. 143, where he explains *toyaṁda* as 'some appliance for drawing water from the well or some place for serving it to visitors'.
43. I. Loewenthal, *Journal of the Asiatic Society of Bengal,* vol. 32, 1863, p. 5.
44. Konow, *Corpus Inscriptionum*, no. 75, pp. 142–5.
45. Ibid., no. 92, pp. 173–6.
46. Ibid., p. 174.
47. Konow is of the view that Thaïdora is a corrupt form of Theüdora (= Greek, Theodoros), the name of a *meridarkha*, described as the donor in a Swat relic casket inscription. Konow, *Corpus Inscriptionum*, no. 1, pp. 1ff. Both the inscriptions come from the Swat region. *Meridarkha* Theüdora, mentioned in the Swat relic casket inscription datable to the mid-first century BC, might be an ancestor of Thaïdora of the Kaldarra inscription datable to the mid-first century CE.
48. Konow, *Corpus Inscriptionum*, no. 24, pp. 65–6.
49. Ibid., no. 94, p. 178.
50. Ibid.

51. Ibid., no. 96, p. 179.
52. Ibid., no. 26, pp. 67–70.
53. Ibid., p. 69.
54. H.H. Wilson, *Ariana Antiqua: A Descriptive Account of the Antiquities and Coins of Afghanistan*, New Delhi: Oriental Publishers, 1971, repr., pp. 69ff.
55. Konow, *Corpus Inscriptionum*, no. 17, pp. 50–2.
56. Alexander Cunningham, *Archaeological Survey Reports*, New Delhi: Archaeology Survey of India, 2000, repr., vol. 2, p. 129.
57. Konow, *Corpus Inscriptionum*, no. 31, pp. 83–6.
58. James Prinsep, *Journal of the Asiatic Society of Bengal*, vol. 3, 1834, p. 318; N.G. Majumdar, 'A List of Kharoshṭhī Inscriptions', *Journal and Proceedings of the Asiatic Society of Bengal*, vol. 20, 1924, no. 38.
59. Konow, *Corpus Inscriptionum*, no. 78, p. 151.
60. Ibid., no. 37, pp. 97–8.
61. Ibid., no. 37, p. 99.
62. *ASIAR*, 1902–3, pp. 163ff.
63. Konow, *Corpus Inscriptionum*, no. 55, pp. 120–2.
64. John H. Marshall, *ASIAR*, 1919–20, pl. XXVII, pp. 8–9.
65. Konow, *Corpus Inscriptionum*, no. 33, pp. 87–8.
66. Ibid., no. 34, pp. 88–9.
67. *ASIAR*, 1912–13, pp. 17ff.
68. Konow, *Corpus Inscriptionum*, no. 35, pp. 89–90.
69. Ibid., p. 89.
70. D.C. Sircar, *Select Inscriptions Bearing on Indian History and Civilization, from Sixth Century BC to Sixth Century AD*, p. 54, 3rd edn., New Delhi: Archaeology Survey of India, 1986.
71. Major rock edict XI, E. Hultzsch, *Corpus Inscriptionum Indicarum*, 1, Inscriptions of Aśoka, p. 18 (Girnar version), p. 63 (Shahbazgarhi version), 80 (Mansehra version), etc.
72. *Śatasahasram dattam, vide* R.K. Mookerji, *Aśoka*, repr., New Delhi, 2002, p. 152, n. 1.
73. James Legge, *A Record of Buddhistic Kingdoms (Being an Account by the Chinese Monk Fa-hien of Travels in India and Ceylon (AD 399–414) in Search of Buddhist Books of Discipline* (repr., New Delhi, 1998), p. 80. See R.K. Mookerji, *Aśoka*, p. 64. However, *contra* B.M. Barua, *Aśoka and his Inscriptions*, Calcutta: New Age Publishers, 1946, pp. 352–3, who is of the view that the evidence of the edicts of Aśoka does not indicate that the Maurya emperor spent so lavishly on charity to the Buddhist *saṃgha*.
74. *Aśokāvadāna*, tr. J.S. Strong, as *The Legend of King Aśoka: A Study and Translation of the Aśokāvadāna*, p. 286. See also E.B. Cowell and R.A. Neil, eds., *Divyāvadāna*, Cambridge, 1886, p. 430; T. Watters, *On Yuan Chwang's Travels in India*, 2 (London, 1904–5), p. 99; Tāranātha, *History of Buddhism in India*, tr. from Tibetan by Lama Chimpa and Alka Chattopadhyaya, Shimla, 1970, p. 65. R.K. Mookerji, *Aśoka*, p. 37n; K.K. Thaplyal, *Aśoka: The King and the Man*, Vārānasī: Aryan Publishers, 2012, pp. 268–9.
75. Major rock edict II, E. Hultzsch, *Corpus Inscriptionum Indicarum*, 1, Inscriptions of Aśoka, p. 72 (Mansehra version), 3 (Girnar version); Major pillar edict VII, D.C. Sircar, *Select Inscriptions Bearing on Indian History and Civilization, from Sixth Century BC to Sixth Century AD* (3rd edn., Delhi, 1986), p. 63.

76. Major rock edict II, E. Hultzsch, *Corpus Inscriptionum Indicarum*, 1, Inscriptions of Aśoka, p. 51 (Shahbazgarhi version), 3 (Girnar version), etc.
77. Major pillar edict VII, D.C. Sircar, *Select Inscriptions Bearing on Indian History and Civilization, from Sixth Century* BC *to Sixth Century* AD, 3rd edn., Delhi, 1986, p. 63.
78. Ibid.
79. Major rock edict II, E. Hultzsch, *Corpus Inscriptionum Indicarum*, 1, Inscriptions of Aśoka, repr., Delhi, 1969, p. 51 (Shahbazgarhi version), 72 (Mansehra version), etc.
80. Ibid.
81. R.K. Mookerji, *Aśoka*, pp. 38–9.
82. See T.W. Rhys Davids, *Buddhist India*, London: PTS, 1903, p. 275; D.R. Bhandarkar, *Aśoka*, 4th edn., Calcutta, 1969, p. 1; A.L. Basham, Emperor Aśoka, in *Indological Studies: D.C. Sircar Commemoration Volume*, ed. S.K. Maity and Uprendra Thakur, New Delhi, 1987, p. 4; K.K. Thaplyal, *Aśoka: The King and the Man*, p. 11.
83. Major rock edict VIII, E. Hultzsch, *Corpus Inscriptionum Indicarum*, 1, Inscriptions of Aśoka, repr., Delhi, 1969, p. 59 (Shahbazgarhi version), 77 (Mansehra version), etc.; R.K. Mookerji, *Aśoka*, repr., Delhi, 2002, p. 69.
84. Major rock edict VIII, E. Hultzsch, *Corpus Inscriptionum Indicarum*, 1, Inscriptions of Aśoka, repr., Delhi, 1969, p. 59 (Shahbazgarhi version), 77 (Mansehra version), etc.
85. E. Hultzsch, *Corpus Inscriptionum Indicarum*, 1, Inscriptions of Aśoka, repr., Delhi, 1969, p. 64 (Shahbazgarhi version), 80 (Mansehra version), etc.
86. D.R. Bhandarkar, *Aśoka*, 3rd edn., Calcutta, 1955, p. 100; K.K. Thaplyal, *Aśoka: The King and the Man*, pp. 216, 230.
87. See Major Rock Edict IX, E. Hultzsch, *Corpus Inscriptionum Indicarum*, 1, Inscriptions of Aśoka, repr., Delhi, 1969, p. 16 (Girnar version), 90 (Dhauli version), 109 (Jaugada version), etc.; Major Rock Edict XI, E. Hultzsch, *Corpus Inscriptionum Indicarum*, 1, Inscriptions of Aśoka, repr., Delhi, 1969, p. 18 (Girnar version), 40 (Kalsi version), etc.
88. See R.K. Mookerji, *Aśoka*, repr., Delhi, 2002, pp. 25–6, who says that in his edicts, Aśoka strives for the moral uplift of the people.
89. For example, the Sānchī stone inscription of Chandragupta II, Gupta year 93. D.C. Sircar, *Select Inscriptions bearing on Indian History and Civilization, from Sixth Century* BC *to Sixth Century* AD, pp. 280–2.
90. According to Richard Salomon, *Indian Epigraphy: A Guide to the Study of Inscriptions in Sanskrit, Prakrit, and Other Indo-Aryan Languages*, New Delhi, 1998, pp. 46–7, Kharoshṭhī script went out of use in South Asia 'in or around the third century AD'.
91. D.C. Sircar, *Select Inscriptions Bearing on Indian History and Civilization, from Sixth Century* BC *to Six Century* AD, pp. 164–7.
92. John H. Marshall, *Taxila*, vol. 2, p. 613.
93. Ibid., p. 612.
94. Ibid., p. 613.
95. E.J. Rapson, *vide* S.K. Chakrabortty, *A Study of Ancient Indian Numismatics (Indigenous System) from the Earliest Times to the Rise of the Imperial Guptas* (*Mymensingh, 1931*), pp. 82–7. Chakrabortty himself takes the ratio between gold and silver as 1: slightly higher than 9.
96. *Vide* R.S. Sharma, *Indian Feudalism* (*c.* AD *300–1200*), repr., New Delhi: Macmillan, 1998, p. 2.

6

Dynamics of *Dāna* in Buddhism

From Subsistence of the Faithful to Sustenance of the Faith

ANAND SINGH

DĀNA IN BUDDHISM is attributed by the intersection of special paradigm of the *saṃgha*, monk, and laity. It consists of a bipolar structure, where the monks followed peripatetic lifestyle and lay persons made donations to them. The monastic rules were originally evolved for fulfilling the *nissaya* (resources) requirements, viz., food, robe, medicine, shelter and propagation of the Buddha's preaching to *bahujana*. Later on, these were transformed, translocated, and transplanted into a settled *saṃgha* context. The process of *dāna* began with the earliest form of monasticism of Buddhism that was not sedentary in character, whereby, the nature of *dāna* changed when settled monasticism developed at the expense of the *saṃgha* of peripatetic monks. When the Buddha renounced home to become a wanderer, an overwhelming transformation occurred in his sedentary and settled princely life. At one end, he was free from all domestic chores but at other, he was to depend on society to support his mendicant life. He laid the foundation of his *saṃgha* by pondering over all these necessities and evolved the mechanism to adjust the two contrasting but interdependent situations. The *bhikkhu saṃgha* had to depend on the laity but with greater aloofness and non-attachment. His ordained followers, i.e. the *Śākyaputtiya samanas* accepted the Buddha as *Bhagava* and *Sattha* (lord and master) and adopted his given system of order which meant survival on alms-begging. The reciprocity between the *bhikkhus* and the *upāsakas* was sui-generis of *dāna* and patronage in Buddhism. The *dāna* relationship and its process might be derived from the existing and antecedent cultures and traditions but the Buddha framed his own regulations, method, and structure as per the requirement of the *bhikkhu*, laity, and the *saṃgha*.[1] Generally, *dāna* had been defined as gift, piety, an act of granting and yielding some material objects or wealth.[2] In the Vedic context, it was an offering to the god during the performance of sacrifice, invariably, cake of cereal, especially rice.[3] The Buddha's ingenious idea of *dāna* was to seek food and robes for his wandering community. It was a reciprocal act of *dānadhamma-dhammadāna,* in which the laity performed under the rubric *of dānadhamma* by giving alms to the *bhikkhus* and the monk community reciprocated by giving him *dhamma* talk. *Dāna* can be of two kinds—*āmisadāna* (material gift) and *dhammadāna* (spiritual gift). The first one was for the laity and the latter was reciprocated by the *saṃgha.*[4] Initially, *dāna* requirements were limited to food, robes, and medicines, but later on lodging also came under it. The requirement of permanent lodging broadened the idea of patronage in Buddhism. The patronage was reciprocity restricted to a relationship between the patron and the recipient of patronage, which involved multifarious concerns such as occasion, recognition, the patron recipient, etc. In Buddhism, patronage concerned with donation towards building of monuments like *stūpas*, *vihāras*, *guhā-vihāras*, and adornments as acts of piety.[5] The pattern and characteristics of donation and patronage were not uniform in early Buddhism but modified and adjusted with the upcoming needs and opportunities. *Dāna* requisites could be discussed under four stages:

1. Foundation and Evolution
2. Transition and Transformation
3. *Bodhisattva* and Body Sacrifice
4. The *Mahāvihāra* Tradition

Foundation and Evolution

Dāna in Pāli tradition involved attributes, conditions, rules, and procedures of *nissayas* which included alms begging, robe, medicines, and shelter. The Buddha initiated rules and procedures dealing with *nissaya* subjects, which later on were adjusted, modified and even compromised by the *saṃgha.* The *bhikkhus* and *upāsakas* were at opposite ends but followed a reciprocal relationship. The *bhikkhu saṃgha* was dependent on the laity for food, robes and other things and in reciprocation, laities' spiritual urge was satisfied by the monks and nuns. This dynamic relation did not emerge instantly but through adjustments and experiments which were later institutionalized. The Buddha and his *saṃgha* initially depended on four *nissaya*, i.e. meals of scraps, robes of rags, lodging at the root of a tree and medicine of strong-smelling urine of cattle (*puttimutta*).[6] The food of *nissaya* categories could be many-fold—*pindiyatopabhojana* (meals of scrap of food), *atirika* (extra), *saṁghabhatta* (meals for the *saṃgha*), *udessabhatta* (for special person), *nimantana* (invitation) and *salakabhatta* (elective).[7] Sujātā, the daughter of

Senāni, was the first lay follower to give Siddhartha food in Uruvela, when he was taking penances for *nibbāna*.[8] After *nibbāna*, Tappasu and Bhallika requested the Buddha to take some rice cake and honey balls, and that act brought blessings and happiness to them.[9] Food was an important element of the *saṃgha* life for gaining strength and leading a healthy life.[10] The alms were described by the Buddha to sustain the body, to keep *saṃgha* life going on and to prevent injury.[11] The *Saṁyutta Nikāya* said that proper food is necessary for the attainment of *bodhi*.[12] The rules for *bhikkhus* during *nissaya* phase, during the non-*vassāvāsa* period was taking up a bowl and outer robe (*pattacīvaram ādaya*) and go out once a day for alms food before noon.[13] The monks were also advised to eat only once (*ekasanabhojana* or *ekabhattika*) for good health, spiritual well-being and comfort.[14] Such visits were known as *pindakathika*.[15] The food could be of any variety—*khadaniya* and *bhojaniya*.[16] The most common word for food was *pinda* (rice ball).[17] Meat was not prohibited by the Buddha, but according to the rules of *Tikotiparisuddha*, killing animals for the occasion was prohibited.[18] In certain cases, group meals (*ganabhojana*) were allowed if one of the seven conditions was fulfilled—at the time of illness, at the time of giving of robes, at the time of receiving of robes, on a journey, on a boat trip, during scarcity of food and at a meal time of all the recluse.[19]

The Buddha accepted alms begging as voluntary patronage by the laity instead of obligatory hospitality. To protect the ever-changing delicate need of food with changing responses from the lay followers, he introduced some prohibitions and preferences. The *Cullavagga* instructs the monks to go to houses for the begging with their eyes cast down and not look at the donor when the alms are being given.[20] The Buddha cautioned the monks to avoid prostitutes, widows, grown girls, eunuchs for alms begging.[21] The *Bhikkhuni Vibhanga* enjoins the nuns to keep the desire in strict control when interacting with male donors. The *saṃgha* made a cautious approach to develop the infant religion. In the process of reciprocation between the monks and society, the early *saṃgha* was even in constant fear of losing its members. They might go back to lay people's life (*hīnāya avattati*). Several reasons are given in the canonical literature when monks or nuns broke the norms or were not watchful to their righteous way of life.[22] Sometimes, *bhikkhus* were put under observation for violating the rules of alms begging and were known as *gihikambhogin* (living like householder).[23] The real testing was when the scarcity of food arose and the monks struggled to receive alms. The *Vinaya Pitaka* mentions such an instance when alms begging became difficult, one brāhmaṇa monk said to the Buddha: 'O venerable, I did not join the *saṁgha* to do this that I should walk around for alms food. If you will provide me food, I will partake, if you do not give, I will leave the *saṁgha*.' He was admonished by the Buddha who reminded him about the *nissaya* rules.[24] The Buddha described four great perils to which any monk could succumb. These were the perils of waves, or being filled with anger, the perils of crocodiles or overeating, the perils of whirlpools or fondness of pleasure and the perils of fish or women.[25] The *Vinaya* literature praises such monks, who, despite all social constraints, got *upasampadā* and became monks, and rebukes those who broke away with the *saṃgha* for an easy, mundane life. The examples of Sudina[26] and Ratthapala[27] were quoted in canonical literature. Sudina, the son of wealthy merchant became a *bhikkhu* after listening to discourses of the Buddha but could not survive and returned to a householder's life. He was the only son of the family, which gave their consent of his monkhood under great strain. Once, because of shortage of alms food, he went to his house for begging. He was identified by his maid who informed his parents. All the family members allured him with good foods, gold and he was even seduced by his former wife. In due time, she bore a son, Bijaka. Sudina, filled with remorse, told the Buddha about the happenings, who rebuked him. Later on, Sudina was charged with *pārajika* offence and was expelled from the *saṃgha*. Ratthapala, despite all the pressure from family and relatives did not succumb. The story of Ratthapala goes in the same direction, who became a monk. Once in dire need he went to his family for alms begging. His parents and wife tried to allure him with all material affluence and requested him to return to lay life. Ratthapala admonished his family members and preached about the futility of abundance.

The second element of *nissaya* was robe. The purpose of wearing the prescribed robe was to be identified as the practitioner of the middle path. The robe protected the monks and nuns from cold, rain, insects, snakes, and diminished the effects of wind and sun.[28] The acquisition of the robe for new entrants in the *saṃgha* focused on that. While giving the robes to monks and nuns, the idea of non-attachment should be in mind and a monk was not to get a new robe from a donor in an improper way.[29] A monk or a nun would not ask an *upāsaka* or *upāsikā* for a new robe except in the case one's robe was stolen or destroyed.[30] The monks were not allowed to ask for yarn or robe material woven by weavers.[31] The monk or nun, who was accepting the robe (*civarapatiggahaka*) must have five characteristics—one should not be partial, with hatred, stupidity or fear and has ability to keep track about the amount of *dāna*.[32] Once the donor commissioned the material of weaving especially for him, he was not allowed to visit the weaver's place for any favour.[33] The Buddha also created a robe fund (*cīvaracetāpana*) in which the laity could donate funds including gold, precious metals, threads, etc.[34] Even regulations were issued by the Buddha to instruct the monks/nuns to avoid any sort of attachment or indulgence for robes. He did not allow *bhikkhuni* Thullananda to ask King Pasenadi for a robe for cold weather.[35]

Medicine was a part of *nissaya*. The monks had no family and they had to help the brotherhood when any such need arose. The Buddha's approach was liberal when dealing with the medical concerns of the monks. The monks used *puttimutta* as medicine.[36] When *nissaya* was expanded into *parikkhāra* requisites, five more items were allowed as medicine—classified butter, fresh butter, oil, honey, and molasses.[37] When a sick monk requested Suppiya for meat broth as medicine, she sent her servants to find some meat but could not because of *māghatā ajjā* (non-slaughter day). She cut off a piece of flesh from her thigh and cooked broth for the monk. When the Buddha came to know, he visited her and admonished the monk who had accepted the broth without verifying its origin and content. He also prohibited the use of human flesh as food.[38] Jīvaka, a great physician of the Buddha's time served the Buddhist fraternity without taking any fees. He was trained by the great physician, Ātreya of Takshaśila and was appointed as the royal physician of Bimbisāra. He treated the Buddha many times and became his friend.[39] With the development of *vihāras*, *ārogyavihāras* were built by patrons within its boundary for the monks and the nuns. The monastery VI of Sārnāth, lying west to Dhāmeka *stūpa* was supposed to be a *ārogyavihāra*. Here, a large number of pestles and mortars had been found during excavation.[40] The existence of *ārogyavihāras* had also been confirmed by a sealing found from Rājghāt. The legend of sealing (*Bhishaka-vihāre therasa bhikkusaṅghasa*) indicated *ārogyavihāra* in a Sthaviravāda *vihāra* at Sārnāth.[41] In all, the probable existence of the sealing suggested donation. Another sealing, referring *ārogyavihāra* had been found at Kumrahar. In its upper half, a tree (*bodhi* tree?) with a conch shell on each side had been depicted and in the lower half, legend in Gupta character (*Śri-Ārogyavihāre bhikshu-saṁghasya*) had been inscribed.[42] It suggested monastic community with a sanatorium. Rājghāt sealing belonged to a monastery which served as *ārogyavihāra* for the monks of Sthaviravāda sect and the *ārogyavihāra* at Kumrahar was a monastery cum sanatorium where *bhikkhus* and *bhikkhunis*, irrespective of their sects, could stay and regain health. The legend '*ārogyavihare*'[43] occurs on a pot-shred from Kumrahar which suggests donation of pots by potters to a *ārogyavihāra* at Kumrahar. Hirananda Sastri also reported a *vihāra*, IA in Nālandā, that could be recognized as *bhishak-śāla* where students of medicine were given training in pharmacy and *rasas* (compound of Ayurvedic medicine) were prepared in it.[44] It seems that the school of medicine was also patronized in Nālandā.

The *Śākyaputtiya samanas* were a community of wanderers in his early days. They had to wander from place to place except in *vassāvāsa* period. The Buddha's original instruction for the monk community was to take shelter on the root of a tree (*rukkhamula*).[45] The gift of *āvāsa* or *vihāra* was the best gift of the *saṃgha*.[46] The Buddha initially conceived selecting a good place for the *vassāvāsa*. It should neither be too far nor too near a village, suitable for coming and going, accessible to people for *dhamma* talk, not crowded, and full of privacy and seclusion.[47] Such residence will be temporary in nature, staked out by the monks themselves and known as *āvāsa*.[48] To make appropriate arrangements, the *saṃgha* deputed *senasanagahapaka* who was concerned with resources and requirements. The allotment for rain retreat was done three times—the earlier (*purimaka*), on the day after full moon of month of Āshāḍha, the latter (*pacchimaka*), a full month after the full moon of Āshāḍha and the intervening (*antaramuttaka*), on the day of *pāvarana*, when the monks were assigned lodging for the next retreat.[49] The transformation of the community of wanderers to a settled monastic organization made *dāna* one of the central concepts of Buddhism, especially in relation to laity.[50] It was mandatory for every monk to reside at one permanent abode during *vassāvāsa*, though some exemptions were given. The seven days excuse was allowed if going to meet his/her fellows—a monk, a nun, a female probationer, a male or female novice or a male or female lay person.[51] They were also permitted to take seven days break in case of illness of fellow monks.[52] When the Buddha was staying in Jetavana *vihāra* at Srāvastī, Udena requested the Buddha to come in the *vihāra* built for him in Kosala. When his journey was delayed, Udena complained and the Buddha acknowledged.[53] The use and disposal of accessories in *vihāra* were not decided by the concerning monks but the *saṃgha*. When sixty small *vihāras* were gifted to the *saṃgha* in Rājagaha, it was clearly instructed that these were the property of *chatuddisasaṃgha* for present and future.[54] The *saṃgha* was not only the main adjudicator of use and disposal of issues concerning lodgings but a final authority on inspecting, approving and allotting, etc.[55] However, for construction and maintenance, an individual monk might be assigned the duty by the *saṃgha*.[56] Even the furniture and other accessories were not private properties of the monks and nuns.[57] In the early phase of Buddhism, as a result of the munificence of kings, *setthis*, and *gahapatis*, a chain of monastic settlements sprang up on the horizon of the Ganga Valley. The earliest *ārāma* donated to the *saṃgha* was Veluvanārama at Rājagaha by King Bimbisāra.[58] Anāthapindika bought prince Jeta's pleasure garden with a hundred thousand gold coins, demanded as a price, and converted it into a huge *saṁghārama* comprising *vihāras*, *parivenas*, wells, etc.[59] The donor of the *ārāma* did not leave his entire proprietary right over the *ārāma* when it was converted from private property to *saṃgha* property. The donor might appoint servants (*āramika*) and superintendents (*āramika-peśaka*) to look after *saṁghārama*. Bimbisāra sought permission of the Buddha to employ servants at Veluvanārama *saṁghārama*. These servants were in large numbers so their village was known as Pilindigāma.[60] The donations of *ārāma* as a permanent abode by laities, inevitably brought certain significant changes in the *nissaya* tradition as well as in the *saṃgha*. Since daily necessities for the monks and the nuns were deposited in the *saṁghārama* by the lay devotees, the tradition of wandering for alms begging deviated from its original and mandatory character. The monks had no requirement to go around for alms. The wandering life was not relinquished by the monks but they ceased to be wanderers. There are evidences that monks returned and occupied the same *āvāsa* or *ārāma* where they earlier resided in the last rain retreat. The circumstance formed a background for the transformation that slowly developed *vāssa* settlements into permanent abodes. The *āvāsa* and *ārāma* were normally for three months sojourn, but tended more and more to become a settlement of semi-permanent nature. It developed a sedentary character of the *saṃgha* which triggered aloofness of monks from laities.[61] The *vihāras* started to become localized and the *bhikkhu* who was an outsider could get hospitality for only a few days. Faxian mentions that if an unknown *bhikkhu* stays in a monastery, he will get full provision for three days only, and then he had to seek his permanent abode.[62] At the initial stage, cooking, storage were not allowed and because of that monks were known as *anagni*.[63] The Buddha himself permitted cooking and storage during famine.[64] The process once allowed, became a rule. If thc storehouses of the monasteries had abundant food, it could be offered to the nuns or vice versa.[65]

The *saṃgha* was conscious of the fact that its very existence stood on the support and mercy of the lay devotees, because of it the Buddha granted special attention to the laity world. He accepted that the *saṃgha* must have the support of the laities for its survival and growth.[66] There was an interwoven relationship between the laity and *saṃgha*. The *upāsaka* would provide to the *saṃgha* food, robes, medicine, and lodging, and in reciprocation, the monk community would fulfil their spiritual quench.[67] It was a sort of exchange between two opposite poles, in which a material gift was given to the *bhikkhus* by the laities and the goodwill of the Buddha, *dhamma* talk, a place in heaven in future, rebirth in good society, etc., would be reciprocated. In reality, such exchanges did not happen, only promises were made for differed exchange.[68] The Buddha said that *manussagaha* were *kamabhogins* (pleasure loving), *kamarama* (fond of pleasure), *kamarata* (delight in pleasure) and *kamasamudita*. It was difficult for them to leave it. These were the radical differences between the *bhikkhus* and *bahujana*. The *bhikkhus* were devoid of all these fetters.[69] The *kamabhogins* could enjoy four types of pleasures—happiness of owning, happiness of wealth, happiness of being without debt and happiness of being without blame.[70] The relation between the *saṃgha* and laity was not unconditional but with caution, restriction and restrainment. When Upali, a native of village Balakand and follower of Nigantha was instructed by his master to refute the teachings of the Buddha, in his conversation with the Buddha he asked if a follower of the Buddha could give *dāna* to others. He replied that Upali should give gifts to Jains as well. Impressed by the catholicity of the Buddha, he became a convert.[71] When the Malla king desired to be the only donor of robes, food, lodging, and medicines, the Buddha assured him that he would be one of such donors.[72] The Buddha explicitly declined to give monopoly to anyone. He did the same while giving *dhamma* talk to Siha, commander of the Lichchhavis. The Buddha said that the visible result of *dāna* for *dāyaka* includes becoming dear and loving to many and gaining an auspicious reputation. One would be self-possessed, untroubled and get a rebirth in heaven after break-up of his life body.[73] However, sometimes, special favours had been showered by him. When Vishakha requested the Buddha to be the donor of the eight articles to the *saṃgha* in perpetuity, i.e. rain cloth, food for the incoming, food for the outgoing, food for the sick, medicine for the sick, food for the sick tenders, conjey and bathing cloths for nuns, he granted permission.[74] But he did not give exclusive rights to anyone. When Prajapati Gautami wanted to donate only to the Buddha, he declined and said one can donate only for the *saṃgha* as a whole.[75]

The examination of Pāli literature also suggests classes of donors for the *saṃgha*. The Buddha told Pasenadi that *dāna* to a good person reaps great reward, while to an immoral one, vice versa.[76] He accepted donation to the monks and the nuns as *punyakkheta* and *kalyānmitta* which was not a passive acceptance of alms for survival but as motivation to progress spiritually.[77] He also said that the monks and the nuns were the most worthy recipients of gifts from the laities.[78] It seems that when a lay follower became a novice, he was well-supported by his family members. Women and female relatives of the monks had substantial contribution in the distribution of robes, alms, and the construction of *vihāras*. Even women donated their *itthidhana* for the building of *vihāras* and other charitable works. Sesavati donated her gold necklace for construction of a *vihāra*.[79] Findly says:

> The potential for householder extravagance in secular life is thus curbed, and the saṃgha became significant institution available as an equalizer in drawing off householders surplus. Being a donor, then, means not only reaping spiritual rewards for giving a gift, but contributing to social equilibrium as well.[80]

Findly's remark could be partially correct when the donors were from affluent class of the society, like kings or *setthis* but majority of the doors including *gahapatis* were from middle class and did not have an extravagant life, what they did was because of sheer devotion and spiritualism. One of the major donor groups in *dāna* reciprocity was women who carved out imminence because of their charity and donations. Because of their material support to the *saṃgha*, they had substantial influence and esteem in the order. The Buddha gave them due respect and accommodated their views in disciplinary practices. Buddhism was successful in redefining the values of a householder's life by introducing egalitarian and prodigious values.[81] Sometimes, the list of donors was so long that they had to wait for their turn. A brāhmaṇa in Andhakavana, who wanted to serve the Buddha and his fellow monks, after waiting for his turn for two months when his turn did not arise, he personally visited the monastery where the Buddha was staying and found conjey and honey balls missing. He sought the permission of the Buddha and offered them.[82] Sometimes, hostile nature of the inhabitants had also been recorded, when people of a brāhmaṇa village Pañcasāla in Magadha refused to give alms to monks, even at the time of festivities.[83] The reciprocation between *dānadhamma* and *dhammadāna* had been explained by the Buddha. The laity not only receives *dhamma* talk from the monks and the nuns but is also assured that virtuous works would be reciprocated in his/her next birth by getting a superior birth, residing in heaven, etc. The laity can attain *sagga* (heaven),[84] *saggathana* (place like heaven),[85] *devaloka* (abode of gods),[86] *dibbathana* (divine places),[87] and *avyapajjha sukha loka* (happy and pleasant world).[88] When the *saṃgha* firmly established its root in the Ganga Valley in the first two decades of the Buddhahood, changes started in the structure of the *saṃgha*. Some modifications and adjustments were introduced due to practical difficulties faced by the monk community during its early expansion but some were interpolated. The *nissaya* commitments were transformed into *parikkhāra* and changes could be seen in all four requisites—*āvāsa*, *pindapata*, *senasana*, *gilanapaccaya*, i.e. robes, food, lodging and medicine.[89] Findly says it was the beginning of 'strict asceticism to indulgent hedonism'.[90] However, at an early stage, the establishment of permanent abode was a practical necessity as the religion was growing, so was the number of the monks and the nuns. The *saṃgha* could be regulated and structured only by institutional setup and permanent structure. When the *saṃgha* became prosperous, some hedonistic tendencies have been referred to, but condemned by the Buddha and canonical literature under *pārajika* and *pācittiya* offences.

Transition and Transformation

In this phase, donations and patronage were directly acquainted with *stūpas*, images and other votive monuments. The emphasis of *saṃgha* life transformed from *Vinaya* to the inculcation of *bhakti*, and its ritual expression could be found in *stūpa* or image. It reflects a deeper change in the spirit of religion.[91] It is presumed that the Buddha himself conceived a plan for the *stūpa* and told Tappasu and Bhallika. He gave them some hair and a pair of nails and made a square pile of his *saṁghati* on the ground. He did the same with the *uttarasaṅga* and with his *samkachchika,* in succession. On the top of this, he put his bowl, inverted, and then put his mendicant staff to resemble it like a *stūpa*.[92] Romila Thapar says:

> The stūpa becomes the symbol of the power of the saṃgha in relation to the patron. It emerges as a major symbol when the worship of sacred sites per se gives way to monuments as the physical manifestation of the saṃgha as an institution. Whereas in the early Pāli canon the vihāras or monasteries are more frequently mentioned, the archaeology of the post Mauryan period refers to the stūpa and the caitya as the major edifices.[93]

The *Mahāparinibbāna Sutta* says that after *mahāparinibbāna* of the Buddha, his body relics were divided into eight parts by Brāhmaṇa Drona, and eight *stūpas* were built (*Vitthārika hontu disāsu thūpa*).[94] The *stūpa* regarded by the Buddha was not incorporating the memory of the lord, but the idea of him. It symbolized the divine presence and the lord himself was supposed to be symbolically present in the sacred mound, enshrining his *dhatu*. Prayers and rituals were performed and boons of all sorts—secular and spiritual—were solicited. To worship and to circumambulate is not only an emotional satisfaction but a spiritual gain so great and enduring that it leads to *nibbāna*.[95] Aśoka is said to have excavated the relics of seven *stūpas*, except of Rāmagāma and built 84,000 *stūpas* throughout his realm.[96] He not only built new *stūpas* but also renovated the old ones. The Niglivā inscription mentions that he enlarged the *stūpa* of Kanakamuni Buddha.[97] He personally visited Buddhist pilgrimages and exempted taxes at Lumbinī.[98] During his regime, large-size *stūpas* were built for public worship and it emerged as a popular institution. *Stūpapūja* became identified with *śarirapūja*. The Buddha exhorted to the monks not to engage themselves with *śarirapūja* but restricted it to the laity.[99] Nāgasena says to Milinda that *śarirapūja* was meant for the laity and the monks should devote themselves to doctrines and disciplines.[100] After a long time, *stūpa* worship got canonical sanction and became an integral part of religion. Initially, the monks were opposed to it but soon became an integral part of *vihāra* life. Reginald argues:

> The identity of stūpa with the physical body of the Buddha is also seen in the iconographic tradition, in which the stūpa is seen as the idealized structure of the Buddha's body. Typically, the ground where the stūpa is built is understood as Vajrāsana, the seat of enlightenment. The base of the stūpa is seen as the Buddha's leg and feet, the dome as his torso, the central axis as his spinal column and the harmikā is as his head.[101]

The *stūpas* were patronized both by the monks and the laities when *upāsaka* rituals intermingled with canonical literature and the canonical idea of *stūpa* as a memorial was transformed into a symbol of the Buddha's presence. The sculptures of Sānchī *stūpas* show worship with music and floral offerings. The laities are shown worshipping *stūpa* but the monks are conspicuous by their absence.[102] In post-Mauryan period, the whole Indian subcontinent was dotted with *stūpas*. The omnipresence of *stūpas* was not only described by Buddhist literature but also by brahmanical sources who saw them with contemptuous and jaundiced eyes.[103] Faxian, Xuanzang, and I-Ching informed about hundreds of *stūpas*. The archaeological remains of such *stūpas* have been found from the north-west part of the Indian subcontinent to the bank of Krishna River in south. All these *stūpas* were patronized by the kings or their queens. In Sānchī, Bharhut, Amarāvatī, Nāgarjunkonda, the *stūpas* were distinguished by huge ornamented *toranadvāras*, large hemispherical domes and sculptured *vedikas*. The miniature *stūpas*, as votive offerings, have been found from all important places of Buddhist pilgrimage. These were placed in open space at the site of main *stūpa* or *mūlgandhakutī* to mark their devotion by lay followers and the monk community. It was donated to the *saṃgha* as a votive offering and put in close proximity to main *caityagraha*. Such votive offerings, both large and small in size, have been found in Sārnāth, Nālandā, Bodhgayā, Ratnagiri, and Lalitagiri.

Image worship was another phenomenon that started in the post-Mauryan age. It is still a debate between Mathurā and Gandhāra schools that which one carved out the first image of the Buddha. It has been accepted that the Buddha image came to existence between the first century BCE or CE. Before image worship, a follower of Buddhism had to make a conscious effort to associate his/her mind with a symbol like the *bodhi* tree, *cakka*, or an empty throne as a representation of the Buddha. The laity could urge to have before him something more directly evocative, expressive, and representative. This spiritual need prompted the urge for designing the image of the Buddha.[104] The representation of god is a formless abstraction and unseen power and very difficult to conceive. Man sees great unseen power and unbounded companionship in his image.[105] The idea of image worship may be influenced by *stūpa* worship which have all ritualism with image worship like circumambulation, obeisance with folded palm, offerings of flowers, garlands, incense, buntings, cloths, blankets and *civara*, *dīpa*, and *vadya*, cleansing and spreading perfumed paste, collecting offered flowers, donation of *chatra,* etc.[106] Early Buddhist sculptures never represented the figure of the Buddha, though the *Bodhisattva* was represented but the suppressed desire for a Buddha image was conveyed by several features of sculptures of Sānchī and Bharhut. The Buddha's footprints are shown, the descent of the Buddha from heaven to earth is shown by a footprint on the lowest rung of a ladder and another one on the topmost. Stella Kramrisch says that in one Sānchī panel, footprints, tree motif, wheel and umbrella have been combined in vertical succession, alluding in a childish way to the bodily appearance of a man.[107] Around the beginning of the Christian era, the laity required something more accessible and direct that could evoke and satisfy their emotional urge. It accelerated image worship in Buddhism. In Nāgarjunkonda, a double shrine has been made—a shrine with a *stūpa* and the other with the image of the Buddha. These shrines stand side by side and provide opportunity to the worshipper to offer worship according to their own inclination. In the caves of Ajantā, Ellora, Nasik, a compromise had been made by carving an image on *stūpa* itself or recessing the image into it.[108] Theravāda became conservative even long after image worship became prevalent in Buddhism. The adherents of this school gave reluctant recognition to it. Theravāda worshipped an image or a casket with relics and gave offerings. Despite the presence of the Buddha image, due importance was not given to image worship by the Pāli commentators. The instruction was given to the meditating monks that they should devote to *caityas* and *bodhi* tree but image worship was not completely ignored. Buddhaghosa mentions *patimāghara* in Sri Lanka in fifth century CE and existence of image worship. The sacred sanctity was given to image by placing *dhatu* inside it. They were stood by *śarirapūja* which was recommended by canonical literature.[109]

Vajrayāna can boast of extensive and varied pantheons of gods who could be invoked for all kinds of perfection and *siddhis*. The deities of various colours and forms were worshipped to discharge various functions. The Vajrayāna had made itself attractive and popular by its interesting tenets, doctrines, and practices. The deities were direct manifestations of *śunya*.[110] The *Advayavajra* denies that the Tantric Buddhism is nothing but idolatry. The Buddhist *sādhanas* give elaborate description and procedure for worshipping the different deities. It was a certain abstract idea which took a different shape of gods and goddesses. The whole process was primarily a mental process and it had nothing to do with the external world.[111] Buddhism had its own interpretation for image worship. It was nothing but the manifestation of and by nature non-existent.[112] The Buddhist *tantras* first acquired strong footing in the sixth and seventh centuries. Initially, they had been handed down in the most secret manner, up to the time of Dharmakirti (600–15 CE).[113] It is said that various cryptic practices entered in Buddhism because Ācarya Asanga, in order to bring different tribal communities into Buddhist fold, embraced their demons, goblins, witches, ghosts, evil spirits, and various deities of mother cult. The intellectual capabilities of ordinary folk were more interested in power of magic based incantations, female ascetics rather than abstract philosophy.[114] Tantric practices were a religious undercurrent flowing from obscure point of time in religious history of India. It is neither Hindu nor Buddhist in origin.[115] The appearance of Tantric Buddhism in the learning and culture of Nālandā in the Pāla period has been attested by the images of Tantric deities recovered from sites.[116] *Bhikkhu* Bala's donation of the Buddha images in Mathurā, Srāvastī, and Sārnāth are one of the earliest donatives' records of image donation in India. *Bhikkhu* Bala, a master of *Tipitikas,* installed a ten feet image of the *Bodhisattva* in Sārnāth in the third year of Kanishka's reign. The image was provided with a huge umbrella.[117] After sometime he caused to set up another *Bodhisattva* image eleven feet and eight inches high. The image was covered by an umbrella. Here, his friend Pusyavuddhi and nun Buddhamitra were associated with the gift.[118] Gregory Schopen remarks:

> the nature of the relationship between Bala and Buddhamitra is curiously unstated. Buddhamitra is the only specifically named individual apart from the satrapas—whom Bala associates with his gift. But he does not say that she was a nun, nor does he indicate that she was his pupil. Buddhamitra although specifically mentioned by Bala, does not mentioned him all in any of her three inscriptions. She indicates that she was a nun but gives no indication of whom her teacher was. This of some significance, since it was a common practice already for monks or nuns to identify themselves by reference to the monastic who was their teacher.[119]

Sārnāth inscription of the third year of Kanishka clearly mentions five important donors of the image—*bhikkhu* Bala, *bhikkhu* Pusyavuddhi, *bhikkhuni* Buddhamitra, *Kshatrapa* Vanaspara and Kharapallana together with the others (*etaye purvaye bhikshusya Pushyavuddhisya saddhyeviharisya bhikshusya Balasya . . . antevāsekehi cha sahā Buddhamitraye . . . trepitika saha kshatrapena Vanasparena Kharpallnena . . .*).[120] In the inscription, the word '*antevāsekehi*' may be used not only for other fellow monks, but also for Buddhamitra, showing she belongs to the monastery of *bhikkhu* Bala. The inscription was caused to be written on behalf of *bhikkhu* Bala, probably under the instruction of Kushāṇa *kshatrapas*. Here, it was pertinent to mention the donation, the donor, and the donee rather than discussing the personal relationship between the monks and the nuns. Srāvastī inscription of the age of Kanishka or Huvishka mentioned the name of *bhikkhu* Bala and *bhikkhu* Pusyavuddhi but did not mention Buddhamitra.[121] It suggests that donations were made on behalf of two monks only. In a similar fashion, Buddhamitra donated an image of the *Bodhisattva* at Kauśambi (. . . *Bodhisatvattvam pratishthapayati bhikkhuni Buddhamitra tripitika* . . .).[122] If in the inscriptions of *bhikkhuni* Buddhamitra the name of *bhikkhu* Bala was not mentioned, it means that they were the individual donations of the *bhikkhuni* who did not find it necessary to inscribe others' names. She did not mention any name, except King Kanishka by whom (probably) the donation was made on her behalf. Schopen contended that in the above inscription, she had been mentioned as a nun, but in Sārnāth she was not referred to. In Sārnāth inscription, the line '*antevāsekehi cha sahā Buddhamitraye trepitika*' indicated that she was living in the same *vihāra*. In *vihāras*, only monks and nuns resided, so she was a nun and master of *Tipitika*. In the Mathurā image inscription of 33rd year of Huvishka, she was directly mentioned as *bhikkhuni* and disciple of *bhikkhu* Bala by *bhikkhuni* Dhanavati who was her niece.[123]

Three separate inscriptions have been discovered which are associated with *bhikkhu* Bala's donation of the *Bodhisattva* image in Sārnāth. The largest inscription has been found on umbrella shaft, one on the front side of the image pedestal and last one on the back of the image, between the feet of the statue.[124] Schopen says that the earliest donations of the Buddha images at Sārnāth, Srāvastī, and Kauśambī came from Mathurā and it was an intentional and well-conceived plan to export images from a central point.[125] It may be true due to several reasons, first, Mathurā had abundant supply of red stone, which was used for carving of the Buddha image. Second, Mathurā was situated on the great *Uttarapatha* and was connected with Sārnāth, Srāvastī and Kauśambī, so it was easy to supply images on these nodal points. Third, despite quarrying of Chunar mines of Vārānasī by Aśoka, it was not used for making of the Buddha image till the emergence of Sārnāth School in the Gupta Empire.

Since Kushāṇa age, hundreds of epigraphic records have been discovered showing image donations by the monks, nuns or lay followers. Gregory

Schopen has studied votive records of Ganga Valley and observed that majority of such donations were made by monastic communities. Of the nineteen individuals who were associated with the donations of images in Mathurā during Kushāṇa period, six were monks, six were nuns, five were lay women and two were lay men.[126] D.R. Sahani mentions that there were twenty-two Kushāṇa and Gupta image inscriptions from Sārnāth, fifteen of them monastic in nature.[127] At Bharhut, nearly 40 per cent donors were either monks (24) or nuns (14). The records of Sānchī show the same trend. Here, out of 437 donatives inscriptions, 136 were monastic donors.[128] Many questions were raised over the donations by the monks and the nuns because private possession of property by the monks and the nuns was not allowed. Two reasons may be observed, that the monks and the nuns were often patronized by their family members, and other patrons like kings. Though the money was donated by the relatives and well-wishers, but donations were made in their name. *Bhikkhu* Bala was patronized by Kharapallana and it may be the chance that he was in direct touch with them.[129] It may have also been observed that *bhikkhus* maintained some private possessions during early Common Era and after their death, their property was not inherited by any individual monk but by the *saṃgha*.

The Śunga-Kushāṇa age began an era of image worship which could be found in *stūpas*, *caityas*, and *vihāras* of the age. The images, bas-reliefs of Bharhut, Bodhgayā, Sānchī, Amaravatī, and other places exhibit illuminating commentary on the mode of Buddhist donations. The images, medallions, coping stone of railings, pillars and posts of gates of Bharhut, Sānchī, Bodhgayā, and Amaravatī not only show the mode of donations but also folk and pictorial tradition, mindset, and ideology of Buddhism of that time. The origin of cult images opened new vistas for donations which were imbibed not only in *madhyadeśa* but also in north-western India. The Kushāṇas patronized Gandhāra and Mathurā schools and built lofty *vihāras* and *stūpas*. Their liberal patronage to Buddhism provided ample opportunities to donate images, *stūpas,* etc. The large finds of stucco, terracotta, and stone sculptures within the complex of *stūpas* shed light on the nature, tradition, and mode of donations.

Bodhisattva and Body Sacrifice

The *dāna* of body and organs has been an important milieu of Buddhism, especially Mahāyāna. The tradition started in the age of the Buddha, when Suppiya gifted a part of her thigh to make soup for the ailing monk. She was admonished by the Buddha who discouraged such tendencies.[130] The scattered traditions in Theravāda could be recorded when Subbha Jivakambhavanika gifted her eyes to a wicked man who was obsessed and had a seditious design against her.[131] Kuṇāla was blinded by Tissarakha.[132] The real development of *dāna* of body could be sought from the emergence of Mahāyāna tradition where the Buddha's *prajna* and *karuṇā* were much wider in scope and much effective in application. In the *Bodhisattva* ideal, humanitarianism superseded the concern for the self well-being. The altruism became a motivating factor of the *Bodhisattva* who differed his own well-being for the well-being of others. The *Bodhisattva* as a human being/animal/fish, etc., tended to sacrifice his eyes, flesh or whole body to mark generosity and compassion. Both Theravāda and Mahāyāna literature mention such examples but in Mahāyāna literature such examples are in abundance. The *Vinaya* literature and Pāli *Jātakas* inform about a number of stories alluded to the *Bodhisattva* and their sacrifices. The *Lalitavistara*, *Rāstrapālaparipracchā Sūtra*, and *Jātakastava* represent a good number of the *Bodhisattva's* sacrifices.[133] The *Avadānaśataka*, *Mahāvastu*, *Divyāvadāna*, Kumaralata's *Kalpanāmaṇditīka*, *Jātakamāla* of Aryasūra, Haribhatta, and Gopadatta inform vividly about body sacrifice of the *Bodhisattvas*. The *Suvarnbhāsottana Sūtra*, *Manicūdāvadāna*, *Lokānandanātaka* of Chandragomin contain stories of king Manicuda and others who donated their bodies for compassionate action. The Chinese literature the *Liudu Ji Jing* (Sutras on Collection of Six Perfections), and Tibetan literature the *mDzangs bLun* (Sutra of the Wise and Fool) draw a proper sketch of the *Bodhisattva's* sacrifice.[134] The *Prajnāpāramita Sūtra* informs that the *Bodhisattva* offered his body, flesh, head, and eyes, even to his detractor who wanted to kill him.[135] The *Nārāyanoparipṛccha Sūtra* even advices the *Bodhisattva* to gift generously without thinking of his body, flesh, and eyes. [136] The *Vajradhvaja Sūtra* says that one should sacrifice all his limbs for the welfare of living beings.[137]

The stories of sacrifice have not only been narrated in literature but also visually depicted in the monuments at Sānchī, Bharhut, Amaravatī, Ajantā, and Gandhāra. Faxian informs that the *Bodhisattva* as King Indra rescued his subject from famine and transformed himself into a dead giant python. When people came to know, they took its flesh to eat and to cure their diseases[138] and Xuanzang[139] mentions the commemorative *stūpa* built in memory of the *Bodhisattva* Mahasatta who gifted his body to a hungry pregnant tigress. He informs that from Udyana to Kashmir, he saw commemorative *stūpas* dedicated to the *Bodhisattvas* who gifted their lives:

> It was here that Ju-lai in his existence as Indra encountered a year of famine with pestilence. In order to save the peoples the Pusa as a Indra changed himself into a great serpent lying dead in the valley: the starving and distressed in response to a voice from the void, cut from his body pieces of flesh which were at once replaced, and all who ate were satisfied and cured. Near this monastery was Su-Mo great tope where Ju-lai in his Indra life in a time of plague changed himself into Su-Mo serpent and all who ate his flesh were cured.[140]

The *Śibi Jātaka*[141] has been the most narrated and depicted *Jātaka*, both in art and literary tradition. Its earliest reference has been found in Pāli *Jātaka*, where King Śibi gifted the flesh of his body to protect a dove from a hawk.

The *Jātakamāla* says that King Śibi gifted both his eyes to a blind brāhmaṇa but they were restored to him through two acts of truth.[142] The *Śibiyavadāna* of the *Avadānaśataka* says that Śibi's eyes were plucked out by a bird and gifted to a brāhmaṇa.[143] The *Kalpanamanditika* of Kumāralata informs that king Śibi offered his flesh to save the life of a dove.[144] The *Avadānakalpalata* of Kshemendra says that king Śibi gave his flesh to free a dove from ransom. Though it was Sakka's test but his body parts were restored.[145] A frieze from Gandhāra shows that King Śibi was removing flesh from his body and placed it on a scale to balance the exact weight of the dove who was ransomed.[146] In Cave number I of Ajantā, he put his entire body on scale but the weight of the dove was not matched. The same story has been depicted at Amarāvatī, Nāgarjunkonda and Mathurā.[147]

The *Maitribala Jātaka* informs that king Maitribala offered his flesh and blood to five *yakkhas*. Though it was test of Sakka and his body was restored by him.[148] The *Lokānandanātaka* of Chandragomin says that king Manicuda gave his flesh and blood to a *rakṣasa*, who was the deity Sakka in disguise, and his crest of jewels to a group of brāhmaṇas. Later, his life was restored by Sakka.[149] The *Divyāvadāna* says that King Chandraprabha gifted his head to brāhmaṇa Rudrākṣa and died. However, Rudrākṣa had no good intentions for this demand. The king gifted his head despite knowing his evil.[150] The *Avadānasārasamuccaya* says that King Sarvaṁdada gifted his head to a brāhmaṇa to give it to another king as a reward.[151] The *Avadānaśataka* informs that King Padmaka sacrificed his life to transform himself into a fish and gifted his flesh and blood to his subjects who were grappling with an epidemic. The king died.[152] The *Avadānasārasamuccaya* says that a merchant killed himself in the ocean so that his drowning companions could use his body to reach the shore.[153]

The *Chaddanta Jātaka* narrates a story of six tusked elephants as a *Bodhisattva*. He had two wives. One of the queens, out of jealousy for the first queen, developed a grudge. She committed suicide with an intention to be born again and become the favourite queen of the king of Vārānasī, so she could avenge her earlier humiliation. After becoming the queen, she pretended to be sick and demanded the tusk of Chaddanta to recover from her sickness. The king sent a hunter to whom Chaddanta gifted his tusk and died.[154] This story has been represented at least in twelve versions, eulogizing his sacrifice to a greedy hunter. Foucher has given a description of all twelve narrations of *Chaddanta Jātaka*.[155] These include *Chaddanta Jātaka* (no. 514), Medallion of Bharhut (second century CE), Medallion from Amaravati, Fresco of Ajanta (Cave no. X, I and II CE), in Counter Steps of Gandhara, *Lieu tu tsi king* (translated by Seng-Houei, 200 CE), Prose Commentary of *Jātaka* (fifth century CE), *Kalpadrumāvadāna*, *Ta che tu luen* (translated by Kumarjiva during 404–5 CE), *Tsa Pao tsang king* (translated by Ki-Kia-ye and Tan Yao in 472 CE), *Sūtralaṅkara* (translated in Chinese by Kumarjiva in 410 CE), and Fresco Cave of XVII Ajanta (sixth century CE). John Strong, while taking the references of Chinese pilgrims, informs about the number of sites in north-west region of the Indian subcontinent where *stūpas* were raised in memory of the *Bodhisattva* who sacrificed themselves for others. He says:

> Stupas of the Bodhisattva were very important in this region. Most famous, perhaps were a set of monuments commemorating Jataka stories that were renowned as the 'four great stupas' of Northern India and which Faxian describes as being large and magnificently adorned with precious substances. The stupa in question marked sites (a) where the Bodhisattva as a King Sibi sacrificed his flesh to ransom a dove from a hawk, (b) who he willingly gave up his eyes when asked for them, (c) when he lays down his body to feed a hungry tigress, and when, as king Chandraprabha, he cut off his head as a gift to a Brahmin.[156]

Reiko Ohnuma has categorized body sacrifices of the *Bodhisattva* on the pattern of its nature and recipient. On some occasion, the recipient is a commoner whose demand is real which brought about under arduous circumstances, like drought, famine, etc. It includes great courage of the *Bodhisattva* showing his utmost generosity and compassion. The ordinary recipient can be categorized into two groups—pitiful and evil. The pitiful recipients (hungry animals, thirsty insects or destitute wanderers) are usually in dire strait and do not demand anything directly from the *Bodhisattva*. The *Bodhisattva* simply encounters their pitiful situation—very often a situation of hunger, thirst, illness or threat of imminent death and decides on his own initiative, to give up his body in order to save their lives. The pitiful recipients are innocents and not conscious of the desire to ask from the *Bodhisattva* to cut off his head, gift his eyes or sacrifice himself.[157] It could be exemplified by the *Jātaka* stories. The *Nigrodhamiga Jātaka*[158] mentions the *Bodhisattva* as a deer, ready to sacrifice his life for a pregnant she-deer. When the king got acquainted with reality, he left hunting and granted immunity to all four-legged creatures. Such acts of pity symbolize generosity and compassion by the *Bodhisattva*. This type of *dāna* showed state-subject relationship in which the king was bound to take extreme steps of sacrificing his life to safeguard the interest of his subjects.

Reiko Ohnuma also classifies 'evil' recipients who make 'direct, explicit and conscious' demands from the *Bodhisattva* to give his body. It was not a situation of dire need but a conscious act of destructiveness and evil. There is no genuineness in the demand, but an act of cruelty. Despite the wickedness of the donee's character and evil design, the *Bodhisattva* intended to gift his body. The *Silavanaga Jātaka* tells about the *Bodhisattva* as an elephant who once gave shelter to a wicked wanderer. At his abode after relishing the hospitality for few days, he left for his home at Vārānasī. In the city, when he came to know about value of elephant's precious tusk, he returned to the forest and demanded the tusk from the *Bodhisattva* and it was granted. He sold it in the market and returned to the forest to demand more and his demand was again accepted. When third time he demanded root of the stump, and the *Bodhisattva* again adhered to his demand. The earth trembled due to his greed and he was killed.[159] The *Divyāvadāna*[160] tells about king Chandraprabha who gifted his head to a greedy Brāhmana Rudrākṣa. He, a dweller of Gandhamadan hill, came to the king to demand his head and he acceded the demand. The *Sasa Jātaka*[161] says the *Bodhisattva*, as a hare, offered his own body to be consumed when Sakka tested him. The *Bodhisattva*, as a hare, was living with his three friends—a monkey, a jackal and an otter—on the foot of a mountain. All four resolved that on the day of the fast, they would eat after giving alms to someone. On the fast day, Sakka tried to test them. The otter gave fish to Sakka. The jackal gifted a dead lizard and a bowl of sour milk and the monkey gave his mangoes. Sasa could not give grass to Sakka, so he jumped into fire to give his body as a food but he was saved by Sakka. The *Hasti Jātaka* informs that an elephant gave his body to a group of travellers who lost their destination. The elephant died.[162] The *Surūpa Jātaka* of *Mahāvastu* mentions a deer king Surūpa who offered his body to a hunter in exchange for a single verse of teaching.[163]

After *mahāparinibbāna* of the Buddha, both Theravāda and Mahāyāna traditions praised generous gifts of body or body organs by the *Bodhisattva*. It was included as one of the *pāramitas* (*dāna-pāramita*). The Pāli *Jātakas* and Mahāyāna literature put it as one of the highest ethical standards. The probable cause was to generate faith among the masses that even in the worst circumstances, the Buddha, in form of the *Bodhisattva* would come to rescue them. The gift of the body deals explicitly with the *Bodhisattva's* three degrees of perfection, especially *dāna-pāramita*. These stories of body sacrifice demonstrate that his *dāna* was complete at the lowest degree when the *Bodhisattva* gave people food, wealth, and clothes. The *dāna* perfection was further fulfilled when the *Bodhisattva* gave away his body organs as his eyes, flesh, and finally, the *Bodhisattva* shows how perfection of *dāna* could be fulfilled at the highest degree when he sacrifices his own life.

Mahāvihāra Tradition

The Mahāvihāra tradition took organizational shape in the Gupta age, when in Nālandā, constellation of monasteries combined under a single umbrella. It introduced new values in monastic life prelude to transformation of conventional character of monasteries, changing the orientation of Buddhist learning from 'study for faith' to 'study for knowledge'.[164] A Mahāvihāra had a place for the chief or abbot though ancient *Vinaya* rules make no provision for it.[165] The *vihāras* now ceased to be propaganda centres, which produced experts in canonical doctrine for the growth of Buddhism. They had been enlarging one aspect of monastic life that was rooted in their ancient tradition of monk scholarship and this process was marked by a re-orientation of monastic learning which withered its cloistered, inbuilt character and turned into a learning that was a liberal and multidimensional.[166] In these Mahāvihāras, a reorientation took place in the old, traditional monk culture which led to disintegrating the basic ideals of the original *saṃgha* tradition. This liberalized culture was the Indian Buddhist culture of the early medieval age.[167] Sukumar Dutt says:

> The traditional learning of the monasteries had been its beginning a cloistered pursuit-learning in canonical lore for the benefit and use of monkhood. But it was progressively liberalized-extended and enlarged in its scope and contents and made available not to monk alone, but to all seekers after knowledge. It was a new development of monastic life and activity and one involved in the complex of conditions and circumstances Buddhism had passed since the beginning of the Gupta era in its long and historic process of decline.[168]

Many reasons could be cited for the origin and rise of this tradition. First, with the emergence of Mahāyāna's culmination in early centuries, the distinction of Buddhism as a non-brahmanical faith started diminishing. It broadened continuous bonds and outward similarity in the form of rituals, patterns of worship and metaphysics between Brahmanism and Mahāyāna.[169] This pattern was fully established in the age of the Gupta kings (275–600 CE). The majority of early Gupta kings professed Brahmanism with Garuda, the mount of Visṇu as their royal insignia. Sometimes, they actively patronized Buddhism and its monasteries, as evident from their epigraphic records. This liberal outlook hastened the assimilative process between Brahmanism and Buddhism, especially Mahāyāna, and the process was complete up to the early medieval age when it reached its zenith with the acceptance of the Buddha as a Visṇu.[170] The Mahāvihāras in this age functioned as *studia generalia,* meant for liberal learning of the scholars from all the religions and disciplines but the monastic character was not fully lost. These Mahāvihāras produced eminent scholars of Mahāyāna as well as Vajrayāna who redeemed Buddhism not only in the Indian subcontinent but also in Tibet, China and South-East Asia. I-Ching says:

> The priests learn besides all the Vinaya works, and investigates the Sutras and Sastras as well. They oppose the heretics as they would derive beasts (deer) in the middle of plain, and explain away disputations as boiling water melt frost. In this manner they became famous throughout Jambudvīpa, received respects above gods and men, and serving under the Buddha, and promoting his doctrine, they lead all the people to Nirvana. Of such persons in every generation only one or two appear. They are to be likened to the sun and moon, or are to be regarded as dragon and elephant. Such were Nagarjuna, Deva, Aśvaghosa of an early age; Vasubandhu, Asanga, Saṅgabhadra, Bhavaviveka in the middle age; and Jina, Dharmapāla, Dharmakirtī, Śilabhadra, Simhachandra, Sthiramati, Gunamati, Prajnagupta, Gunaprastha, Jinaprabha (or

Paramaprabha) of late years. None of these great teacher was lacking in any kind of qualities secular or sacred. The men free from covetousness, and practicing self-content lived matchless lives. Men of such characters have scarcely been found among the heretics or other people.[171]

Nālandā was the first Buddhist establishment of the Mahāvihāra type. It attracted monk scholars from India and abroad for higher studies. The Mahāvihāra of Nālandā acquired fame in the Gupta age and its glory finally ended in the twelfth century CE. The Chinese pilgrims gave a list of the kings who built *vihāras* and donated land for its maintenance. Xuanzang says that Śakraditya built *saṁghārama* at Nālandā. His son Buddhagupta built another *saṁghārama* to its north. Tathagatgupta constructed a monastery east from it and in the post Gupta age, while Baladitya built a *saṁghārama* on north-east side.[172] The Pālas ushered in a new era in the Mahāvihāra tradition by the foundation of Odantapurī, Vikramśilā, Somapurī, Jagaddala and Ratnagirī, the Tibetan sources of Tāranāth, Bu-ston, and Dharmmasvamin gave vivid account of these Mahāvihāras, teachers, and their scholarship. The Pālas patronized these Mahāvihāras in a very special fashion with each Pāla king trying to establish his own Mahāvihāra and continued to patronize the Mahāvihāras established by their predecessors.

While examining the nature of endowments and patronage of these Mahāvihāras, it has been found that in *dāna* of the traditional *nissaya* requisites, the role of lay followers was minimized and the state became the main patron. However, the role of the laity was not abandoned altogether but such vast establishments with thousands of teachers, novice monks, and staff required organized administration and revenue generation. The king donated land to these monasteries to utilize their revenue for day to day requirements of the monks in the monasteries. Xuanzang informs that the revenue of 100 villages was endowed to serve the requirements of novice monks and teachers.[173] I-Ching says Nālandā had its own administrative setup which governed some 200 villages free from taxation.[174] Similar references have been found for Odantapurī,[175] Vikramśilā,[176] and Somapurī Mahāvihāras.[177] Due to the emergence of land as the main economic commodity in early medieval age, kings of different ages patronized these Mahāvihāras by donating villages. The donation records of Nālandā, i.e. inscriptions of the kings, and monastic, royal, official, and *Jānapada* seals suggest that sacred complex of state-monastery-peasant was formed. The kings patronized these monasteries by issuing the grants of villages which were implemented by their respective offices. The offices of *Kumaramaty-Adhikarana, Adhikarana*, *Vishay-Adhikarana*, *Nay-Adhikarana*, *Dharma-Adhikarana*, etc., have been mentioned in inscriptions of Nālandā.[178] These offices implemented the revenue grants issued by the respective kings to the concerned monastery/monasteries. The monasteries maintained affiliation with these villages by corresponding with their seal impressions. The numerous seals with *Dharmachakra* symbol and legend

Śri-Nālandā-Mahavihariy-ārya-bhikshu-saṅghasya also mentions names of the villages.[179] The villages maintained their relations by posting their representatives at Mahāvihāra. In the legend of the *Jānapada* seals, the name of the village to which the seals belongs is given first, either in locative singular or compounded with the term *Jānapada* which follows it (*Purika-grama-jānpadasya*).[180] An economic hierarchy was established to fulfil the ecclesiastical requirements of the sacred complex of Nālandā. This hierarchy can be examined with the help of inscriptions and seals.

1. Royal Inscriptions and Seals
2. Official Seals
3. Monastic Seals
4. *Jānapada* Seals

Royal Inscriptions and Seals

A number of inscriptions referring the donations or votive in nature have been found during the excavation at Nālandā. One of the earliest inscriptions found in the Nālandā complex near monastery no. 1 belongs to Samudragupta (350–75 CE). This inscription was issued by Gōpasvāmin, the *Mahāsenapati* and *Akshapataladhikrita* from his victorious camp at Nirpura on the second day of *Magha* in his fifth regnal year. It mentions gift of village Chandrapushkaraka/ Pushkaraka *grāma.*[181] This is supposed to be first inscription dealing with the grant of village to Nālandā monastery. The Nālandā seal of Kumargupta-III contains pieces of string or cloth which originally passed through it and were fastened to the document to which the seal was attached.[182] A copperplate inscription of Vainyagupta found at Gunaighar, in district Tippera of Bangladesh records a gift of land from victory camp at Kripura which was made at the instance of his feudatory Maharaja Rudradatta.[183] The seal fastened at it resembles Nālandā seal of Vainyagupta suggesting that Nālandā seal was also used for village donation. Most of these seals give personal information of the Gupta kings and their genealogical hierarchy but the cause to issue has not been mentioned. The inscription of Samudragupta indicates that such type of village grants may have been made by his successor but paucity of direct evidence questions such motives. The twenty-six Gupta seals have been discovered.[184] The seals of Buddhagupta, Narsiṁhagupta, Kumargupta-III, Vainyagupta, etc., are of special relevance. These seals are only genealogical in character but the inscriptions on which these seals have been fastened might give records about the village grants of patronage of *stūpas vihāras*, etc.

The seals of Harshavardhana and Bhaskaravarmana also have been found in Nālandā.[185] The donations of villages are not mentioned on these seals, but Xuanzang informs that Harsha remitted the revenue of about 100 villages for the endowment of Buddhist monks at Nālandā.[186] The Gōhsrāwaṅ stone inscription of Devapāladeva mentions Yaśovarma Vihāra of Nālandā.[187] The

Nālandā stone inscription of Yaśovarmmadeva records that Malada, the son of minister of Yaśovarmmadeva, gifted ghee, curd, a lamp, and pious water mixed with four-fold fragrance and a permanent endowment (*akshaya nīvi*). Malada also distributed delicious food and scented water to *bhikkhus* and purchased a *layana* and other things from revered *saṃgha* and returned them back to the monks. He patronized the *saṃgha* because of the venerable monk, Pūrṇṇendrasēna.[188] The nature of permanent endowment is not known. It may be the particular village in vicinity of Nālandā. The Nālandā copperplate inscription of Dharmapāladeva informs the grant of village Niguha in the Gayā *vishaya* of Nagara *bhukti* and Jambunadi *vithi*. The purpose of grant has not been discovered but the revenue of the village seems to be meant for the monks of Nālandā Mahāvihāra.[189] The Nālandā copperplate inscription of Devapāladeva was issued in his 39th regnal year on the twenty-first day of the Kartika month. This inscription is one of the most illustrious in the history of Nālandā, mentioning friendly relations between the Pāla ruler and the Śailendra king Bālaputradeva. Devapāladeva was requested to build a monastery at Nālandā and for the *bhikkhus* of *chatuddisasaṃgha*, copying of Buddhist texts, and upkeep of the *vihāra* in the future, five villages should be granted. The Pāla ruler granted five villages, Nandivanaka, Manivataka, Natika, Hastgrama, and Palamaka for Nālandā Mahāvihāra.[190] The Pālas not only granted villages to Nālandā but also to other Mahāvihāras.

Official Seals

The name of different offices inscribed on official seals indicates elaborate system of revenue administration related to Nālandā Mahāvihāra. The offices like *Kumarāmatya-Adhikarana*, *Adhikarana*, *Vishya-Adhikarana*, *Nay-Adhikarana*, *Dharma-Adhikarana*, *Hatta-Mahajana*, *Rajvaiśya*, etc., have been mentioned with the name of the villages and their territorial divisions. Most of the seals belong to the early medieval age, between seventh to tenth centuries of Common Era.[191] The references of offices show that village grants were made from provincial to subdivision level. The office of *Kumarāmatya* was provincial while *Nay* was a subdivision. Hirananda Sastri says that the words like *Brahmananam*, *Traividyasya*, *Chaturvaidyasya,* inscribed on seals do not corroborate to individuals but functionaries related to the Mahāvihāra. These terms are used for experts in various disciplines like, *Traividyasya* means expert in three disciplines, *Brahmananam* and *Chaturvaidyasya* may be for experts in brahmanical knowledge, appointed in the monastery to impart Vedic knowledge.[192] The term *agrahara* may have been used for the grants specifically meant for the scholars of the *Vedas* and brahmanical texts, not for all scholar monks of *chatuddisasaṃgha*. One strange phenomenon is that no seal of any guild organization of *sresthin*, *sārthavāha*, etc., have been found, though *Rajvaiśyas* have been mentioned.[193] It shows that the representation of donations and grants of guilds and other mercantile community did not have substantial value or amount, and king's patronage was in abundance. *Rajvaiśyas* and *Hattamahājanas* were mercantile communities at the village level, probably engaged in economic transaction with monasteries. Some seals mention place, administrative units and some in fact, inform the places from where or for the particular division village grants have been made. Twenty-three such legends have been discovered showing geographical identities. Some of the seals are—*Rājagrihē vishay-ādhikaranasya,*[194] *Gaya-vishay-ādhikaranasaya,*[195] and *Sravasti-bhuktai nay-ādhikaranasya.*[196] The legends inform that grants were made not only in adjoining regions of Nālandā but in far off areas of Srāvastī.

Monastic Seals

The seals of the Nālandā Mahāvihāra, approximately, 775 excluding fragments have been found in different monasteries. The majority of these, 690 seals, have been found in monastery no. IX, suggesting it as the record room of administrative head office. These seals are identical, in which the upper portion is occupied by the *Dharmachakra* symbol and in the lower portion the legend, *Sri-Nālandā-Mahavihariye-arya-bhikshu-saṅghasya* has been engraved. These seals bear two characteristics, the majority bears legend containing the name of the monastery and the assembly of the monks and others also have the name of the village connected with the monastery.[197] The first symbolizes Nālandā as '*dharma-ratna-lekhana*' (Jewel of *dhamma* and its writing) and '*Prājňapāramit-ādisakala-dhamma-ratna-sthānīya*' (abode of propounder of *dhamma*) because it was a place from where thousands of *bhikkhus* learnt and preached Buddhism not only in India, but abroad too.[198] The seals referring the names of the villages directly mention the patronage and grant of the village to a monastery of a particular sect or monks of four quarters or for other purposes. One fragmented seal of Śakraditya mentions monks of all four quarters (*chaturddisey-arya-mahabhikshu saṅghasya*).[199] Some records mention specific sects or monasteries. One seal of Baladitya of Nālandā represents the *bhikkhus* of *gandhakutī*, built by Baladitya in Nālandā (*Sri Nālandā-Echa Baladitya-gandhakudya varika-bhikshunam*)[200] and some to monasteries in charge of distribution of *civara* (*chivarkajya panaya bhikshu saṅghasya*).[201]

Jānapada Seals

The seals with the legend *Jānapada* found in Nālandā are possibly corporate seals, informing about the corporate office of a particular village in the Mahāvihāra. The legend of the seals like *Śri-Nālandā-Pratibaddha Āgami grāma-vihārastha janapadsy*[202] and *Śri Nālandā-pratibaddha Mamnayika-grāma jānapadsya*[203] show that *Jānapada* was an office distinct from the inhabitants of the village mentioned in the legends. The term *pratibaddha* means that *Jānapada* was attached to a *vihāra*. The names of the villages to which *Jānapadas* belonged have been mentioned in the legends of the seals found from the Mahāvihāra. Hirananda Sastri says that there may be two *Jānapadas*, one being subordinate to other like in Jakkurika.[204]

The *Jānapadas* were probably responsible to pay the assigned revenue of the villages and to maintain administrative relations with the Mahāvihāras. The mode of payment is not clearly known. Hwui-Li records:

> The king of the country respects and honours the priests and has remitted the revenue of about 100 villages for the endowment of the convent. Two hundred householders of these villages, day by day, contribute several hundred piculs (1 picul=133lbs) of ordinary rice, and several hundred cattis (1 catty = 160 lbs) in weight of butter and milk. Hence the students here, being so abundantly supplied, do not require to ask for four requirements.[205]

The remains of Mahāvihāras, their inscriptions, and sculptures bear witness to kings as a conspicuous category of donors on a very large scale. It has been widely discussed and speculated that such grants were basically legitimatization processes, perpetuated by successive rulers. Majority of such royal grants may fall in this category but some of the royal grants could not be considered as a means of legitimacy. Here, faith was the only motive. Similarly, majority of donations of common people had not been recorded in seals or inscriptions. These donations were purely religious and the motive was generally personal. The Mahāvihāra tradition led some very significant changes in the functioning of *vihāras*, in the domain of land grants and their management in the middle and the lower Ganga valley. One interesting aspect of such grants is that they generally do not mention unfertile or marshy lands. It is presumed that only fertile lands were granted, showing that land was not with a purpose to expand the horizon of agriculture but as a resource to feed and fulfil four requisites of *nissaya*. It also encouraged radical changes in land ownership, land revenue, and its administration. The donation of land grants was possibly a conscious policy adopted by the Gupta rulers to

TABLE 6.1: Some *Jānapada* Seals and its Villages[206]

S. No.	Jānapada *Seals*	*Village*/Jānapada
1	S.1, 374	Purikā
2	S.9, R.92	Vārakīya
3	S.9, R.92	Brāhamani
4	S.9, R.92	Udradvara-sthane
5	S.9, R.159	Valladiha
6	S.9, R.16	Mamnayika
7	S.9, R.92	Navaka
8	S.9, R.144	Angami

maintain the free flow of revenue to the Mahāvihāras and to penetrate their administration, the rural areas with some sort of religious sanctions. The Vardhans and the Pālas continued the policy of the early Guptas. Nālandā and other Mahāvihāras, as centres of Mahāyāna and Vajrayāna helped to consolidate it. K.R. Srimali says:

> Mahāyāna glorified dāna mahima (glories of gift making), bhumi (land), and kshetra (domain) in a calculated and conscious manner. In contrast to the arhat of the Hīnayāna sect, whose sole objective was merely the nibbāna of the self, the Bodhisattva of Mahāyāna was an Avalokitesvara, who worked for happiness and salvation of entire suffering humanity. The underlying assumption of the concept of the Bodhisattva is that he becomes the Buddha in a specific period and at a specific place. The theologians ascribed a regional base to that world and designated it as a Buddhakshetra.[207]

In the ancient land of Magadha, the broader question still left is that it helped in the cultivation of the forest and the marshy lands as in the case of the other parts of India or not. However, it cannot be denied that the main motive of the kings who patronized Nālandā and other Mahāvihāras was to promote them as great centres of learning. The Nālandā inscription of Devapāla desires it as a great centre of learning both by preaching Dharma-(*Prajnārmit-ādi-Sakala-dharma-ratna-sthāniya*) and by writing (*dharma-rantna-lekhana*).[208] Altogether the reciprocity among kings, monks, and common people not only strengthened social harmony but also inculcated Buddhist learning not only in the Indian subcontinent, but also in other parts of Asia.

Notes

1. E.B. Findly, *Dāna: Giving and Getting in Pāli Buddhism*, Delhi: Motilal Banarsidass, 2003, pp. 2–3.
2. Romila Thapar, 'Dāna and Daksina as Forms of Exchange', in *Cultural Pasts: Essays in Early Indian History*, ed. Romila Thapar, Delhi: Oxford University Press, 2000, p. 522 (*Dāna* is different from *dakṣina*, which indicates gift made to the performer of Vedic sacrifices. It often consisted of gifts to the priests, maybe a cow, bull or other valuable objects. Thapar, 'Dāna and Daksina as Forms of Exchange', p. 528. It also connotes with *ista*, which means spiritual merit acquired through donations at the time of sacrifice, Manu, IV.226.
3. J.C. Heesterman, *The Ancient Indian Royal Consecration: The Rājasūya Described According to the Yajus Texts and Annoted*, s' Gravenhage: Mouton and Co., 1957, pp. 49, 174.
4. *Aṅguttara Nikāya*, III, 49–51.
5. Romila Thapar, 'Patronage and Community', in *Cultural Past: Essays in Early Indian History*, p. 590.
6. *Vinaya Pitaka*, I.58; *Dīgha Nikāya*, III.137; *Aṅguttara Nikāya*, I.117 (*Pindiyalopa-bhojana pamsukuluavara, rukkkhamulasenasana and puttimutta bhesajja*).
7. *Vinaya Pitaka*, I.58.
8. *Dhammapadaatthakatha*, I.71.
9. *Mahāvagga*, III.90.

10. *Saṁyutta Nikāya*, I.32; *Majjhima Nikāya*, I.247.
11. *Dīgha Nikāya*, III.130.
12. *Saṁyutta Nikāya*, V.64–7.
13. *Vinaya Pitaka*, I.57–8 (The *saṃgha* also arranged bowl, which was distributed under supervision of *pattagahapaka* according to seniority of the monks. The hoarding of the extra bowls was not allowed and could not be replaced, if not molded at least from three places, *Vinaya Pitaka*, III.242–7. It was made of either iron or clay. The bowls of gourd, skulls, gold, silver, pearl, beryl, crystal, bronze, glass, lead, copper or wood were not allowed, *Vinaya Pitaka*, II.114–15).
14. *Majjhima Nikāya*, I.124; *Dīgha Nikāya*, I.204 (They were also instructed for alms begging to go early in the forenoon but not too early, *Majjhima Nikāya*, I.84. Return not too late in a day, *Vinaya Pitaka*, I.70).
15. *Majjhima Nikāya*, III.88, *Saṁyutta Nikāya*, I.76 (The *bhikkhus* should go out and partake food only once for good health, spiritual well-being, and contentment—*ekasanabhojana* and *ekabhattikas*, *Majjhima Nikāya*), I.124, *Dīgha Nikāya*, I.204, II.72.
16. *Saṁyutta Nikāya*, IV.122; *Aṅguttara Nikāya*, III.30.
17. *Majjhima Nikāya*, I.31 (Sometimes *yañña* is also referred for food, *Suttanipāta*, 461, 484).
18. *Dīgha Nikāya*, I.5 (Raw meat as well as human flesh and flesh from elephants, horses, dogs, snakes, lions, tigers, panthers, bears, hyenas and wolves were prohibited), *Majjhima Nikāya*, I.368–9.
19. *Vinaya Pitaka*, IV.71–5.
20. *Vinaya Pitaka*, 2.213, 216 (The *Cullavagga* says about a monk who went for alms begging in house without proper knocking and information. The woman of the house was lying naked on her back in the inner apartment. The husband seeing the monk, accused him of seducing his wife and beat him. The women came out in monk's defence but the husband did not listen. Thereafter, the Buddha made more stringent rules for alms begging. *Vinaya Pitaka*, II.215–16).
21. *Vinaya Pitaka*, I.70.
22. *Saṁyutta Nikāya*, IV.103–4.
23. *Vinaya Pitaka*, II.107–8.
24. *Vinaya Pitaka*, I.57–9.
25. *Majjhima Nikāya*, I.459–62, *Aṅguttara Nikāya*, II.123–6.
26. *Vinaya Pitaka*, III.11–21.
27. *Majjhima Nikāya*, II.54–64.
28. *Dīgha Nikāya*, III.130 (The Buddhist monks and nuns took vow not be naked. *Majjhima Nikāya*, I.77–83).
29. *Dīgha Nikāya*, III.224.
30. *Vinaya Pitaka*, III.210–13.
31. Ibid., III.256–7.
32. Ibid., I.283.
33. Ibid., III.257–60.
34. Ibid., III.213–15 (In addition to robe, funds *Chandaka*, an additional voluntary collection, especially for the nuns has been mentioned. It was strictly for the robes. *Vinaya Pitaka*, IV.250–3).
35. Ibid., IV.255–7.
36. Ibid., I.96; *Majjhima Nikāya*, I.316.

37. Ibid., I.58, 96, 199 [These were counted as *aharattham*, not as substantial food resources. *Vinaya Pitaka*, I.199. These five medicines can be used *kale* (right time) or *vikale* (wrong time) *Vinaya Pitaka*, IV.85–6].
38. Ibid., I.216–20.
39. Debiprasad Chattopadhyaya, *Studies in the History of Science in India*, vol. I, Delhi: Ashajyoti Press, 1992, pp. 14–19.
40. Vasudeva Sharan Agrawala, *Sārnāth*, Delhi: ASI, 1980, pp. 24–5.
41. *Journal of Numismatic Society of India*, XXIII, 2, Numismatic Society of India, 1960, p. 409.
42. K.K. Thaplyal, *Studies in Ancient Indian Seals*, Lucknow: Akhil Bhartiya Sanskrit Parishad, 1972, p. 214.
43. A.S. Altekar and V. Mishra, *Report of Kkumrahar Excavation 1951–5*, Patna: K.P. Jayasawal Institute, 1959, pl. XXXV, p. 107.
44. Hirananda Sastri, *Nālandā and its Epigraphic Material*, Delhi: ASI, 1999, p. 23.
45. *Vinaya Pitaka*, I.58.
46. Ibid., II.147.
47. Ibid., I.38–9.
48. Sukumar Dutt, *Buddhist Monks and Monasteries of India*, Delhi: MLBD, 2000, p. 58.
49. Findly, *Dāna: Giving and Getting*, pp. 148–9.
50. Uma Chakravarti, *Social Dimensions of Early Buddhism*, Delhi: OUP, 1987, p. 58.
51. *Vinaya Pitaka*, I.139–42.
52. Ibid., 1.142, 148 (Rain retreat is also allowed when there is danger of wild animals, crocodiles, robbers and demons, *Vinaya Pitaka*, I.148–9).
53. *Majjhima Nikāya*, I.139–42 (But, forest dwelling was not allowed for the nuns because of security reasons. *Vinaya Pitaka*, II.274).
54. *Vinaya Pitaka*, II.147.
55. Ibid., III.149–55.
56. Ibid., II.159–60, 278.
57. Mohan Wijayratna, *Buddhist Monastic Life: According to Texts of Theravada Tradition*, tr. Claude Grangier and Stevan Collins, Cambridge: Cambridge University Press, 1990, p. 26.
58. *Mahāvagga*, I.22.17–18.
59. Ibid., III.5.6.
60. Ibid., V.1.15.4.
61. Dutt, *Buddhist Monks and Monasteries*, p. 92.
62. Samuel Beal, *Si-yu-Ki, Buddhist Record of the Western World*, Delhi: LPP (reprint), 1995, p. xxxi.
63. Patrick Olivelle, *The Origin and Early Development of Buddhist Monachism*, Colombo: M.D. Gunasena, 1974, p. 15.
64. *Vinaya Pitaka*, III.207–10.
65. Ibid., II.269–70.
66. Anand Singh, 'Early Buddhist Order and the Lay World', in *Transformation in Indian History*, ed. S.Z.H. Jafri, Delhi: Anamika Publication, 2009, p. 117.
67. Narendra Wagle, *Society at the Time of the Buddha*, Bombay: Popular Prakashan, 1966, p. 154.
68. Kenneth Boulding, *The Economy of Love and Fear: A Preface to Grants Economics*, California: Woodsworth Publishing Company, 1973, pp. 2–3.
69. *Aṅguttara Nikāya*, IV.438.

70. Ibid., II.69.
71. *Majjhima Nikāya*, I.371–89, *Aṅguttara Nikāya*, I.160–2.
72. *Vinaya Pitaka*, I.247–9, II.156.
73. *Aṅguttara, Nikāya*, III.38–40.
74. *Vinaya Pitaka*, I.290–4.
75. *Majjhima Nikāya*, III.253–7.
76. *Saṁyutta Nikāya*, I.98–100.
77. Nathan Katz, *Buddhist Images of Human Perfection*, Delhi: MLBD, pp. 186–7.
78. *Suttanipāta*, no. 488.
79. *Dhammapada Commentary*, V.35.
80. Findly, *Dāna: Giving and Getting*, p. 61.
81. Ibid., pp. 3–4.
82. *Vinaya Pitaka*, I.220–2.
83. *Saṁyutta Nikāya*, I.113–14.
84. Ibid., I.23.
85. Ibid., I.32.
86. *Aṅguttara Nikāya*, II.59.
87. *Saṁyutta Nikāya*, I.21.
88. *Aṅguttara Nikāya*, IV.244 (In Buddhist literature, detailed list of rebirths taken by virtuous people engaging in *dāna* has been provided, such as among wealthy nobles, brahmanas and householders of worth. Among the four royal gods with handsome physique, among the Tavatimsa gods, among the Yama gods, in Tusita heaven, in Nimmanarati heaven, in Paranimmitavasavattin gods and among the Brahma world with happy and contended life, *Dīgha Nikāya*, III.258–60 and *Aṅguttara Nikāya*, IV.239–41).
89. *Saṁyutta Nikāya*, IV.288; *Aṅguttara Nikāya*, I.247, II.26–7.
90. Findly, *Dāna: Giving and Getting*, p. 112.
91. Dutt, *Buddhist Monks and Monasteries*, p. 110.
92. Thomas Watter, *On Yuan Chwang's Travels in India* (*AD 629–45*), vol. I, Delhi: LPP, 2004, p. 112.
93. Thapar, 'Patronage and Community', p. 595.
94. *Mahāparinibbāna Sutta*, V.24 (Eight *stūpas* were built by The Lichchhavis of Vaiśalī, the Śakyas of Kapilavastu, the Mallas of Pāvā, the Mallas of Kuśinagar, the Bulis of Allkapp, the Koliyas of Rāmagāma, the brāhmaṇas of Vetthadvipa and Mauryas of Pippalivana or Ajātaśatru of Magadha).
95. *Mahāvastu*, II.362.
96. Akira Hirakawa, *A History of Early Buddhism: From Sakyamuni to Early Mahāyāna*, Hawaii: University of Hawaii Press, 1990, p. 101.
97. *Corpus Inscriptionum Indicarum: Inscriptions of Aśoka*, Delhi: Indological Publishing House, 1969, vol. I, p. 165.
98. Ibid., p. 164.
99. *Mahāparinibbāna Sutta*, V.29.
100. *Milindapanho*, IV.24–7.
101. Reginald A. Ray. *Buddhist Saints in India: A Study in Buddhist Values and Orientation*, Oxford: OUP, 1994, p. 326.
102. John Marshal, *The Monuments of Sanchī*, 3 vols., Delhi: Agam Kala Prakashan, 1983, repr, vol. 1, p. 184.
103. Dutt, *Buddhist Monks and Monasteries* [The *Mahābhārata* says that the earth will be covered with '*edukas*' (structure of contempt), i.e., *stūpas*, instead of with temples of gods. *Mahābhārata, Vanaparva*, VV.13074–6, Asiatic Society], p. 186.

104. Ibid., p. 189.
105. Binoytosh Bhattacharya, *Indian Buddhist Iconography*, Calcutta: K.L. Mukhopadhyaya, 1968, p. 656.
106. *Mahāvastu*, II.362–4.
107. Stella Kramrisch, *Indian Sculpture*, Delhi: MLBD, 1933, p. 24.
108. Dutt, *Buddhist Monks and Monasteries*, p. 192.
109. Walapola Rahula, *History of Buddhism in Ceylon: The Anuradhapura Period, 3rd century* CE*–10th century* AD, Colombo: M.D. Gunasena, 1966, pp. 125–6.
110. Bhattacharya, *Indian Buddhist Iconography*, p. 656.
111. Ibid., p. 661.
112. *Advayavajrasaṁgraha*, vol. 660, tr. Haraprasad Sastri, GOS, No. XL, Baroda, 1927, p. 51.
113. A.K. Warder, *Indian Buddhism*, Delhi: MLBD, 2008, pp. 485–6.
114. K.T.S. Sarao, *Decline of Buddhism in India: A Fresh Perspective*, Delhi: Munshiram Manoharlal, p. 138.
115. Sashibhusangupta Dasgupta, *Obscure Religious Cults*, Calcutta: K.L. Mukhopadhyaya, 1962, p. 27.
116. A. Ghosh, *A Guide to Nālandā*, Delhi: ASI, 1950, p. 22.
117. *Epigraphia Indica*, vol. VIII (1905–6), p. 173.
118. Ibid., pp. 180–1, *Epigraphia Indica*, vol. IX (1907–8), pp. 290–1.
119. Gregory Schopen, *Indian Monastic Buddhism*, Delhi: MLBD, 2010, p. 247.
120. *Epigraphia Indica*, VIII (1905–6), p. 176.
121. Ibid., pp. 180–1.
122. *Epigraphia Indica*, vol. XXIV (1937–8), pp. 210–12.
123. *Epigraphia Indica*, vol. VIII (1905–6), p. 182.
124. Ibid., p. 179.
125. Schopen, *Indian Monastic Buddhism*, p. 248.
126. Ibid., p. 249.
127. D.R. Sahani, *Catalogue of the Museum of Archaeology at Sārnāth*, B(b)1, B(b)59, B(b)60, B(b)172, B(b)179, B(b)293, B294, B295, Calcutta, 1919.
128. Gregory Schopen, *Indian Monastic Buddhism*, pp. 30, 48–9.
129. Anand Singh, *Buddhism at Sārnāth*, Delhi: Primus, 2013, pp. 46–50.
130. *Vinaya Pitaka*, I. 216ff.
131. *Therigātha*, VV.366–99.
132. John S. Strong, *The Legend of King Aśoka: A Study and Translation of Aśokavadāna*, Delhi: MLBD, 2008, pp. 275–7.
133. Reiko Ohnuma, *Bodily Self-Sacrifice in Indian Buddhist Literature*, Delhi: MLBD, 2009, pp. 6–8.
134. Ibid., pp. 20–1.
135. Etienne Lamotte, *Le traite de la grande vertu de sagesse de Nāgārjuna*, 5 vols., Bibliothique du Muśeon 18, Louvain: Bureaue du Museon, 1944–8, p. 143.
136. *Siksasamuccya* (Shantideva), tr. Cecil Bendall, *A Compendium of Buddhist Doctrine*, Delhi: MLBD, 1990, p. 21.
137. Ibid., pp. 25–6.
138. Watter, *On Yuan Chwang's Travels in India*, vol. 1, p. 235.
139. Samuel Beal, *Travels of Fa-hien and Sung-yun from China to India (450* AD*–518* AD*)*, Delhi: LPP, 2004, repr., p. 33.
140. Watter, *On Yuan Chwang's Travels in India*, vol. 1, pp. 234–5.
141. *Jātaka*, no. 499.
142. *Jātakamala*, pp. 8–9.

143. Mary Cumming, *The Lives of Buddha in the Art and Literature of Asia*, Ann Arbor: Centre for South and Southeast Asian Studies, University of Michigan, 1982, pp. 75–83.
144. Ohnuma, *Bodily Self-Sacrifice*, p. 275.
145. Leslie Grey, *A Concordance of Buddhist Birth Stories*, London: PTS, 1994 (The king's name in this literature is Sarvaṁdada), pp. 361–5
146. Ohnuma, *Bodily Self-Sacrifice*, p. 5.
147. Mary Cumming, *The Lives of Buddha*, pp. 74–83.
148. *Jātakamālā*, pp. 55–71.
149. Grey, *A Concordance of Buddhist Birth Stories*, pp. 239–40.
150. *Divyāvadana*, Edward B. Cowell and Robert A. Neil, ed., *The Divyāvadāna: A Collection of Early Buddhist Legends*, Amsterdam: Oriental Press, 1970, pp. 314–28.
151. *Avadānasarasammuccaya*, tr. Michael Hahn, *Der grosse Legendenkranz (Mahājātakamala): Eine Mittelalteriliche buddistischu legendensammlung aus Nepal.* Wiesbaden: O. Harrassowirz, 1985, pp. 532–50.
152. J.S. Speyer, *Avādānaśataka: A Century of Edifying Tales Belonging to Hinayana*, vol. I, 2 vols. in one, The Hague: Mouton and Co., 1958, pp. 168–72.
153. Michael Hanh, *Haribhatta and Gopadatta, Two Authors in Succession of Āryasūra: On the Rediscovery of Parts of Their Jātakamālās*, second edn., Studia Philologica Buddhica Occasional Paper, I Tokyo: International Institute of Buddhist Studies, 1992.
154. *Jātaka*, no. 514.
155. A. Foucher, *The Beginning of Buddhist Art and Another Essay in Indian and Central Asian Archaeology*, Delhi: Asian Educational Services, 1994; repr., p. 196.
156. John S. Strong, *Relics of the Buddha*, Delhi: MLBD, 2007, p. 53.
157. Ohnuma, *Bodily Self-Sacrifice*, pp. 53–4.
158. *Jātaka*, no. 12.
159. *Jātaka*, no. 72.
160. *Divyāvadāna*, p. 316.
161. *Jātaka*, no. 316.
162. J.S. Speyer, *Jātakamālā, Hasti Jātaka, The Gātakamala or Garland of Birth Stories by Aryasura, Sacred Books of Buddhists*, Delhi: MLBD, 1990, pp. 281–91.
163. J.J. Jones, *The Mahāvastu*, 3 vols., Sacred Books of Buddhists, 16, 18 and 19, London: PTS, 1949–56, vol. 1, pp. 240–2.
164. Dutt, *Buddhist Monks and Monasteries*, p. 319.
165. Sukumar Dutt, *Early Buddhist Monachism*, Delhi: MLBD, 1996, pp. 143–4.
166. Dutt, *Buddhist Monks and Monachism of India*, pp. 322–3.
167. Ibid., p. 318.
168. Ibid., p. 319.
169. Ibid., 321 (Bu-ston mentions this liberal thing by citing *Sūtralaṅkara*—'In order to vanquish and to help others and to obtain knowledge for himself, the good monk is earnestly applied to study, science of logic (Hetuvidya) and of grammar and literature in order to vanquish one's adversaries (in controversy), the science of medicine (Cikitsavidya) and Arts (Silpakarmavidya), for administrating help to others and that of metaphysics (Adhyatamavidya) to acquire knowledge of himself', p. 196, E. Obermiller, *Blue Annals,* pt. I, p. 44).
170. Ibid., pp. 196–7.

171. J. Takakusu, *A Record of the Buddhist Religion as Practised in India and the Malaya Archipelago (AD 671–695)*, Delhi: Munshiram Manoharlal, 1998, p. 181 [Kasyapa says that dragon and elephant are not separate identities but understood as Dragon-Elephant. In India, the best quality of elephants are known as dragon (naga) elephant. J. Takakusu, *A Record of the Buddhist Religion*, p. 181].
172. Hirananda Sastri, *Advayavajrasaṁgraha*, pp. 14–15 (Nālandā, as a Buddhist monastic settlement first developed in the age of the Buddha. Xuanzang informs that Nālandā was purchased by 500 merchants for 10 *kotis* of gold pieces and gifted to the Buddha who preached the *dhamma* here at Pavarikambavana for three months. Its one satellite area, Sarichak was famous for the birth of the great monk, Sariputta and another great monk, Mahamoggalayana was also born in Nālandā. Samuel Beal, *Records of the Western World*, vol. II, pp. 175–7).
173. Samuel Beal, *The Life of Hiuen-Tsiang* by Shaman Hwvi Li, Delhi: LPP, 2008; repr., pp. 112–14.
174. J. Takakusu, *A Record of the Buddhist Religion*, pp. 175–9.
175. Debiprasad Chattopadhyaya, *Taranath's History of Buddhism in India*, Delhi: MLBD, 1970, pp. 262–4 [Odantapuri Mahāvihāra was founded by Pala king Gopala (660–705 CE). The Tibetan legend says that monastery was built upon a lake that became dry by miracle.]
176. Ibid. (Vikramśilā Mahāvihāra was founded by Dharamapala. Nandulal Dey identifies it with Patharghata of Bihar, Nandulal Dey, *Vikramśilā Monastery*, JASB, n.s., vol. V, 1909, p. 278.)
177. Ibid. (This Mahāvihāra was founded by Devapāla. It was in Paharpur, of Rajshahi district of Bangladesh), p. 266.
178. Hirananda Sastri, *Advayavajrasaṁgraha*, p. 34.
179. Ibid., pp. 36–7.
180. Ibid., 32, 45, S.1, 374.
181. Sastri, *Epigraphia Indica*, vol. XXV, p. 50 [The inscription was issued by Gopaswamin, the *Mahasenapati* and *Akshapataladhikrita* (chief commander and chief of records) on instruction of Samudragupta. No royal seal was attached to it. Hiranand Sastri identified Nripura as a *mauza* 1.5 miles away from Nālandā comprising four *talukas*, Nripur, Chak-nripur, Jalalpur and Tajubigha. The name of *Vishya* (district) in the inscription is not clear. The gift village has not been identified yet. Probably it was situated near a pokhara (tank) and so may derive the name Chandrapokhara, pp. 77–8].
182. *Corpus Inscriptionum Indicarum*, vol. III, p. 356.
183. *Indian Historical Quarterly*, vol. VI, no. 3, 1930, pp. 45–60.
184. Sastri, *Epigraphia Indica*, p. 64.
185. Ibid., pp. 67–70.
186. Samuel Beal, *The life of Hiuen-Tsiang*, pp. 112–13.
187. Sastri, *Epigraphia Indica*, p. 91.
188. *Epigraphia Indica*, XX (1929–30), pp. 38–9.
189. Ibid., XXIII, pp. 291f.
190. Sastri, *Indian Antiquary*, vol. XXI, pp. 257–8 [Hirananda Sastri identified the five villages as, Nandivanaka and Manivataka in the Ajapura *naya* possibly, represented by Naunwen (Nandivanaka), Manianwan (Manivataka), Ajaipur (Ajaypura) village in the Ajai Hisse Chaharam *mauja* of Bihar. Natika and the Pilipinka have been identified as modern Nai Pokhar village and Pilkhi *maujan* respectively, Sastri, *Indian Antiquary*, p. 95, Identification of rest of villages are still not known].

191. Ibid., p. 33.
192. Ibid., pp. 33–4.
193. Ibid., p. 34.
194. *Nalanda Museum*, S.I, 749.
195. Ibid., S, I, 829.
196. Ibid., S, I, 821.
197. Hirananda Sastri, *Indian Antiquary*, pp. 36–7.
198. Ibid., pp. 36–7.
199. *Nālandā Museum*, S.1, 848, Pl. II, e.
200. Ibid., S.1, 675, Pl. III, a.
201. Ibid., S.9, R.15, Pl. III, d.
202. *Nālandā Museum*, S.9, R.144.
203. *Nālandā Museum*, S.9, R.16 (K.P. Jayaswal says that *Jānapada* was a corporate body).
204. Sastri, *Indian Antiquary*, 1999, p. 33.
205. Samuel Beal, *The Life of Hiuen-Tsiang*, pp. 112–13.
206. Ibid., pp. 32, 45.
207. K.M. Shrimali, 'Religions in Complex Societies', in *Religion in Indian History*, ed. Irfan Habib, New Delhi: Tulika Publication, 2007, p. 54.
208. Sastri, *Indian Antiquary*, pp. 36–7.

7

History Gleaned from Inscriptions

Recording Buddhist Endowments with Guilds at Nasik

KIRAN KUMAR THAPLYAL

NASIK, THE FIND-SPOT of the two inscriptions under consideration[1] recording Buddhist endowments with guilds, was in ancient times known by the name of Govarddhana.[2] It was a flourishing town in early centuries of the Common Era, and was a centre of administration, religion, trade and industry. It is also known for its rock-cut caves meant as residences for the monks. A number of inscriptions are recorded on them, most of which either state that the caves meant for residence of the Buddhist monks were the gift of pious donors, or record the endowments made in favour of the Buddhist monks residing in those caves, or in favour of the Buddhist *saṃgha* located nearby. Only a few of them record donations to the brāhmaṇas. A number of inscriptions belong to the Śakas and the Sātavahānas, and are datable to a few early centuries of the Common Era.[3] Below, various aspects of history as gleaned from these two epigraphs recording Buddhist endowments with guilds at Nasik are discussed.

Nasik Cave Inscription of Ushavadāta

Of the two inscriptions under discussion, the first one was recorded in a cave at Nasik by Śaka Ushavadāta (Ṛishabhadatta), who was the son-in-law and the general of Kshaharāta Śaka King Nahapāna, and son of Dīnīka who, in the absence of any title for him, is to be taken as a commoner. It deals with Ushavadāta's donations to the Buddhist monks residing in the cave that bears the inscription. After mentioning the gift of 8,000 roots of coconut, it also mentions the offering of 70,000 *kārshāpaṇas* to the brāhmaṇas, which he paid in the form of its equivalent—2,000 gold coins, as a way of honoring the commitment that he had made earlier. This statement, incidentally, provides an important information, the only one of its kind in the inscriptions, that the ratio between silver coins and gold coins at the time of the recording of the inscription was 35 : 1.[4] Taking into consideration that the silver coins were those issued by Nahapāna, whose silver coins have been found in a fairly large number,[5] and gold coins would have been the ones issued by the Kushāṇas. Rapson states: 'If we take the weights of the *kārshāpaṇa* and the *suvarṇa* as 36 and 124 grains respectively, we shall find that the ratio of silver to gold at this time was approximately as 1 to 10. . . .'[6] The inscription, thereafter, mentions the endowment made in favour of the Buddhist monks detailed below.

From the inscription, it is known that the cave accommodated twenty Buddhist *bhikhhus*, the fulfilment of whose needs was the concern of Ushavadāta. The primary material needs of the *bhikkhus*, like other human beings, are food, clothing, and shelter. Shelter was provided by the rock-cut cave; and with a view to meet the other two needs, Ushavadāta made two endowments, one each with two weavers' guilds. One of the guilds was to provide light meals to the twenty monks residing in that cave, and the other was to provide clothes to them. The inscription gives significant information that the contract with the guild, of which the nature, terms, and conditions will be mentioned below, was proclaimed in the *nigama-sabhā*, and as per the custom, was inscribed on the tablet for future reference. The *nigama*, it appears, was a larger economic corporation than the *śreṇī* which was a craft-guild, and would have had some control over the craft-guilds.[7] This is also supported by the evidence of an inscription from Nagarjunakonda, edited by D.C. Sircar.[8]

The endowments were in the nature of permanent, fixed deposits (*akshaya-nīvi*), in which the principal sum deposited was not to be withdrawn, only the interest was to be used for doing the needful. This was in keeping with the common practice followed in ancient India throughout the centuries regarding such deposits with guilds. The guilds, thus, only partly performed the functions of modern banks. In ancient India, there is no instance of money being deposited with the guilds in the form of what we today call savings bank account, or in the form of deposits for earning compound interest to be paid to the depositor or credited in his account; all the deposits made with guilds were meant only for getting some pious and charitable work done out of the interest accruing from the sum deposited, according to the wishes of the one who made the endowment. The guilds were bound to carry out the work in perpetuity with the agreed upon rate of interest, irrespective of the fact whether the cost of the things relating to the acts to be performed by the guild would increase or decrease, and perhaps even if the guild would migrate to some other place.[9]

The total sum deposited by Ushavadāta was 3,000 *kārshāpaṇas*.[10] Of these, 2,000 *kārshāpaṇas* were deposited with one weavers' guild and 1,000 *kārshāpaṇas*, with another weavers' guild. The amount of 2,000 was deposited with interest at the rate of 1 per cent per month, i.e. 12 per cent per annum. It is stated that out of the annual interest of 2,000 *kārshāpanas*, which comes to 240 *kārshāpaṇas* per annum, each of the twenty *bhikkhus* residing in that cave was to be provided one robe annually; thus, the cost of the robe for each *bhikkhu* was twelve *kārshāpaṇas*. It is understood that in case a *bhikkhu* left the cave, or died, another *bhikkhu* was to be admitted in his place, making the total as twenty. Out of the interest of the 1,000 *kārshāpaṇas* deposited with another weavers' guild at the rate of ¾ per cent per month, the said twenty monks were to be provided light meals.[11]

It is significant that in the inscription of Ushavadāta at Nasik, not one but two guilds engaged in the same craft, viz., weaving. It is difficult to agree with the view[12] that the Nasik guilds were engaged not in weaving, but in trading the manufactured cloth, since the epigraph categorically mentions both the guilds as *kolīka-nikāya*, 'guild of weavers'. The presence of two weavers' guild at that place may be due to one of the following:

1. One guild became too large and so, was branched off into two separate guilds.
2. The breaking of the guild into two was the result of internal bickering.
3. A new guild was founded by recruiting new members, as one guild was not able to produce cloth sufficient to meet the demand of the people.
4. A weavers' guild migrated from elsewhere to that place where a guild of weavers already existed; there is an important instance of a silk-weavers' guild migrating *en masse from* Lāṭa in Gujarat to Daśapura (modern Mandasor) in western Malwa in the Gupta period.[13]

From the existence of the two weavers' guilds at Nasik, it can be assumed that it was a great centre of weaving and would have catered not only for the people residing at Nasik, but also those residing at other places. It is difficult to say if they or one of them, produced quality cloth and had a share in the export of such cloth to the Roman Empire, with which India had brisk trade, particularly from the first century BCE to third century CE and which was a great buyer of costly quality Indian cloth.

On the basis of the endowments made in favour of the Buddhist monks, one is likely to infer that the donor, Śaka Ushavadāta, was a Buddhist. But this very inscription, as seen above, also mentions the offering of 70,000 *kārshāpaṇas* to brāhmaṇas, and another inscription from Nasik,[14] likewise, records his donations to the brāhmaṇas as well as to the Buddhists. It appears that Ushavadāta was cosmopolitan in religious matter and patronized the followers of Buddhism as well as brahmanical religion equally. He, being a

Śaka would have aimed at, and perhaps succeeded in, earning the goodwill of the followers of both the religions. It is too well known that Kushāṇa ruler Kanishka, who was not far removed from Ushavadāta in time, was a devout Buddhist who organized the Third Buddhist Council; however, the depiction of Buddhist, Brahmanical, Iranian and Greek deities on his coins indicates his cosmopolitan outlook with regard to religion. It is possible that the members of the weavers' guilds, at least majority of them, were the followers of Buddhism and Ushavadāta thought that they would be more interested in the endowments relating to the Buddhist monks and would try their best to fulfil their obligations meticulously. It may be stated that Buddhism was popular with the artisans, most of whom belonged to the śūdra *varṇa*, and also with members of the trading community, most of whom belonged to the vaiśya *varṇa*. The status of these two *varṇas*, in the brahmanical *varna*-hierarchy was lower than the brāhmaṇas and the kṣatriyas, and therefore, by joining Buddhism, which did not lay much emphasis on *varṇa*-hierarchy, they acquired a better status in the society. It has been observed[15] that the fortune of Buddhism and business community waxed and waned together.

Perhaps, this inscription of Ushavadāta dealing with the two endowments in favour of the Buddhist monks is the only ancient Indian epigraph which mentions in clear terms the rate of interest, as it was in practice in a given time and region. Some law-givers[16] have prescribed monthly rates of interest to be paid by the brāhmaṇas, kṣatriyas, vaiśyas, and śūdras as 2 per cent, 3 per cent, 4 per cent, and 5 per cent, respectively. The mention of two different rates in the inscription needs explanation. As stated,'Difference in the rates of interest would be understandable, if the two guilds were located at two different regions, or if they belonged to two different periods, or if they pursued two different crafts or callings, or even if there would have been two different donors'.[17] But in the case of the inscription under discussion, there is identity regarded as *deśa* (place) which is Govarddhana (modern Nasik), *kāla* (time) which is year 42, and the *pātra* (recipient) of the benefit of the endowments which are the Buddhist monks, the *dātā* (donor) is the same, viz., Ushavadāta, the occupation of the members of the two guilds with whom the endowments were made was the same, viz., weaving, and the source of information about the endowments is also the same, viz., the Nasik inscription of Ushavadāta. In such circumstances, two rates of interest appear curious.

In the absence of any evidence for the difference in the rate of interest, one can only guess, and the following possibilities may be suggested:

1. The guild with which the money was deemed safer, paid interest at a lower rate in comparison to the other one which was deemed not so safe.
2. The guild with which greater amount (2,000 *kārshāpaṇas*) was deposited, paid higher rate than the other one with which lesser amount (1,000 *kārshāpaṇas*) was deposited.

3. The guild which paid higher interest was either the newly established one, or it had migrated from elsewhere, and was keen to enter into business even by paying higher rate of interest.
4. The guild which offered higher rate of interest dealt with costly quality cloth and earned high profits, and the other one dealt with coarse cloth and earned low profits, and Ushavadāta for some reason or the other, wanted to patronize both of them.
5. One weavers' guild could pay higher interest as it supplied its own manufactured cloth to *bhikkhus* directly, without any middlemen; while the other weavers' guild had to arrange for light meals, perhaps, through some other agency, dealing with catering for food and paying to it a sizeable amount of the interest accruing from the endowment.[18]
6. The light meals were to be provided daily,[19] and as such, there would be no accumulation of interest, while the robes were to be provided annually, the interest calculated on monthly basis was compounded, and so the guild which was to provide cloth paid higher interest than the one who arranged for light meals.

Whatever be the reason for the difference in the interest rates, one thing is certain that even the higher rate of interest, i.e. 1 per cent per month mentioned in the case of one guild is lower than the lowest one, viz., 1.25 per cent per month, which is considered as the just rate by some ancient authorities.[20] In the case of the rate of interest, as in some other cases, it is often difficult to decide whether what is mentioned in the ancient texts was actually in practice at the time and the region they were composed in, or it is what their authors wished the rates to be, or whether they were merely following some ancient tradition. In contrast, as per the evidence of the inscription under discussion, there cannot be any doubt that at the beginning of the second century CE, in the region around Nasik, for some reason or the other discussed above, there was no uniform rate of interest, but at least two separate rates of interest, 1 per cent per month in one case, and ¼ per cent less than that, i.e. ¾ per cent per month, in another. It can also be assumed that the exorbitant interest rates of 2 per cent, 3 per cent, 4 per cent and 5 per cent per month, respectively for the brāhmaṇas, kṣatriyas, vaiśyas and śūdras, as mentioned by some ancient authorities (above) were normative, rather than followed in actual practice, although there is hardly any doubt that there were different rates of interests for different *varṇas*.

The Nasik inscription of Ushavadāta indicates that the area around Nasik was within the kingdom of the Śaka King Nahapāna, a fact which is corroborated by the evidence of the find of other inscriptions from the site. Like some other ancient inscriptions, it throws light on the bank-like function of the guilds as they accepted permanent endowments in which the principal sum was kept intact and used only the interest accruing on them, as per the wishes of the one who made the endowment. It shows that Nasik, with two weavers' guilds, was a great centre of weaving. The inscription under discussion mentions Ushavadāta's endowments made in favour of the Buddhist monks as also offering of money to the brāhmaṇas, which shows his cosmopolitan outlook in religious matters. The purpose of the inscription was to record the endowments made in favour of twenty Buddhist monks residing in a cave at Nasik, but it provides some significant data relating to the various aspects of history—political, religious, and economic, of the period to which it belongs.

Nasik Inscription of the Time of Īśvarasena Ābhīra

Another inscription from Nasik, dealing with the endowments made with a guild in favour of the Buddhist monks, belongs to the time of the Ābhīra King Īśvarasena, and is datable to 258–9 CE.[21] It refers to the fixed deposits made with four different guilds by one Vishṇudattā, a woman of the Śaka race, with a view of providing medicines to the sick *bhikkhus* of the Buddhist *saṃgha* located at Triraśmi hill, near Nasik. The break-up of the endowments was: 1,000 *kārshāpaṇas* with the guild of the *kularikas* (potters), 2,000 with the guild of the *udayaṁtrikas* (workers fabricating hydraulic engines, water clocks, etc.), an amount (the portion mentioning it is mutilated) with the guild of *tila-pishakas* (oil-millers), and a sum of 500 *kārshāpaṇas* with another guild, the name of which is mutilated. Thus, while the inscription of Ushavadāta, discussed above, takes care of the food and cloth for the monks, the present inscription is meant to take care of their health.

As expected, in the flourishing town of Nasik, there were a number of guilds of different crafts. In ancient India, some guilds lasted for a long period, during which kings and even dynasties changed. However, it cannot be ascertained whether all, or any of these four guilds had also existed in the first quarter of the second century CE, during the reign of Nahapāna, when Ushavadāta made the above-mentioned endowments with the two weavers' guilds. It is possible that during the time of Ushavadāta, amongst the various guilds that were located at Nasik, the weavers' guilds were the most prosperous and therefore, were chosen for making endowments by the Śaka chief. It is likely that the prosperity of the weavers' guild was because they exported quality cloth to Roman Empire with which India had close commercial contacts during that time, and earned much profit from that. In the Nasik inscription of the time of Īśvarasena, under discussion, four endowments were made to four different guilds, total sum being more than 3,500 *kārshāpaṇas*, all for performing a single act, viz., providing medicines to the ailing monks of the Buddhist *saṃgha*. No weavers' guild is mentioned for making endowments.[22] It is not known whether or not both or one of the weavers' guild of the time of Ushavadāta continued to exist during the reign of Īśvarasena Ābhīra, but if they existed, they were not favoured with the permanent endowment, may be because they were not in good shape as the export of quality cloth to Roman Empire had declined considerably by that time.

In the Buddhist *saṃgha,* care was taken that a *bhikkhu*, on falling ill, gets proper medical treatment. It is known that in the sixth century BCE, the services of Jīvaka, a distinguished royal physician, were also available to the Buddha and the *saṃgha.* Since, only for providing medical treatment to the *bhikkhus*, four endowments with a fairly large sum of more than 3,500 *kārshāpaṇas* were made, suggests that the number of the *bhikkhus* falling ill must have been considerable, and also that the number of the *bhikkhus* in the *saṃgha* located near Nasik would have been quite large. It can be said that the rock-cut cave which accommodated twenty monks during the time of Ushavadāta, must also have done so, during the reign of Īśvarasena, and those monks would have been the members of the *bhikkhu saṃgha* located at Triraśmi hill, near Nasik.

The aim of these two inscriptions was to record endowments in favour of the Buddhist monks. The composers of the inscriptions would have hardly thought that the information that they were giving about the nature and form of the endowments, would be in future an important source for throwing significant light on the various aspects of history and culture of the Deccan during the second and the third centuries of the Common Era.

Notes

1. D.C. Sircar, *Select Inscriptions*, I, 1965, no. 58, pp. 164ff; E. Senart, *Epigraphia Indica*, VIII, pp. 88ff.
2. This is the name in the inscription of Ushavadāta discussed below.
3. For example, inscriptions of the time of Nahapāna; Sircar, *Select Inscriptions*, no. 58, pp. 164ff, which is the subject of the present paper; ibid., no. 59, pp, 167ff; and ibid., no. 60, pp. 170–1; of Gautamīputra Sātakarṇi, regnal year 18; ibid., no. 83, pp. 197ff; another inscription of the same king, year 24; ibid., no. 84, pp. 200ff; of Vāsisṭhīputra Pulamāvi, year 19; ibid., no. 86, pp. 203ff; of the same ruler, year 22; ibid., no. 87, pp. 207ff; of Yajnasri Sātakarṇi; ibid., no. 89, pp. 211–12.
4. Ibid., pp. clxxxiv–clxxxv.
5. Over 13,250 coins of Nahapāna have been found at Jogalthembi in the Nasik district, Maharashtra, of which more than 9,270 were restruck by the Sātavāhana ruler, Gautamīputra Sātakarṇi. See E.J. Rapson, *Catalogue of the Coins of the Andhra Dynasty, the Western Kšatrapas, the Traikûþaka Dynasty and the 'Bodhi' Dynasty*, in the British Museum, London, pp. lxxxviii–lxxxix.
6. Ibid., p. clxxxv.
7. For details, see K.K. Thaplyal, *Guilds in Ancient India*, New Delhi, 1966, p. 111.
8. *Epigraphia Indica*, XXXV, p. 4.
9. For an important epigraph providing information regarding the migration of a silk-weavers' guild from Lāṭa in Gujarat to Daśapura (modern Mandasor) in Madhya Pradesh, see Sircar, *Select Inscriptions*, no. 24, pp. 299ff.

10. *Kārshāpaṇa* was originally a coin with the weight of one *karsha*, which was equivalent to 80 *raktikās* or 146.4 grains. In the case of the inscription under discussion, it would refer to the silver coins of Nahapāna, based on the standard weight of 36 grains, as Nasik was located within his territory.
11.. The word used in the inscription is *kuśaṇamūla* at one place, and *kuśaṇamūla* at another. This word has not been translated by Senart (*Epigraphia Indica*, VIII, p. 82) and by R.C. Majumdar (*Corporate Life in Ancient India*, 3rd edn., Calcutta, 1969, p. 32). D.R. Bhandarkar thought that *kuśaṇa* was a coin-designation named after the Kushāṇas (*Carmichael Lectures*, 1921, 199). R.K. Mookerji takes it to mean 'money for outside life' (*Local Government in Ancient India*, 2nd edn., Oxford, 1920, p. 97), and G.L. Adhya (*Early Indian Economics*, 1st edn., Bombay, 1966, p. 86) for minor expenses. We have followed Sircar (*Select Inscriptions*, p. 166, n. 3) who takes it to mean money for light meals (*kuśāṇa mūlyam*). See also, Thaplyal, *Guilds in Ancient India*, p. 90, n. 37.
12. H.P. Ray (*Monastery and Guild—Commerce under the Sātavāhanas*, Delhi, 1986, p. 130). She is of the opinion that the textile was produced at Ter, where there is evidence of textile manufacture, and that possibly the Nasik guilds 'were primarily responsible for the organization of trade'.
13. Sircar, *Select Inscriptions*, pp. 299ff. However, in this case, it is not known whether or not any silk-weavers' guild already existed at Mandasor.
14. Ibid., no. 59, pp. 167ff.
15. Deepak Lal, *Hindu Equilibrium*, I, Oxford, 1988, p. 23.
16. *Manu*, VIII, 142; *Yājñavalkya*, II, 38.
17. Thaplyal, *Guilds in Ancient India*, pp. 176–7.
18. Unless it is presumed that some members of the guild knew the art of cooking and themselves prepared the light meals.
19. It can be presumed that the arrangements for light meals would have been made for the four months of rainy season, when the *bhikkhus* for *vassāvāsa* would stay at one place; for the rest of the month, they would move from place to place disseminating Buddhist teachings.
20. *Gautama-dharma-sūtra*, XI. 29; *Arthasāstra* of Kauṭilya, 3.11.1.
21. *Epigraphia Indica*, VIII, pp. 89ff.
22. Unless it is assumed that the guild, the name of which has been mutilated, might have been one such.

8

Ascetic Donations at Early Buddhist Sites

Transgression of Monastic Code or Case of Reciprocity Redirected

SUSHMA TRIVEDI

CHARITY IS A UNIVERSALLY appreciated feature of the religious systems; with certain specifications it takes the form of *dāna* in Buddhism. It is considered as a cornerstone of the Buddhist philosophy as it sows the seeds of detachment from worldly possessions, the basic requirement for the attainment of higher soteriological goals. *Dāna* in Buddhism is very complexly conceptualized, yet a most simply performed ritual. The act generally involves two parties: the *saṃgha* as a community of the monks, individual monks, too, as the recipients, and people coming from all walks of life as donors. Sometimes, it becomes a tripartite affair with the donor, recipient and merit gainer, as the idea of merit transfer seems to have been fully developed in early Buddhism.[1] Among all the contemporary Indian religions, Buddhism probably had the most evolved *dānic* tradition, with meticulously laid rules abiding both on the donors as well as on the recipients and outlining their mutual obligations. *Dāna* emerges as an all pervading phenomenon as it is a controller of order in the society,[2] helps relocate wealth and purifies thoughts and actions of people as donors. Hence, *dāna* has a wide-ranging implication, from transformation of a person to the transfer of wealth; from survival and growth of the faithful to the sustenance of faith.

Dāna is eulogized in many ways and the Buddhist lay ethics are deeply rooted in it. It is one of the virtues (*pāramita*) to be perfected by an aspiring Buddha, the most potent means to remove all sorts of worldly sufferings which ensures birth in higher realms. The Buddha makes an ardent appeal to donate for the *saṃgha* when he says, 'They are the most incomparable fertile field for all to sow the seeds of merit.'[3] The householders are impressed at a psychological level to be generous donors. In his exposition to queen Mallika, the Buddha speaks about a woman who had all the negative qualities but gave alms to monks or brāhmaṇas prophecies that all her negativity would be nullified and in spite of all this, she may be rich, affluent and high in the social order.[4] With such indirect references, it is emphasized that a small act of *dāna* as *karma* stands out against the many unfair deeds of a man and protects him/her from sufferings incurred through bad deeds[5] and motivates them to refrain from such things.

The problem arises when the monk emerges as a donor, not of *dhamma*, the task which has been delegated to him, but as a donor in the worldly sense, evidenced in the votive inscriptions of the early Buddhist sites. It raises questions about the character of the Buddhist monk, validity of monastic laws and veracity of monastic ethics. Already, in recent times the institution of Buddhist *dāna* has come under scholarly percussion, sometimes viewed as a cleverly devised scheme to support the comfortable living of the monks and the nuns. But the point which is missed is that the monastic community was not just a passive recipient but an active participant in the act of *dāna*, they strove to make themselves gift-worthy, to prove themselves as the spiritual leaders of the society and at times they also put in their efforts towards the furtherance of faith by contributing to the creation of permanent icons. Indeed, the patrons and lay followers were too generous and Buddhist establishments have always been pretty rich and prosperous. The canonical texts enumerate endless list of items being received by the *saṃgha* by way of donation, which included from the very basic necessities such as robes and food, to valuables such as gold, silver, pearls, jewels, monastery, and gardens in great numbers.[6] Normally, the inmates of such wealthy establishments making small donations here and there should not have come as a surprise. However, the functioning of the *saṃgha*, the complex proprietary rights and stringent monastic laws make it an enigmatic issue, attracting such queries as to how the celibate men left such largesse in the archaeological records.[7]

The ascetic donations have been an intriguing feature as they do not occur as sporadic appearances but are omnificent features at almost all the early Buddhist sites. The enormity of their number and the proportion of their contribution among the total donors is surprisingly high. Bharhut is the earliest site dating back to a couple of centuries before the Christian era. The *stūpa* and its surroundings have yielded about 123 readable dedicatory records out of which 38 have been caused by ascetics that amount to 31 per cent of the total.[8] The caves at Kanherī bear around 29 readable votive inscriptions, including 12 by the monks and the nuns, almost 42 per cent. Though Mathurā is prolific in Jain votive inscriptions, there are 21 legible Buddhist donations and 14 out of them are made by the monks.[9] Similar inscriptions have been noted from Bhattiaprolu, Nasik, Amaravatī, Nāgarjunkonda, Sārnāth and many other places, all dating before the fourth to the fifth century CE. Sānchī is the site which has brought forth the issue of ascetic donations to the foray. Marshall[10] has documented more than 800 votive inscriptions from balustrade, gateways, railing pillars, and stairways of the *stūpas*. The monks and nuns appear as donors in 249 of these inscriptions, making a contribution of about 30 per cent of the total. In fact, at all these places, the ascetics constitute the single largest community of the donors, while the rest include lay followers, royalty, official class, traders, and bankers.

Ideally, a gone forth person is supposed to have no personal resources to fund such ventures, neither can it be believed that so many erring monks and nuns would have publicly proclaimed their wrong deeds, not stopping at that only, they would even try to immortalize it by getting it engraved in stone. The glorification of the act of *dāna* and respect for the donor ascetics lends credence to the view that this might not have been a transgression of monastic code. This paradoxical phenomenon has generated immense interest in the wealth of the Buddhist monks. It has been suggested that the monks and nuns accumulated great wealth, continued their right to inheritance of family property and indulged in moneylending and business,[11] all the while living the life of an enlightened and impeccable ascetic within the precincts of a monastery. These assumptions are based on the *Mūlasarvāstivāda Vinaya* that grew and is believed to have been compiled in the north-western periphery of India.[12] It has been rightly described as an immense pot-power of Buddhist discipline.[13] It has nearly folkloric character in which the local traditions and customs seem to have been accommodated in a big way. It is admitted that the influence of the *Mūlasarvāstivāda Vinaya* in Indian Buddhism is marked from Gupta period onwards from the fifth to the seventh century CE,[14] whereas the most of the archaeological material pertaining to monastic donations belong to an earlier period. The possession of personal property by the monks is inferred through circumstantial evidences related to the ritual of death and the funeral of a dead monk. An often repeated clause in the *Vinaya* text about something incurred or obtained by means of his (monks) own property[15] is also taken as an indication of possession of personal property by the monks. Before delving any further into the monastic donations, this rubric of personal property needs to be unravelled, otherwise, if accepted, the issue becomes, a non-issue at the very onset.

One rule that is held steadfastly throughout the Pāli *Vinaya*, never found with *anujanāmi* or 'I allow' enjoinder, is about handling of gold and silver by the monks and the nuns. Its assertive repetition suggests that the rule must have been severely enforced too. It states that a monk or a nun should neither accept or seek gold or silver for themselves,[16] nor personally handle the money assigned to them for specific purpose.[17] It is also not allowed to get someone to receive it for him or allow it to be kept in deposit for him.[18] It is treated as an offence for the monks and the nuns to engage in various transactions in which gold and silver are involved.[19] The Buddha emphatically denies permission to accept or make use of gold and silver, and says, 'I have allowed carriages and servants if they are needed, yet I have never said in anyway whatever that gold or silver may be sought after or accepted'.[20] Even in the *Mūlasarvāstivāda Vinaya*, there is not much flexibility shown in this regard. At the request of Mendaka, a much respected lay follower and prominent benefactor of the community, the travelling monks may be permitted to accept *kārshāpaṇa* as travelling expenses. The Buddha, without relaxing the rule made a provision that the *kārshāpaṇa* might be received by a novice or an attendant selected for the purpose.[21]

There are certain narrations in the *Mūlasarvāstivāda Vinaya* which raise doubts about the efficacy of these laws and seem to indicate that the private property and possession of gold and silver by the monks wa validated by the Buddha himself. The interpretation of these passages require very scrupulous dealing because it would have serious bearing on not only later monachism, but the entire history and tradition of Buddhist monachism. It is about a childless lay follower who wrote his entire wealth in the name of the *saṃgha*. Besides his other possessions, the Buddha instructs that gold and gold coins be divided in three parts and the part which belongs to the *saṃgha* and also the sum received from 'selling' books related to other faiths, are part of the wealth may be divided among the monks.[22] A closer scrutiny would reveal that the items received by the monks individually were all allowable, such as clothes, vessels of hide, water jars, pill bottles or things that were used for ritualistic purposes such as colours and pigments, gems and conch shells with spirals turning to the right (like hair of the Buddha). Specifications regarding the conch shells point out that the articles were to be used for religious purposes. Even gold coins and uncast gold might have been put to similar use by the monks. According to the Buddhist tradition, there were two types of offering made by the devotees, one is of respect and other is material offering, which included among other things, silks, flags, and necklaces of gems.[23] This has been supported by archaeological evidences as well. At Delverzinīepe, a Buddhist site very close to Gilgit from where the manuscripts of *Mūlasarvāstivāda Vinaya* have been recovered, in Central Asia, a hoard of gold objects have been found which contain gold bars with inscriptions, and some of them mention *samanas* as the owners of the bars.[24] It is believed that these gold bars were meant for making sculptures of the Buddha or decorating cult objects because some unfinished objects of this nature were part of the hoard.

One more point in the concerned passage needs attention that is the use of the word '*vikriya*', which has been literally translated as 'selling'. It would be difficult to implicate this translation for a monk or a nun as it was already prohibited for *abhikkhu* to engage in any one of the various kinds of buying and selling that involves gold and silver and is consistently maintained in the

Vinaya tradition of various schools. The Tibetan *Mūlasarvāstivāda Vinaya* has the word 'transforming' for '*vikriya*'[25] and this term seems to be better qualified to explain the act in accordance with the monastic rules. As per the instructions, whatever was given was not to be thrown away by the monks but if not usable, should be either given over to the *stūpa* for veneration or exchanged for legally permissible things.[26] The procedure to be followed is also detailed. The task was to be performed by *kappiyakāraka*[27] of Pāli *Vinaya* and *kappiyakāraka*[28] of the *Mūlasarvāstivāda Vinaya*, an official of the monastery appointed for this purpose. This could be the regular storekeeper of the monastery or an available householder or a devotee. It is made very clear that whatever was to be procured in exchange through *kappiyakāraka*, must fall in the category of allowables for the inmates of a monastery. Another dimension of the discussion of personal property held by the monk centres round the issue of inheritance of a dead monk's belongings. Generally, the possessions of a dead monk reverted back to the *saṃgha* and the *saṃgha* presided over its division.[29] But, if the monk has been sick, he may assign his bowl and robe to the co-resident, who waits upon him during his illness, before completing his time. There are certain peculiar cases, both in Pāli and in the *Mūlasarvāstivāda Vinaya*, where the deceased member of the *saṃgha* is exposed as being very rich and in possession of property of considerable worth, even by the standards of worldly people. In the case of Pāli *Vinaya*, the monk's belongings included a large supply of *bhikkhu's* requisites and property.[30] It was decided that the small supply of requisites may be divided among the *saṃgha* that were present at that time, but his property and large quantities of requisites were to belong to the *saṃgha* of the four quarters. With the *saṃgha* of four quarters, it is probably meant that the *saṃgha* was as a corporate body. There is an account of accurate valuation of the dead monk Upananda's property and *Mūlasarvāstivāda Vinaya's*, which included three lakh gold coins. That even took the king by surprise who ordered a raid on the cell of the monk and confiscated his property. But the verdict on its dealing was very ambiguous. First of all, to get the property released from state control, a message was sent by the *saṃgha* that according to the monastic law, 'the fellow monks are the beneficent "*sabrahmachariamesha lābhah prāpadyate*"'.[31] Thereafter, the co-residents were invited to divide among themselves the dead monk's requisites but there was no mention of three lakh gold coins.

Without referring to the context, the real intention of placing the story of Upananda in the *civarvastu* section could not be apprehended properly. Monk Upananda, the Śakyan is a fairly known figure through the *Vinaya* literature, though not for good reasons. He symbolizes infirmity and like Devdatta, is a habitual wrongdoer. Many of the laws, too, were formulated against the conduct of Upananda. Eight out of thirty[32] rules involving forfeiture (*nissaggiya*) and seven out of ninety-two rules entailing confession (*pācittiya*) were laid down to refrain other monks from behaving the way[33] Upananda did, which brought disrepute to the *saṃgha* and was sharply criticized by the lay people. This Upananda, who could not be cured because of his greed, is said to have left a hoard of gold coins. At this juncture, the Buddha narrates the account of his previous life when he was a greedy jackal (*rigal*).[34] The comparison of Upananda with *rigal*, not a very noble animal in the Indian tradition, itself gives a hint that neither Upananda nor his deeds were to be appreciated and followed by the monks. Incidentally, it would be appropriate to look into the matter of how discrepancies appeared over the time in various traditions, as Pachow[35] has noticed in his comparative study of patīmokkha of different traditions. It is often repeated in the *Vinaya* that no demand is to be placed with or no untimely gift is to be accepted from a person who is not a relation of a *bhikkhu*.[36] In the Tibetan version, it is presented as if a layman or a laywoman sends for a weaver not related to them to make a garment for a monk,[37] it would be an offence. It is apparently a misinterpretation because in all such cases, the concern is about the donor not being related to the monk or the nun, not for the weaver not being related to the donor. Similar might have been the case of Upananda, as probably in entire *Vinaya* tradition there is no other monk found to be owning three lakh gold pieces. Therefore, it should be treated as an isolated occurrence and it would not be justified to employ it for large scale generalization.

An extensive survey of the monastic law makes it absolutely clear that an ordinary monk or a nun lived a life of moderation and rejoiced in the fewness of desires. They were neither inclined to accumulate wealth nor allowed to do so. While dealing with the votive records of early Buddhist sites, we are primarily concerned with these ordinary monks and the nuns. Still, it is sometimes believed that the rules of *patīmokkha* were less binding.[38] *Patīmokkha* laid down the fundamental principles of a monk's life which were the guiding force of Buddhist monachism, described as 'monastic glue' holding the *saṃgha* together.[39] Significance of *patīmokkha* rules for higher attainments is reiterated time and again, and the monks were warned against any laxity in its following. It is counted among *śila* or morality in the *Dīgha Nikāya*. It is stated that a *bhikkhu* practices self-restraint by the perfection of *Patimokshasamvara śila*.[40] *Patīmokkha* is a regulatory code that has been formulated to 'firmly establish *saddharma* and to protect the *Vinaya*'.[41] It is not the ochre colour robe or the shaven head, neither the begging bowl, but the practice of *patīmokkha* rules that distinguished a Buddhist monk from ordinary people. It was stressfully prescribed for a monk to constantly and regularly practice it as it is unenduring, and any breach in conduct could allow lust to creep in,[42] undoing his efforts. One of the qualities that an elder monk should be endowed with to be appointed as an exhorter of the nuns is that he should live restrained by *patīmokkhasamvar*.[43] Abiding by these rules symbolized the integrity of a monk and it is not at all convincing to presume that infringement of these rules would have been so rampant, yet might have gone unnoticed. The system could not have survived so long without guarding its fundamental principles.

The applied form of monastic ethics depended upon a meticulously crafted mechanism of checks and balances. Internal discipline of the *saṃgha* placed several barriers at different stages to avert the monks and the nuns from deviating from their path. The *Vinaya* rules regarding the procurement and possession of requisites, various kinds of offences, their repentance and punishments were compiled as *sikkhāpadas* that a trainee monk had to learn and practise in his day to day life. This was the preparatory and preliminary stage of checks. The second embankment against the waywardness of the monks was placed in the form of observance of *upostha* ceremony every fortnight. It was the formal meeting of the *saṃgha* where all the assembled *bhikkhus* recited *patīmokkha*. This was not just a ritual performance but its recitation required active participation and honest response from the assembled monks, evidenced in the way the whole act was carried out. To begin with, the senior most *bhikkhu* recited the *nidānuddeso* or introduction and invited fellow monks to announce their purity, and for guilty monks to reveal their offences.[44] In this way, after every fifteen days, a monk's conduct came under the scrutiny of the *saṃgha*. It was one of the preliminary functions of the assembly, before starting the formal meeting, to ensure that none of the *bhikkhus* were guilty of offences.[45] This must have discouraged the *bhikkhus* from repeating the offence as it would have led to their expulsion from the assembly. In the *Nidāna* part itself, it is made clear that if any *bhikkhu*, when proclamation to reveal one's offence thrice, still remains silent and does not confess his offence, becomes guilty of telling a conscious lie, *sampajānamusāvād*.[46] Clearly, telling a conscious lie or hiding the truth was viewed as a grave offence, as it was probably the only overlapping offence that was a part of both *pācittiya*[47] and *pārajika*[48] rules. *Pācittiya* offence involved confession by the guilty monk but *pārajika* entailed expulsion from the *saṃgha*, obviously an offence of the most serious nature. The internal evidence of *Nidāna* suggests that the monk, even after being called thrice up to maximum times, does not reveal his offence, then, since no more chance could be given to him, he may not be subjected to *pācittiya* but be treated as having committed the *pārajika* offence.

Pāvarana ceremony, held at the end of the rain retreat took the detective and corrective measures of the *saṃgha* for the monks' behaviour to a new level. It was held for the resident monks of that *āvāsa*, where a monk invited his co-residents to point out his faults. This was a kind of peer review by the monks who lived together day and night through the *vāssa* period of three months. Under such conditions, even a very clever monk would have found it difficult to hide his accumulations or wrongful possession of wealth from his fellow inmates. Furthermore, there was also a set of minor disciplinary proceedings to be initiated against the guilty monks and here too, the punitive measures were no less severe. Confession of guilt was the basic sentiment underlying monastic discipline and a monk was morally and psychologically motivated for it. Even then, if he was bent on not doing so and the offence had been brought into the cognizance of the *saṃgha*, the *saṃgha* steps into castigate the guilty monk. It carries out *āpattiya adassane ukkhepaniya-kamma*, i.e. the act of suspension for not acknowledging one's fault.[49] The monk, put under suspension, was to be treated as an outcast, he was not allowed to dine or dwell with the *saṃgha* and this information was to be circulated from *āvāsa* to *āvāsa*. His rights to perform *upasampadā* (initiation), give *nissaya* and give exhortation were withheld and he was not to receive reverence or courtesy from the other *bhikkhu*.[50] This public disgrace was probably aimed to send a message across the community to refrain from such acts.

It is, thus, affirmed that the monastic code was a well-braced and well-fortified system in itself to meet the challenges posed by the offender monks. The *saṃgha* took every care to uphold the monastic ideal of non-possessiveness, no worldly attachments and unfettered from passion, that were the hallmarks of a monk's life. Preservation of these features of the ascetic's life were crucial to his personal reputation as well as for the prospects of the *saṃgha*. A monk, acting like a householder was condemned and criticized by the people who looked up to them. It also repelled the donors. The *saṃgha* could not afford to ignore the demeaning behaviour of monks for very practical reasons. The material well-being of the *saṃgha* was directly linked to the morality of the monks. Under such circumstances, accumulation of wealth by the monks and nuns seemed to be a farfetched imagination by any standards. Indeed, the *saṃgha* engaged in trading and moneylending for the growth of its resources, but it did it as a corporate body. The financial dealings were not done by the monks within their individual capacity, but were undertaken as a collective act by the *saṃgha*. Monks did take part in the proceedings but they only exercised the designated authority of the *saṃgha*. A large number of seals and sealing have been found at various archaeological sites, which belong to the *saṃgha* and often bear the name of the monastery, but not of individual monks.[51]

The way of living for the monks actually did not present them with any sort of incentive or temptation towards increasing their possessions or holding on to their wealth because they were not left with any opportunity to enjoy that wealth. A monk was to use his bowl till the time it was mended in five places[52] and could not keep an extra bowl for more than ten days.[53] Only under dire circumstances, a monk or nun was allowed to accept extra and out of reason robes.[54] Similarly, medicines to be used by them were not to be kept for more than seven days.[55] Making a hoard of bowls[56] and for that matter, any of the requisites was an offence that had to be confessed by the monk or the nun, and forfeit the articles to the *saṃgha*.

Several explanations determining the character and locating the actual source of monastic donations have been put forward. Kern was so much averse to the idea that the monks and the nuns could be the donors that he totally rejected it.[57] He doubts the correctness of the reading. There are not two or three, but thousands of such inscriptions and the writing is loud and clear, leaving no room for such outright rejection. Bühler has worked extensively in the collection and interpretation of the epigraphical material from Sānchī and in his opinion, the monks and the nuns might have obtained by begging, the money required for making the rails and the pillar.[58] It does not seem very convincing because first, the ascetics were prohibited from handling the money themselves; second, most of them were not the residents of the place where they made donations. Collecting money at one place and carrying it over to some other place to make a donation seemed hard, compliable with the monastic living. It is believed that rather than begging, there could have been some more dignified way to arrange resources for such donations. Sometimes, it is also proposed that the monks lawfully owned some property which served the purpose of gift-making.[59] Vijay Nath seems to endorse this view and he further adds that donations might have been made by appropriating some of the property already dedicated to the *saṃgha*.[60] It is doubtful if such an occurrence would have gone unnoticed and no rectifying measure would have been taken by the *saṃgha*. Moreover, appropriation of the *saṃgha's* property for one's own benefit was too serious an offence to have been ignored for a long time.

Accepting that monks could neither retain or generate private wealth, nor accept or handle money and gold, this phenomenon had been defined as the mixing of labour.[61] Right to property was generated by the mixing of labour to the original property and the monks and the nuns earned the credit to get their names engraved as donors by actually working at the sites. Judging by the uniformity of pattern, technique and homogeneity of decoration of Sānchī, Bharhut, Nāgarjunkonda, and Amarāvatī, it is obvious that these were delivered by the hands of skilled professionals and were not the creations of amateurs. It was supervised by the monks appointed for the purpose designated as *navakammika*, who performed this duty on behalf of the *saṃgha*. One of the Kanherī cave inscriptions gives an illustrative account of this arrangement.[62] It records the donation of a *caitya* building by the merchant brothers Gajasena and Gajamitra. The overall construction was looked after by five senior monks assigned with the task by the *saṃgha*. Another monk was responsible for executing the work and whose teacher acted as an overseer. The work was carried out by stone masons, stone cutters, and polishers. Such inscriptions are common at almost all sites, i.e. Sānchī,[63] Bharhut,[64] and Nāgarjunkonda.[65] On the basis of the *Jātaka* narration, it is supposed that monks continued to enjoy their property and worldly comforts and, therefore, could make donations.[66]

In all probability, the actual source of donations made in the name of the monks and the nuns were the donors. But these benefactors of the community generally provided the four requisites to the monks individually and larger donations were made to the *saṃgha* as a corporate body which held exclusive rights over its appropriation and disposal. These votive records of monastic community seem to be the manifestation of some form of reciprocity of the lay community towards the monks and the nuns as their spiritual guides. Before implying reciprocity into this aspect, it needs to be redefined in the special reference to the Buddhist *dāna* tradition. Modern anthropological theories of reciprocity explain it in terms of gift exchange and are based on conclusions drawn from empirical studies of mostly primitive societies.[67] Archaeologists incorporate the exchange of ideas too in their concept of reciprocity.[68] Buddhist *dāna* was performed in a civilized society, one of the parties being highly enlightened and the whole act was much sentiment-loaded. Another difference is about the object dualism which is a precondition and the question of equivalence of the value of the objects exchanged is the central issue of the concepts of reciprocity.[69] To some extent, object dualism is there but the nature of the two objects offered is completely dissimilar. One of the parties makes material *dāna* (*āmisdāna*), while the other offers a spiritual one (*dhammadāna*), which is immeasurable and invaluable. It might be accepted as reciprocity in a restricted sense but may not necessarily involve exchange in physical form as the Buddhist *dāna* is self-generative. In Findly's observation, *dāna* was instrumental in activating transformation,[70] transformation in both the donor and receptor. It would be pertinent to exemplify this point with a monk's resolve to make the offering fruitful and worthy, 'We will practice the way proper to recluse so that our designations may be true and our claims genuine and so that the service of those whose robes, alms food, resting place and medicinal requisites we use shall bring them great fruit and benefit.'[71]

In order to understand the role of reciprocity in the context of the monastic donations, it is important to study the circumstances which led to the genesis of the reciprocity. According to theorists, sociability, underlying the principle of reciprocity,[72] is expressed in two ways—intimacy and courtesy.[73] Ideally speaking, the first parameter is improbable for an ascetic to meet out and the second gives limited scope to the laity. Still, this was the axiomatic position whereas, the engaged form of the Buddhist monachism was somewhat different even in its early phase. Therefore, sociability and courtesy are the two vantage points from where the relationship between reciprocity and monastic donations will be explored.

There are no direct evidences, either in the canonical texts or epigraphs which could throw light on the mechanism of monastic *dāna*. Nevertheless, a careful analytical study of these votive records yields vital information regarding the various aspects of such donations. A majority of these inscriptions are one line statements, containing the name of the donor, the name of the place and if made jointly, also the relations among the donors. This meagre information could be amplified by the application of the method of deconstruction. Derrida's deconstruction has two features, one is splitting the text and the other is looking into the productive silences or present absences.[74] Because the epigraphs are too brief, the splitting of text would not be of much help but searching for the present absences may definitely lead to the real intent and purpose of the donation. Information, thus procured is corroborated with textural references to the present the actual nature of monastic donations, instead of laying undue emphasis on the personal wealth of the monks.

Buddhism is basically a monastic religion, promising a better birth in the future life and good fortune in the present. For the lay devotees, it generally reserves the right to the highest soteriological attainment, only for going forth. It is said in the *Muni Sutta*, 'the blue necked peacock which flies through, never approaches the speed of the swan'. Similarly, the householder can never resemble the monk.[75] Like other faiths, Buddhist monachism required a person desirous of joining the order, to leave behind his family, wealth and all worldly attachments. Ideally, a monk should wander alone like lion, not be caught in a net.[76] Solitude as being the most essential for the spiritual progress of the monks, is reiterated in the Buddhist texts. The Buddha, enumerating the factors of non-decline of a *samana* says that so long as the *bhikkhu* delights in the forest seats, so long they may be expected not to decline but to prosper.[77] It is prescribed that residence of the monk must be located at a distance from the village and town. This distance should be a stone's throw away or water's throw away from the last living quarters of the village.[78] The strong recommendation of solitude, particularly in the Buddhist context, does not translate into fierce aversion for sociability of the monks or social life being looked down upon. It was actually not possible because the very survival of the monastic community depended upon its proximity with the lay society. It is so because solitude was the necessary precondition for meditation and meditation was the kernel of Buddhist practices, from which all the spiritual attainments sprouted and blossomed. Elaborating upon the meditation path, it is noted that a monk is delightful in solitude because in this state his mind is not distracted by unsuitable visible objects, he is free from anxiety and he abandons enjoyment.[79]

Significantly, perhaps, no other Indian religion is so much socially concerned and society-oriented as Buddhism is. In fact, a very close and regular interaction with the society was maintained. Votive inscriptions from the early Buddhist sites are illustrative of this character. In return, it garnered abounding social support which may be counted as the single most important reason for its sustenance and survival amidst the changing political and cultural scenario. It has been aptly remarked that a monk renounced his life in society but did not renounce his concern for the society.[80]

Buddhist philosophy is termed as applied philosophy.which is preeminently concerned with sentient beings, for the welfare of all and for the benefit of all. Sukumar Dutt has rightly observed that isolation from the society is never a cue of Buddhist monachism.[81] *Dāna* bridged the gap and made it possible for both the communities to reach out to each other. Findly has pointed out the integrative function of *dāna*.[82] The mechanism of *dāna* demanded a thorough involvement of both the parties, leading to the development of interdependent, intercommunity relationships. It is interesting to note that lay people made their presence felt in an impressive way in all the monastic codes. Not only heed is paid to their opinion and is taken into consideration, but at the time of formulation of the rules, rules are also moderated according to the public opinion.[83] While admonishing the monks for their unseemly behaviour, the Buddha is often found repeating the sentence, 'It is not for pleasing those who are not yet pleased'.[84] Here pleasing has the meaning of conversion.[85] Monks are more openly warned in these words of the Buddha, 'This will not conduce, *bhikkhus* either to the converted, but rather to the increase of the unconverted beings not converted'.[86] Sometimes, it is (wrongly) interpreted that in this way that the *saṃgha* tried to entrap donors. But the concern is primarily for the goodwill, not for the goods. This was a necessary prerequisite for the furtherance of faith as well as for the association of more and more people as donors and adherents. A Buddhist monk could seek *dāna* only made out of goodwill, as instigated or hinted, *dāna* was not only prohibited but counted among the most serious offences.[87] Acceptance of the monks and the nuns by the society was of vital importance, the inflow of *dāna* was consequential to it.

Regular alms tour and preaching sessions brought the monks in contact with the lay people. The monk was expected to be moon like, ever new to the families,[88] always a stranger among the families,[89] and to be compassionate impartially.[90]A particular kind of relationship fostered and grew between the donor and the donee. This had generally evaded the attention because of the universal perception that recluses shunned all social ties. This might have been the ideal proposition but their real implication was quoted differently. This relationship between the monastic community and the society is visible in the Buddhist texts and its results are manifest in the donative records of these early Buddhist sites. The *Vinaya* literature itself is replete with instances where a certain monk is supported by a certain householder,[91] a certain monk lives in dependence upon a certain householder,[92] and a certain monk is a regular diner with a certain family.[93] In several cases, the monks had their regular support at different stations. Venerable Upananda was supported by a certain laity when he stayed at Srāvastī and when he visited Rājagaha, he had a family there, upon whom he lived as a dependent.[94] This kind of regular interaction, for sure, must have generated some feelings for each other and is reflected in the episode of a dispute between the monk Sudhamma and the householder Kitta. Venerable Sudhamma was residing in dependence upon the householder,[95] Kitta. Whenever the householder wished to invite other monks, he always made a special reference of Venerable Sudhamma. Once he extended invitation to some other monks before honouring Sudhamma, as he usually did. Sudhamma reacted and there was some unpleasantness between the two. Here, Sudhamma reacted because he was probably hurt for he might have developed the feeling of possessiveness for Kitta. In another incidence, when the family in Benāras, which supported Venerable Pilindavaccha, was aggrieved by the kidnapping of their two children, the Venerable Pilindavaccha brought back the children by exercising his psychic power,[96] though the monks were prohibited from showing their psychic power to the ordinary people.

Similarly, what lay people felt for ascetics was something more than reverence. They seemed to be always eager to serve the community in whatsoever way it may suit them, and it definitely extended beyond providing the requisites. They performed different duties for the *saṃgha* in the capacity of assigner of lodgings, distributor of robes, handler of robe-funds, and other forms of monetary donations.[97] These were all obviously, voluntary acts but were serious business for the *saṃgha*, as tasks were assigned to the householder in a due procedure of the *saṃgha* in a formal act.[98] The donors of the lodgings were not only satisfied by making donations, but ever remained concerned about the monks taking residence in those lodgings.[99] There are the iconic householders, Mendaka and Kitta. Mendaka, knowing that the Buddha was travelling with a great company of monks, prepared to follow him and gave the command to his servants:

> Load them, my men, a quantity of salt and oil, and rice, and hard food, and come and let one thousand two hundred and fifty cow keepers came with one thousand two hundred and fifty cows. Wherever we find the blessed one there will we supply him with fresh milk.[100]

This sensitivity of Mendaka and his persuasions led the Buddha to allow monks to accept provisions for their journey.[101] A *patisāraniyakamma* (act of reconciliation) was carried out against the monk Sudhamma whose behaviour humiliated the householder Kitta.[102]

This makes it clear that these relationships were not merely functional relationships, devoid of any feelings but there might have always been an emotional undercurrent sustaining it. Among the votive inscriptions, there are a number of epigraphs which record joint donations by the ascetics and the lay persons. One such inscription from Amarāvatī reads as follows:

> The gift of a chief pavilion to the order by perfumer (Gadhika), the merchant (Nāniya) Sridata (Sridatta) son of the merchant Dhamilla . . . of the pupil (Sisiha) of the *achariya*, Sāriputta, the Mahavansaliva.[103]

The foremost significance that this record emits is that there was a close relationship between the ascetic and lay donors that was based on cordiality, goodwill and respect for each other. The basic purpose of this epigraph seems to be to pay respect to *Ācarya* Sāriputta, who was perhaps not even present at the site of donation and his name was probably added at the instance of his pupil who was part of the donor party. The lay people among the donors include a person himself a merchant, and belonging to a family of merchants. The donation was also of considerable worth of a chief pavilion, as compared to a single crossbar, rail of a pillar. The most important inference that can be drawn from the writing is that this one and other such donations reflect the financial status of the lay people of the donor party and not of the ascetics. The other thing that is even clearer is that the monetary part of the donations was handled by the lay people.

There is another inscription from Amaravatī belonging to the same category:

> The erection of a slab by Hamgi (Samghi), the daughter of Bhayant Bodhi . . . of the nun resident in Kevuryra.[104]

It has all the details of the lay donor but none of them have the name of the nun. This would not have been in the case of joint donation, where both the parties had equal share of contribution. Either these monks and the nuns were travelling with these lay people or it was some gift, meant for these ascetics that was invested this way, hence, also bore their name. Similarly, some of the donations make the *saṃgha* itself a party to the *dāna*. A Kanherī cave inscription mentions the gift of a cistern by the goldsmith Samidatta of Kalyana, together with the *saṃgha*.[105] When the epigraph is deconstructed, its meaning is obvious that the money Samidatta intended to give to the *saṃgha* is utilized to construct a cistern.

At Sānchī and Bharhut, there are few donations with multiple donors, probably very few of the nature where lay and monastic community perform the act of *dāna* together. Perhaps, the donations are so small that instead of joining names, they did it separately. There are groups of donations made by the people coming from the same place, clustered at a certain part of the monument. These donors include ordinary people, lay worshippers and ascetics.[106] There are fourteen such inscriptions from Sānchī where all the donors come from Ujjain, including ascetics and yet another group of donors includes eight donations made by commoners as well as some nuns.[107] The donative record of the nun from Ujjain has words:

> *Ujjeniye Mitye bhicchu . . .*

That translates into gift of the nun Mita in Ujjain. The most interesting thing to be noted is that the nun was not accompanying the touring party. Apparently, the gift was made by some member of the party who was physically present in Sānchī in the name of the said nun. The most classic example of redirection of reciprocity is seen in the inscription of monk Bala, recording his donation at Sānchī[108] and Sārnāth.[109] Out of this comparatively larger writing, monk Bala emerges as the main donor. His qualification as the knower of the *Tipitikas* is mentioned in all these inscriptions. In the Sārnāth inscription, names of Kushāṇa Kshatrapa Kharapallana and Vanaspara are always added as joint donors. In all probability, Kharapallana and Vanaspara were the disciples of monk

Bala, they were the actual donors who might have done this to commemorate the visit of Bala to Sārnāth, falling in their territory. Generally, these small donative records do not contain names of rulers, but where the kshatrapas' names appear in epigraphs, the names of Kushāṇa rulers are mentioned with due respect. This fact also points out towards the actual donors.

Two similar inscriptions of Kanherī[110] strengthen the idea of indirect donation by ascetics. Both the records have been caused by a merchant, a son of Venunudi (Vishnunandiṇ) together with a monk. The first one mentions the place of residence of this lay donor and the merit is shared by his father, his mother, his brother, and all of his relatives. The second inscription, most probably recorded by the same son of Vishnunandiṇ, has names of Hālanika, Dhāma, Buddhakāya, and of a monk whose name is not legible. All the merit seekers from this donation of a cave are either family or friends of Vishnunandiṇ, except the monk. The only logical inference that could be drawn from these two epigraphs is that the monk was the teacher of the family and this was the way they acknowledged his spiritual guidance.

There are large number of monastic donations which are made with the family members of monks and nuns, or refer to their relationship. First, we need to locate the position of the family and other relations in the monastic paraphernalia. Field petty is a marked feature of Buddha's preaching. There is always an emphasis upon the fulfilment of social obligations and on honouring the responsibilities towards family. Buddhism visualizes a prominent role of filial piety in the maintenance of social order. It is said that society degenerates and anarchy prevails when people fail to perform filial duties towards mother and father, and fail to show regard for the elders in the family and clan.[111] Also, there are the three things praised by the enlightened and the awakened ones—*dāna*, *pabbajja*, and serving one's mother and father.[112] In *Sigālovāda Sutta*, the Buddha gives an exposition on how the relationships in an ideal Buddhist society should be maintained.[113] Though this is meant for the householder, it seems that even the monks and the nuns were not completely exempted from such obligations. The general perception is that the recluses completely severed their ties with their families. In Buddhism too, a monk is required to leave his family and relations.[114] Family and kin are counted among the ten impediments in the path of perfection that a monk should severe.[115] But the difference of viewpoint and the beauty of Buddhism lies in the explanation as to how this impediment is to be removed. It is said that when they are sick, they are an impediment for him. Therefore, that impediment should be severed by curing them with nursing.[116] It indicates that after going forth, a monk may not have remained in everyday physical proximity with his family, but care and concern for them was neither seen as gregarious behaviour nor was it condemned, rather it was expected of him.

The Buddha himself is seen acknowledging relations at several occasions. A novice entering the order who had previously been a follower of a different faith had to undergo a *parivāsa* period extending over four months, but an exception was made for the entrants belonging to Śakya clan.[117] Similarly, when Rahula asked for his inheritance from the Buddha, he did not shy away from fulfilling a father's obligation. He gave him his begging bowl, the property of an ascetic father. At some other times too, the Buddha relaxed monastic rules for *samana* Rahula.[118]

The monks and the nuns maintaining contact with their families was treated as normal, this can be inferred from the *Vinaya* texts. Many of their acts would have incurred offences for them if they had not been performed in reference to their relations. The Buddha, while judging the behaviour of an erring monk, always asked the monk whether the lay person involved in the act was related to the monk or not. If that person was a relative, the act would not be considered as an offence because it was believed that one who was a relation knew what was suitable or unsuitable[119] for him/her. For a Buddhist monk particularly, getting things by persuasion,[120] suggestion,[121] and indirect talk[122] were termed as wrong livelihood and were not allowed. But these clauses were waived off, in case the provider was a relation of the monk.[123] This way the monk continued to share a special relationship with his family ever after entering the order.

The issue of relationship of a monk or a nun with his or her family was dealt with utmost sensitivity by the monastic lawmakers. It was said that the mother and father should be treated like preceptors, that is, to be accorded highest reverence. If they lived within the kingdom and looked to their son for help, it should be given. If they had no medicine, he should give them his own. If he had none, he should set in search of it as alms and give that.[124] For three months a year, the monks settled into a sedentary life for *vassāvāsa* and their activities were usually confined within the *āvāsa*. Under certain circumstances, a monk was allowed to break his *vāssa*. It is felt that these exceptions were made because the community was dependent on the laity[125] and the prospect of material gains was never overlooked.[126] But there were also nobler reasons for it. It was legitimately broken to grant the wish of a donor who was to enter to go with the army, or on journey, ill or dying, or a wish arising in a pregnant woman.[127] The psychology behind the exceptions made for the break of *vāssa* was exemplified in the exception made for a monk whose mother, father or relation was sick. He was allowed to go to see and nurse them but return within seven days.[128] Even a monk's obligations towards his extended family were taken into cognizance. The uncle of a certain monk fell ill in army and desperately wished to see him.[129] The wish of the uncle was honoured, though seeing an army officer was an offence for a monk.

It seems that the monks and the nuns were never discouraged from nurturing their family bonds. Enough space was created for this within the monastic code. Family was actually not excluded from the whole scheme of ultimate attainment of a monk. A monk aspiring for higher spirituality depended upon and practised four sublime attitudes, the *Brahmavihāras*, i.e. *maitrī*, *karuṇā, mudita*, and *upekkha*. A monk developed these attitudes by practising on, through four types of persons—dear ones, unfortunate or evil doers, neutral, and the hostile.[130] Dear ones included family and relations, and having compassion and loving kindness for family was not considered an inappropriate act but was a desirable condition for a monk's soteriological progress. The nature of this bonding was different from the bonding of lay people. Equanimity was the basis of a monk's relations, either within the community or outside. He was to be 'compassionate impartially'.[131] Hence, retaining family ties, conditioned with equanimity, were never a hindrance for a Buddhist monk in his spiritual journey.

On the other end of the spectrum of this relationship stood the family members of the goneforth. To observe the response of the family towards the goneforth member and the reciprocity generated by his care in the family members is the most crucial as it gives us important clues about the real source and nature of monastic donations. The response is most demonstrative in the narration of the young monk of Rohana.[132] He stayed in Korandanka monastery for his rain retreat and was put up in the cell built by his father. He was requested to have his meals at their place. His mother prepared and served him meals for next three months. But, his parents could not recognize him and the young monk neither gave them any hint regarding their relations, nor showed any signs of emotions for them. Afterwards, when the mother came to know from the preceptor of his son that the young man who dined at their place for three months was her son, she was not found lamenting upon the fact or regretting that she could not recognize her son or even that his son never said, 'I am your son, you are my mother'. On the contrary, the lay woman was pleased to know that her son had perfected the preaching of the Buddha and conducted himself in an exemplary manner, following into the steps of the great saints. The mother laid prostrate, with her face in the direction in which her son had gone and worshipped.

Obviously, the monks and the nuns were extolled and respected by their families. Having a goneforth member was supposedly a prestige enhancer for the family. They felt a sense of pride and by proclaiming it, they themselves felt honoured. There is an inscription from Sānchī which records the gift of a pillar by all the relatives of venerable Nāgila.[133] The donors did not wish to publicize their own names but were contented just by the mention of their relationship with the monk. Another interesting inscription is from Kanherī. The donor Ananda is a monk and for his introduction he does not mention names of his father or mother, as is customary, but of his elder brother who was an *ācarya*, a senior in the order.[134] In a similar inscription from Sānchī, the donor herself keeps a low profile, highlighting her ascetic son: the gift of the mother of the venerable Rahila, the Saphinayaka.[135]

Understandably, when the family cherished this relationship and valued the care and concern extended to them by the goneforth member, they seem to be naturally eager to reciprocate this gesture in addition to their regular *dāna*. But there was restricted scope for this, as whatever was to be received by a monk or a nun should confine within the periphery of 'allowable' things, which were very few. Though the Buddha was generous enough to relax a number of rules where family was concerned, he sanctioned untimely gifts from family, some extra acquirements from them and gaining something by putting forward the demand to their relations but never so extravagant as to allow them to receive money or gold. This is well conclusive with the nature of monastic donations because among more than thousand such inscriptions, there is perhaps none that refers to an ascetic donation in monetary terms, though some donations as Kanherī include endowment.[136] Most likely, these votive inscriptions indicate towards a new opening through which this reciprocity felt for the monks was directed towards the monument in the form of their contribution and was caused to be engraved in their names. The content and context of the epigraphs effectively affirm this assumption. There is a sculpture inscription from Amarāvatī, where three generations of females of the same family make this donation.

Gift of the upright slabs by the nun Saṁgharkshita living in Devparvana and by her daughter, the nun *saṃgha* (Hamgha) and by the latter's daughter Jiyava.[137]

Two of the women appear to be fully ordained members of the *saṃgha* and the last one, the youngest was a lay person. In all likelihood, Jiyava was the person responsible for the donation and the most important person in the epigraph was her grandmother whose place of residence was also inscribed. The same site had yielded an inscription of a donor party of five people out of which three were lay persons and two ascetics, one of the lay persons was related to an ascetic.

> Gift of the nun Buddharakshita . . . antevsini of the ther bhadanta Budharakshita, the overseer of works, the Chaityas who lived at Rajgriha, together with her daughter and of Dhanadina and Saṁgharakshita.[138]

This whole writing was made out to appear as if the donor was *Bhikkhuni* Buddharakshita. The monk Buddharakshita emerges as the focal figure with two honorifics prefixed to his name, and his place of residence being mentioned, but the actual donor might have been the daughter of the *Bhikkhuni* Buddharakshita, otherwise, there seems to be no logical explanation for her name being added to this inscription.

In the votive records with family affiliations, no standard formulae of donation are followed, rather they relate to a multitude of relationships of monks and nuns, i.e. a brother.[139]

Gift of Bhicchu Upanijha, a sister[140] . . . the sister of the monk (Pavejita) Sidamita (Siddhartha) who lived at . . . A mother[141]

The gift of Bhikkhuni Roh, daugther of Sujta . . . A father:[142]

A cave and a water cistern, the gift of the nun (*pavaitika*) Spa (Sarpa), the daughter of lay worshipper Kulapiya (Kulpriya) Dhamanaka (Dharma), the Dhenukakatiya . . . A granddaughter:[143]

Gift of a slab at the northern entrance by . . . Bhadanta Nga . . . and by his female pupil (Antevsini) Buddharakhita (Buddharakshi) and by her grand daughter Chulabuddharakmit (Kshudra buddharakshita) . . . A brother-in-law.[144]

Gift of Arya Kuramigi, followed by Gift of Kurmigi, sister-in-law of Imdagimitra (Inaragnimitra), the son of . . . Ka . . . A son:[145]

Gift of Bhikhuni Isidsi, the inhabited of Kada, mother of Saṁgharakshita . . . A daughter:[146] Gift of nun Budhdarakshita . . . together with her daughter. . . .

The consistency of the appearance of family relations, so near as father and mother and so distant as granddaughter and brother-in-law, seem to be indicating towards some kind of ritual performed by the family members to felicitate their goneforth relatives. Some records give an impression that many of the monks and the nuns whose names have been engraved as donors may not have been there at the time of donation.

One relationship which was openly encouraged and carefully guarded by the monastic law was that of pupil and teacher. It was probably the closest human bonding involving physical proximity, recognized by the *saṃgha*. It is also the most fervently celebrated relationship in donative records all across the early sites, reflecting upon the dynamics of in-community understandings and associations of the ascetics. In order to grasp the essence of this relationship and its connotations in perspective of *dāna*, the whole procedure of admission to order, ordination, and training of a monk or a nun needs to be carefully viewed. A person desirous of joining the order first of all chooses an Upadhyaya or preceptor for himself or herself.[147] The Upadhyaya introduces the neophyte to the *saṃgha* at the formal ceremony held on the occasion. This initiation in general is known as a *pabbajja*. After this, the young entrant lived with his Upadhyaya Saddhaiviharika or *antevāsini* and was to train in six rules, i.e. the five *śilas*, and one rule against eating at the wrong time,[148] for two years. After successful completion of this period, he graduated to become a *nav* or novice and his curriculum is extended to ten *sikkhāpadas*.[149] Still, he lives in *nissaya* or spiritual tutelage with a senior monk, probably with the same Upadhyaya he was with at the time of his *pabbajja*. Nissaya may last for ten years or less[150] and after this the *nav* became a fully ordained monk or nun. A fully ordained monk has to abide by the 227 rules of *Bhikkhu Vinaya*, the *patīmokkha*.[151]

In the entire corpus of votive inscriptions pertaining to ascetics, the most frequently appearing monastic designations are those of *antevasina* and *Sadhaiviharika, Sisya, Arya, Bhadanta* and *Thera*. Most often *thera* and *bhadanta* are in communion with *Saddhaiviharin* or *Antevasina*. The content of this category of inscriptions has the same distinct features. There is a correlational order of hierarchy among the donors. These epigraphs not only enlist donations but also record tributes paid by the ascetics lower in rank to the senior one involved in the act. To decipher the real purpose of these donations and to figure out the real donor, it would be pertinent to look into the sentimental and practical aspects of pupil-teacher relationship as envisaged and practised in the Buddhist monachism. The Buddha gives lengthy exposition on how this relationship was to be conducted. It is said that an Upadhyaya should consider the Saddhaiviharika as his son, he should share whatever he has with Saddhaiviharika, attend to him when he is sick and take his care in every way.[152] Likewise, the Saddhaiviharika was to consider his Upadhyaya as a father, to attend him in every possible way and observe strict conduct towards his Upadhyaya.[153] There are two points crucial to this union. First, *pabbajja* was conferred on youth not less than fifteen years of age, hence it is assumed that the newly admitted must be usually around of 15–16 years of tender age and living together with their preceptors, usually would have developed emotional attachment for the teacher. Second, Upadhyaya was responsible for the spiritual growth of his *antevāsini*.[154] A novice's monastic career hinged onto his relationship with his Upadhyaya. He could be turned down by his Upadhyaya if he is not found respectful and affectionate towards his preceptor.[155] This emotional bonding and formal compulsion is reflected in monastic donations and convincingly lead us to the possible actual donors.

For a proper understanding of hundreds of inscriptions in the name of senior monks and of pupil-teacher combination, the Nāgarjunkonda inscription may serve as a point of reference. This *āyaka* pillar inscription, caused by the Mahātalvāri Chāmtitisiri of the Ikshvaḳu Royal family has lines as, 'Reverend Ananda who knows the Dīgha . . . and the *Majjhima Nikāya* by heart, a disciple of the masters of the Aryan Saṁgha . . ., who are preachers and preceptors of the Dīgha, the Majjhima and of the five Mtukas.'[156]

There are two persons represented in the inscription, one by whom it has been caused, that is Chāmtitisiri, and for whom it has been caused that is, Reverend Ananda. The basic intention of the lofty praise in the epigraph was to pay tribute to her teacher. There are hundreds of such epigraphs from Sānchī, Bharhut, Kanherī, and Amarāvatī. A majority of these inscriptions qualify the names of the senior monk with their competence and proficiency in doctrine such as *Sutrantik*,[157] *Pitakin*,[158] *Panch Nikyin*,[159] *Traipitakpdhyaya*,[160] *Bhānaka*,[161] etc.

> *The gift of the monk . . ., who knows the five Nikāyas and of his antevsin.*[162]

Another inscription from the same site has:

> *Gift of Bhadanta Arya Rishipalata, the Bhānaka, the overseer of the works (Navakamika).*[163]

These inscriptions give an impression that either the senior monks were a party to donations or they themselves made these donations. The typological similarity with Nāgarjunkonda inscriptions points towards a greater possibility of these inscriptions being commemorative inscriptions meant for them, but not by them.

The structure of epigraph demonstrates that besides merit seeking, the objective of these donations was also to honour the preceptors and senior monks and nuns. The internal evidence of the epigraphs is of immense importance. A large number of monastic donations have two names: the donor is referred as a simple monk or nun whereas, the teacher is addressed as *thera* or ācarya or both at the same time, such as this from Sānchī:

The gift of monk Pratishthana the antevsin of āya Tishyaka.[164]

A similar one from Amarāvatī sculpture:

The Gift of the two female pupils antevsini of Arya Kamya.[165]Also as Mahthera[166] and Mahvinayadhara.[167]

These 'monks' and 'nuns' might have been probationers as they regularly presented themselves as *antevāsini* or *Saddhaiviharin* of some senior monk. These probationers were not fully ordained members of the order and their initial training in six *sikkhāpadas* and ten *sikkhāpadas* was very simple. These rules only entailed good conduct on their part and as *patīmokkha* was not binding on these novices, they could still retain their worldly and same worldly possessions. Therefore, they could easily and legitimately be the donors. Even in those epigraphs where the novices are not present in the frame, their role in donations is clearly visible like:

The gift of the ṭhera, the venerable (Arya) Nga a monk of Ujjain.[168]

The language of the inscription makes it obvious that this might not have been a first person's account because generally the formula followed in such epigraphs is the inhabitant of so and so place—*ndinagar kbajasa bhicchuno dnam* and not as *theras Ayangas bhicchuno ujenikas dānam.*

There are some inscriptions that, even more strongly, propose the novices as the donors on part of their perceptions. An inscription from Kanherī records:

Gift of the ācarya Buddharakshita with the wish that all living beings may become Buddha.[169]

In another epigraph, the donor monk eulogizes his teacher as *tripitakopdhyya.*[170] In the monastic discipline, *ācarya* and Upadhayaya are two relative terms, they relate a novice to his preceptor. A monk is chosen as an Upadhyaya or *ācarya* by a person entering the fold of *dhamma* as a regular member. Generally, the monk neither addresses himself in these terms nor the other people do, only the person training under him to become a full-fledged monk addresses him with these words. Sānchī *stūpa* II has yielded three inscriptions regarding the donations of a monk Buddharakshita. In one of the inscriptions, he is simply mentioned as monk Buddharakshita,[171] in the second one as Buddharakshita, the *Sautrantika*[172] and in the third one as Buddharakshita who knows the five *Nikāyas*.[173] The spatial proximity of these two records makes us inclined to believe that they are for one and the same person. One equally learnt monk, Buddharakshita, noticed that Bharhut is mentioned as the knower of five *Nikāyas*.[174]

At Sānchī *stūpa* I, there are three records of donations by a monk Aryaparsanaka[175] at three different places. Palaeographical study of Bühler has proved that they are not the copies of the same inscription but are separate inscriptions.[176] Aryaparsanaka is known from Sānchī *stūpa* also.[177] It seems that Aryaparsanaka was a monk of high repute, the addition of Arya to the monk indicates that his disciples of followers made these donations to show their respect. Otherwise, Aryaparsanaka would have made a consolidated donation at that one site, instead of splitting it into many. This might have been a common practice at that time. From Sānchī there are two donative records of the monk Bhanduka:

The gift of monk Bharduka, son of Gopt[178] and there are four donations made by the pupil of Bharduka, all addressing him as Arya. It could be derived that the first two donations were made by the mother of Bhanduka and the rest by his *antevasin*.[179]

This circumstantial evaluation and analysis proves that most of the monastic donations were 'credited' donations, not actually involving the fully ordained monks and the nuns in the business of transactions. Yet there might be same direct donations through legitimate means, duly approved by the monastic code and probably devised for practical reasons. One such measure was the allotment of stipend for outside life of the monks. This information is gleaned from the votive inscriptions of Nasik and Kanherī. In a Nasik inscription,[180] an instruction is given by the donee investor that the monks should be paid a certain amount of money for *kusana* out of the interest incurred on the capital. The word *kusana* has generated curiosity and has been explained in various ways. Although, no exact parallel to this word is found in literary sources, but some concern is definitely shown for a travelling monk in canonical literature, in the form of some extra share of things.[181] At the insistence of Mendaka, the eminent lay follower, the Buddha allowed travelling monks to accept provisions for their journey.[182] These might have been some extra resources collected by the monks. End of *vāssa* was also an occasion for the monks to receive some extra things. At the *pāvarana* ceremony, the host families who had supported the monk during his rain retreat presented him with gifts and these were received by the monk in his individual capacity. Although the preeminence of the *saṃgha's* right over the property of the order is established, but a monk's rights were not completely ignored. Gifts were also made to the *saṃgha*, with special reference to a particular monk.[183]

This way, the *saṃgha* and the monk both became recipients, but in case of assigned gifts, the right to disposal was not exclusively held by the *saṃgha*, perhaps, the use of it was to be decided by the designated monk. In some cases of assigned *dāna*, rules were modified to ensure that the *dāna* reached the named monk. There was a category of individual *dāna* or *pudgalika dātum*, and the individual was allowed the ownership of such *dāna*.[184] These monastic donations were probably the metamorphic manifestations of assigned gifts and individual *dāna*.

The conclusion may be drawn that even after playing such an important role in creation of object of veneration, this lithic testimony of votive inscriptions does not stand against the character or conduct of the Buddhist monks and nuns. It may be affirmed that the solemn desire of the ascetics was fulfilled through perfectly legitimate means. If sieved out, a majority of monastic donations emerge as credited donations and the result of redirected reciprocity and individual *dāna*.

Notes

1. Richard Gombrich, 'Merit transfer in Sinhalese Buddhism: A case study of the interaction between Doctrine and Practice', *History of Religions*, vol. 11, no. 2, 1971, pp. 203–19.
2. *Dīgha Nikāya, Pathikavagga, Cakkavattisutta*, 102.
3. *Dīgha Nikāya, Mahāparinibbāna Sutta*, 159.
4. *Aṅguttara Nikāya*, IV.197.
5. *Saṁyutta Nikāya*, III.2.10.
6. P.L. Vaidya, ed., *Saddharma Pundarika*, Darbhanga: Mithila Institutes, 1960, pp. 38–9.
7. Gregory Schopen, *Buddhist Monks and Business Matters*, Honolulu: University of Hawaii Press, 2004, p. 19.
8. H. Luders, *A List of Brahmi Inscriptions from Early Tribes to about AD 400*, Berlin: 1912; repr., Indological Book House, Vārānasī, 1973, pp. 66–90.
9. Ibid., pp. 102–9.
10. John Marshall and Alfred Foucher, *The Monuments of Sānchī*, New Delhi: Swati Publications, 1982, vol. II, pp. 301–83.
11. Schopen, *Buddhist Monks*, pp. 170–92.
12. M. Winterwitz, *History of Indian Literature*, Calcutta: Calcutta University, 1933, vol. II, p. 231.
13. Sylvan Levi, *History of Indian Literature*, New Delhi: Motilal Banarsidas, 1992 repr., p. 233.
14. Schopen, *Buddhist Monks*, p. 173.
15. Herman Oldenberg, ed., *The Vinaya Pitakam*, vols. III, IV, *Sutta Vibhanga*, London: William and Norgate, 1882; Nissaggiya XXVI, III, VI, VII, VIII, etc.; *Pacittiya* XIX.2, XXXIX.3.
16. I.B. Horner, tr., *The Book of Discipline*, vol. VI, *Parivar*, London: Luzac and Co. Ltd., 1966; *Sutta Vibhanga*, III.237, *Paimokkha, Nissaggiyapacittiya*, XVIII.
17. *Sutta Vibhanga*, X, 1.3.
18. Ibid., XVIII.

19. Ibid., XIX, *Parivar*, p. 19.
20. *Cullavagga*, XII, 1.4.
21. Nalinaksh Dutt, ed., *Gilgit Manuscripts*, vol. III, pt. 1, *Mūlasarvāstivāda Vinayvastu*, Calcutta: Calcutta University Press, 1947, *Bhaisajyavastu*, p. 248.
22. Ibid., pt. 1.
23. *Mahāvastu*, 11, 489.
24. Bongard Levin, p. 211; G. Bangard Levbin and A. Vigasin, *The Image of India*, Moscow: Progress Publications, 1984, p. 221.
25. S. Bagchi. ed., *Mūlasarvāstivāda Vinaya*, p. 357, n. 5.
26. *Cullavagga*, VI, 19.1.
27. G. Bagachi, ed., *Mūlasarvāstivāda Vinayavastu*, vol. I, Darbhanga: Mithila Vidyapeeth, 1967, p. 357, n. 5.
28. *Mūlasarvāstivāda Vinayvastu*, IV, p. 266.
29. *Mahāvagga*, VIII, 27.5.
30. Ibid.
31. *Mūlasarvastivāda Vinaya*, II, p. 232.
32. *Sutta Vibhanga, Nissaggiya*, VI, VIII, IX, X, XVIII, XX, XXV, XXVII.
33. Ibid., *Pacittiya*, IX, XLVII, XLIII, XLIV, XLV, XLVI, LIX.
34. *Mūlasarvāstivāda Vinaya*, II, pp. 233–4.
35. W. Pachow, *The Comparative Study of the Pratimoksha, Santiniketan: Sino Indian Cultural Society*, 1955, p. 116.
36. *Sutta Vibhanga, Nissaggiya*, VI.
37. W. Pachow, *The Comparative Study*, pp. 116–17.
38. Schopen, *Buddhist Monks*, p. 12.
39. Charles S. Prebish, 'Vinaya and Prtimoksha: The Foundation of Buddhist Ethics', in *Studies in the History of Buddhism*, ed. A.K. Narain, Delhi: B.R. Publishing Corporation, 1980, p. 248.
40. *Dīgha Nikāya, Cakkavattisutta, Patnika Vagga*, 110.
41. *Aṅguttara Nikāya*, XVIII, 2.
42. *Viśuddhimagga*, I, 101.
43. *Sutta Vibhanga*, XXI, 1.
44. *Pātimokkha*, Stanza 10 (Vinaya, vol. I, p. 4).
45. Ibid., Stanza 3 (ch.).
46. *Pātimokkha, Nidanudesso.*
47. *Sutta Vibhanga*, VIII.
48. *Pātimokkha*, IV.
49. Cullavagga, I, 25.1.
50. Ibid., I, 27.1.
51. Debal Mitra, *Ratnagiri*, New Delhi: ASI, 1983, vol. II, p. 390.
52. *Sutta Vibhanga, Nissaggiya*, XXII, 1.3.
53. *Parivar, Sutta Vibhanga*, III, 195–6, 260.
54. Ibid., *Mahāvibhanga*, VI, 135.
55. *Pātimokkha, Nissagiyapcittya*, 1.
56. H. Kern, 'The Inscriptions of Junnar', *Indian Antiquary*, vol. VI, p. 40.
57. G. Bühler, 'Votive Inscriptions of Sanchi', *Eigraphia Indica*, vol. II, 1894, p. 93.
58. Ibid., pp. 93–4.
59. John Marshall and Alfred Foucher, *The Monuments of Sānchī*, New Delhi: Swati Publications, 1982.

60. Vijay Nath, *Dāna: Gift System in Ancient India (c. 600 BC–AD 300), A Socio-economic Perspective*, New Delhi: Munshiram Manoharlal, 1987, p. 79.
61. Romila Thapar, *Cultural Past, Essays in Early Indian History*, New Delhi: 2000, p. 589.
62. Luder's, no. 987, p. 102.
63. Alexander Cunningham, *Bhilsa Topes*, Vārānasī, Indological Book House (Indian Edition), 1966, no. 62, p. 136.
64. H. Luders, *A List of Brahmi Inscriptions*, Berlin, 1912, repr., Vārānasī, Indological Book House, 1973, no. 987, p. 102.
65. *Epigraphia India*, vol. XX, no. F, p. 23, C1, p. 17 and C2, p. 20.
66. Himanshu Prabha Ray, *The Winds of Change*, New Delhi: Oxford University Press, 1994, p. 149.
67. B. Malinowksy, *Argonauts of the Western Pacific*, London: Routledge and Kegan Paul, 1912.
68. Colin Renfrew, *Archaeology*, London: Paul Bahn, 1991, pp. 307–11.
69. Takie Sugiama Lebra, 'An Alternative Approach to Reciprocity', *American Anthropologist*, vol. 77, p. 554.
70. Ellison Banks Findly, *Dāna-Giving and Getting in Pāli Buddhism*, New Delhi: Motilal Banarsidass, 2003, p. 180.
71. *Majjhima Nikāya*, XXXX.2.
72. C. Levi-Strauss, *The Elementary Structures of Kinship*, Boston: Beacon Press, 1969, pp. 58–9.
73. Takie Sugiyama Lebra, *An Alternative Approach to Reciprocity*, Hawaii: Hawaii University Press, 1974, p. 552.
74. Glenn Ward, *Post Modernism*, Chicago: McGraw Hill Company, 2003, pp. 106–7.
75. Dines Anderson and Helmer Smith, eds., *Sutta-Nipāta*, London, 1913, p. 221.
76. Ibid., p. 213.
77. *Dīgha Nikāya, Mahāparinibbāna Sutta*, 136.
78. Bhikkhu Nyānmoli, tr., *The Path of Purification, Viśuddhimagga*, II, 36, London: Shambhala, 1976.
79. Ibid., II, 54.
80. Harvey B. Aronson, *Love and Sympathy in Theravāda Buddhism*, Delhi: Motilal Banarsidass, 1980, p. 11.
81. Sukumar Dutta, *Early Buddhist Monachism* (*600 BC–100 BC*), London: Kegan Paul, Trench, Trubner and Co. Ltd., 1924, p. 25.
82. Findly, *Dāna-Giving and Getting*, p. 61.
83. *Vinaya Pitaka* (*Sutta Vibhanga*).
84. *Sutta Vibhanga*, VII.1.
85. I.B. Horner, tr., *Book of Discipline, Sutta Vibhanga*, vol. III, London: Humphrey Milford, 1940, n. 1, p. 3.
86. *Cullavagga*, 1, 16.1.
87. *Viśuddhimagga*, 1.78.
88. *Saṁyutta Nikāya*, II.197.
89. *Viśuddhimagga*.
90. *Saṁyutta Nikya*, II.197.
91. *Sutta Vibhanga, Nissagiya*, VIII.
92. *Cullavagga*, 1, 18.1.
93. *Sutta Vibhanga Nissaggiya*, XVIII.1.
94. Ibid., XVIII, 2; 5.

95. *Cullavagga*, 1, 18.1.
96. *Sutta Vibhanga, Nissaggiya*, XXIII.1.
97. *Cullavagga*, VI.21.
98. Ibid., VI, 21; *Parivar*, XV.204.
99. *Sutta Vibhanga, Nissaggiya*, XXVII.
100. *Mahāvagga*, VI.34, 18.
101. Ibid., VI, 34.21.
102. *Cullavagga*, I, 18.1
103. Luders, no. 1230, p. 144.
104. Luders, no. 1240, p. 146; no. 152, p. 148.
105. Ibid., no. 986, p. 102.
106. Bühler, nos. 148 to 161.
107. Bühler, nos. 219, 229, pp. 380–1.
108. Luders, nos. 926, 927, p. 94.
109. Luders, no. 19, p. 92.
110. Ibid., nos. 1001, 1003, pp. 104–5.
111. *Dīgha Nikāya.*
112. *Aṅguttara Nikāya*, III.45.
113. *Dīgha Nikāya, Sigālovāda Sutta.*
114. *Dīgha Nikāya, Silakhandavagga, Sammanaphala Sutta*, 191.
115. *Viśuddhimagga*, III.29.
116. Ibid., III.49.
117. *Mahāvagga*, I, 38.1.
118. *Sutta Vibhanga.*
119. Ibid., III, 211; *Nissaggiya*, VI, p. 2.
120. *Viśuddhimagga*, I.73.
121. Ibid., I.74.
122. Ibid., I.78.
123. *Parivar, Sutta Vibhanga*, III.211.
124. *Viśuddhimagga*, III.49.
125. I.B. Horner, *Book of Descriptive Discipline*, p. 4, XVI, XVII.
126. Schopen, *Buddhist Monks*, p. 173.
127. *Sutta Vibhanga Pacittiya*, XLVIII.2.
128. *Cullavagga*, III, 7.1–8.
129. *Sutta Vibhanga, Pacittiya*, XLVIII.2.
130. *Viśuddhimagga*, IX.77–82.
131. *Saṁyutta Nikāya*, II.197.
132. *Viśuddhimagga*, III.35–42.
133. Bühler, no. 84, p. 106.
134. Luders, no. 999, p. 104.
135. Bühler Topel, no. 137, p. 371(a).
136. Luders, no. 999, 1016, 1020.
137. Luders List no. 1262, p. 150.
138. Ibid., no. 1250, p. 149.
139. Luders, no. 294, p. 27 (Sānchī).
140. Luders, no. 1234, p. 145 (Amrāvatī).
141. Luders, no. 1263, p. 150 (Amrāvatī).
142. Luders, no. 1020, p. 107 (Kanheri).
143. Luders, no. 1295, p. 155 (Amrāvatī).

144. Luders, nos. 942, 943, p. 96.
145. Luders, no. 590, Sānchī.
146. Luders, no. 1250, p. 148.
147. *Mahāvagga*, 25.6, *Book of Descriptive*, vol. II.
148. Ibid., 56.1.
149. Ibid., 25.6; 26.2.6.
150. Ibid., 32.1.
151. *Sutta Vibhanga.*
152. *Mahāvagga*, 26.2–6.
153. Ibid., 25.6, 25.9.
154. Ibid., 26.1.
155. Ibid., 26.6.
156. *Epigraphia Indica*, vol. XX, no. 1, p. 17.
157. Bühler, no. 59, p. 103 (Sānchī); Luders, no. 797, p. 80 (Bharhut).
158. Luders, no. 773, p. 76, no. 856, p. 8 (Bharhut); Luders, no. 989, p. 103 Kanheri (Sānchī).
159. Bühler, no. 66, Tope I, p. 104, Luders, no. 867, p. 87 (Bharhut).
160. Luders, no. 989, p. 103 Kanheri (Sanchi).
161. Luders, no. 789, p. 79 (Sānchī); no. 762, p. 75 (Sānchī).
162. Bühler, no. 66, Tope I, p. 104.
163. Luders, no. 773, p. 76.
164. Marshall, *The Monuments of Sanchi*, no. 229, p. 322.
165. Luders, no. 1237, p. 147.
166. Luders, no. 1272, p. 151.
167. Ibid., 1270, p. 151.
168. Bühler, no. 206, p. 385 (Tope I Sānchī).
169. Luders, no. 992, p. 103.
170. Ibid., no. 989, p. 103.
171. Bühler, no. 302, p. 388.
172. Bühler, no. 59, p. 400; no. 62, p. 401.
173. Luders, no. 867, p. 87.
174. Ibid.
175. Marshall, *The Monuments of Sanchi*, nos. 144, 148, 149, p. 314.
176. Bühler, p. 385.
177. Marshall, *The Monuments of Sanchi*, p. 314.
178. Bühler, no. 16, p. 98, 256, 384.
179. Ibid., no. 103, pp. 108, 110, 122, 207, 303, 379, 388.
180. E. Senart, *The Inscriptions in the Caves of Nasik*, E.I., vol. VIII, N. 12, pp. 81–2.
181. *Mahāvagga*, VIII, 9.3.
182. Ibid., VI, 24.30.
183. *Mahāvagga*, V, 13.7, VI, 19.1–2.
184 *Cullavagga*, X.151.

9

The Matrix of Patronage

Vikramaśilā Mahāvihāra

KRISHNA KUMAR MANDAL

TIBETAN SOURCES REFER to five great Mahāvihāras located at Vikramaśilā, Nālandā, Somapurī or Pahārpur, Odantapurī, and Jagaddala, known for the Vajrayāna tradition. Vikramaśilā, the great centre of Vajrayāna learning founded by King Dharmapāla, identified with the site of Antichak is situated in the Bhagalpur district of Bihar on the right bank of the river Ganges. Excavations at Antichak, in the Bhagalpur district of Bihar between 1960–9 and 1977–82, have yielded remains of the huge Vikramaśilā monastery. It was square in plan, each side measuring 330 m. with a series of 208 cells, 52 on each of the floor sides, opening into a common verandah. In the centre was a cruciform *stūpa* and a cluster of votive *stūpas*. To the north of the monastery, a number of scattered structures, including a Tibetan and a Hindu temple, have been found. The entire area is spread over more than 100 acres. The excavations also uncovered a mix of Buddhist and non-Buddhist images, such as that of Śiva, Uma-Maheśwara, Śiva and Parvati, Bhairava, Mahisasuramardini, Cāmundā, Ganeśa, Karttikeya, the Navagraha, Vrsabha, Visṇu, and Surya.[1] Vikramaśilā enjoyed its safe position and liberal patronage by the Pāla kings and local rulers, as gleaned from the inscriptional and sculptural data discovered in the excavations at Antichak. Patronage network in India, as elsewhere, lies embedded in particular socio-political systems, which in turn rests on deeply pervasive and culturally patterned conception of power and authority. Where this power emanated from and how it gained authority and legitimacy is the central concern of discussion about this Mahāvihāra. Conceptions of legitimate authority were never fixed in time and space but kept changing and depending on variables.[2] Patronage, therefore, may be interpreted in the context of power structure and the nature of polity.

One can locate certain broad features of feudal formation in early medieval India from the Gupta and especially from the post-Gupta period onwards. Its basic features include granting of virgin and cultivated lands, transference of peasants, extension of forced labour to restriction on movement of the peasants, artisans, and merchants, and the paucity of coins, retrogression of trade, abandonment of fiscal and criminal administration to the religious beneficiaries, the beginning of remuneration in revenues to officials and, the practice of the obligatory services to the *samanas*. The new society was marked by the appearance of a substantial class of landlords and numerous classes of servile peasantry. The emerging pattern was strengthened during the period of the Pālas in early medieval Bihar. The Pālas created many religious intermediaries in the land ownership system. Nālandā owned 200 villages in the second-half of the seventh century.[3] Their number was increased by five under Devapāla in the ninth century.[4] Odantapurī, Vikramaśilā, and Jagaddala may similarly have possessed hundreds of villages,[5] which indicates an elaborate series of relations attached with these villages. More likely, monasteries of this variety would frequently be given jurisdiction over the proximate area as an extension of their endowment and part of the feuds assigned to them. The consequence was that monasteries had responsibility for the maintenance of law and the setting of litigation, not simply of their own officials, but also over the villages under their aegis.

Monasteries and temples formed wider economic units. It has been suggested that like other Mahāvihāras, Vikramaśilā Mahāvihāra might also have been assigned for financial support by the state.[6] This led to accommodation of 10,000 monks and students; the evidence for grants of villages is clear and definite. But we have no such definite evidence for Vikramaśilā Mahāvihāra, the total population of which would have constituted about 1,000 people.[7] According to Lama Tāranāth, during the period of King Rampāla (*c*.1076 CE–*c*.1132 CE) when Abhyankara Gupta was its head, there were 108 professors and 1,000 inmate student monks.[8] Another estimate puts the number of students between 1,000 and 10,000.[9] The number of monk scholars at Vikramaśilā in the twelfth century CE is estimated to have been 3,000.[10] This population of about 3,000 people must have been dependent on the revenue collected from villages, assigned by the state for the purpose.[11] The area surrounding the Mahāvihāra was settled for about 2,000 years before the Mahāvihāra took its shape and is evident in the settlement at the neighbouring excavated sites of Oriup[12] which clearly appears to have been resettled after a long period during *c*.600 CE and continued throughout the existence of Mahāvihāras. This reflects that this Mahāvihāra received patronage and reciprocated in injecting the rhetoric of ethical responsibility into the political dialogue. The Pālas had no claim over the kṣatriya status when they first appeared, and contemporary evidence indicates that they have been śūdras or even outcastes. The *Manjusrimulkalpa* makes it clear.[13] The political strategy adopted by Gopala, strengthening the dogmatic base of Mahāyāna Buddhism, was laced with tantric ritualism and local deities could influence popular opinion in favour of the sponsoring regime. Vajrayāna Buddhism was patronized by Pāla rulers, chiefly for legitimizing purpose but later on they shifted to brahmanical sources.[14] It was royal attention that was given to the Buddhist institutions like Vikramaśilā Mahāvihāra. The Mahāvihāra administered its estate and established loyalties in a manner closely analogous to members of the circle of the vassal of an overlord. The Mahāvihāra relied on patronage as a land grant.

Archaeologist B.S. Verma had reported the finding of about 40 inscribed seals and sealings, 9 of which were surface collections and the rest were discovered in the stratified contexts during regular excavations.[15] Despite the scantiness of epigraphic data from Antichak, it is efficient to provide a clue to interpret the nature of patronage to the Mahāvihāra. The reported data can be classified as follows:

(a) A royal inscription (Antichak pillar, *prasasti* of Sahura), which was found engraved on a pillar within the precincts of the monastery during the excavations at Antichak.[16]
(b) Inscriptions on seals and sealings.
(c) Inscriptions on dedicatory *stūpas*.
(d) Dedicatory inscriptions on sculptures/sculpted fragments.

The Antichak pillar, *prasasti* of Sahura belongs to the twelfth century CE. The royal inscription on a pillar at Antichak introduced the line of rulers in the Antichak area of Bhagalpur as follows:

1. Kesara is referred to as *Rājadhirāja*, *Parmeśvara*, *Divyamurti* and *Sakalabhumipatipradipah*.
2. Hanasana is described as lord Cakrapani incarnate.
3. Sahura as Sahavara appears as a friend of the King of Gauda and the victor over the army of the Vangas (possibly the Senas). He might have been a dependent of the Pālas, and not their vassal.
4. Masanikesa.

The Antichak inscription introduces *Rājadhirāja Parmeśvara* Kesara as an early king of the family. In his family was born Hanasana, considered to be an incarnation of Visṇu. After him came Sahura or Sahavara, who was received by the lord of Gauda, and received the latter's grace. He subdued Sonadamana sent by the king of Vangas and established an image in the *vihāra* built by Rajyapāla. He was followed by Masanikesa under whom Manjusri wrote the present eulogy. Though Sahura or Sahavara was a Buddhist, the epigraph exhibits considerable brahmanical influence in the form of references to Cakrapani, Bharga, Krshna, Gauri, and Laksṃī. They are from the Rajmahal hills via Colgong—Patharghatta up to the Santhal *parganas*, which is hilly and forested and inhabited by a large number of different tribes. The tribals of the area appear to have avenged the weakness of the Pālas after Nayapāla. Under Kesara, they appear to have wielded some political influence in and around the Patharghatta region. They might have accepted suzerainty of the Pālas for the sake of convenience. Thus, these are reflections of the formation of local state and the formative beginning of this region.

The later Pālas were in search of allies and found one in Sahura or Sahavara. Masanikesa was his son and a patron of Manjusri, the composer of this epigraph. Manjusri was a Buddhist, as suggested by D.C. Sircar. Sahura laid the foundation of greatness of his family. Nothing is known after him about the dynasty from any source. It seems that with the destruction of the University of Vikramaśila, the dynasty of Masanikesa came to an end. It may be reasonably assumed that Sahura got installed therein, one image in the Vikramaśila Mahāvihāra complex, as the area was in proximity which is otherwise illogical. This inscription indicates that Vikramaśila complex was able to attract patronage from a local ruler in the twelfth century CE. The motive behind the patronage was to get legitimacy because it was a central concern for these local rulers since they did not derive it from the traditional kṣatriya lineages. D.C. Sircar, on the basis of the non-Sanskrit names in the Antichak inscription, suggests that they were probably descendants of an aboriginal tribe.[17] They sought to legitimize their authority, getting a monastery constructed and installed therein an image in the Vikramaśila Mahāvihāra complex in an area near to it. *Prasasti* text in the inscription was quite consciously devised and developed as a legitimizing instrument[18] in the post-Gupta period in Bihar. Its function was, thus, twofold: First, as legitimizing the authority, the newly emerging ruling families and second, by virtue of their contents they are a major source of history, i.e. for reconstructing the dynastic history and more importantly for situating the dynasty in changing ideological and socio-religious contexts.[19] Such kind of patronage ensured the extension and consolidation of authority.

On the basis of the reported epigraphic records, inscriptions on seals and sealings have been located and tabulated as follows:

The inscriptions described below indicate that the earliest inscriptions belong to the ninth and tenth century CE, inscribing Sri *Rajyagrha-Mahāvihāra*

Sl. No.	*Legend*	*Dating*	*The Donor*
1.	*Vibhukasya* (seal of Vibhuka)[20]	12th century CE	Not mentioned. Apparently non-monastic, no royal background
2.	*Salakasya* (seal of Salaka)[21]	12th century CE	-do-
3.	Two line inscription: Sri Var in the first line and Vasya in the second line (seal of person called Varadeva)[22]	12th century CE	-do-
4.	Three line inscription Line 1: *Pa Mari Ji* Line 2: *La Tam Pukha* Line 3: Sa[23]	11th –12th century CE	-do-

(*Contd.*)

(*contd.*)

Sl. No.	*Legend*	*Dating*	*The Donor*
5.	Si na (seal of a person called Silna?)[24]	12th century CE	Not mentioned. Apparently non-monastic, no royal background
6.	*Puve* (seal of a person called *Puve?*)[25]	12th century CE	-do-
7.	*Sri Vijayaraja* (seal of Sri *Vijayaraja*)[26]	12th century CE	-do-
8.	*Sri Purusottamapala* (seal of *Purusottamapala*)[27]	12th century CE	-do-
9.	Three line inscription Line 1: *Sri Rajyagrara* (ha) Line 2: *Mahavihare* Line 3: blurred[28]	9th –10th century CE	Seal of a monastery
10.	Three line, damaged inscription Line 1: *Sri Mjjaya* (or *Rajjaya*) Line 2: *Vihara*[29]	12th century CE	-do-
11.	*Maharsi*[30]	11th century CE	Not mentioned. But apparently non-monastic, non-royal background.
12.	*Vasukara* (seal of a person called *Vasukara*)[31]	10th–11th century CE	-do-
13.	*Saharasa* (seal of a person called *Sahara*)[32]	11th century CE	-do-
14.	*Sahara* (seal of a person called *Sahara*)[33]	11th century CE	-do-
15.	Three impressions on a seal, one of them reading *Chedi* (seal of a person associated with the *Chedi dynasty?*)[34]	12th century CE	A person associated with the Chedi dynasty?
16.	*Chandra* (seal of a person called *Chandra*)[35]	12th century CE	Non-monastic, non-royal
17.	Two lines: Line 1: *Aya* Line 2 : *Sau*[36]	12th century CE	-do-
18.	*Dinna* (seal of a person called *Dinna*)[37]	12th century CE	-do-
19.	Two line legend reading *Mahasramana*[38]	12th century CE	A monk?
20.	*Bajala* (seal of a person called *Bajala*)[39]	12th century CE	Non-monastic, non-royal
21.	Three line inscription Line 1: *Siddhama-Dina* Line 2: *Aditya Vermanah* Line 3: *Suya Gatim Mantri*[40]	12th century CE	One of the donors was probably a minister
22.	Three line inscription Line 1: Siddhama Line 2: blurred, probably referring to *Vakratanam Sri*	11th–12th century CE	One of the donors was probably a minister

(*Contd.*)

(*contd.*)

Sl. No.	Legend	Dating	The Donor
	Line 3: blurred, probably referring to Kheta or *Gtedanada Mantri*[41]		
23.	Blurred inscriptions Line 1: *Siddhama-Sakhena* Line 2: *Devadasasa* Line 3: only *Gotrasakha* is readable[42]	11th–12th century CE	Non-monastic, non-royal
24.	*Puhasa* (seal of a person called *Puha*)[43]	12th century CE	-do-
25.	*Srivara* (seal of a person called *Srivara*)[44]	11th–12th century CE	-do-
26.	*Maha* (seal of a person called *Maha*)[45]	12th century CE	-do-
27.	Legend in two lines Line 1: Pari?ata Line 2: *Sri Madhava* (seal of a person called *Sri Madhava*)[46]	12th century CE	-do-
28.	Legend in two lines Line 1: *Sri* Line 2: blurred[47]	12th century CE	-do-
29.	*Saharasa* (seal of a person called *Sahara*)[48]	12th century CE	-do-
30.	Legend in two lines Line 1: *Sri* Line 2: *Devasya* (seal of a person called *Sri-Deva*)[49]	12th century CE	-do-
31.	*Sri* (seal of a person called *Sri*)[50]	12th century CE	-do-
32.	*Sahara* (seal of a person called *Sahara*)[51]	12th century CE	-do-
33.	*Uttarantaka* (seal of a person called *Uttarantaka*)[52]	12th century CE	-do-

and suggesting thereby, 'Great monastery of royal house'. That the present relics unearthed at Antichak belonged to a Buddhist monastery is also indicated by the depicted motif on the seal: a *Dharmacakra* flanked by a deer on each side. It shows up in the symbolism depicted on the monastic sealings; during this age, virtually, all monastic sealings recovered from various monasteries are symbolic representations of the religious affiliations of the *vihāra*. Location of the Mahāvihāra referred to in this seal is not known. It does not suggest the royal house that patronized it, or the kind of relationship this Mahāvihāra had with Vikramaśila Mahāvihāra. Similar is the case with another monastery—*Sri Mjjaya*, referred to in the twelfth century CE seal. It is generally suggested that *Rajjaya-vihara* is an incorrect rendering of *Rajavihara*, meaning a royal monastery and it may be a reflection of the regional/local language formation which is a specific feature of early medieval society. But the context suggests that it is a royal monastery. One may keep in mind that such surprising alterations of narrative content are comprehended only in the face of equally dramatic transformations of the socio-linguistic expectations and audience appeal. The narrative changes in the case are reflective of Sanskrit, to transmit socio-political values, and an indication of the social composition of those versed in their language.[53] In fact, Angika language is the local dialect of Bhagalpur and its adjoining area. Scholars have tried to trace the origin of Angika from the Middle Indo-Aryan language, Prakrit.[54] A simplified and colloquial form of it is called Avahattha (i.e. Apabhrasta), who was the direct ancestor of the Eastern New Indo-Aryan languages. This literary Apabhramsa-Avahattha is known by a mass of literary records. From a study of these it is evident that it had local forms in separate regions of the country. These regional forms gave rise to different Eastern Indo-Aryan dialects some time about 1000 CE.[55] Rahul Sankrityayan has indicated that this language was in vogue in the Bhagalpur region when Vikramaśila Mahāvihāra was flourishing.[56] This is indicative of the changing nature of patronage patterns with the transformation of language.

Two seals datable to the twelfth century CE indicate that the Vikramaśila complex has some interaction with persons having association with the royal court. Both the seals contain the name of more than one individual, simultaneously. Therefore, it was probably a joint seal. In the first seal, the names of two persons are engraved, one of which was a *mantri* (minister) named Gtedanada. The second inscription, besides containing the name of an individual called Aditya Vermanah, also contained the name of Suya Gatima Mantri. None of the seals inform of the king with whom they were associated. A seal of another *ranaka*, Srideva from the site of Vikramaśila Mahāvihāra under the charge of a feudal lord, Srideva, had some political authority in the area. It is evident from the three inscriptions that the *ranaka* in the districts of Monghyr and Bhagalpur were in charge of local administration under the Pālas and did not fail to take advantage of the weakness of their overlord.[57] No doubt, there is very little evidence for a state exercising control over a precisely delimited territory with the help of a bureaucratic command structure, where the contours of power relation and jurisdiction of the officials are defined. This kind of patronage could sustain the ruling elite's strategies of domination and consequently, help the consolidation of authority.

Legends on the other seals and sealings do not help in locating the nature of relationships they had with the Mahāvihāra. None of the persons mentioned in the seals and sealings had any expressed affiliation to Buddhism, except the terracotta seal with the legend *Mahāsramana* probably belonged to a Buddhist motif. On the seal belonging to *Sri Purusottamapala*—a trident having a flag tied in the middle and kept horizontally, the bottom, a humped bull in sitting posture upon a pedestal—indicates that this person was influenced by Śaivism.[58] Buddhist and Śaiva potentates at the Mahāvihāra show how the ethical positions of each religious tradition configured the rhetorical gestures of their respective supports. The Indian Śaiva system of the Pasupatas appropriated aspects of Buddhist nomenclature and iconography as well. Buddhist esotericism is the pale imitation of Śaivism, as it has sometimes been described. In fact, tantrism/esoteric Buddhism is a form of medieval Buddhism that internalized, appropriated, re-affirmed, and re-arranged the structure most closely associated with the system of power relation, ritual authentication, aesthetics, gift-giving, clan associations, and a sense of dominion that defined post-Gupta Indian polities.[59] Even Buddhist monarchs supported the Śaiva ascetic, as shown in the Bhagalpur plate of Narayanpāla of 900 CE.[60] It seems that kings ruled in the name of Śiva as the lord of the world (*lokeśvara*) to establish their legitimacy. Once the relation of being a part of the deity has been accepted, the myths of divinity extended to the king, so that an attack on the king would be tantamount to an attack on the rule of Śiva. Thus, the politics of patronage would legitimize power and help the emergence of a stratum of ruling elites.

It is significant to note that many donors, who do not ascribe their official title and did not claim to be the monks or the nuns, were probably from subaltern background. That applies to the person named Sahura, whose name appears on four seals: two in the eleventh century CE and two in the twelfth century CE. That he could not be equated with the rulers called Sahura where *prasasti* is engraved in a pillar inscription of Antichak, is indicated by the fact that no royal epithet has been used for him. This kind of patronage involved marked cultural innovation, based on the emergence of new social groups who identify themselves as patrons of new aesthetic forms. Such common people, perhaps, looked to men of substance for the performance of services that were important for the everyday life of the community. Patronage of religious establishment, thus, provided a major channel for status enhancement to those who wanted to move up within the hierarchical, caste society.

During the Antichak excavations, four inscribed dedicatory *stūpas* were discovered as follows:

The four inscribed dedicatory *stūpas* belonged to the twelfth century CE. The *stūpa* has a legend in *bhikkhuni* characters. This script was probably used by Buddhist monks only, so we may draw inference that this *stūpa* was donated by a monk. Other donors have left neither their association to religion nor their social background. It might be possible that they were from common

Sl. No.	*Legend*	*Dating*	*The Donor*
1.	*Sridhamma*[61]	12th century CE	Not mentioned. But apparently, non-monastic, non-aristocratic
2.	*Hadrava*[62]	12th century CE	-do-
3.	*Sridha*[63]	12th century CE	-do-
4.	Legend in the *Bhikuni* character[64]	12th century CE	Probably a monk

sections of the society. Although the community of monks was normatively superior to the laity, it was dependent on the laity's for protection, and in return the laity acquired spiritual merit. Its significance lies in the fact that it indicates continued pilgrimage to this site even during its decadent phase. In this context, we may bear in mind that the concepts of purity and power are two inseparable perceptions.[65] Anthropological case studies reveal that aspirant ruling chieftains build and control popular cultic shrines and pilgrimage centres, and through this process automatically became associated with the enshrined deity. As its human representatives, they acquire the much needed religious sanction and popular backing for their political command.[66] The nexus that was created between power, religious institutions, and the people continued throughout.

A fairly good number of inscribed images has been reported at Antichak but only four inscriptions on the sculptures/sculpted fragments contain the name of donor. The following are the sculpted fragments.

Two inscriptions on the sculpted fragments of the eleventh century CE record 'Sonar Mancika', which according to B.S. Verma, 'probably means goldsmith's throne'. These images were probably located in the same shrine within the Mahāvihāra through the patronage to the Mahāvihāra in the said century. The donor has not recorded the motive behind donation. The name of the deity whose image was donated, as the name of the religious centre where this image was installed has not been mentioned either. Artisans as patrons, indicate social mobilization in a period of social change with upward mobility. Such patronage reflects the respect meted out to artisans where they are wealthy, as is also indicated in Buddhist texts to the *gahapati*, even if an artisan profession had been given the status of *ucch kula* or high family (*Aṅguttara Nikāya* II, 363). This, not withstanding in contemporary brahmanical *Dharmasutra*, where they are ranked low (Gautam, X. 60; Manu, X. 99–100; or even the *Arthshastra*, 138). When trade declined, the impoverishment of this group led to a lowering of their status, and this group supported religious sects which the brāhmaṇas regarded as heretical. Revival

Sl. No.	*Cultic identity of the sculpture/sculpted fragments*	*Period*	*The Donor*
1.	Pedestal of an unidentifiable broken image[67]	11th century CE	A goldsmith?/Artisanal?
2.	Pedestal of an unidentifiable broken image[68]	11th century CE	A goldsmith?/Artisanal?
3.	*Tara*[69]	12th century CE	Pratihara Sri Udayavara/ a person associated with the Pratihara dynasty of northern India
4.	*Mansasa*[70]	12th century CE	Chandra/Non-monastic, non-aristocratic

of trade by the tenth to eleventh centuries, and the improved economic climate, evidently stimulated mercantile construction of Buddhist institutions once again, as is evident in the inscriptions of Bihar.[71] The reference to Chando Saudagar in Aṅga region confirms the emerging process. Chando Saudagar, overwhelmed by profit, decided to go to Sri Lanka along with his family members for a vacation from where he procured items of trade, particularly spices. Chando Saudagar's venture for trade in the sea is amply reflected in Buddhist and foreign sources.[72]

Adding to it, an inscription on an image of Mansa records the legend 'Chandra' which was probably the name of a donor. The name of the deity whose image was donated, or the image of the religious centre which this image was installed in, has not been mentioned. The inscribed image of Mansa, the Snake-Goddess pointed its integration into the institutional form of Buddhism. This autochthonous deity had strong local roots. Finds of terracotta figurine of a pair of snakes (*naga/nagin*) with a human head from Champa belonging to the Śunga period (185 BCE to 75 BCE)[73] and a fragment of a door-jam of a Visahari temple, made of black granite with snake engraved on it belonging to the eighth and ninth centuries CE also from Champa,[74] clearly suggests the continuance of snake worship from the beginning of the historical period to the early medieval period. In Bhagalpur, about sixteen temples of Goddess Visahari are known, for which Mansa temple of Champanager, in the west of Bhagalpur, is the most important. The story of the *Champeya Jataka*[75] centres on a puissant serpent king Champeya of Aṅga, who, devoid of his magnificence was caught by a serpent charmer who made him dance for his shows. Abundance of snakes of different varieties influenced the religious beliefs and practices of the people of ancient Aṅga. Lord Śiva and Visṇu, who were closely associated with snakes, thus, came to be worshipped by the people of Aṅga in one form or the other. A popular Bihula-Visahari[76] salutation song in Angika, while describing the geographical boundaries of Aṅga, mentioned this place as the abode of both lord Śiva and Visṇu. The spiritual spread of these deities and cults provided the emerging local/translocal lineages and assured dimension of territoriality as their principal patrons. Chandra might have been from the lower sections of society as the tradition of snake-worship was embedded in the masses of the Aṅga region, particularly the subaltern people who were the worst sufferers of the evil effects of snakes. Present popularity of Mansa/Visahari worship among the subaltern population of Bhagalpur region is a reflection of the tradition, albeit with some modifications which came to effect from time to time. Interestingly, most of the temples of Goddess Visahari, dotting present Bhagalpur district are being patronized by Modi or Sahu families belonging to Baniya (trading class) and the following subaltern sections of the society. Thus, patronage centred around locality deities, and their shrines or establishments, may be understood in the context of the need to create larger community identities by transcending kinship consideration.

Autochthonous chiefs, without the support of a kṣatriya status for legitimacy, extended patronage to the locality deities, and the patronage simultaneously led to the formation of locality.

A twelfth century inscription on an image of Tārā records that this image was the Deyadharma of *Mahayana-Anuyayinah Paramopaska Sri Upadhayaya* and parents in the front rank. So the donor was a lay follower of Mahāyāna and he probably belonged to the Pratihara lineage of northern India. This is the only epigraphic example of long distance pilgrimage to this Mahāvihāra; and Vikramaśila, at that time was the centre of Mahāyāna, Tantrayāna, Vajrayāna, and Sahajayāna.[77] The Mantrayāna was the last version of Indian Buddhism to develop and sustain a canon of scripture, long after the canon of the early schools or of the Mahāyāna were verified as received authority by a longer or smaller segment of the Indian community. Consequently, esoteric monks were required to build on the previous models to the extent that they could, but the foundations of their new categories of scripture required them and other representing the institution to formulate a new mythology of revelation, so there was a space for a Mahāyāna lay follower to assert his Mahāyāna identity, therefore, the relationship between Mahāyāna and esoteric Buddhism cannot be overlooked.[78] In this guise, esotericism became a part of the socialization system that turned from disparate background into member of a culture unified by monastic rule, ritual cosmology, and doctrine.

In terms of epigraphic findings, eleventh and twelfth centuries CE appear to be the most prolific for Antichak and they indicate patronage to this institution from different sections of society but we do not find any seal issued by women, in fact it needs serious interpretation. Conformity and reconfiguration are something religious traditions are continually required to negotiate. Buddhist institutions could not capitulate certain aspects of the *Varnāsrama* model but other facts were seen definitively negotiable, particularly if it bought them closer to sources of support and social legitimacy. The decline of women's participation was a part of this process, and from the seventh century onwards, we see an erosion of women's involvement, particularly in the virtually total eclipse of the office of the nun (*bhikkhuni*) in north India. More broadly, though, the early medieval period saw the dramatic deterioration of support for and involvement of women in Buddhist activities at all levels, whether in the monastery, in the lay community, or in the newly evolving Siddha systems.[79] Vikramaśila Mahāvihāra which was one of the most renowned centres for Tantric Buddhism was no exception to it. Tantrism, as the product of brahmanical colonization of the tribal areas through the process of land grants, gave rise not only to serfdom in the outer circle, but also recognized social and feudal hierarchy.[80] No doubt the *Tantric Cakra* opened its door to all sections of people, irrespective of *varṇa*, sex, and other considerations, but social hierarchy and inequality still persisted in the Mahāvihāra. The intellectuals of the Mahāvihāra were often of high castes[81] and the Mantrayāna was decidedly deleterious to religions aspiration of those women desiring participation as independent and equal persons. Thus, Buddhism no longer held the place of pride previously accorded, and the monks felt themselves under pressure to conform to the dominant paradigm—the *Varnāsrama Dharma*, the affirmation of caste and stages of life.[82]

Archaeological material can be particularly useful in the exploration of marginal or marginalized strata of the society. The depersonalization essential to the hagiographical process is part of a larger ritual and literary field; for Indian hagiography appears to require that process of legitimacy extended either from an ancestral lineage, or its immediate analogy, the religious lineage. Epigraphical data throws light on the variation in women's position in Buddhism over this duration. The early tradition, evident in Sānchī, Amarāvatī, Bharhut, Takshaśila, Gandhāra, Sārnāth, Vajrāsana, and the other great sites demonstrate flourishing nun communities.[83] These are the sites where *bhikkhunis* commanded sufficient resources or sufficient prestige to act as a cipher for others, had resources to erect railings, and have their names inscribed in dedication statues.[84] A review of the epigraphical material for the early medieval period does not indicate the enthusiastic participation of women at this level, and it has already been observed by Falk that nuns were increasingly in short supply. Her observations are affirmed by the surviving inscriptions.[85] For example, Huntington's review of seventy-seven inscribed and dated sculptures from the 'Pāla-Sena' schools, both Buddhist and Hindu, list no nuns at all. The only inscription by a woman claiming religious affiliation as a committed lay woman (*upāsikā*), comes from a pre-Pāla fourth-century image.[86] Of the other Buddhist images, inscriptions record donations by two queens, a princess, the wife of a chieftain, a vintner's daughter, the wife of a wealthy donor, a monk's mother, and four otherwise undistinguished wives of gentleman of means.[87] All the women listed in these inscriptions identified themselves through their relations to men. This information is reinforced by the data from the Kurkihar bronze hoard; a group of specifically Buddhist statuary. Of the 93 inscriptions listed, 42 provide names of donors: 9 are clearly donated by women (no nuns), while 33 are by men (10 clearly by monks), yielding 22 per cent women, the highest archaeological percentage in the early medieval period.[88]

These findings reinforce the suggestions available from the numerous personal sealings found. As many as 173 personal sealings were listed, by Hirananda Sastri, of the medieval Buddhist educational system. Of these, only three identify women—Srimat-Siyadevi, Sri-Ijjadevi, and Sridevi. All of them were well-respected ladies, as is indicated by their names.[89] Among the largest class of other personal materials from the 109 'unhistorical votive inscriptions', only one name could possibly be construed as feminine, Krsnatuka and is otherwise unspecified religiously.[90] The data appears to confirm the statement of the Chinse monk, I-Ching, that nuns were allowed no specific provision in monasteries of his acquaintance. His rather cavalier attitude that women should just do as they were told, appears as a reinforcement of the late seventh-century unwillingness to engage women's participation.[91]

The textual sources of the period are solely those of esoteric hagiography. The surviving literature shows the fallacy of assuming equal participation of women in the Indian esoteric system. The literature configures the ritual system as diverted towards males and privileging male response. Out of the hundreds of ritual manuals from the esoteric texts surviving in Sanskrit, translated into Tibetan, Chinese, Newar, Uyghur, and other languages; out of the hundreds of exegetical works describing the ritual systems in those several languages, out of the lineages—living and dead—in Tibet, Nepal, Burma, Nan-chao, China, Japan, Mongolia, Sri Lanka, and many other places, esoteric specialists have yet to uncover a single text or lineage that preserves instructions about *yogic* or sexual practices that relate to women's position. Those texts treating specifically sexual rituals, describe them in a manner anatomically impossible for women to perform, if they were to be the primary agents.[92] Beyond that, several surviving texts admittedly authored by women discuss the ritual and meditative system from the viewpoint of the male. In this context, the best example of this is the *Vyakatabhavanugata-tattva-siddhi*,[93] a text that has been lauded by one feminist as 'a gemlike treatise' because it ostensibly articulates an affirmation of the female body. Yet the first chapter of the work actually affirms not the female body but how the body might be manipulated and employed by a *yogic* in search of his own goal. In this way, early medieval women were persuaded to leave Buddhist religious life behind and retreat to the home, as their society exhorted them and frequently forced them to. Buddhist authors and institutions—male and female—internalized, articulated and espoused these *Varnāsrama Dharma* paradigms, since there appeared to be neither another option nor an alternative sense of direction. The ritual focus of surviving literature, attributed to women of the period, simply reinforces the virtual unanimity of the decision and provides us with little recourse but to assume that they accepted this position as they saw the door of the Buddhist religion grow narrower before their eyes.

The foregoing discussion reflects that Vikramaśila Mahāvihāra grew up of liberal patronage of Pāla and local rulers. The forms of patronage as gleaned from the inscriptions and sculptural data discovered in excavation at Antichak, highlights Vikramaśilā Mahāvihāra in the context of power structure as well as the formation of regional/local state and the need to legitimize the emerging political structure that took place in early medieval Bihar. The nature of patronage was multidimensional. The process of local state formation and power elite, involving patronage for one and validation for other, i.e. patronage and legitimation at local level. Individual or group patronage emanated from the desire to acquire upward mobility in the making and to gain acceptance for the assured status. Besides, common people, too, perhaps looked to a man of substance for the performance of services that were important for the everyday life of the community. Patronage of Vikramśilā Mahāvihāra, thus, provided a major channel for status enhancement to those who wanted to move up within the hierarchical, caste society. The nexus that was created between state power, the Mahāvihāra and the people continued throughout. The structure of legitimation reflects both cultural basis of power and its religious domain. The autochthonous deities such as Mansa—the Goddess of snakes and Visahari had strong local roots. The spatial spread of these deities and/or the centre, provided the emerging local lineages an assured dimension of territoriality as their principal patrons. Patronage centred around local deities and their shrine's establishment may be understood in the context of the need to create larger community identities by transcending kinship consideration. Autochthonous chiefs, without the support of a kṣatriya status for legitimacy, extended patronage to local deities. Patronage extended to the local autochthonous deities in Vikramśilā Mahāvihāra indicates the process of regional/local formation. Available data at Antichak do not record any donation by women. The social invisibility of women implied the acceptability of an entrenched brahmanical society premised on *varṇa* caste/ideology.

Notes

1. *Indian Archaeology: A Review, 1974–5*, p. 7; *1975–6*, p. 7; *1976–7*, p. 11; *1977–8*, p. 15; *1978–9*, p. 43 and *1979–80*, p. 13; Radha Krishna Choudhary, *The University of Vikramaśilā*, Patna: The Bihar Research Society, 1975; Ram Chandra Prasad, *The Archaeology of Champa and Vikramaśilā*, Delhi, 1987; Sukumar Dutt, *Buddhist Monks and Monasteries of India*, Delhi, 1988, pp. 358–2, 364–9, 374–80; Miranda Shaw, *Passionate Enlightenment*, New Delhi, 1994, p. 21; Giovanni Verardi, *Hardship and Downfall of Buddhism in India*, New Delhi, 2011, p. 365; Himanshu Prabha Ray, *The Return of the Buddha*, New Delhi, 2014, pp. 187–8; K.K. Mandal and Asha Kumari, 'The Destruction of *Vikramaśila Mahāvihāra–Revisit*', in *Studies in History and Archaeology of Vikramaśila Mahāvihāra*, Rajiva Kumar Sinha and Om Prakash Pandey, Varanasi, 2015, pp. 222–7.
2. Barbara Stoler Miller, ed., *The Power of Art Patronage in Indian Culture*, Delhi, 1992, pp. 3–4 (Introduction); Maurice Godelier, *The Enigma of the Gift*, Chicago, 1999, pp. 11–15.
3. *Epigraphia Indica*, XXIII, 47, 11.17–24; J. Takakusu, tr., *A Record of the Buddhist Religion* (I-Tsing's account), Oxford, 1896, p. 65.
4. *Epigraphia Indica*, XVII.17.
5. Ibid.
6. Ram Sharan Sharma, *Indian Feudalism*, New Delhi, 1980, p. 91; Ronald M. Davidson, *Tibetan Renaissance*, Delhi, 2008, p. 29; Rajiva Kumar Sinha, 'The Making of Vikramaśila Mahāvihāra: Material Milieu and Socio-Religious Context (783 CE–1150 CE)', in *The Indian International Journal Buddhist Studies*, no. 10, 2009, p. 138.
7. R.S. Sharma, *Urban Decay*, New Delhi, 1987, p. 162.
8. Sinha and Pandey, *Studies in History*, p. 138.

9. Raman Kumar Singh, *Palakalina Vikramaśila Mahāvihāra*, Delhi, 2005, p. 21.
10. S.R. Goal, *Buddhism in Indian History and Culture*, Jodhpur, 2004, p. 187.
11. Sharma, *Urban Decay*, p. 162.
12. S.N. Sahay, 'The Oriup Excavation', *The Journal of the Bihar Puravid Parishad*, Patna, 1978, p. 15.
13. *Manjusrimulakalpa*, LIII, pp. 680–90; LIII, p. 883; T. Ganapati Sastri, *Aryamanjusrimulakalpa*, Trivandrum, 1920, pp. 631–2.
14. Asha Kumari, *The Making of Early Medieval Bihar (AD 650–1150)*, Unpublished Ph.D. Thesis, T.M. Bhagalpur University, Bhagalpur, 2011, p. 205.
15. B.S. Verma, *Antichak Excavations*, pt. 2 (1971–81), Delhi, 2011, p. 159.
16. *Epigraphia Indica*, 1963–4; B.P. Sinha, *Dynastic History of Magadha*, Delhi, 1977, pp. 228–9.
17. R.S. Sharma and K.M. Shrimali, eds., *Comprehensive History of India*, vol. IV, pt. I, New Delhi, 1992, p. 597.
18. B.P. Sahu, 'Legitimation, Ideology and State in Early India', in *The Changing Gaze*, New Delhi, 2013, pp. 195–6.
19. Asha Kumari, *The Making of Early Medieval India*, p. 206.
20. B.S. Verma, *Antichak Excavations*, p. 160.
21. Ibid., p. 162.
22. Ibid.
23. Ibid.
24. Ibid.
25. Ibid.
26. Ibid.
27. Ibid.
28. Ibid.
29. Ibid., p. 165.
30. Ibid.
31. Ibid.
32. Ibid.
33. Ibid.
34. Ibid.
35. Ibid.
36. Ibid.
37. Ibid., p. 167.
38. Ibid.
39. Ibid.
40. Ibid.
41. Ibid.
42. Ibid.
43. Ibid., p. 169.
44. Ibid., p. 167.
45. Ibid., p. 169.
46. Ibid.
47. Ibid.
48. Ibid.
49. Ibid.
50. Ibid.
51. Ibid.

52. Ibid.
53. Sheldon Pollock, 'The Sanskrit Cosmopolis, 300–1200 CE: Transculturation, Vernacularization, and Question of Ideology', in *Ideology and Status of Sanskrit, Contribution to the History of the Sanskrit Language*, ed. Jan E.M. Houben, Delhi, 2012, pp. 197–48.
54. Maheshwari Singh 'Mahesh', 'Anga and Angika', in *Glories of Bhagalpur*, ed. A.K. Sinha, Bhagalpur, 1984, pp. 1–19; Tej Narain Kushwaha, *Angika Bhasa Ka Itihas*, Hyderabad, 1981.
55. R.R. Diwakar, ed., *Bihar Through the Ages*, Patna, 2000, pp. 349–400.
56. Rahul Sankrityayan, *Ganga Puratattwank*, Sultanganj, 1933, pp. 214–7.
57. Ram Sharan Sharma and K.M. Shrimali, eds., *A Comprehensive History of India*, pt. 1, p. 598.
58. Giovanni Verardi, *Hardships and Downfall of Buddhism in India*, p. 367.
59. Ronald M. Davidson, *Indian Esoteric Buddhism: A Social History of Tantric Movement*, Delhi, 2004, p. 115.
60. E. Hultzsch, 'The Bhagalpur Plate of Narayanapala', in *IA*, 1886, p. 15: pp. 304–10.
61. B.S. Verma, *Antichak Excavations*, p. 171.
62. Ibid.
63. Ibid.
64. Ibid.
65. S. Wadley, 'Power in Hindu Ideology and Practice', in *The New Changing Identities in South Asia*, ed. David Kenneth, The Hague, 1977.
66. Herman Kulke, 'Tribal Deities in Princely Courts', in *Folk Culture*, II, Institute of Oriental and Orissan Studies, pp. 13, 23.
67. B.S. Verma, *Antichak Excavations*, p. 175.
68. Ibid.
69. Ibid.
70. Ibid.
71. L. Susan Huntington, 'The "Pala-Sena" School of Sculpture', *Studies in South Asian Culture*, vol. 10, Leiden, 1984, pp. 203–50; A. Banerjee-Sastri, 'Ninety-three Inscriptions on the Kurkihar Bronzes,' in *Journal of the Bihar and Orissa Research Society*, vol. 26, no. 3, pp. 236–51, 299–308; Om Prakash Srivastava, 'Situating Urban Centres in Early Medieval Northern India', *General Presidential Address*, U.P. History Congress, 22nd Session, Vāranasī, 2011.
72. *Jātaka*, vol. III, no. 359; E.B. Cowell, ed., *Jātaka Stories*, vols. I–VI, Delhi, 1990; Louis de la Valle Poussin and E.J. Thomas, eds., *Mahaniddesa*, vol. I, pp. 154–5; vol. VI, pp. 414–25.
73. *IAR*: *1968–9*, pt. XIII B.
74. Rajiva Kumar Sinha and Om Prakash Pandey, eds., *Manjusha Art*, Varanasi, 2008, p. 40.
75. *Jataka*, vol. IV, p. 506.
76. Nundo Lal Dey, *The Geographical Dictionary of Ancient and Medieval India*, New Delhi, 1984, pp. 44–6.
77. Radha Krishna Choudhary, *The University of Vikramaśila.*
78. Ronald M. Davidson, *Indian Esoteric Buddhism*, p. 144.
79. Ibid., p. 91.
80. R.S. Sharma, 'Material Milieu of Tantrism', in *The Feudal Order*, ed. D.N. Jha, New Delhi, 2002, pp. 451–2.

81. Giovanni Verardi, p. 316; David N. Gellner, *Monk, Householder and Tantric Priests*, New Delhi, 1996, pp. 332–3; Vinlent Eltischinger, *Caste and Buddhist Philosophy: Continuity of Some Buddhist Argument against the Realist Interpretation of Social Denominations*, New Delhi, 2012, pp. 164–6.
82. Ronald M. Davidson, *Indian Esoteric Buddhism*, p. 91.
83. B.C. Law, 'Bhikshunis in Indian Inscriptions', *EI*, vol. 9 (1939–40), pp. 31–4; Anand Singh, *Buddhism at Sārnāth*, New Delhi, 2014, pp. 38–60.
84. Luders' List, *EI*, *X*, New Delhi, repr., 1952.
85. Nancy A. Falk, 'The Case of the Vanishing Nuns: The Fruits of Ambivalence in Ancient Indian Buddhism', in *Unspoken Worlds: Women's Religious Lives in Non-Western Cultures*, ed. Nancy Falk and Rita Gross, San Francisco, 1979, pp. 207–24.
86. Susan L. Huntington, 'The "Pala-Sena" Schools of Sculpture', pp. 203–4.
87. Ibid.
88. Ananta Prasad Banerji-Sastri, 'Ninety-three Inscriptions on the Kurkihar Bronzes', *JBORS*, vol. xxvi, no. 3, 1940, pp. 246–7.
89. Hirananda Sastri, *Nalanda and Its Epigraphic Material Memoirs of the Archaeological Survey of India*, Delhi, 1942, pp. 58–64.
90. Ibid., p. 112.
91. J. Takakusu, tr., *A Record of the Buddhist Religion*, p. 80.
92. Ronald M. Davidson, *Indian Esoteric Buddhism*, p. 97.
93. *Vyaktabhavanugata-tattva-siddhi*, pp. 169–72, 176.

10

The Culture of 'Generosity' and the Ethics of Altruism

PADMASIRI DE SILVA

THE PRACTICE OF giving is universally recognized as one of the most basic human virtues, a quality that testifies to the depth of one's humanity and capacity for self-transcendence. In the teachings of the Buddha, too, the practice of giving claims a place of eminence, one which singles it out as being, in a sense, the foundation and seed of spiritual development. In the Pāli *Suttas*, we read time and again that the 'talk on giving' (*dānakathā*) was invariably the first topic to be discussed by the Buddha in his 'graduated exposition of the Dhamma'.[1] Venerable Bodhi also says that whenever the Buddha delivered a sermon to an audience comprising of people who had not yet regarded him as a teacher, he would start by emphasizing the value of giving. Teachings on moral excellence, the law of *kamma* and the 'renunciation' quest would be offered later. In fact, the act of giving is a miniature self-expression of what goes on to make more demanding acts of self-sacrifice, and at the deepest levels considered as '*dana pārami*' (the perfection of giving) in the *samsāric* quest of a *Bodhisattva*.

One central assumption motivating ethical theory in the analytic tradition is that the function of ethics is to combat the inherent egoism or selfishness of individuals. Indeed, many thinkers define the goal of morality as 'selflessness' or 'altruism'.[2] Moral behaviour is, at the most general level, altruistic behaviour, motivated by the desire to promote not only our own welfare but the welfare of others.[3] In the West, especially due to the writings of Max Weber, there is a tendency, to see in Buddhism, a dichotomy between working for one's own good and that of others: 'Salvation is an absolutely personal performance of the self-reliant individual. No one and no social community can help him'.[4] But the Buddhist *Suttas* take the position, 'that by protecting oneself, one protects others; protecting others, one protects oneself'. Venerable Nyanaponika has developed this point in greater detail.[5] Both the good and the bad are infectious. In fact, Erich Fromm sees 'acquisitiveness' and 'generosity' as two cultural orientations manifested in the 'having mode' and the 'being mode'.

Erich Fromm, in his work *To Have or To Be*? makes an important distinction of character, way of living and culture with these two orientations: the acquisitive personality/the 'having mode' which concentrates on material possessions and power based on greed and aggression; 'being mode' which manifests in the pleasure of shared experience, love, productive and generous, and an expression of a creative and humanistic temperament. *Dāna* is referred to as 'giving' and *cāga* is used in the following way: (1) abandoning, giving up, renunciation; (2) liberality, generosity. While *dāna* is basically related to almsgiving, and offering robes, food, etc., to the monks, the monks in turn give back a noble gift to the lay people through sermons and that is the *dhamma*, which according to the Buddha excels all other gifts.[6] Laymen also may be involved in the production of *dhamma* books or writing books on the *dhamma*, contributions to the erection of a temple and a temple-building fund is also a form of material gift. Donating must also adhere to the rules for the *saṃgha* like offering proper gifts at the proper time. Personal qualities of generosity are associated with an inward disposition, which makes possible still more demanding acts of self-sacrifice. It was also associated with the entire Buddhist path of the eradication of greed.

In fact, the eradication of greed is an important 'function' of giving and generosity. This disposition also helps to weaken the clinging (*upādāna*) to wealth and material objects, and the possessive structure of self-centred behaviour. At the level of moral excellence, the defilements of covetousness and avarice lose their power, and we build up positive emotions of liberality and compassion. At the psychological level, motivational factors develop for leading a balanced and righteous life (*sama cariya, dhamma cariya*). Both the evils of miserliness and wastefulness thin out with this lifestyle. This develops positive character strengths which are a base for the spiritual path. The Buddha also praises the person who earns in the righteous way and gives to the needy.[7] More than the size of the wealth or gift given, real generosity emerges from the heart. Giving security and freedom from fear is also the highest form of *dāna.*[8] Unhealthy forms of giving, like for insulting a person, for fame and publicity, for obtaining favours and in a spirit of competition and envy for others are all counterproductive, and destructive. When some of these are practised with desires in disguise and deception, there is an additional layer of ignorance. Practice of mental culture helps the person to have motives which are transparent to the person practicing the art of generosity. Moral excellence and mental culture provides the base for spiritual upliftment. It is also an additional strength to differentiate between the different varieties of giving. Three important forms of *dāna* are as follows: giving of material things (*āmisadāna*), the giving of fearlessness (*abhayadāna*), and the giving of the *dhamma* (*dhammadāna*).

Today, contexts for 'giving' have widened—not merely in terms of wealth but giving one's time, energy, creative planning, travel, and so on, due to the complexities of our times: tsunami, bushfires, floods, earthquakes, people struck by dire poverty, starvation, and disease. I was deeply struck by a group of kids in Melbourne who came to the platform during a fund-raising musical evening, and handed over their pocket money collected in small 'saving boxes', for the tsunami fund. They learnt for the first time that one can 'get' something by 'giving': not something tangible but a spirit of joy, having done something wonderful. The factors of the donor's motive, spiritual purity of the recipient, and the kind and size of the gift are the normal evaluative factors in a Buddhist setting. But the volition/motive of the donor is the most important and here, it is an innocent, disinterested, and spontaneous disposition that is valued.

The suffering around is so tense that some volunteers, social workers, and compassionate psychologists/therapists succumb to what is described as 'compassion fatigue'.[9] The advice of the Buddha in such a context is that, compassion has to be blended with wisdom, a sense of realism and equanimity—which is the balancing principle across loving kindness, compassion, and altruistic joy. We are living in a time when there are contradictions in contemporary cultures and we need a humanistic culture that could heal the cracks. Universities have courses on ethics, management faculties have integrated ethics into their fold and every serious research project has to satisfy an ethics committee. But in the recent economic crisis, the obvious casualty is ethics and values. These are the contradictions, when we do not have ethics integrally linked to a 'way of life'. This was the Buddha's insight that ethics, its practice, and mindfulness/caring, and wisdom go together.

But there are new signs of promise to revive the humanistic culture of generosity in the West, at a global level. Peter Singer in his recent work *The Life You can Save* raises the question: Most of us are absolutely certain that we wouldn't hesitate to save a drowning child and we would do it at a considerable cost to ourselves. Yet, while thousands of children die each day, we spend money on things that we take for granted, and we would hardy miss them if they were not there. Is that wrong? If so, how far do our obligations to the poor go? Peter Singer's best reason for the benefits that are reaped by the giver is the giving in contexts like the suffering children in Africa and such activities bring meaning and fulfilment to life:

> You may have to make some adjustments to your spending, but quite possibly you will find that some of those adjustments make no difference to your well-being. Instead of having to spend money to keep up appearances because otherwise people will think you can't afford to buy new clothes or a new car, or renovate your home, you now have a good reason for keeping things that you find comfortable and serviceable: you have better use for the money.[10]

Singer concludes that a collective effort to help the world's poorest people would give greater meaning and fulfilment to our lives. Singer was the pioneer in formulating the discipline of *Practical Ethics*, several decades back, but following this new dimension of caring for others, we may agree with Martin Seligman that what we need is not just ethics but the ethics that we 'care for'. When a mother rushes into a burning building to save her child, she is not acting from an ethical principal but because the life of the child is important to her—because she cares about the child. Seligman, after having quoted this example turns to a new perspective on ethics by the Princeton philosopher, Harry Frankfurt—understanding of what we care about is the great unanswered question. This is a dimension I wish to locate in the Buddhist perspective of generosity (*dāna*). Singer hardly examines the Buddhist perspective on 'global compassion'. He says that the 'Golden Rule' (to which we refer below) is found in all the major religious traditions, including Buddhism.[11] But, Buddhism has its own perspective of generosity, altruism, and global compassion. In a dialogue between the Dalai Lama and Paul Ekman, there is an extended discussion of the subject.[12]

The ethics of care is relatively a new tradition in the West which differs from the alternative moral theories of Kantian ethics, utilitarianism, and virtue theory. *The Ethics of Care* presents a new perspective on ethics, relevant to personal relations, as well as political and global concerns. It is a work which does not see a split between, on the one hand, values such as justice, equality, and individual rights, and on the other hand, values such as care, trust, mutual consideration, and solidarity. It is very important, in the light of the concerns of the present essay which extends from a personal, family-based dimension to global dimensions. Ethics of care values emotions such as sympathy, empathy, sensitivity, and responsiveness. Also, this focuses on the relational and interdependent relations as in family relations in Buddhism rather than the self-interested, independent rational agents.[13] The ethics of care is summed up in these celebrated words of the Buddha: 'Even as a mother would risk her own life, to protect her own child, just so one should cultivate a Boundless Heart towards all living beings.' In fact, Seligman looks at the collapse of values in the background to the current financial crisis and observes, 'the downturn was caused by the mathematical wizards and greedy people who profited hugely in the short run by selling derivatives that they knew would crash and burn in the long run'—and Seligman in a lighter vein raises the question—'would courses in ethics help?'[14] It is a paradox that ethics in academia may not bring results, unless people become passionate about moral life. They are all aware of the simple lessons about honesty and integrity which have been drowned by the pathologies of the current culture of economics, and I have suggested a number of diagnostic tools to reveal, diagnose, and explore remedial measures.[15]

Seligman has a way of bringing back 'caring' to ethics in his concept of 'character strengths' and he is also credited with the pioneering project on 'positive emotions'. In this study, instead of focusing on the management of emotions described as 'negative', we shall look at the place of altruistic emotions associated with 'generosity', which would also examine the roots of greed and how we could restore the human dimension of moving out of greed towards the more humanistic dimension of positive emotions. It is said that Seligman explored what he described as character strengths and virtues, and it was an attempt to explore these qualities valued across China, India, Greece, and Rome to the contemporary Western cultures. Working with a number of other psychologists, their focus was six character strengths: wisdom/knowledge, courage, humanity, justice, temperance, and transcendence.

Out of these virtues, not one character strength is more fundamental than the others, but has to be blended with wisdom and our sense of humanity. The background to this development is found in the humanistic psychologists like, Abraham Maslow, Carl Rogers, and Erich Fromm. More recently, positive psychologists have found empirical support for the humanistic psychology of these three psychologists. As the president of the psychological society, Seligman declared that for the last half century, psychology has been consumed with a single topic of mental illness, and urged psychologists to follow the mission of the earlier humanistic psychologists for developing virtues and character strengths in normal life. This perspective falls in line with the Buddha's focus on character-strengths and virtues in normal life. The Buddha also brought ethics and psychology together. The perspective of 'positive psychology' offers a meaningful basis to focus on 'generosity', and in Buddhism, we have the four sublime virtues of *mettā, karuṇā, mudita, upekkhā* (loving kindness, compassion, altruistic joy, and equanimity) which come under Seligman's character strength of 'humanity'. The four sublime states can strengthen the internal forces of the body to fight against grief and inculcate calm. It is known as grief counselling.[16] It also runs through this dimension of 'humanity', and in this article, we are looking at the altruistic emotions associated with generosity and moving out of greed. People do not, in actual life, summon a deductive calculus of moral logic to guide their lives. To reach even the most sublime impersonal truths (as in the 'Buddhist quest), or to act in accordance with the most desirable moral rules (as with Kant and the utilitarians) people struggle with the emotions and desires that obstruct them and generate and cultivate the most ennobling sentiments and attitudes. In the words of Profit, 'the struggle is to live creatively, like producing a work of art'.[17] During recent times, ethics teachers have been using novels and short stories to display the excitement, conflicts, and creativity embedded in our moral lives, and the recent emphasis on ethical realism and moral psychology proves the point. In fact, in the Buddhist quest, there is a three-fold linkage running through the practice of giving/generosity (*dāna*), moral excellence, and mental culture. When one discusses questions about the logic and ethics of generosity in general, such concerns have to be located in the mutual nourishment of three levels.

Giving (*dāna*) can also be identified with the personal quality of generosity (*cāga*). This angle highlights the practice of giving, not as the outwardly manifest act by which an act is transferred from oneself to others, but as the inward disposition to give, a disposition which is strengthened by the outward acts of giving and which in turn, makes it possible, still more demanding the acts of self-sacrifice. Generosity is included in the essential attributes of *sappurisa*, the good of a superior person, along with such qualities as faith, morality, learning, and wisdom. Viewed as the quality of generosity, giving has a particular intimate connection with the entire movement of the Buddhist path. For the goal of the path is the destruction of greed, hate, and delusion, and the cultivation of generosity directly debilitates greed and hate, while facilitating that pliancy of mind that allows for the eradication of delusion.[18]

In terms of the Buddhist path of liberation, out of the three bases for the performance of meritorious deeds (*punnakiriyavatthu*), giving is the first, the other two are moral excellence and mental culture.[19] These qualities may interact. For instance, a person who practices mental culture would have an enhanced perspective on giving. Giving is also regarded as a base that can counteract greed and selfishness. When a person has moral and spiritual strength, it is easy to give.[20] One has to avoid miserliness, as well as carelessness and wastefulness, and contribute to a culture of giving. It is a cultivation of character that blends *dāna* (generosity), *śila* (moral excellence), and *paňňa* (wisdom). Apart from the functions of giving, motivation is the real nexus to discover the humanistic facet of positive emotions. Giving can be very mechanical, in fact it can degenerate, if one throws a coin at a beggar thinking that he is a nuisance. Also if one gives to be known, giving for reputation can have mixed results. In line with our interest in 'patronage' and 'giving', there is a relevant image in the Buddhist sermons: The donor is also described as the one who keeps an open house for the needy (*anavatadvaro*). He is like a wellspring (*openabhuto*) for recluses, brāhmaṇas, the destitute, wayfarers, wanderers, and beggars. Being such a person, he does meritorious deeds. He is munificent (*muttacago*) and is interested in sharing his blessings with others (*danasamvibhagarato*). He is a philanthropist who understands the difficulties of the poor (*vadannu*).

From the point of view of humanistic values linked to the practice of giving (*dāna*), the most relevant criterion for evaluation of these acts should be the factor of volition (*cetanā*), as in Buddhist ethics motive/intention is the criterion for distinguishing good and bad or skilful and unskilful actions: 'Buddhist teaching devotes special attention to the psychological basis of giving, distinguishing among different states of mind with which one may give. A fundamental distinction is made between acts of giving that lacks wisdom and those that are accompanied by wisdom, the latter being superior to the former'.[21]

Acts of giving with the aim of liberation, understanding *kammic* law of cause and effect, along with the awareness that both the giver and recipient are impermanent, are considered as actions rooted in a deep understanding, and having wisdom. An important feature in this process is, by constantly making the right type of giving a disposition, one builds character, and that means the whole person undergoes positive change. I wish to focus on a special type of transformation. As my counselling work has been in the area of emotions, the character building in the context of giving is linked to what Seligman calls 'positive emotions'. I wish to introduce the notion of 'emotionally generous people'. It is said that such people continuously bring happiness, love, and positivity to others. This is what I call the 'giving character' as opposed to the hoarding, and possessing things. In fact, this giving is more than an action but a way of being beautifully exemplified in Fromm's work *To Have or To Be*. According to Fromm, in the present period of crisis, there are two ways of being: there is the 'having mode', concentrated on material possessions and power, and based on greed, envy, aggressiveness, and a second alternative, with the pleasure of shared experience, rooted in love. The having mode has generated a crisis around the world today, and it is the mode of gambling and risk-taking which has thrown people and countries on the verge of bankruptcy.

Thomas Nagel says, 'altruism is any behaviour motivated merely by the belief that someone else will benefit or avoid harm by it'.[22] In fact, one sense of altruism in popular usage is giving more weight to the preferences of others than our own.[23] A second sense of altruism is as follows: Giving equal weight to the well-being of all sentient beings, including oneself as counting for one. It has been observed that altruism in this second sense is found in a good deal of utilitarian philosophy, and that a similar strain is found in Buddhism. Singer, in his book *The Life You Can Save* also gives other strands of altruism. One is the 'Golden Rule': Do unto others as you would have them done to you, which implies to count the desires of others as if they were our own. Singer observes that though this axiom is well known from the words of Jesus, it is found in Buddhism, Hinduism, Confucianism, Islam, Jainism, and Judaism. He also cites Bill Gates' philosophy of giving—doing the most good in the world as a whole.

For a Buddhist lay person entrenched in routine life, there is an interesting tension between the concept of universal benevolence and the feeling for the suffering and the good that they are obliged to do for the family, close friends, those in their village, monks, and recluses, and even animals, their pets. If one goes through the *Sigālovāda Sutta*, one sees the network of relations pointing out that have special obligations to the elders, the aging and so on. In giving advice to the kings, the Buddha presented a broader group of improving the living conditions of people. It is necessary to bring a sense of realism in any attempt to resolve these points of tension. 'It is important that we be clearly aware of the difference between "particular kinds of affection" and the "most extensive benevolence", which later is an expression of altruism.' The utilitarian philosophy had remained as Singer's ethics for a long time. From my own perspective, it is necessary to integrate the personal and impersonal viewpoints. On this possible integration, there are different responses. Kupperman says that the utilitarian variety of 'impersonal altruism' sounds too hydraulic, treating concern as if it were a quantifiable and divisible liquid.[24] Yet, in its historical role as a political philosophy, it was limited to a particular country and had no global appeal. The difficulty is to achieve some kind of integrity in human life, without either overwhelming its personal core with a pervasive impersonality or bulldozing the impersonal standpoint in the name of what one must personally do. The discovery of an alternative that we can live by, I take to be the task of ethical theory.[25]

Lafollette, in the *Companion to Ethics*,[26] in an article on 'Personal Relationships' says that such an ethic of personal relations can empower an impersonal ethic. His position is that we can neither develop moral knowledge nor the empathy necessary for an impartial morality, unless we experience intimate relationships. There is, in fact, an important difference between the 'impersonality ethic' in Buddhism and utilitarianism:

1. An ethical theory which requires the dissociating of preferences and desires from individuals, and the agglomeration of them (utilitarianism).
2. An ethical theory which recommends to individuals the restructuring of their motivational economies with the aim of transcending personal craving and desires (Buddhism).

Expanding on this distinction, Flanagan says that truly living, according to the tenets of Buddhism or any other very impartial, impersonal (in the second sense) or detached form, requires an extremely complex and disciplined kind of character, possibly richer and more complex than required to live as a liberal individualist.[27] What Flanagan emphasizes is that being a person, an agent having a point of view is a necessary pre-condition to move towards the ultimate goal of *nibbāna*.[28] It must be mentioned that even the perfected *arahant* has an enriching repertoire of positive emotions of empathy, compassion, and altruism in turning the minds of people towards a way out of suffering. He does not reap any good *kamma*, as there is no need for it. But in the lives dominated by altruism in the world today, there are many icons with a diversity of styles.

Notes

1. Bodhi Bhikkhu, *Dana: The Practice of Giving*, Kandy: BPS, 1995, p. 1.
2. W. Schroeder, 'Continental Ethics', in *Blackwell Guide to Ethical Theory*, ed. La Follette, Oxford: Blackwell, 2000, p. 396.
3. J. Rachels, 'Naturalism', in *Blackwell Guide to Ethical Theory*, ed. La Follette, Oxford: Blackwell, 2000, p. 81.
4. Max Weber, *The Religion of India*, Glencoe: Free Press, 1958, p. 213.

5. Padmasiri de Silva, *Buddhism, Ethics and Society*, Clayton: Monash Asia Institute, 2000, pp. 25–6.
6. *Dhammapada*, V.354.
7. *Suttanipāta*, V.87.
8. Lily de Silva. 'Giving in the Pāli Canon', in *The Practice of Giving*, ed. Bodhi Bhikkhum, 1995, p. 11–24.
9. Elsa Gringold, 'Compassion Fatigue and How to Avoid It', in *The Power of Compassion*, ed. Marion Kostanski, Melbourne: Victoria University, 2005, pp. 43–7.
10. Peter Singer, *The Life You Can Serve*, Melbourne: Text Publishing, 2009, p. 184.
11. Ibid., p. 16.
12. Paul Ekman, ed., *A Conversation Between The Dalai Lama and Paul Ekman: Emotional Awareness*, New York: Henry Holt and Company, 2008, pp. 185–225.
13. Verginia Held, *The Ethics of Care, Personal, Political and Global*, Oxford: Oxford University Press, 2012, pp. 44–6.
14. Martin Seligman, *Florourish*, North Sydney: William Heinman, 2012, p. 229.
15. Padmasiri de Silva, 'The Pathological Facets of the Culture of Economics: Does Ethics offer a Path to Recovery and Strategies for Social Welfare', in *East-West Philosophy Conference*, Honolulu, 2011.
16. Padmasiri de Silva, *Introduction to Mindfulness-based Counselling: The Magic of the Ordinary & the Elegance of Small Things*, Colombo: Sarvodaya Vishva Lekha, 2008, pp. 22–4.
17. Padmasiri de Silva, *Environmental Philosophy & Ethics in Buddhism*, London: St. Matins Press, 1998, p. 89.
18. Bhikkhu Bodhi, *Dāna: The Practice*, pp. 1–2.
19. *Aṅguttara Nikāya*, IV.241.
20. *Majjhima Nikāya*, I.449.
21. Bhikkhu Bodhi, *Dāna: The Practice*, p. 4.
22. Thomas Nagel, *The Possibility of Altruism*, Oxford: Clarendon, 1970, p. 16.
23. William Hare, 'The Attack on Open-mindedness', *Oxford Review of Education*, vol. VII, no. 2, pp. 119–29.
24. Joel Kupperman, 'The Emotions of Altruism, East and West', in *Emotions in Asian Thought*, ed. Marks Joel and Ames Roger, Albany: Suny Press, 1995, p. 125.
25. Thomas Nagel, *Other Minds*, New York: Oxford University Press, 1995, p. 171.
26. Peter Singer, *Rethinking Life and Death: The Collapse of Our Traditional Ethics*, New York: St. Martin's Press, 1994, p. 191.
27. O.J. Flanagan, *Varieties of Moral Personality: Ethics and Psychological Realism*, Cambridge: Harvard University Press, 1991, p. 78.
28. Ibid., pp. 78–9.

11

Dāna-Deya Dharma

Donation in the Buddhist Records of the North-West (*c.* Second Century BCE–Third Century CE)

SARITA KHETTRY

THE CONCEPT OF *dāna* was pre-Buddhist in date. It has been defined and interpreted differently in brahmanical and non-brahmanical religions. Dāna, or gifts normally involve exchange of items that are imbued with 'value' in society. It has been suggested that the exchange of gifts served a magical-cum-religious function in early Indian society.[1] The gift exchange also operated as a major mode of circulation of wealth, and as a process of legitimizing or reinforcing social and moral ties between individuals and/or groups of people. The mode and magnitude of gift-exchange, however, never remained static in any society nor did its function remain the same always. The mode, magnitude and function of the gift undewent changes corresponding to the changes in the social and economic patterns of the society. Some of the *Smṛti* literature refers to six elements of *dāna*, and these include the *dātā* (donor), the *pratigrahītā* (recipient), *śraddha*, the appropriateness of the gift, and the place and time, for making the gift.[2]

In Buddhism, much emphasis is given to the concept of *dāna*. The emergence of Buddhism in the sixth century BCE produced a large number of renouncers and wandering monks who lived exclusively on alms. Such alms (*bhikśā*) are described as *dāna* in the early Pāli and later Sanskrit Buddhist texts. Reference to terms such as *dānapati* (munificent giver of alms), *dānavato bhikkhu, dānagga* (a house where alms or donations are given), *dānādhikar* (supervision in charge of alms distribution), *dānavatthu* (object for a gift), *dānaraho* (worthy of a gift), *dānupatti* (rebirth of an alms-giver according to his wish) are found in the Pāli literature. *Dāna* is even classified as *dhammadāna* (gift of spiritual blessings) and *āmisadāna* (gift of temporal blessings).[3] *Dāna* in the Buddhist context, thus, seems to comprehend the elements of compassion and charity. It was understood more in the sense of alms and charity rather than ritual gift.

In the Pāli Buddhist canon we come across the concept of *dāna pāramita* which is variously explained as *bahur bhānda pariccāgo* (sacrifice of external goods and property), *aṅga pariccāgo* (sacrifice of limbs), and even *jīvita pariccāgo* (sacrifice of life).[4] It clearly emphasizes the element of sacrifice entailed in *dāna*. It is also significant to note that during the time of the Buddha, donation of *ārāmas* (early settlements for the monks) were given by the wealthy laymen in or near a town looked after by the donor himself[5] as found in the Buddhist texts. One such *ārāma* was Veluvana at Rājagaha. It is said to be the first gift of a *ārāma* to the Buddha by King Bimbisāra. Reference to a large number of *ārāmas* like (i) Jīvakārāma at Rājagaha, (ii) Ambapālivana at Vaiśalī, (iii) Udambari-kārāma near Rājagaha, (iv) Kukkutārāma, Ghositārāma and Pāvārikāmbavana at Kauśambī, (v) Jetavanārāma near Srāvastī, (vi) Badarikārāma at some distance from Ghositārāma, and (vii) Nigrodhārāma at Kapilvastu are found in the Buddhist texts.

The earliest epigraphic reference to *dāna* is found in the Aśokan inscriptions, dated in the third century BCE and are mainly written in Prakrit language and Brāhmī script. In this connection, the 4th Pillar Edict (Delhi-Topra version) of Aśoka (*c*.273–72–236 BCE) is worth mentioning: '*dānan dāhanti pālatikan upavāsan va kachanti*', 'they will bestow gifts or will undergo fasts in order to (attain happiness) in other (world)'.[6] In the Ninth Major Rock Edict (Mansehra version), *dāna* or gifts are said to have been made to the *samanas* and brāhmaṇas. This was a part of *dharma-magala* (*dharma-mangala*).[7] The gift of mango-orchard, or a garden (or a grove), or an alms-house, or anything else is recorded to have been given by Kāruvākī, the second queen of Aśoka and the mother of Tīvara (*yat atra dvitīyāyām devyām dānan-āmravātīkā vā aramam vā dānagrhan vā, yat vā api anyat kincit ganayate*) in the Queen's (Allahabad) Pillar Edict.[8] Aśoka is said to have been given the gift of cave to non-Buddhist sects like Ājīvikas in the Barabar hill in Gayā district of Bihar.[9] The expression for this gift is not the substantive *dāna* but the participle *dinā* (Skt. dattā). A close look at the Aśokan inscriptions suggests that the concept of *dāna* was restricted to the sense of charity, as in early Buddhist texts.

A large number of inscriptions written in Kharoṣṭhī script and Gandhārī Prākrit were discovered from different areas of north-western part of the Indian subcontinent. These inscriptions were mainly Buddhist (belonging to *c*. second century BC to third century CE) and donative in nature. The present essay aims at highlighting the nature of the concept of *dāna* in the Kharoṣṭhī inscriptions of the north-western part of the Indian subcontinent. The area concerned includes the territories, now politically in Pakistan (Pak-Punjab, North-West Frontier Province, Sind, and Baluchistan), Jammu & Kashmir (partly occupied by Pakistan), Punjab and parts of Haryana and Himachal Pradesh, and also eastern Afghanistan. Buddhism reached the area of our study by the third century BCE or at least during the reign of the Mauryan King Aśoka, as suggested by the epigraphic and literary sources.[10] Since then, it was the predominant religion till about the fifth century CE. Thereafter, it was still a major living force till the middle of the seventh century CE. The region was under the political control of Bactrian Greeks/Indo Greeks, Scythians, Parthians, and the Kushāṇas during the period concerned. It was not always unified politically, though culturally it was very much a part of India.

The Indo-Greek rulers (*c.* second century BCE to the first century BCE) who were sympathizers of Buddhism did not make any endowment in the favour of Buddhism. Some of the vassal rulers and rich devotees during the reign of Menander (I or II) made donations in the favour of religion. Two groups of Kharosṭhī inscriptions[11] on a damaged soapstone casket, discovered at Sinkot in Bajaur (situated along the western border of Pakistan's North-West Frontier Province, to the west of swat), records that the casket was consecrated twice. The original consecration was performed by Vijakamitra during the reign of Minedra (Menander I or II). He installed the (supposed) relics of Śākyamunī in a *stūpa*. Later, the container was broken and the relic no longer remained an object of worship. The casket was then reconstructed by Vijayamitra. Both Vijakamitra and Vijayamitra were called themselves as *apraca-rājās*. The epigraphic and numismatic data suggests that *apraca-rājās* were the rulers of Bajaur region in the first century BCE and the second century CE. Probably one of their predecessors (Vijakamitra) served under the Indo-Greek ruler, Menander I or II.

The Takshaśilā inscription[12] of the year 78, during the reign of Moga (identified with Scytho-Parthian King Maues) perpetuates the enshrinement of the relics of Lord Śākyamunī and the establishment of a Saṁghārama in a section of town of Takshaśilā (called Kshema) by Patika, who was the son of Liäka-Kusulaka, the Kshaharāta and *kshatrapa* of Chukhsa (identified with Sind-Sagar doab) for the worship of all the Buddhas, worshipping his mother and father, for the increase of the life and power of the *kshatrapa*, together with his son and wife, worshipping all his brothers and his blood-relations and kinsmen. The interesting point is that the inscription describes Patika as Mahadānapati (the great gift lord). It is a private donation of Patika, the Kshatrapa of Chukhsa who served under the Scytho-Parthian king, Maues.

An interesting epigraphic record comes from Bīmarān, a small village six to seven miles west-north-west of Jalalabad. The inscription (in Kharosṭhī script) inscribed on a steatite vase was found inside a relic chamber. The inscription states that it was the gift of Śivarakshita, the son of Mūjavaṅda presented for the relics of the Lord, in honour of all the Buddhas (*Śivarakshita, Muṅjavadaputrasa danamukhe niyadide Bhagravabudhatra śarirehi sarvabudhana*).[13] The identity of Śivarakshita is unknown. We know a person of the same name from the Shahdaur inscription. The name Śivarakshita is also found on a seal from Takshaśila. The coins which were found in the *stūpa*, belonged to the Azes family with the legend *mahajasa dhramikasa rajatirajasa Ayasa*. On the basis of this numismatic evidence, it is usually implied that the vase was deposited in the days of Azes I or II. However, there is a controversy regarding the exact date of the vase.[14]

A number of feudatory chiefs made a number of endowments in the favour of Buddhism in the Scytho-Parthian age (first quarter of the first century BCE to the middle of the first century CE). A Kharosthī inscription is found on the casket of soapstone, whose exact provenance is not recorded. It might have been found in northern Pakistan. The inscription records that in the year 77 of the great King Aya, the relics of Lord Śākyamunī were established by Mātrava, the army commander who was the son of Subhutika and the nephew of the king of Avaca in an area where such relics had not been established before, in the village called Atha, or at a village consisting of eight concentrations of settlements 'in the acceptance of the Kaśaviya (Kāśyapīya) teachers'.[15] It is clear from the inscription that the donor of the casket was undoubtedly Mātrava, identifiable with Vijayamitra.[16] Another inscription is a Buddhist dedication of a relic casket containing bodily relics of the Buddha in Kharoṣṭhī script of the Scythian period (*c.* first century BCE to the first century CE).

It perpetuates the installation (*pradithaveti*) of the supposed body relics of the Buddha, a previously unestablished place by Itravarman (Indravarman) in the year 25 as well as in the year 63 of a dead or past king called Aya (Azes). He creates divine merit (*brammapujo*) for himself and for his relatives.[17] The donor of the casket was Indravarman, the son of Vishṅuvarman, the *apraca-rājās* who was the younger brother of Vijayamitra, who served as the stratega under an unspecified emperor, either Azilises or more likely Azes II in 5 CE.

It is interesting to note here that only in one inscription of the Scytho-Parthian period, we find the word *dānamukhe* having the meaning of donation or gift. The Mahadānapati (the great gift-lord) occurs in one of the inscriptions of the period concerned. However, most of the inscriptions of this period had the term *pradithaveti* (established) instead of *dāna* or *dānam*.

The Kushāṇa period (*c.* second half of the first century BCE to *c.* third century CE) is one of the most important phases of history of the Indian subcontinent. Like their predecessors, some of the Kushāṇa rulers were patrons of Buddhism. A large number of Buddhist donations were found in various places in the Kushāṇa Empire. The earliest reference to the word *deya-dharma* in the sense of meritorious gift is found in the Shāh-jī-kī-dherī casket of Kanishka I. It is a royal donation made by the Kushāṇa King Kanishka in acceptance of the Sarvāstivādin teachers. The inscription on the casket records that this perfume box is the meritorious gift of Mahārāja Kanishka in Kanishkapura, for the welfare and happiness of all beings. [. . .] sa . . . the superintendent of construction of the refectory in Kanishka's Vihāra, in

Mahāsena's saṅghṅrāma (*Acaryena sarvasti-vadina pratigrahe . . . jasa Kani Kanishka-pure nagare ayaṅ gaṅdha-karanne deya-dharma/sarva-satvana hita-suhartha bhavatu/ . . . sa agiśala ṅavakarmia nashkasa vihare Mahasenasa saṅgharame.*)[18]

A Kharosṭhī inscription, belonging to the eleventh year of the reign of Kanishka I, was discovered from Zeda, a village near Unn. The inscription records that a well was dug during the reign of Mahārāja Kanishka and a gift of water-giver by Hipeä Dhiä was found, for the increase of the Sarvāstivāda, in honour of the Kshatrapa Liäka, for the benefit of his mother (*khade kue muronasa marjhakasa Kanishkasa rajami toyanda cha bhui danamukha Hipeadhisa sarvastivadativadhase pujane Liakasa kshatrapasa upakachaa madu kata dana anugrahena vudhasa Saghamitrarajasa*).[19] The interesting point is that this gift (*dāna*) is made at the request of the elder Saṅgharāja. As the name indicates the donor of water giver was Greek in origin. The term *dānamukha* and *dāna* both occurs in this inscription.

Another Kharosṭhī inscription which is worth mentioning here is the Manikiala inscription of the year 18. Manikiala is a village in the Rawalpindi district of Pakistan. The above mentioned Kharosṭhī inscription is found in one of the cells of a *stūpa* discovered at Manikiala. The epigraph records the general Lala as the donation master in his own *vihāra* who establishes the supposed relics of the Buddha during the reign of Kanishka I (. . . *Gushanavaśasanvardhaka Lala danaṅayago Veśpaśisa kshatrapasa horamurtosa tasa apanage vihare horamurto etra nama bhagava Buddhajhava pratistavayati . . . navakarmigena*).[20] The inscription referred to a word *horamurta*, which has been explained by Professor Luder as a Scythian word with the same meaning as Sanskrit *dānapati* (the gift-lord). A bronze casket was discovered from the same site, which contains a Kharosṭhī inscription. It states that the casket was the gift of the Kapiśa Kshatrapa, the son of the Kshatrapa Granavhryaka (*kaviśia kshatrapasa G(r)anavhryaka Kshatrapa putrasa danamukha*).[21]

During the Kushāṇa period, we come across a large number of donative inscriptions on the images of the Buddha and *Bodhisattva* in the north-western part of the Indian subcontinent. These inscribed images contain the word such as '*dānamukhe*', '*dānam*' (gift of), *deyadharma-parityagena*, etc. A class of donors who were ranked as mendicant monks (*bhikkhus*) and nuns (*bhikkhunis*) in the Buddhist community or *saṃgha* are associated with the above mentioned terms. In this connection, we can refer to the eighteen Kharosṭhī inscriptions, edited by Sten Konow that record images of the gifts and in which the names of the donors are preserved. Of this eighteen, more than two-thirds (or thirteen) record the gifts of the monks.[22] Excavation conducted at Lorian Tangai yielded a number of the Buddha and *Bodhisattva* figures. Of these, four inscribed images are mentioned by Konow. He assigned the *stūpa* to the second century CE.[23] All the images were the gift of the monks. We can refer to the eight inscribed images of the Buddha from Jaulian monastery. According to Sir John Marshall the images with which the inscriptions are associated, and the inscriptions themselves may be assigned to the second half of the fifth century CE but they are a part of the redecoration of much older *stūpas*.[24] Mention should also be made of one inscribed image of the *Bodhisattva* from Shahr-i-Napursan (situated between Rajar and Utmanzai) in which the term 'śramaṇa' is used before the name of the donor, one inscribed image from Yakubi (in Peshawar in Pakistan) which represents the 'miracle of Srāvastī' and the donor is the monk.[25] Again, of the nine dated Gandhāran sculptures[26] (in which the Shāh-jī-kī-dherī Casket is included), three were the gifts of the monks. In this connection, mention should be made of a Brussels Buddha of the year 5, published by J.C. Harle.[27] It belonged to a Brussels art dealer, M. de Marteau. Its provenance is not known, but according to Harle, it is reported to have come from near Peshawar. The panel displays a seated figure of the Buddha (Amitabha?) who is flanked by an image of Maitreya (or Mahāsthānaprāpta) on his right and that of Avalokiteśvara on his left. Representations of Indra and Brahmā can be noticed in the background. If the year 5 is correctly referred to the era of 78 CE, the panel belongs to 83 CE or 82–3.[28]

The Kharoṣṭhī inscription on the pedestal has been translated as follows: In the year 5, on the fifth day of the month of Phalguna; the pious gift of Budhanada learned in the three Pitakas: may it be for the honouring of his deceased(?) father and mother (*Sa(m) 4 1 phagunasa masasa di pamcamī Budhanadasa trepitakasa dānamukhe madapidarana adhvadidāna puyaya bhavatu*).[29] The interesting point is that the monk who is the donor is well-versed in the three *Pitakas*. The second dated inscription where the donor (probably a Buddhist teacher Śramaṇa Dharmapriya by name) is a monk, is found on the pedestal of the image of the Buddha. This image of the Buddha hails from Mamane-dherī[30] (a small ancient mound in Charsada, Peshawar in Pakistan).The Mamane-dherī Stele is now in the Peshawar Museum. The inscription has been read as follows: Anno 89, in the month of Mārgaśirsa, the fifth day, at this term was bestowed this religious gift by the Śramaṇa Dharmapriya, in honour of . . . his teacher Buddhapriya, for the bestowal of health on his fellow disciples (Sam 20 20 20 20 4 4 1 *Mā(rgaśi) ras(ra) masi 4 1 iśe kshunami niryaide ime deyadhar(me) Dharmapriena shamanena . . . (puyae) upajayasa Budhapriasa puyae samanuyayana arogadakshin*).[31] The third dated inscription appears on a standing image of the Buddha, recovered from the ruined *stūpa* of Lorian Tangai and now preserved in the Indian Museum. The inscription contains the following two lines: Anno 318, the 27th day of Praushthapada, gift of Buddhaghosa, the companion of Samghavarma (Sa 111 100 10 44 *Prothavadasa di* 20 4 111 *Buddhaghosa dānamukhe Saghorumasa sadavigarasa*).[32] Here also, we find the donor of the image is a monk. In three other dated inscriptions, the status of the donor is unclear and in two of them the donor is a layperson and in the Shāh-jī-kī-dherī casket, as mentioned above, the donor is a royal personage. It is worth mentioning here that even if in all three of the dated inscriptions in which the donor's status is unclear, the donor is assumed to be a lay person, this would still mean that almost 60 per cent of the inscribed images from the north-west now known were given by the monks. It is also interesting to note that of the eight dated Gandhāran pieces, two earliest dated images were the gifts of the monks.

It is worth noting here that women fell into two divisions in Buddhism: those who remained in the world as lay votaries of the religion (*upāsikā*) and those who renounced the world and became *bhikkhunis*. The name of the nuns (*bhikkhunis*) did not appear as donors in the area of our study. The exact reason is yet to be known. It may be that the north-western part of the Indian subcontinent has always been open to foreign influence and occupation and this influence and occupation may have determined a different attitude towards the participation of women in monastic lives. The reference to the first category of women (*upāsikā*) is found in the Pāli text as giving alms to *bhikkhus*. In the *Udāna Suppavāsa*, the daughter of the Koliyan king is said to have 'invited the order of the monks headed by the Buddha to seven days food'.[33] Likewise, according to the *Therigāthā*, Sela performed a grand feast of offering and worship to the Buddha.[34] Examples can be multiplied in this connection. Whether royal women of Kushāṇa society took part in any kind of donation is not known to us. The account of Bardesanes gives us the true picture of Kushāṇa women which is as follows: 'Among the Bactrians, who are called Kushāṇas, the women adorn themselves with goodly garments of men, and with many ornaments of gold and pearls, and their male and female servants minister to them more than to their husbands; and they ride horses caparisoned with gold and precious stones. And these women do not observe chastity but have connection with their slaves and with strangers who may have come to their country, and their husbands do not blame them, and they have no fear, for the Kushāṇas regard their wives as mistresses.[35] However, a number of Kharosthī inscriptions of the Kushāṇa period mention the names of women who were associated with the Buddhist donation (*dāna*). A Kharoṣṭhī inscription[36] of *c.* first to second century CE on the halo of an icon of the Buddha records its installation by the wife Moma (*momadarae*), the wife Balasoma (*Balasomabhayae*) together with the wife Anakara (*san Anakara–bhayae*) at the Dharmarājikā Vihāra, founded by Aśoka. This monastery can be easily identified with the Dharmarājikā monastery of Takshaśilā, mentioned in a few inscriptions from Takshaśilā.[37] Its ruins have been found in this locality. Konow refers to another Kharoṣṭhī inscription on the pedestal of a sculpture from Jamālgarhi which records that the sculpture was the gift of the mother (or Ambā), together with the wife of Vāsishnha, in honour of all beings and for the benefit of health of the master (*anbae sa Vasenhabhariae danamukhe sarvasatvana puyae sāmiasa cha arogadakshiniae*).[38] From the ruins of Takshaśilā, the ancient city of Sirkap, a circular stone box was discovered. Inside the stone box is found a small hollow crystal figure of a *haṁsa* or goose, containing a thin gold plate inscribed with Kharoṣṭhī characters. The inscription perpetuates the gift of Śira, depositing a relic of the Lord in the *haṁsa* of her mother, the *haṁsa* of her father. Might it become its place when a corporeal birth comes (*śirae bhagavato dhatu matu hasisa pitu hasase Loo tasa siati yo ha dehajati*).[39] It is clear from the inscription that Śira was a rich lady, for only few women could afford a gold plate for affixing the inscription and an artistic crystal figure to accommodate it. Probably, she also financed the making of the relic-box and the *stūpa* to house it. Her pious deed was based on the belief in its efficacy to secure Buddhahood for her departed parents. The names of several laypersons were also associated with donation of images and other objects as evidenced by Pālānūdherī Jars inscriptions and Ghazdherī Pedestal inscription.[40] At least one of the inscriptions refers to a Brāhmaṇa Vāsudeva as the donor of the well as a meritorious gift (*maharajasa masasa di . . . iśe kshunanmi khanavide kuve Vasudevena Indraputrena brahmanena Obharavastavena Danasya avaptir astu*).[41]

A thorough analysis of the above data leads to several observations. The Kharoṣṭhī inscriptions, which are the main source of our study give us the true picture of the concept of *dāna* in the cosmopolitan society of the north-western part of the Indian subcontinent. Compared to other inscriptions of the period concerned, of other regions, the objects of benefactions in north-western India include a wide variety. Digging of wells, dedication of tanks and wells constitute objects of donation in a number of records. Among others, reference to *ārāma* or grove, *parivāra* or enclosure, and *yasti* or staff are also available. Yet other category of gifts include objects such as lamps, ladles, jars, silver vases, plates, caskets, etc. Finally, the dedication of icons and sculptures, and also of relics and religious structures, constitute a separate category of objects. The aims and objects of the donation are also present in the north-western inscription. The donations are mainly given to acquire religious merit. Sometimes, donation is made for the purpose of *pūjā* (worship). The *pūjā* may be directed towards all the Buddhas, the Pratyeka Buddhas, and Arhats. This is well attested by a number of Kharoṣṭhī inscriptions, like Takshaśilā Copperplate inscription of Patika of the year 78, Bīmarān Vase inscription, a casket inscription of the time of Vijayamitra, the ruler of Avaca, etc. All these inscriptions record that these divinities were worshipped at the time of giving donation by the donor. As evident from Kharoṣṭhī inscriptions belonging to the Scytho-Parthian period, donation is made in honour of venerable persons like parents (Takshaśilā Copperplate inscription of Patika of the year 78, Takht-i-Bāhī inscription of the year 103), brothers, relatives, and friends (Shahdaur inscription of Damijada). The Kharoṣṭhī inscriptions also record the offering of gift by the donor for the increase of life and strength (Jamālgarhi Pedestal inscription). Much more interesting are the Kharosṭhī inscriptions which indicate that ordinary people could attain *nirvāna* as a result of performing meritorious acts. In this connection, we may refer to the Kālawān inscription of the year 134 (of the Azes era) or 76–7 CE. Here a meritorious act in favour of the Sarvāstivādin teachers was considered to be of help for a lady donor to attain *nirvāna*.[42] Here, the evidence of Takshaśilā Silver Scroll inscription of the year 136, discovered in one of the chambers to the west of Dharmarājika *stūpa*, may also be cited. The date of the inscription corresponds to 78–9 CE. It records the enshrinement of the relics of the Buddha by Urasaka, a Bactrian resident, in the chapel of the Dharmarājika *stūpa* at Takshaśilā. It is stated in the inscription that this act of munificence would help the donor in the attainment of *nibbāna*.[43] The second Kharosthī inscription is found in one of the *stūpas* of Hadda (it is situated about five miles to the south of Jalalabad). The epigraph records the deposition of relics by one Sanghamitra in a *stūpa*. Here, gift is considered as an equipment for the attainment of *nibbāna* for all beings.[44] Thus, the Kharosthī inscriptions of the area concerned, highlights the objects of the donation, the name of the donor, the recipient of the gift and time, and space of the donation. Probably, *dāna* was an integral part of the society from *c.* second century BCE to third century CE.

In the early Christian centuries, the north-western part of the Indian subcontinent saw the rise of Mahāyānic traits. According to this system, the *Bodhisattva* ideal was open to all regardless of whether one was a monk or not and, importantly, regardless of whether one was a layman or laywoman. In place of the great emphasis on *śila* (i.e. moral discipline and restraint) advocated by early Buddhism, the Mahāyāna gave primacy to *dāna*. Indeed, *dāna* was ranked first in the list of the Mahāyāna's 'six perfections' (or *pāramitas*) of practice. Hence, *dāna* or giving is considered as the cardinal principal of Mahāyāna Buddhism. If one did not want to practice the monastic life, one could still practice Buddhism, gain merit through giving, and mount the successive stages of the *Bodhisattva* to finally reach enlightenment. The laity on their part in order to get the fruit of *dāna* started making material offerings to the *saṃgha*. With the advent of Mahāyāna, the *Vinaya* rules were relaxed pertaining to the acceptance of more opulent variety of alms by the monks.[45] During this period a necessity was felt for the laity's support, not only for daily simple alms but for funds for construction of more permanent and ever-larger monastic complexes.

Notes

1. Ganpathy Subbiah, *Roots of Tamil Religious Thought*, Pondicherry: Pondicherry Institute of Linguistic and Culture, 1991, p. 134.
2. Romila Thapar, *Ancient Indian Social History: Some Interpretations*, New Delhi: Orient Longman, 2006, p. 94.

3. Vijay Nath, *Dāna: Gift System in Ancient India: A Socio-Economic Perspective*, Delhi, 1987, p. 17.
4. Ibid., p. 18.
5. Sukumar Dutt, *Buddhist Monks and Monasteries of India*, Delhi: Motilal Banarsidass, 1988, p. 58.
6. E. Hultzsch, 'Inscriptions of Aśoka', in *Corpus Inscriptionum Indicarum*, vol. I, Calcutta, 1925, pp. 123, 125.
7. D.C. Sircar, *Select Inscriptions Bearing on Indian History and Civilization*, vol. I, repr., Calcutta, 1965, p. 28.
8. Ibid., p. 69.
9. Ibid., pp. 76, 111.
10. R.G. Basak, ed., *Aśokan Inscriptions*, Calcutta: Progressive Publishers, 1959, pp. 71–2; *Divyāvadāna*, pp. 433–4.
11. N.G. Majumdar, 'The Bajaur Casket of the Reign of Menander, EI', 1937–8, vol. XXIV, pp. 7ff.
12. Sten Konow, *Corpus Inscriptionum Indicarum*, vol. II, pt. I–Kharoshthi Inscriptions with the Exception of Those of Aśoka, Calcutta, 1929.
13. Konow, *Corpus*, pp. 50ff; E. Errington, J.Criib and M. Claringbull, *The Cross Roads of Asia, Transformation in Image and Symbol in the Art of Ancient Afghanistan and Pakistan*, Cambridge: Cambridge University Press, 1992, pp. 189–92.
14. From the point of view of Palaeography, the Bīmarān Vase is contemporaneous with the Mathurā Lion Capital, the date of which is given towards the end of the first century BCE or early first century CE.
15. B.N. Mukherjee, 'A Casket inscription of the time of Vijayamitra, the ruler of Avaca', Calcutta: Indian Museum Bulletin, 1986, pp. 9ff.
16. According to our record, Vijayamitra was the ruler of Avaca in the year 77 of the era of Aya, identifiable with Azes I. The reckoning began in *c.*58 BC. So Vijayamitra was a ruler in *c.* 19–20 CE, during whose reign the enshrinement of the relic of the Master took place.
17. R. Salomon, 'The "Avaca" Inscription and the Origin of the Vikrama Era', *Journal of the American Oriental Society*, American Oriental Society, vol. 102, no. I, 1982, pp. 59–8.
18. B.N. Mukherjee, 'The Shāh-jī-kī-dherī Casket Inscription', *British Museum Quarterly*, vol. XXVIII, London, 1964, pp. 38–6.
19. Konow, *Corpus*, pp. 142–5.
20. Ibid., pp. 145–50.
21. Ibid., pp. 150–1.
22. Ibid., nos. XXXVI, 1, 2, 4, 5, 6, 7, 8; XL, XLII, XLIII, XLIV, LVIII, LXXXVIII.
23. Ibid., p. 106.
24. Ibid., pp. 92–6.
25. Ibid., no. LVIII, pp. 123–4; no. LXVI, p. 131.
26. Gandhāra Sculpture in the Government Museum and Art Gallery, Chandigarh, 2002, pp. 9–11.
27. J.C. Harle, 'A Hitherto Unknown dated Sculpture from Gandhāra: A Preliminary Report', in *South Asian Archaeology*, ed. J.E. Van Louizen-de-Leeuw and J.M. Ubaghs, 1973, Leiden Brill, 1974, pp. 128–35.
28. There is a controversy about the date of this panel. According to recent discovery, Kanishka may be dated to *c.*127 CE. If that is the case, then the panel may be dated to *c.*132 CE.

29. G. Fussman, Documents Epigraphiques Kouchans, III, Buddha de 1'5; Bulletin de l'E'cole Francaise du Extreme-Orient, vol. LXI, 1974, pp. 54–8.
30. Konow, *Corpus*, p. 171.
31. Ibid., p. 172.
32. Ibid., p. 107.
33. *Udāna*, Sacred Book of the Buddhists, II, VIII, 17, Oxford, 1948.
34. *Therigāthā*, *Pslams of the Sisters*, XXX, London: Pali Text Society, 1909.
35. B.N. Mukherjee, *The Rise and Fall of the Kushāṇa Empire*, Calcutta, 1968, p. 373.
36. B.N. Mukherjee, 'A Kharoshṭhī inscription of the Kushāṇa age referring to Aśoka', *Journal of the Epigraphical Society of India*, vol. XVI, Mysore, 1990, pp. 31–3.
37. Konow, *Corpus*, pp. 77 and 90. A story in the *Divyāvadāna* also alludes to the foundation of this monastery by Aśoka.
38. Konow, *Corpus*, p. 113.
39. Ibid., p. 83.
40. Ibid., pp. 120, 122–3.
41. Ibid., p. 155.
42. John Marshall, *Taxila*, vol. I, Cambridge, 1951, p. 327.
43. Ibid., p. 256.
44. Konow, *Corpus*, pp. 157–8.
45. Vijay Nath, *Dāna: Gift System in Ancient India*, p. 78.

12

Almsgiving in Buddha's Utterances

A Pāli Textual Examination

ARUNA K. GAMAGE

THE TERM *DĀNA* has a wider connotation in the Pāli canon. The sub-commentary of *Dīgha Nikāya* defines it as the things or positions, which are fit for offering.[1] Significantly, the intention for offering also has been considered as *dāna* in some Theravāda exegesis.[2] Even though the most popular meaning of this term is 'offering', it occurs as a homonym in the Pāli canon as well as in the post-canonical literature. The *Abhidhānappadīpikā* recognizes *dāna* to convey several meanings, such as 'purification, cutting or breaking off, giving; a gift, a donation; almsgiving, charity, liberality, the fluid that flows from an elephant's temples, when in rut'.[3] Furthermore, the *Suttanipāta* commentary mentions that *dāna* (giving), *yañña* (brahmanical sacrifice) and *yāga* (sacrifice) are synonymous in some contexts.[4] Early Buddhism speaks of two types of donations, namely, worldly-goods and doctrine. The following statement can be found in *Aṅguttara Nikāya*, 'There are, o, monks, two kinds of donations. What are these two? The donation of worldly-goods (*āmisadāna*), and donation of *dhamma* (*dhammadāna*). Out of these two kinds of donations, the latter is foremost'.[5] It is apparent that the donation of worldly-goods is a physical and tangible activity whereas the donation of *dhamma* is utterly an intellectual and intangible activity. According to the commentary of *Aṅguttara Nikāya*, *āmisadāna* means the donation of four requisites, namely, clothing, food and drinks, medicines, and lodgings. Also, *dhammadāna* means enlightening others with the doctrines that lead to attain deathlessness.[6] However, it can be noted that the references for 'donation of *dhamma*' are very limited in number in early Buddhism in comparison with the references for the 'donation of worldly-goods'. There are considerable amounts of attestations that can be found in the Pāli canon which explore the significance, efficacy, positive consequence, and necessity of *āmisadāna* in various ways. In contrast, no scope or process is mentioned for *dhammadāna* in the Pāli canon. Thus, it would not be hasty to state here that early Buddhism does not lay much emphasis on the 'donation of doctrine'. The term *dāna* immensely occurs in the Pāli canon as an isolated term. Thus, one may think that the exact meaning intended by this term in such accounts is undetermined since it does not have any specification (as *āmisadāna* or *dhammadāna*). However, the scrupulous examination of contexts and phraseology of such occurrences reveals the fact that the isolated use of the term *dāna* in the Pāli canon always stands for 'donation of worldly-goods', namely, food, beverages and so forth. In order to get the vivid picture of this fact, we can scan one specific passage of the *Dāna Sutta* of the *Aṅguttara Nikāya*.

There are eight donations (*dānāni*) existing in this world. One gives [1] as a 'tit for tat' (*āsajja*); [2] one gives from fear (*bhayā*); [3] one gives as repayment for, which s/he has been previously given (*adāsi me iti*); [4] one gives expecting future reciprocation from the receiver (*dassati me iti*); [5] one gives because 'donation' is accepted as a good manner in the world (*sāhudānaṃ iti*); [6] one gives with the belief 'I cook but these receivers (i.e. monks) do not cook, it is not fit that I who cook should give nothing to those who do not cook' (*na arahāmi pacanto apacantānaṃ dānaṃ adātuṃ iti*); [7] *one gives expecting the fame (kitti-saddo abbhuggacchati iti*); [8] one gives because one wishes to adorn and equip one's heart (*citt'ālaṅkāra-citta-parikkhār'atthaṃ*).[7]

It is quite difficult to assume that the factors mentioned above refer to 'donation of doctrines' (*dhammadāna*), and a close examination of those factors suggests that the eight intentions of donors of 'worldly-goods' are meant here. With the exception of the last (i.e. number eight), all the other factors reveal about the 'donations' performed by someone with a contaminated or with an unwholesome intention. Number one speaks of a 'donation' with the intention of 'tit for tat; *āsajja*'. Interestingly, the commentary explains this donation in a positive viewpoint. However, semantic examination of *āsajja* leads us to a reluctance to consider it as a reasonable exegesis. Furthermore, this term has occurred in many canonical accounts to convey a negative sense.[8] For instance, *āsajja* occurs in three accounts in the Pāli canon in the sense of 'having confronted with' or 'having annoyed' (*ghaṭṭetvā*).[9] Number two refers to a 'donation' that is performed out of fear while number three and four are reminders about a mere reciprocation. Although number five refers to a sort of awareness of a donor, it does not reveal any deep attentiveness about the positive consequence of donation. Here, what one knows is only that 'donation' is a good activity. In number seven, the donor does not have the intention for the accumulation of merits or elimination of unwholesome traits such as greed and avarice through the process of 'donation' whereas, expects dignity and popularity. The last (i.e. number eight), evidently refers to an actual donation with proper intention. Number six provides an indestructible proof for what we mentioned at the very outset of the previous passage. It speaks of 'cooking' or 'boiling' of the things before the donation. If the donation of doctrine had been intended here, there would not have been any necessity for such a preparation before offering. What is necessary to cook before offering to someone is not 'doctrine' but foods or 'raw materials of foods'. It is awkward to presume about cooking or boiling in a doctrine. Now, it is clear that eightfold donations; *dānāni* mentioned above, refer to the 'donation of food'. Food is, in fact, one of the constituents of 'worldly goods: *āmisa*'. Accordingly, it can be concluded, considering the foregoing facts that the isolated use of the terms *dāna/dānāni* without precedent adjectives or specifications, typically refers to the 'donation of foods and other worldly goods (*āmisadāna*)'. Thus, the term almsgiving will be used throughout this article to denote *āmisadāna* (in addition, seven factors related to the almsgiving, which slightly differ from the contents of the discourse discussed above, are given in the *Dānamahāpphala Sutta* in the *Aṅguttara Nikāya*).[10]

Since *dāna* used in isolation in the Pāli canon to denote the 'donation of foods and other worldly-goods', it is worthwhile to pay our attention to its scope. The *Mahāsudassana Sutta* of the *Dīgha Nikāya* portrays the nature of pre-Buddhist almsgiving, performed by King Mahāsudassana. This almsgiving consisted of eight components, namely, food, drink, raiment, vehicle, bed, woman, bullion, and gold.[11] As the commentary of this discourse records, these objects were donated for both temporary and permanent consumption of the receivers.[12] It is rather surprising about the sixth factor of this list since it speaks of women who donated for both temporary and permanent consumption as a component of almsgiving. It seems as a conventional norm that existed in ancient India. Perhaps, it might be a special treatment offered to visitors and guests by the kings. However, the *Pārājika-pāḷi* sheds light on this factor, furnishing an account to assume that 'sexual intercourse has been considered as the "best donation" by some people'. One female devotee, as this text relates, held a belief as 'she who offers sexual (intercourse) pleasure to the others, performs the utmost almsgiving'.[13] However, it should be noted here that Buddhism had not accepted this as a mode of noble donation, and no single Pāli canonical proof can be found that supports to believe that the Buddha permitted this kind of almsgiving. Ten constituents that are fitting to offer to recluses and brāhmaṇas[14] for almsgiving are repeatedly mentioned in the Pāli canon, viz., food, drink, clothing, vehicle, wreaths, perfumes, ointments, bedding, dwelling, and accessories, which are connected with lighting lamps.[15] Since recluses (*samana*s) are also mentioned as the receivers of these items, it is necessary to examine who they are. In fact, this term stands for both Buddhist and non-Buddhist recluses. As *Mahāvagga* of *Vinaya Pitaka* records, abstinence of using wreaths, perfumes, and ointments is one of the precepts of *sāmaṇera-dasasīla* (ten precepts for Buddhist novices).[16] Moreover, as the *Majjhima Nikāya* states, when a Buddhist monk follows the spiritual path described in many discourses, leading to *nibbāna*, it is one of the initial necessities to refrain from using the three factors underlined here.[17] One may see a contradiction between the previously mentioned 'ten constituents for offering' and this precept. However, it is useful to consider the phraseology of this precept. In fact, what this precept statement semantically suggests is, a novice or a monk should avoid using (*dhāraṇā*) or be adorned with (*maṇḍanā*) garlands, perfumes, and ointments, and no prohibition is conveyed in this precept to accept those things. The prohibition is regarding the usage but not regarding the acceptance. Buddhist monks, as Theravāda exegeses insist, can accept garlands, perfumes, and ointments for offering them to sacred monuments such as the *Bodhi*-tree, Buddhist relic shrine, etc.[18] Again, if we examine the semantic sense of the fourth item of the list mentioned above (i.e. *yānaṃ*), it suggests that the 'vehicle' is worth offering to the monks as a component of almsgiving. In contrast, according to the *Mahāvagga* of the *Vinaya Pitaka,* the monk who travels by a vehicle, unless he has any sickness, commits a *dukkaṭa* offence.[19] Both singular and plural forms of *yāna* (*yānaṃ* and *yānāni*, respectively) can be found in various places in the Pāli canon and fortunately, it has been interpreted in *Vinaya Pitaka* itself. Significantly, the latter source speaks of three kinds of vehicles.[20] These two Pāli canonical proofs seem to contradict each other. That is to say, while *yāna* is accepted in the canon as an item of worth offered to Buddhist monks, a disciplinary rule has been promulgated that forbids the use of vehicles for monks. It is interesting to pay attention towards the ahistorical interpretations for this term provided by the Theravāda tradition (perhaps, with the purpose of solving this disagreement). The commentary on *Dīgha Nikāya*, for instance, states as '*yāna* in this context, means *sandals*'.[21] This interpretation reminds the pragmatics, a specific branch of the tree of modern linguistics wherein, the study of 'contextual meaning' mostly dealt with.[22] Anyhow, the usage of sandals is also one of the necessities for the monks to prevent their feet from injures when they walk in faraway and thorny places. In addition, Buddhism permits each monk to use two pairs of *sandals*, namely, one for outdoor use and the other one for indoor use.[23] Another set that consists of four constituents for almsgiving can be found in many places in the canon, viz., robes, alms-food, lodgings, comforts, and medicines for sickness.[24] However, this list is more popular, thus, often adduced in current almsgivings in Sri Lanka.

The receivers of almsgivings are often referred to in the Pāli canon as recluses, and brāhmaṇas. Nevertheless, this usage is not constant. Some canonical attestations use the term *pabbajita* (one who entered to homelessness),[25] *bhikkhu* (monk)[26] and also in some contexts, an extended list can be found that consists of six types of receivers for almsgiving. In addition to *samana* and brāhmaṇa, this list adds *kapaṇa* (poor people), *addhika* (wayfarers), *vaṇibbaka* (mendicants)[27] and *yācaka* (beggars).[28] The first and the second items are foods (*annaṃ*) and drinks (*pānaṃ*), respectively, in the aforementioned list that consists of ten items for almsgiving. The second list, however, seems to have put both of these under the common heading *piṇḍapāta*.[29] As the commentary of *Niddesa* interprets, it is meant 'any kind of food'.[30] Interestingly, the Theravāda tradition offers a wider connotation for this term. As the several commentaries insist, *piṇḍapāta* stands for sixteen-fold items that can be eaten or drunk, etc., namely, boiled rice, sour gruel, barley meal, fish, meat, milk, curds, ghee, butter, oil, bee honey, molasses, rice gruel, something that can be crunched, something that can be tasted, and something that can be licked.[31] This interpretation clarifies the fact that the scope of *piṇḍapāta* goes far beyond its literal meaning in Theravāda Buddhism. Food and drinks are of paramount significance for every living creature for the survival and enrichment of both physical and mental aspects, thus, these two factors hold a very specific place in the early Buddhism. When Buddhism speaks of almsgiving, the efficacy of offering food and drinks are specially insisted. In some accounts, these two factors encapsulate under *āhāra*: foods. As the Buddha and some of his leading disciples (*arahants*) categorically mention, 'all beings sustain on foods'.[32] The physical body of beings does not remain without foods.[33] Accordingly, the other items of almsgiving such as clothing and bedding represent a secondary place in comparison with foods, and the latter holds a prominent place. Another specification for the physical body is *odana-kummās'ūpacayo*, which is heaped up and grown with the nourishment of boiled rice and junket.[34] This phrase visibly reveals the contribution of rice and milk for the survival of the body. Even though this Pāli phrase literally means only rice and junket, for the convenience of utterance[35] it is justifiable to consider that it pragmatically implies all the foods and drinks.

The *Anna Sutta* of the *Saṁyutta Nikāya* emphasizes the necessity of *anna* in the way of posing an interesting question, as *anna* is highly desired by both humans and divines. Who is that being who does not enjoy *anna*?[36] The literal meaning of *anna* is food, or the things that can be eaten.[37] It is palpable that in the first list discussed, in the previous passage, *anna* represents all the eatable things and *pāna* denotes all the drinkable things. However, in this context, it is logical to mention that *anna* stands for 'foods and drinks'. As this statement relates (even though this comes in the form of a query, the syntax of the verse suggests it as a form of declaration) not only to human beings, but divine beings also who become delightful on receiving food. Besides, the figurative statement that appears in the *Kiṁdada Sutta* of the *Saṁyutta Nikāya* as 'One, who gives food, gives strength'[38] categorically exposes the effectiveness of food for the survival and sustainability of all the living creatures. Accordingly, the effectiveness and benefit one can gain through the process of donating food is vehemently eulogized in the Pāli canon. Hunger and thirst are two immutable phenomena for all living creatures. It is significant to note here that these two factors are considered as diseases (*ābādhā*/*parissayā*) in early Buddhism.[39] On this ground, foods function as medicines. Therefore, one who donates foods can be interpreted as one who treats a diseased person. The receiver who is satiated with foods can be compared to a recovered person. As the *Padhāna*

Sutta of the *Suttanipāta* says, 'hunger and thirst belong to the third army of the evil-one'.[40] On this basis, it is reasonable to say, figuratively, that one who donates foods, is a creator of rival force in the consciousness of the receiver, in order to conquer 'the third army of the evil-one'. The *Abhidhānappadīpikā* recognizes *khuddā* and *jighacchā* as synonyms for hunger. These two terms often occur in the Pāli canon. In addition, we are able to recognize the other two synonyms that have not been listed in Pāli traditional lexicons and modern dictionaries. The specialty of these two terms is that they properly depict the natural gravity of hunger, viz., *vihiṃsā* and *sūcikā*. As the dictionary sub-voices suggest, the first term would mean 'malice', 'hostility', 'cruelty', 'intention of harm', 'spitefulness', etc.[41] The literal meaning of *sūci* is 'needle',[42] and, *kā* is apparently a suffix that gives lesser meaning. Interestingly, as Pāli commentarial tradition makes out, these two terms are synonyms for hunger. The Pāli canon repetitively insists that one who wishes to attain to the position of complete annihilation of defilements (*nibbāna*), should be very cautious of foods, since exceeding consumption of the latter would be a great obstruction for that purpose. However, such a person is instructed to take food in order to vanquish *vihiṃsā* (*vihiṃsūparatiyā*).[43] As *Viśuddhimagga* interprets, *vihiṃsā* is a synonym for hunger, since it afflicts the body as well as the mind.[44] *Sūcikā* occurs in the *Petavatthu*, in the sense of hunger. As the commentary of the latter recognizes, hunger is called *sūcikā* in the sense of piercing both body and mind.[45] These two terms properly portray both physical and mental detrimental effects of hunger. According to the exegeses offered for *vihiṃsā* and *sūcikā* hunger makes manifold afflictions both to body and mind. On this basis, as we mentioned above, the one who bestows foods can be identified as the one who treats these physical and mental illnesses.

It is unnecessary to explain the physical and mental harmfulness of hunger here since a mass of scientific research that explores its negative influence has already been put forward for several decades. Thus, offering food to vanquish the receiver's hunger is considered as a great conduct of accumulating merits in early Buddhism. If we pay our attention to the contents of the two canonical texts *Vimānavatthu* and *Petavatthu*, most of the accounts in them illustrate the positive outcomes of donation and negative consequences of stinginess, respectively. While the former text shows the luxurious life of divine beings who have attained that position as a result of almsgiving in their previous existences, in contract, the latter text demonstrates the miserable livelihoods of the people who have got birth in hell, in consequence of avoiding donation due to tightfistedness they had in their former births. Significantly, the contents of the two texts mentioned above are substantiated by some other discourses of the Buddha that appear in the first four *Nikāyas*.[46] For instance, the *Cūlakammavibhaṅga Sutta* mentions that one who donates the things mentioned above could easily get rebirth in heaven with supreme facilities or in the human realm with the highest lavishness. On the contrary, one who refrains from such donations will get rebirth in hell or in the human realm surrounded with many discomforts.[47] On the other hand, the efficacy of almsgiving, as Buddhism clearly points out, depends on the donor's intention also. That is to say, good intention and manners of the donor will bring him a more prolific hereafter. It is apt to pay our attention to the *Cūlapuṇṇama Sutta*, where we read two fold almsgivings, viz., *asappurisadāna*: donation of unworthy people,[48] and *sappurisadāna*: donation of worthy people.[49] When the 'almsgiving' is performed in an improper manner (*asakkacca*), without the donor's direct involvement (*asahatthā*), without enough reverence (*acittīkatvā*), with humility (*apaviddhaṃ*),[50] without believing, the fruit of donation (*an'āgamana-diṭṭhiko*)[51] belongs to the first category, and, the almsgiving performed in accordance with the completely opposite manner, that of the first, belongs to the second category. As the *Pāyāsi Sutta* relates, the chieftain Pāyāsi is said to have been reborn in a lonely mansion as he practised *asappurisadāna* whereas, his disciple Uttara got admission to a higher heaven in consequence of giving *sappurisadāna*.[52] However, an interesting fact here is that the owner of the gifts was Pāyāsi and Uttara was his agent, appointed by him, to maintain the almsgiving properly. Pāyāsi, even if he was the owner had no faith or necessary respect on this charitable process. Uttara bestowed the charitable goods, even though he did not own them, with due faith and veneration at the almsgiving.

Ajita, one of the six teachers (*cha satthāro*), firmly emphasized the futility of almsgiving. According to him, the latter is not capable of producing merit.[53] In contrast, Buddhism strongly protests against this opinion and unanimously accepts the positive outcome of almsgiving. As several discourses of the Pāli canon record, the Buddha's physical body was endowed with thirty-two marks of a great man (*mahāpurisa-lakkaṇāni*).[54] According to the *Lakkhaṇa Sutta* of the *Dīgha Nikāya*, these marks are identical only to the Buddha and the 'wheel roller' monarch (i.e. king *cakkavattī*).[55] This discourse is also of ethical significance since it gives a comprehensive analysis of these signs, revealing the reasons that have influenced the possession of each mark, sufficient to pay our attention here on the inheritance of *sattussado*; seven convex surfaces.[56] It means to have perfectness in seven places of the body, namely, on both hands, both feet, both shoulders and trunk.[57] As this discourse says, both these supreme persons acquired this Mark in this very life, as a *remnant* of the consequence of donating delicious foods and drinks to others in their previous human lives. Almsgiving, as Buddhism points out, is a process of acquiring wholesome deeds (*kuśala-samādāna*), thereby it produces immense merit (*puñña*).[58] Merit is of importance for living beings since it produces manifold positive consequences for the progress of secular and spiritual life. As a number of discourses of the *Saṁyutta Nikāya* relate, merits enable to make an excellent hereafter,[59] and, they contribute to refine the consciousness of the donor.[60] This refinement of human consciousness is an indispensable basic factor to develop mental concentration, which is, accepted as a higher stage in spiritual progress, i.e. the path leading to *nibbāna*. Thus, it is the typical custom of the Buddha, which enlightens a person to begin with an explanation of the outcome of generosity (*dānakathā*) before describing subtle doctrinal factors.[61] Almsgiving makes a proper ground to the person for the decrement of some ignoble traits, which are concealed in human consciousness such as greed (*lobha*), desire (*taṇhā*), covetousness (*kadariya*) and avarice (*macchariya*). Especially, greed is considered as one of three unwholesome roots (*akuśala-mūla*) that function as the main barriers for one's supra mundane uplift. As Venerable Śāntideva poetically says in *Bodhicaryāvatāra*, greed is one of the formless enemies that enslave the person, secretly residing in human consciousness.[62] Therefore, almsgiving is a veritable phenomenon that facilitates the donor to accumulate merit and minimize the power of all these ignoble traits simultaneously.

The *Dānamahāpphala Sutta* of the *Aṅguttara Nikāya* remarks that the almsgiving which is performed, being out of inferior expectations (*nas'āpekho*) and longing (*napaṭibaddha-citto*) yields immense benefits. As this discourse exemplifies, one who wishes to get the highest fruition of an almsgiving should donate 'worldly goods' (particularly foods and drinks), expecting nothing but the spiritual edification of one's own mind: *citt'ālaṅkāra-cittaparikkhār'atthaṃ*. Therein, the latter fragment of the sentence is used by the Buddha to specify the almsgiving, which is of the highest efficacy. It is therefore, this fragment which is worth analysing. Obviously, this consists of three main units, namely, *cittālaṅkāra*, *cittaparikkhāra* and *atthaṃ*. Again, the first two units possess two subunits, viz., *citta alaṅkāra* and *citta parikkhāra*, *citta* in both these sub-units refers to the 'mind', *alaṅkāra* and *parikkhāra* literally mean 'decoration' and 'requisites', respectively. The last unit *atthaṃ* occurs here in the sense of 'to' or 'for'. Accordingly, literal meaning of the whole fragment is 'for the decoration and requisition of mind'. Some Mahāyāna treatises also speak of this factor such as *Śrāvakabhūmi* of Asaṅga, and *Abhidharma-kośabhāśya* of Vasubandhu.[63] Rhys Davids translates this as 'to adorn and equip one's heart' and E.M. Hare as 'to improve the mind, to equip the mind'. Again, Lamotte, in his translation of *Mahāprajñāpāramitāsūtra* (The Treatise on the Great Virtue of Wisdom), renders this fragment which is also available in Sanskrit sources mentioned above, as 'to adorn the mind of the *ṛddhis*; to ripen the mind of members of the Path'.[64] It is imperceptible how Hare translates the term, i.e. *cittālaṅkāra* as 'improve the mind'. It is apparent that he renders *alaṅkāra* as 'improve' (!?), however, it should be mentioned here that this meaning is not supported by any Sanskrit/Pāli canonical source, commentarial exegesis or by a lexicon. Nonetheless, the rendering offered by other two scholars seems apt for *alaṅkāra*.[65] It suggests that almsgiving enchants the donor's mind, supporting to plant the bliss in his/her mind. According to the *Mahānāma Sutta* of the *Aṅguttara Nikāya*, the recollection of donation (*cāgaṃ*)[66] leads to preventing one's mind from the influence of lust, hatred, and delusion. Moreover, the happiness yielded in consequence of donation becomes supportive to rectify the donor's mind (*ujugataṃ*)[67] and removing its crooked tendencies. When the mind is rectified, one gains inspired knowledge in the goal (*attha-vedaṃ*), inspired knowledge in the doctrine (*dhamma-vedaṃ*),[68] and joy (*pāmojjaṃ*). Because of joy zest (*pīti*) arises leads to arise of physical tranquility (*kāyo passambhati*) thereby one feels happiness (*sukhaṃ*) and a happy mind becomes concentrated (*samādhiyati*).[69] Both Davids and Hare render *parikkhāra* as 'equip', whereas Lamotte's rendering which is given as 'ripen' looks unfitting. Commentarial exegesis mention three meanings of this term, viz., retune, decoration and unit.[70] Dictionaries have listed several and diverse meanings for *parikkhāra*. *The Dictionary of Pāli Language* provides 'surrounding, retune, decoration, furnishing, requisite, utensil, apparatus, furniture, household stuff',[71] in addition, *The Pāli-English Dictionary* gives 'all that belongs to anything, makeup, adornment, accessory' for this term.[72] It is clear that these dictionaries have influenced those aforementioned scholarly renderings for *parikkhāra*. For none of these interpretations yields a satisfactory sense for *parikkhāra* in this context, it should not be out of place here if we draw our attention on the Sanskrit lexicons. *Parikkhāra* appears in Sanskrit as *pariṣkāra*. Tāranāth, in his classical lexicon named as *Śabdastoma-mahānidhi*, interprets this term as 'the activity that attaches merits of existing object'.[73] Furthermore, *Sanskrit-English Dictionary* gives 'purification' for *pariṣkāra*, while *Practical Sanskrit-English Dictionary* provides 'purification by initiatory rites' for it.[74] Thus, it is possible to convey these connotations of *pariṣkāra* from its Pāli corresponding term *parikkhāra*. Therefore, on this basis *citt'ālaṅkāra-cittaparikkhār'atthaṃ* can be interpreted as 'for the adornment and purification of mind'. The sub-commentary of *Dīgha Nikāya* furnishes an enlightening explanation, which is further supportive to believe the substantiality of the underlined meaning of this fragment. As it says, bliss, delight, zest and other wholesome mental concomitants arise[75] in the mind of the donor when they recollect on the almsgiving performed; equally, greed, hatred, jealousy, avarice and other unwholesome mental concomitants become far distant from the donor's mind.[76] In this manner, almsgiving, which is instrumental to increase the uncontaminated traits[77] and to ward off opposite traits,[78] is supportive to adorn and purify the developed mind.

The Buddha categorically states in the aforementioned *Dānamahāpphala Sutta*, the one who performs almsgiving *citt'ālaṅkāra-cittaparikkhār'atthaṃ*, for the adornment and purification of mind, after death will get rebirth in *Brahma-kāyika* realm[79] and thereafter, become a non-returner (*anāgāmī*).[80] It is needless to explain the spiritual supremacy of the non-returnership since it has been already well explored to the world by both oriental and occidental scholarship. However, one factor will suffice to realize the command of this position. In Buddhism, it is the penultimate spiritual attainment, which is attained, having cut-off five unwholesome mental bondages, thus, such a person will never come back to this world, and, will attain to the final liberation therein. It is clear with the foregoing factors, the efficacy of almsgiving. Briefly, the almsgiving, as emphasized, in Buddhism, offers both secular and supra mundane prosperity to the donor.

Notes

1. *Dīyatīti dānaṃ*—*Dīgha Nikāya-aṭṭhakathā-tīkā*, II.256.
2. *Dīyati anenāti vā dānaṃ pariccāga-cetanāy'etaṃ adhivacanaṃ*—*Aṅguttara Nikāya-aṭṭhakathā-tīkā*, II.58, Dhammapāla explains the meaning of *dāna* in the sense of 'giving' in a sophisticated manner as follows: *dānanti dātabbaṃ, sa-vatthukā vā cetanā dānaṃ, sampatti-pariccāgass'etaṃ adhivacanaṃ* (*dāna* means that it should be given, or it means the intention of giving that occurs, together with its all mental requisites. This is a synonym for the donation of wealth)—*Itivuttaka*, II.131, *dānaṃ vuccati avakhaṇḍanaṃ* (*dāna* means cutting off), *Viśuddhimagga*, 58.
3. *Dānaṃ cāge made suddhe khaṇḍane lavane khaye*—*Abhidhānappadīpikā*, 82.
4. *Yañño yāgo dānanti atthato ekaṃ*—*Suttanipata-aṭṭhakathā*, II.132.
5. *Dvemāni bhikkhave dānāni. katamāni dve? āmisadānañca dhammadānañca. imāni kho bhikkhave dve dānāni. etad'aggaṃ bhikkhave imesaṃ dvinnaṃ dānānaṃ yadidaṃ dhammadānaṃ*—*Aṅguttara Nikāya*, I, 91; in addition to this statement, the same idea occurs in *Itivuttaka*, I, 98, 102, and, with a slight difference in *Aṅguttara Nikāya*, IV, 364. According to the three hundred and fifty-fourth verse of *Dhammapada*, 'donation of doctrine excels all the other donations; *sabbadānaṃdhammadānaṃjināti*'.
6. *Āmisadānanti cattāro paccayā diyyanakavasena āmisadānaṃ nāma, dhammadānanti idhekacco amatapattipaṭipadaṃ kathetvā deti, idaṃ dhammadānaṃ nāma*—*Aṅguttara Nikāya-aṭṭhakathā*, II.159. See also, *Itivuttaka-aṭṭhakathā*, II.131 for *dhamma-dāna*. The literal meaning of *āmiṣa* in Sanskrit is flesh, and in some contexts, it stands for meat. See: *dāvoṣṇakharavāto'yaṃ-śvāsavadbhātipaśyata, tat dagdhasattvadurgandho-'pyantar'āmiṣagandhavat*—*Bhāgavata Purāṇa*, 10.12.23, trans. The hot fiery wind is the breath coming out of his mouth, which is giving off the bad smell of burning flesh because of all the dead bodies he has eaten, *loke vyavāyāmiṣamadyasevā-nityā hi jantorna hi tatra codanā, vyavasthitisteṣu vivāhayajña-surāgrahair āsunivṛttiriṣṭā*—ibid., 11.05.11, tr. In this material world, the conditioned soul is always inclined to sex, meat-eating and intoxication. Therefore, religious scriptures never actually encourage such activities. Although the scriptural injunctions provide for sex through sacred marriage, for meat-eating through sacrificial offerings and for intoxication through the acceptance of ritual cups of wine, such ceremonies are meant for the ultimate purpose of renunciation. However, the term *āmisa* seems to have undergone semantic evolution when it comes to Pāli since it is used in the Pāli canon to denote possessions or worldly-goods. See for further explanations: Richard F. Nance, 2012, USA, p. 142.
7. *Aṅguttara Nikāya*, IV.236, same factors occur under *dānavatthu* (bases of donation) in *Dīgha Nikāya*, III.258.
8. *Āsajjadānaṃ detīti patvā dānaṃ deti. āgataṃ disvā taṃ muhuttaṃ y'eva nisīdāpetvā sakkāraṃ katvā dānaṃ deti, dassāmīti na kilameti*—AA, IV.122.

9. *Āsajjāti ghaṭṭetvā-Majjhima Nikāya-aṭṭhakathā*, 282, *Aṅguttara Nikāya-aṭṭhakathā*, IV.171, *Jātaka-aṭṭhakathā*, IV.47. See also, *āsajjāti . . . paribhuyya* (. . . abused)—*Theragatha-aṭṭhakathā,* I.86, *āsajjāti . . . bādhetvā* (. . . restricted)—*Theragātha-aṭṭhakathā,* III.172, *āsajjāti āsādetvā* (. . . harassed)—*Saṁyutta Nikāya-aṭṭhakathā*, I.179. Nonetheless, this term has another meaning. See: *āsajjāti patvā* (. . . having attained)—*Saṁyutta Nikāya-aṭṭhakathā*, I.133, *āsajjāti samīpaṃ . . . gantvā* (. . . having approached)—*Suttanipata-aṭṭhakathā,* II.384, *āsajjāti . . . upagantvā* (having come closer)—*Jātaka-aṭṭhakathā,* V.342, ibid., VI.194.
10. *Aṅguttara Nikāya*, IV.59–62.
11. *Annaṃ . . . pānaṃ . . . vatthaṃ . . .yānaṃ . . . sayanaṃ . . . itthiṃ . . . hiraññaṃ . . . suvaṇṇaṃ—Dīgha Nikāya*, II.179.
12. *Ye . . . vicaritvā . . . ohāya, atthikā gahetvā gacchanti—Dīgha Nikāya-aṭṭhakathā,* II.629.
13. *Yā methunaṃ dhammaṃ deti sā aggadānaṃ deti—Vinaya Pitaka*, III, 39, Cf. *nānā nibandhaiḥ suratopacāraiḥ krīḍāsukhaṃ janma-phalaṃ narāṇām* (the highest benefit of receiving human-life is the pleasure of sexual intercourse, applying diverse methods)—eighth verse, Oliver Hellwig, p. 116.
14. *Samaṇassa vā brāhmaṇassa vā—Dīgha Nikāya*, III.258.
15. *Annaṃ pānaṃ vatthaṃ yānaṃ mālāgandhavilepanaṃ seyy'āvasatha-padīpeyyaṃ—Dīgha Nikāya*, III.258; *Majjhima Nikāya,* III.205; *Saṁyutta Nikāya*, III.248, *Aṅguttara Nikāya*, II.203; ibid., IV.60; ibid., 239, V.271. Interestingly, the term *padīpa*; lamp, does not directly occur here, but it speaks of *padīpeyya*, literally things that connect with the lamp. However, as Pāli commentarial exegeses mention, *padīpeyya* stands for oil, i.e. the fuel for lamps. See: *padīpeyyanti padīpatelaṃ—Dīgha Nikāya-aṭṭhakathā*, III.994.
16. *Mālā-gandha-vilepana-dhāraṇa-maṇḍana-vibhūsanaṭṭhā nāveramaṇī*—V.I.83.
17. *Majjhima Nikāya*, I.180.
18. *Dīgha Nikāya*, III.923–4, as the *Brahmajāla Sutta* of *Dīgha Nikāya* states, the Buddha abstained from wearing, adorning, or ornamenting himself with garlands, scents, and unguents—*mālā-gandha-vilepana-dhāraṇa-maṇḍana-vibhūsanaṭṭhānā paṭivirato samaṇo Gotamo-Dīgha Nikāya*, I.5, Rhys Davids, p. 5.
19. *Na bhikkhave yānena yāyitabbaṃ. yo yāyeyya āpatti dukkaṭassa—Vinaya Pitaka*, I.191, *dukkaṭa*: *wrong-doing, a minor offence*—Bhikkhu Sujato, p. 16.
20. *Yānaṃ nāma vayhaṃ ratho sakaṭaṃ sandamānikā—Vinaya Pitaka*, III.49, *Vinaya-aṭṭhakathā*, II.334, *Vinaya Pitaka*, IV.201 adds another two types of vehicles when defining the term *yāna*. See: *sivikāpāṭaṅkī*, see *Pali-English Dictionary*, 602; *vayha*—portable bed, ibid., 564; *ratha*—chariot, ibid., 659; *sakaṭa*—cart, ibid., 677, *sandamā nikā*—chariot. However, it is doubtful to consider whether these renderings given in *Pāli-English Dictionary* bring the exact meanings of those given in *Vinaya Pitaka.* Literal meaning of *vayha* is something that can be carried, Sanskrit equivalent (*vahya*) of this term does not use a vehicle, and it is hard to believe that it refers to a vehicle. However, the commentaries identify it as a kind of vehicle. See: *Vinaya-aṭṭhakathā*, II.334, *Dīgha Nikāya-aṭṭhakathā*, I.82 is influenced by *Vinaya-aṭṭhakathā*, II.334, *Vinaya Pitaka,* IV.201.
21. *Yānanti upāhanaṃ—Dīgha Nikāya-aṭṭhakathā*, III.993, indeed, sandals are the 'vehicles' for monks; *upāhanā pana pabbajitassa yānam'eva*—ibid., I.82.
22. George Yule, p. 3.
23. *Vinaya Pitaka*, I.188.

24. *Cīvara-piṇḍapāta-senāsana-gilānapaccaya-bhesajjaparikkhārā—Aṅguttara Nikāya*, IV, 366. (Same statement with accusative ending in *Niddesapali*, I.73, and with genitive ending in *Aṅguttara Nikāya*, II.250, Ud 06). Woodward translates this statement as 'robes, alms-food, bed and seat, comforts and medicines for sickness'. See, F.L. Woodward, Verses of Uplift, p. 8.
25. *Aṅguttara Nikāya*, IV.366, *pabbajitoti pabbajjaṃ upagato—Theragātha-aṭṭhakathā*, I, 85.
26. *Majjhima Nikāya*, I.33; *Aṅguttara Nikāya*, II.251.
27. It is hard to differentiate *yācaka* and *vaṇibbaka*, depending on the existing sources, *pauper—Pāli-English Dictionary*, 596, mendicant—Dictionary of Pāli Language, 549.
28. (*Samaṇabrāhmaṇa*)-*kapaṇ'addhika-vaṇibbaka-yācakānaṃ—Dīgha Nikāya*, I.137, ibid., II.354; ibid., III.76, *Itivuttaka*, 64, *kapaṇā* means who are stricken with poverty, *addhikā* means wayfarers, *vaṇibbakā* means those who motivate others for donations to them by illustrating positive consequences of offering and, wishing them for a hereafter. *yācakā* means those who directly beg foods and other materials from others by mentioning the amount. *Kapaṇāti duggatā daliddamanussā. addhikāti pathāvino, vaṇibbakāti ye itthaṃ dinnaṃ, kantaṃ, manāpaṃ, kālena anavajjaṃ dinnaṃ, dadaṃ cittaṃ pasādeyya, gacchatu bhavaṃ brahmalokanti-ādinā nayena dānassa vaṇṇaṃ thomayamānā vicaranti. yācakāti ye pasatamattaṃ detha, sarāvamattaṃ dethāti-ādīni vatvā yācamānā vicaranti*—DA, I, 298, see also for *vaṇibbaka* (K.R. Norman, The Group of Discourses, p. 169).
29. *Piṇḍapāta* literally means 'lump [of food] dropping (Bhikkhu Ñāṇamoli, p. 32)'. However, this term occurs to denote any type of food in the Pāli canon.
30. *Piṇḍapātanti yaṃ kiñci āhāraṃ—Niddesa-aṭṭhakathā*, II, 462, see also *Majjhima Nikāya-aṭṭhakathā-ṭīkā*, I.168 BE, whereas, *Majjhima Nikāya-aṭṭhakathā*, I.174 *piṇḍapātanti odanaṃ* (*piṇḍapāta* means boiled rice).
31. It is doubtful if the English renderings that are given in the article represent the accurate meanings intended by these Pāli terms. *piṇḍapātoti odano kummāso sattu macho maṃsaṃ khīraṃ dadhi sappi navanītaṃ telaṃ madhu phāṇitaṃ yāgu khādanīyaṃ sāyanīyaṃ lehanīyanti soḷasa piṇḍapātā—Dīgha Nikāya-aṭṭhakathā*, III.1014, *Aṅguttara Nikāya-aṭṭhakathā*, III.53, *Niddesa-aṭṭhakathā*, 123, *Pāli-English Dictionary*, 222: *kummāsa*—junket, *Pāli-Sanskrit-English Dictionary*, 588: *kulmāṣa*—gruel, *Pāli-English Dictionary*, 673: *sattu*—barley meal, *Pāli-English Dictionary*, 552: *yāgu*—rice gruel, rice milk (to drink), *Pāli-Sanskrit-English Dictionary*, 1307: *yavagū*—rice gruel, sour gruel made from rice or from any other kind of grain such as barley.
32. *Sabbe sattā āhāraṭṭhitikā—Dīgha Nikāya-aṭṭhakathā*, III.211; ibid., 273, *Aṅguttara Nikāya*, V.51, ibid., 55, *Paṭisambhidamagga-aṭṭhakathā*, I.5, ibid., 122; ibid., 174; ibid., II.34.
33. *Ayaṃ kāyo āhāraṭṭhitiko āhāraṃ paṭicca tiṭṭhati an'āhāro no tiṭṭhati—Saṁyutta Nikāya*, V.64.
34. *Kayo . . . odanakummāsupacayo—Dīgha Nikāya*, I.76, ibid., I.208, *Majjhima Nikāya*, I.500, ibid., II.17, *Saṁyutta Nikāya*, V.370, *Odanakummāsūpacayoti odanenac'eva kummāsena ca upacito vaḍḍhito* (*odana-kummās'ūpacayo* means, that which is heap up and grown up with boiled rice and junket)—*Dīgha Nikāya-aṭṭhakathā*, I.220. See: *Dictionary of Pāli Idioms*, p. 309 where, *odana-kummāsa* is rendered as 'rice and curry'.
35. *Vacanasiliṭṭhatā*: 'the ease of utterance'. Pāli commentaries often examine the places where pragmatic interpretations are necessary in order to recognize some Pāli canonical statements properly. Pragmatics investigates intended meaning of an utterance that

goes beyond the range of its literal meaning. In such places, Pāli exegetes the use of specific terms such as *vacana-siliṭṭhatā, desanā-matta, desanā-sīsa, Majjhima Nikāya-aṭṭhakathā*, II.70, *Saṁyutta Nikāya-aṭṭhakathā*, II.328, *Saṁyutta Nikāya-aṭṭhakathā-ṭīkā*, I, 350. However, this type of statement cannot be found in this context.

36. *Annam'ev'ābhinandanti ubhaye devamānusā atha ko nāma so yakkho yaṃ annaṃ n'ābhinandati—Saṁyutta Nikāya*, I.32. Here, the commentary remarks that anna means a special designation for four requisites namely food, clothing, shelter and medicine. *annanti annasaññito catubbidhopi paccayo—Saṁyutta Nikāya-aṭṭhakathā-ṭīkā,* I.120 and, furthermore, it says *yakkho* occurs in this contexts denotes a 'living creature'; *yakkhoti satto*—ibid., *yakkha* used to denote some contexts in the Pāli canon. As *Saddanīti* enumerates, this term has been used in the Pāli canon, in five senses (see: Msn 284 BE).

37. *Annanti odano kummāso sattu macho maṃsaṃ*; *anna* means boiled rice, junket, barley meal, fish and meat—*Niddesa,* II.495, *annantiyāgu-bhattaṃ*; *anna* means rice gruel and boiled rice—*Vinaya-aṭṭhakathā*, III.923, *annanti khādanīya-bhojanīyaṃ*; *anna* means something that can be crunched and eaten—*Saṁyutta Nikāya-aṭṭhakathā*, II.349, *annāni . . . bhojanāni*; *anna* means foods that can be crunched—*Jataka-aṭṭhakathā,* A, III.522 *anna*—food; *Pāli-Sanskrit-English Dictionary*, 129, *annād bhavanti bhūtāni*; beings are born from food—Patikonda Vishwambara Nath, p. 124, however, the etymological expression appears in *Taittirīya Upaniśad* shows that *anna* directly refers to the eatable things. See: *adyate'tti ca bhūtāni tasmād'annaṃ tad'ucyata*: *anna* is so called because it is eaten by beings and the beings eat them—S. Sitarama Sastri, pp. 120–1. See also: Because it is eaten by beings and because it eats beings, therefore it is called food—'Taittiriya Upanishad, Swami Nikhilananda, consciouslivingfoundation.org/ebooks.

38. *Annado balado hoti—Saṁyutta Nikāya*, I.32.

39. *Tena kho pana manussānaṃ chaḷeva ābādhā ahesuṃ, sītaṃ uṇhaṃ jighacchā pipāsā*: at that time people had only six diseases, namely, cold, hot, hunger, thirst . . . A, IV.138, see also: ibid., V.109; ibid., 121, *jighacchāpipāsā . . . vuccanti pākaṭa-parissayā*; *hunger and thirst are called obvious dangers—Niddesa*, I, 13, *jigacchā paramā rogā*: Hunger is the worst of diseases—*Dhammapada*, V.203. K.R. Norman translates this, as *'greed is the worst of diseases'*. See *Word of the Doctrine*, K.R. Norman, p. 30.

40. As this discourse counts that hunger and thirst are the third force of the evil one; *tatiyā khuppipāsa*-Sn 76, *khuppipāsā* is a compounded term and it refers to *kṣutpipāsā* in Sanskrit. See *adhivāsayiṣyāmi kṣutpipāsāṃ*: I will endure hunger and thirst—*Śiksasamuccaya*, Nagarjuna Institute of Exact Methods, University of the West, 2003, 30.

41. *Hurting, injuring, injury—Pali-English Dictionary*, 643, see also *Dictionary of Pāli Language*, 570.

42. *Dictionary of Pāli Language*, 485, piercing, perforating, a needle—, 1696 *Pāli-Sanskrit-English Dictionary*, a needle, hairpin—*Pāli-English Dictionary*, 721.

43. *Dīgha Nikāya*, III.130, M I 10, ibid., 273, ibid., II.27, ibid., 139, ibid., III.2, *Saṁyutta Nikāya*, IV.104, ibid., 176, *Aṅguttara Nikāya*, I.114, ibid., II, 40, *Vibhanga*, 249, Pug. 25 Rhys Davids translates *vihiṃs'ūparatiyā* as 'to prevent injury'—Rhys Davids, p. 122, and Ms Horner translates as 'for keeping it (i.e. *body*) unharmed'—Middle Length Sayings, vol. I, p. 13, but Woodward gives the accurate meaning as 'for allaying the pangs of hunger'—E.M. Hare, p. 277.

44. *Vihiṃsā nāma jighacchā ābādhaṭṭhena—Viśuddhimagga*, I.31 BE. See: hunger is called discomfort in the sense of afflicting—Bhikkhu Ñāṇamoli, op. cit., p. 33, *vihiṃsā nāma abhuttapaccayā uppajjanaka khuddā*; hunger that emerges in the consequence of refraining from eating—*Niddesa-aṭṭhakathā,* II.344, *Dhammasangani-aṭṭhakathā* 403, also: *Majjhima Nikāya-aṭṭhakathā-tika,* I.168 BE.
45. *So sūcikāya kilamito*: he who stricken with *sūcikā*—Pv. 29, *vijjhanaṭṭhena sūci-sadisatāya sūcikāti laddhanāmāya jighacchāya kilamito nirantaraṃ vijjhamāno*: being frequently pierced with hunger which is designated as *sūcikā* since it pierce the person('s body and mind) just as a needle—*Petavatthu-aṭṭhakathā*, I, 071
46. *Aṅguttara Nikāya*, IV.79–82.
47. *Majjhima Nikāya*, III.205.
48. *Asappurisa*: a low, bad or unworthy man—*Pāli-English Dictionary*, 87.
49. *Sappurisa*: a good, worthy man—*Pāli-English Dictionary*, 680.
50. *Chaḍḍetukāmo hutvā vammike uragaṃ pakkhipanto viya*: in a way of throwing something, just as throws an iguana to an anthill—*Majjhima Nikāya-aṭṭhakathā,* VI.81.
51. . . . *no phalapāṭikaṅkhī hutvā*: without believing the consequence of donation—*Majjhima Nikāya-aṭṭhakathā*, IV.81.
52. *Dīgha Nikāya*, II, 355, see also: Heaven and Hell, Bimala Charan Law, p. 128, Rhys Davids, pt. II, 373.
53. *Dattu-paññattaṃ dānaṃ—Dīgha Nikāya*, I, 55, it is a doctrine of fools, this talk of gifts—Rhys Davids, pt. I, p. 74.
54. *Dīgha Nikāya*, I, 106; *Majjhima Nikāya*, II.143, Sn 107.
55. *Dīgha Nikāya*, III.141–78.
56. *Seven convexes—Dialogues of the Buddha*, III, p. 144, seven convex surfaces—Maurice Walshe, p. 446. Sanskrit correspond appears in Mahayana Sūtra-s as *saptotsadakāyaḥ*. See: BSB, Nagarjuna Institute of Exact Methods, University of the West, p. 17.
57. *Ubhosu hatthesu . . . ubhosu pādesu . . . ubhosu aṃsakūṭesu ussadā honti, khandhe ussado hoti—Dīgha Nikāya*, III.151. Commentarial exegeses point out the exact locations of these Marks. *dve hattha-piṭṭhiyo dve pādapiṭṭhiyo dve aṃsakūṭāni khandhoti imesu sattasu ṭhānesu paripuṇṇo maṃsussado assāti sattussado—Dīgha Nikāya-aṭṭhakathā*, II.448, *Majjhima Nikāya-aṭṭhakathā*, III.378.
58. *Dadato puññaṃ pavaḍḍhati—Dīgha Nikāya*, II.136, *Aṅguttara Nikāya*, II.35, ibid., 65, ibid., III.36, Ud 85, *Itivuttaka*, 89.
59. *Puññāni paralokasmiṃ patiṭṭhā honti pāṇinaṃ—Saṁyutta Nikāya*, I, 18, 32, 57, 58, 59, 72, 93, 97. *Aṅguttara Nikāya*, III, 41.
60. *Attano santānaṃ punanato . . . puññaṃ*; *puñña* is so called since it refines (donor's) own consciousness—Itivuttaka-*aṭṭhakathā*, I.78.
61. *Dīgha Nikāya*, I.110, *Majjhima Nikāya,* I.379, *Aṅguttara Nikāya*, IV.186, *Udanā* 49, *Vinaya Pitaka*, I, 15.
62. BCA, Nagarjuna Institute of Exact Methods, University of the West, 2004, IV.28–9, p. 41.
63. *Citt'ālaṃkārārthaṃ cittapariṣkārārthaṃ. . . tad dānaṃ*—BSB, Nagarjuna Institute of Exact Methods, University of the West, 2006, 43.09, *cittālaṅkārārthaṃ cittapariṣkārārtham . . . dānaṃ dadāti*—Abhidharmakośabhāśya, 588.8. See: to adorn the mind (*cittālaṃkārārtham*) of the *ṛddhis*; to ripen the mind (*cittapariṣkārārtham*) of members of the Path, Étienne Lamotte Leuven, p. 530.

64. *Cittālaṅkāra-cittaparikkhār'atthaṃ*—to improve the mind, to equip the mind—E.M. Hare, p. 35, See also: *Dīgha Nikāya*, III.258, A IV.236, to adorn and equip one's heart—Rhys Davids, pt. III, p. 240. See Lamotte, op. cit., p. 530, Pāli commentarial exegeses offered this fragment to connect the latter with the tranquility and insight. See *citt'ālaṅkāra-cittaparikkhāranti samatha-vipassanā-cittassa alaṅkārabhūtañc'eva parivār'atthañca*; for the adornment and protection in the consciousness of tranquility and insight—*Dīgha Nikāya-aṭṭhakathā*, III.1044, see also *Aṅguttara Nikāya-aṭṭhakathā*, IV, 33.
65. See *Pāli-English Dictionary*, 79, *Sanskrit-English Dictionary*, 94.
66. *Cāgaṃ anussarat i*—*Aṅguttara Nikāya,* III.287.
67. *Ujugatam'ev'assa tasmiṃ samaye cittaṃ hoti cāgaṃ ārabbha*—ibid.
68. Ibid., *Aṅguttara Nikāya-aṭṭhakathā,* II.337, *atthaveda* and *dhammaveda* are referred to as happiness that arose on the commentaries and canon, respectively, whereas, *Majjhima Nikāya-aṭṭhakathā–ṭīkā*, I.277 says these two terms are meant 'knowledge in causes and conditions' (*atthavedanti . . . hetuphalevedaṃ*) and 'knowledge in causes' (*dhammavedanti . . . hetumhi vedaṃ*).
69. *Aṅguttara Nikāya*, III.287.
70. *Parivāro . . . alaṅkāro . . . sambhāro*—*Vinaya-aṭṭhakathā*, III.550, *Itivuttaka-aṭṭhakathā*, II.463, see also *Dīgha Nikāya-aṭṭhakathā*, I.297, *Paṭisambhidāmagga-aṭṭhakathā*, III.607.
71. *Dictionary of Pāli Language*, 342.
72. *Pāli-English Dictionary*, 423.
73. *Vidyamāna-vastuno guṇāntarasya sarjan'ādau saṅskāre*—ŚSN, 282.
74. *Sanskrit-English Dictionary*, 603; *Pāli-Sanskrit-English Dictionary*, 423.
75. *Pāmojja-pīti-somanass'ādayo uppajjanti*—*Dīgha Nikāya-aṭṭhakathā-tiīkā*, III.339.
76. *Lobha-dosa-issā-maccher'ādayo vidūrī bhavanti*—ibid.
77. *An'ukūla-dhamma-paribrūhanena*—ibid.
78. *Paccanīka-dhamma-vidūrībhāva-karaṇena*—ibid.
79. *The company of the devas of Brahmā's hosts*—Hare, op. cit., p. 25.
80. *Aṅguttara Nikāya*, IV.62.

13

Dānadhamma and *Dhammadāna*

Confluence of Material and Spiritual Aspects of Generosity

NEEKEE CHATURVEDI

THE PRACTICE OF generosity in Buddhism is rooted in its commitment to ethics and compassion. Sometimes, religious rituals, though 'seemingly unlikely sources',[1] can throw valuable light on the linkages of the religious and temporal. The term *dāna* is etymologically derived from the root *dā*, which means to give, making *dāna* the act of giving or bestowing. Buddhaghosa defines it as '*dānam vuccati avakhaṇḍanaṃ*'[2] (*dāna* is giving away or distribution). For the survival and sustenance of the Buddhist Order, donations were crucial but gradually, many different forms of *dāna* emerged and coalesced into the umbrella term *dānadhamma.* Generally, an act of giving or donation, in the religious context, evokes the imagination of the Order in the role of its recipient. This is largely true in the economic sense but a deeper inquiry into the material aspect gives way to a more nuanced understanding of the donor in Buddhism. Also, as one delves into the spiritual aspects of *dāna* in Buddhism, a distinctive worldview of non-material forms of exchange emerges, finding its pinnacle in the concept of *dhammadāna. Dhammadāna* refers to the imparting or sharing of spiritual tenets of Buddhism and is accorded a very high position among the various forms of giving.[3]

An anthropological essay 'The Gift'[4] by Marcel Mauss enunciated the role of exchange of gifts and reciprocity in building human relations. In Indian context, brahmanical practices[5] and land grants[6] garnered the interest of scholars. Some academic studies delved into the socio-cultural aspects of religion.[7] *Dāna* formed an important practice in Buddhism. It attracted scholars for its special dimension due to a greater emphasis on monastic life.[8] Findly writes, 'The experience of interdependence and the practice of accommodation are rich benefits of *dāna* practice, a doctrine set up, in part, as an exchange: householders give according to the teachings on donation called *dānadhamma*, and renunciates return householder's offerings with a gift of teaching called *dhammadāna*.'[9] The merit accrued by the donor also forms an important spiritual aspect of *dānadhamma*. Perhaps, the dependence on *dāna* played a significant role in the transformation of consciousness of the monks and the nuns as well. Many studies on Buddhist monasticism deal with the practice of giving only incidentally, while the specialized works on *dāna* do not take into account the interplay of social and economic factors. This inquiry seeks to understand the socio-economic as well as religio-spiritual functions underlying the centrality of the practice of *dāna*. It has tried to understand *dānadhamma* and *dhammadāna* as reciprocal practices. The material and spiritual significance of their interconnectedness can best be understood, not in specialized isolation, but in the context of the core Buddhist teachings. Primarily through a study of Pāli texts and some epigraphic evidence, interesting aspects of the relationship of the laity and the *saṃgha* within the framework of the practice of *dāna* have been dealt with.

Dhamma: Ethics, Practice, Guidance

The term *dhamma* (*dharma*) is used in different orders in the two key terms of this paper, in one as a suffix and in the other as the beginning. It does bring a slight variation of implication, connoting the ethical practice of *dāna* in *dānadhamma* and spiritual guidance or Buddhist teachings in *dhammadāna*. Even in a general context, *dhamma* is imbued with diverse meanings, the variety and richness inherent in them has been systematized by Lama Anagarika Govinda. He writes that 'the Buddha's *dhamma* is, as experience and as a way to practical realization, a religion; as the intellectual formulation of this experience, a philosophy; and as a result of self-observation and analysis, a psychology. Whoever treads this path acquires a norm of behaviour that is not dictated from without, but is the result of an inner process of maturation and that we—regarding it from without—can call morality.'[10] In the *Mahāparinibbāna Sutta*, the Buddha is said to have asked the monks and the nuns to seek refuge in *dhamma*, 'Therefore, Ananda, be islands unto yourselves, refuges unto yourselves, seeking no external refuge; with the *Dhamma* as your island, the *Dhamma* as your refuge, seeking no other refuge.'[11] He further elaborates:

> When he dwells contemplating the body in the body, earnestly, clearly comprehending, and mindfully, after having overcome desire and sorrow in regard to the world; when he dwells contemplating feelings in feelings, the mind in the mind, and mental objects in mental objects, earnestly, clearly comprehending, and mindfully, after having overcome desire and sorrow in regard to the world, then, truly, he is an island unto

himself, a refuge unto himself, seeking no external refuge; having the *Dhamma* as his island, the *Dhamma* as his refuge, seeking no other refuge.[12]

I.B. Horner outlines the evolution of its meaning:

> Whatever the exact meaning or meanings of *Dhamma* may have been at one stage in the history of Early Buddhism or at one part of sayings or another, it is a fair enough description to say, that *Dhamma* concerned the inner life of Gotama's followers, their conscience, their mental training, and outlook, and later stood for the body of teaching they were to believe and follow. . . .[13]

This passage not only brings out the significance of *dhamma* for a practitioner but also highlights the importance of ethical practices. *Dhamma* is not looked upon as an autonomous, universal law existing independent of an individual and his actions. In many of the *Suttas*, *dhamma* is envisaged as the path of righteousness in all walks of life.[14] The most righteous person is defined in the *Majjhima Nikāya* as one who harms neither oneself nor others and is, therefore, implied to be beneficial for oneself as well as others.[15] The wayfarer upon the Buddhist *pathas* has to consciously inculcate spiritual values, 'the inner process' of Lama Govinda, to which *dānadhamma* and *dhammadāna* are great facilitators for both the laity and *saṃgha*. 'While the benefits of giving and getting *dāna* and *dhamma* are immense, it is the ritual form of this exchange itself which continues to have its own power to teach and transform.'[16]

Dhamma also constitutes a holistic system of thought and practice, of which *dāna* forms an important component. The *Bodhisattva*, a being who aspires for enlightenment, or depicted as a Buddha-to-be, is essentially endowed with an extraordinary generous attitude. Many of the *Jātaka* stories, narrating the previous births of the Buddha depict him engaged in magnanimous actions.[17] Born as Prince Vessantara, he gave away the royal elephant on a request and later gave away his children, and then his wife too. These tales illustrate that a *Bodhisattva* must give freely, be it material objects, family members and even body parts.[18] In due course, the quest for perfection was stratified into ten *pāramitas*, or virtues of perfection, the first being the *dāna pāramita*. The *Viśuddhimagga* charts out the path to attain perfection through four *Brahmavihāras*, viz., *mettā* (loving kindness), *karuṇā* (compassion), *muditā* (loft joy), and *upekkhā* (equanimity).[19] Thus, *dāna* is integral to the Buddhist teachings and emanates from ethical conduct (*śila*) and compassion (*karuṇā*). Although, it does not figure in the core teachings like the *atthāngika magga*, yet numerous *dānakathās* (discourses on generosity) extol its indispensable intrinsic worth.

Dānadhamma: Material Means, Spiritual Ends

Dāna, in its various forms like gifts, alms, and donations, has played a significant role in the historical growth and sustenance of Buddhism. Buddhism emphatically recommended renunciation. Contrasting the spiritual potential of a householder and a renunciate, the *Muni Sutta* of the *Suttanipāta* states:

> For all its crest and neck so blue
> The peacock never can match in flight
> The swan, nor layman emulate
> An almsman, when in lonesome wilds
> The sage is plunged in Reverie.[20]

Mohan Wijayaratne traces the roots of primacy of 'renouncers' in its opposition to the emphasis on worldly life and rituals of Brahmanism.[21] The rise of this new movement was spiritually strengthened by the *bhikkhus* and the *bhikkhunis* who came to be specifically addressed as a part of the Buddhist *saṃgha.* They came to be revered by a large section of lay people who were called *upāsaka*s and *upāsikā*s. Thus, the followers of the Buddha formed a composite entity of the monks and the nuns on one hand, and lay devotees, on the other, who continued to be the dispensers of worldly duties. There must have been diverse motivations for being attracted to Buddhism, ranging from an escape from personal hardships, or desire to emulate, to a genuine appreciation and comprehension of the doctrinal thrust. In the ideal sense, though, reverence and devotion to the teachings was expected to have existed as spiritual basis that brought together the Order and the laity. Whatever the initial motivation might have been, they were all expected to exert towards a purer way of life. On this spiritual *bhoomi* (ground), the ties of the two seemingly different paths are cemented further by *dānadhamma*, by forging a socio-economic relationship.

The *pañca-sikkhāpada* (five precepts) enjoins a monk to abstain from taking what is not given (*Adinnādānā veramaṇī sikkhāpadaṃ samādiyāmi*). The ideal for a monk was the state of *anūpalitto,* detachment to sensual attachments as well as the world just like a lotus remains unsullied by the proximate mud and water.[22] Thus, an interaction of the ascetics with the laity was not a hindrance in their spiritual journey if a proper mental attitude had been cultivated. The Buddhist Order could not exist in exclusion because of the large numbers that joined it and also because, unlike other preceding and contemporary ascetic traditions, young were also encouraged to renounce.[23] This required a mechanism for influx of resources to sustain a young and numerous community not permitted to do remunerative work or amass material gains. Even though the monks and nuns were to lead simple, peripatetic lives of meagre needs, they needed food and clothes, if nothing else. They needed medicines in case of sickness. It soon became clear to the wandering ascetics that at least in some part of the year they needed a shelter to shield them from the vagaries of nature. As the order moved from peripatetic to coenobitic mode of organization[24] through the custom of *vassāvāsa*, material support emerged as a pressing need and economic reality. Though *dānadhamma* was a natural consequence to seek support from the society, the economic aspect was also appended by norms of a social nature.

The socio-economic premise that provided the monks and the nuns to seek alms and material support for sustenance lay in their effort to spread the teaching of deliverance from suffering. A few months after attaining enlightenment, the Buddha is said to have told his small band of disciples, 'Monks, take to the road; travel for the good of the many; travel for the happiness of the many, out of compassion for the whole world; travel for the good, benefit, and happiness of men and gods. Preach the doctrine'.[25] The underlying objective of 'the good of the many' provided a social connection with the potential donors. The instruction to travel did not mean that the itinerants were constantly on the move. Rather, it was a common practice for the preachers to indulge into brief sojourns in villages, where the teachings were imparted. It was a social custom in the villages to arrange hospitality for them.[26] The Pāli canonical literature is replete with the *Suttas* that illustrate arrangement of feasts, sermons, stay, etc., for the Buddha and his disciples.[27] The sages were endowed with these amenities as part of *dānadhamma* but they were not to put undue demands and act in the manner of a bee who gathers nectar but leaves the flower unharmed. '*Yathāpi bhamaro pupphaṁ vaṇṇagandham aheyaṭhayam Paleti rasam ādāya evaṁ gāme munī care.*[28] Although the scriptures zealously urge consistent exertion, the rules of discipline forbade the Buddhist monks and nuns to use bodily labour or miraculous powers to generate income. Sloth was inexcusable in the realm of spiritual exercise but humility was inculcated through dependence on the generosity of the laity for even basic necessities. The lure of lucre was regarded as an impediment to religious life. *Pācittiya* rule 40 gives the instruction that, 'Monks must not eat food which they have not received from someone else's hands. If a monk does eat food which he has not been received from someone else's hands, he commits an offence in the *Pācittiya* category.'[29] They could receive material things like food, clothes, bowls, and medicines but only as much to meet immediate needs. Under no circumstances, the early canon permits taking money.[30] Thus, there was a clear economic basis to the evolution of *dānadhamma* in Buddhism. The rules clearly stated that the dignified manner, undemanding equanimity, and proper attire distinguished alms seeking from begging. This was meant to invoke generosity of the laity through the spiritual force of the Buddhist practitioners. The spiritual energy foregrounds material seeking in a subtle yet strong manner wherein the monks and nuns were perceived as 'worthy of offerings, worthy of hospitality, worthy of gifts, worthy of respect; the greatest field of merit in the world'.[31]

Kuśalakamma—In Giving, We Receive

The mental cultivation of the donor was equally important, making ethical practice indispensable in the characteristic Buddhist manner. Buddhism identifies three motivational roots of unwholesome deeds (*akuśalakamma*)—*lobha* (greed), *dosa* (hatred), and *moha* (delusion). *Dāna* is of central importance as it helps to overcome the first root of greed (*jayet kadaryaṁ dānena*).[32] 'Greed is wrapt up with egoism and selfishness, since we hold our personalities and our possessions as "I" and "mine". Giving helps make egoism thaw: it is the antidote to cure the illness of egoism and greed'.[33] There is another motivation for generosity that can be found in the first ethical precept summarized as respect for all forms of life. In order to help life, one is required to abstain from causing injury and to help the less fortunate through the acts of well-meaning charity. The *Sāmaññaphala Sutta*,[34] discussing the ethical life of an individual, says that the first step in the ethical life of a follower of the Buddha should be to avoid causing injury to life, be compassionate to all beings and behave in such a way as to bring about the welfare of all beings.[35]

Pāṇātipātam pahāya pāṇātipātā paṭivirato hoti nihitadaṇdo nihitasattho lajjī dayvpanno sabbapāṇabhutahitānukampī vihārati.[36]

There is another Pāli term, *cāga*, an ethical quality rooted in the wholesome root (*akuśalakamma*) of non-greed (*alobha*). It leads to a disposition for making gifts and sharing in accordance with one's means and ability.[37] Accompanied by *saddhā, aila, suta*, and *pannā, cāga* becomes a quality which elevates its possessor to a higher spiritual level.[38] A person well-disposed for practising generosity (*cāgasampanna*) is described as 'One whose mind is free from the taint of avarice (*macchera-mala*), who is freely generous, open-handed and pure-handed, who delights in relinquishing, and expects to be besought, in the form of looking for opportunities to give'.[39] It is further elaborated that the giver must have benevolence towards the recipient of the gifts, an attitude that eliminates any ill feeling and helps to overcome the second unwholesome root of hatred (*dosa*). When one readily, voluntarily, parts with one's possessions as a pursuit of joy, the third unwholesome root of unwarranted attachment (*moha*) is also overcome. Such a spiritual journey is facilitated by *dānadhamma* but only when the giver pays heed to its ethical foundations.

Generosity is linked to virtuous giving. The act should be executed wholeheartedly. Any reluctance or holding back tarnishes the giver (*maccheraṃ dadato malaṃ*).[40] The simple gifts of a virtuous householder with an innocent heart are far superior to grandiose gifts accrued by vile and vice.[41] During a discussion on what makes the gift worthwhile and superior, the Buddha enunciates four categories of gifts based on their underlying virtuosity.

A gift may be clean and pure from the side of the donor but not from the side of the recipient. This happens when the donor is virtuous but the recipient is corrupt and given to vices. Again, a gift may be clean and pure from the side of the recipient but not from the side of the donor. It happens when the recipient is virtuous but the donor not so. Again, a gift may be unclean and impure from the side of the donor as well as from the side of the recipient. It happens when both the donor and recipient are corrupt and given to vices. Lastly, a gift may be clean and pure from the side of the donor as well as recipient. It happens when both of them are virtuous and pure.[42]

Having described the various types of virtues attached to the gift, the last category is declared to be the best gift. Thus, the gift, donor and recipient are imbued with ethical connotations and one should strive to practise this *dhamma* accordingly.

Although the practice of alms seeking and gift-giving envisaged social harmony and cooperation, it was a distinct possibility that many times the giver and the recipient would come in conflict. There were social modes of expressing displeasure with each other in the context of a conflict of either the monks or nuns with the lay donors. 'Lay people contributed to the community's support, indeed they assumed full responsibility for it, and this gave them the right to criticize monks or nuns who deviated from right conduct.'[43] Even the canonical scriptures find deviant monks unworthy of being supported. The *Dhammapada* strongly says that it is better for an unrestrained, irreligious person to swallow a red hot iron ball than to receive charity from others.[44] Such instances of public criticism could have not only economic but far-reaching social and religious repercussions. It was expected that such aspersions were cast in earnestness, but false accusations were not accepted meekly by the monks or the nuns. The baseless rumour mongers were punished by their refusal to accept his or her alms. This was known as 'the act of overturning the bowl'; where an overturned bowl was symbolically placed outside the offender's house to declare that his alms were no longer acceptable.[45] The *Cullavagga* lists some other offences of a lay worshipper that made him unworthy of a donor. If someone tried to prevent devotees from offering gifts to monks, tried to drive them away, insult them, tried to harm the Order, his acts could be taken cognizance as an offence for which suitable punishment could be inflicted.[46] Thus, *dānadhamma* also served the social function of ensuring smooth cohesion between the Order and laity by instilling the likelihood of exemplary conduct by the monks and nuns as also faithful support by the society at large.

Besides the worldly functions pertaining to sustenance, customs and social cohesion, *dānadhamma* has significant transcendental applications also. Among the three ways of acquiring merit, *dānamayapuñña* (the practice of generosity) is the first, the other two being *sīlamayapuñña* (the practice of virtue), and *bhāvanāmayapuñña* (the practice of meditation).[47] There are many stories that donations to the *saṃgha* resulted in manifold material returns[48] but attaining spiritual evolution and earning merit for future lives was an unmatched benefit. For this purpose donations to the *saṃgha* were highly extolled in its depiction as '*puññakhettraṁ anuttaraṃ*'.[49] Through the practice of charity, not only could one earn social approval and harmonious existence in present life, but also accumulate merit for future lives. One could also transfer merit to dead relatives and mitigate *kammic* repercussions of oneself and the family. Prince Vessantara could earn a place in heaven due to his meritorious deeds of charity.[50] As the yield of seeds sown in a fertile field is abundant, so are the great benefits of giving gifts to a deserving recipient.[51] In later literature, there is a mention of *pāramita* as the perfect exercise of the ten virtues of the *Bodhisattva*, the first of these is the *dāna pāramita*.[52] It confers upon the giver two blessings, inhibiting selfish tendencies and fostering selflessness. Thus, practising generosity led one to spiritual growth and was to be pursued conscientiously by the members of the laity as well as the *saṃgha*; the latter practised it mainly in the form of *dhammadāna*.

Dhammadāna: Spiritual Giving, Spiritual Giver

Sabbadānam dhammadānam jināti
Sabbam rasam dhammarasam jināti[53]

Dhammadāna or giving, in the form of spiritual instruction, is considered to be the most superior gift. The *Itivuttaka* accords a superior status to the giving of spiritual advice (*dhammadāna*) in contrast to a donation made of material things (*āmisadāna*).[54] The giving of the *dhamma* means a discourse on the doctrine of the Buddha, given with an undefiled mind; the content and intent of the discourse is to eliminate suffering. Its objective is to promote good in the present life, to do good in the life to come, and to ultimate deliverance. By means of such discourses, those who are not following the path of Buddhism enter it, while those who have entered it make greater headway.[55] There is a methodical pathway for *dhammadāna* in the *Cariyapiṭakaṭṭhakathā*. The discourses should elaborate on giving, virtue, and heaven, on the defilement inherent in sense pleasures, and on the benefit in renouncing them. The intensity and comprehensive nature of the *dhamma* discourses were to be adjusted according to the evolutionary spiritual state and understanding of the recipient. *Savākabodhi*, disposed towards the enlightenment of disciples, was given a discourse elaborating upon the noble qualities like going for refuge, restraint by virtue, guarding the doors of the sense-faculties, moderation in eating, application to wakefulness, application to serenity (*samathā*), etc., to name a few. *Paccekabuddha*, the ones who were disposed towards enlightenment and those who were enlightened, discourses establishing, and purifying them and elaborating upon the greatness of the spiritual power of the Buddhas, and explaining the specific nature, characteristic, function of the ten *pārami* in their three stages were given. 'Thus the Great Man gives the gift of the *Dhamma* to beings'.[56]

Buddhism is largely viewed as a monastic religion, even though it enjoyed the support of a large number of lay worshippers. This view finds its basis in the importance of renunciation in Buddhism over a worldly life. There are many verses that depict the renunciate's spiritual journey far more untrammelled and unburdened and, therefore, more successful than a householder. A householder is like a tree with many branches getting entangled here and there, thwarting its growth while the monastic rises high like a straight bamboo shoot.[57] The economic dependence of the monastic can be more easily sustained as a social convention if the monastic is able to compensate in some form. Since remunerative work is forbidden, practices involving physical labour, trading and bartering of goods are out of question. To combine the charitable disposition of the laity with reverence, the renunciates should confer upon them a unique gift, something that the householders cannot beget from elsewhere. With this socio-economic understanding, the Buddhist tradition of generosity tapped into its spiritual reservoir. The teachings and consequent merit and blessings could only be imparted by a spiritually trained renunciate, making him worthy of receiving, through the practice of *dhammadāna.*

The exemplary conduct and wise words of the Buddha's disciples were responsible, in no small measure, for attracting large numbers into the Buddhist fold. They imparted discourses for the religious benefit of others. They were compared to 'the moon coming out from behind the clouds'[58] as they dispelled ignorance through their wise words. Not infrequently did the seekers come to the monks and the nuns, but they were also invited to deliver sermons. Even the begging rounds were opportunities for preaching the doctrine, which sometimes resulted in having a favourable effect on initially hostile persons.[59] Several monks earned a great repute being the religious counsels to the laity. A large number of the nuns have also been praised for their skills and adeptness in preaching the Doctrine.[60] Khemā,[61] Dhammadinā Therī,[62] Kajangalā Therī[63] were some celebrated names. The function of *dhammadāna* had been to encourage, sustain, and support the faith of the laity through spiritual guidance and it augmented the inner progress of the preacher. Thus, the practice of giving discourse created a social bond with the laity and was conducive to the spiritual exertion of both the giver and the receiver.

There is one more important side of these spiritual givers, though it is not under the scope of *dhammadāna.* The epigraphic and archaeological remains furnish evidence of donations by several monks and nuns. Records of their charity are immortalized for posterity in votive inscriptions at several Buddhist sites. Thus, in this context, the material and spiritual pathways converge far more symbiotically than in any other form. Buddhist monuments owed much to the donations but it is a startling revelation to find the names of both the monk and the nun figures prominently in the list of donors from many *vihāras* and *stūpas.* Amaravatī,[64] Mathurā,[65] Sānchī,[66] Bharhut,[67] etc., have yielded many inscriptions to bring to light the material gifts made by the members of the spiritual organization. It is after renouncing the worldly possessions that the monks and the nuns have recorded these donations. Although this is not the focus of this study, there are many conjectures regarding the source of their wealth.[68] It could have been their own money, despite the injunctions of the *Vinaya* or sourced from the property before entering the Order or perhaps was procured by goading the relatives. There is no concrete evidence regarding the resources of these spiritual donors, but there is enough indication of a unique correlation. The laity was limited to the role of recipient of teachings and the giver of material objects while the monks and the nuns practised the giving of spiritual as well as material gifts.

It can be concluded that the practice of *dāna* arose out of economic needs but soon acquired a spiritual paradigm due to the religious frame work. It was conducive to social harmony and monastic organization. In the context of Buddhist practice, it enhanced the spiritual evolution of an individual. The system that developed around the practice of *dāna*, or giving, sought to create a balance between the material and spiritual needs. It led each one to create merit through a spate of good deeds, to sustain spiritual seekers, and find support to move towards a higher spiritual plane. There are many aspects of interrelationship between the householders, the monks and the nuns regarding the practice of generosity which creates a viable socio-economic mechanism, while the ultimate aim of final liberation is never lost sight of. The interrelationship of *dhammadāna* with the larger corpus of *dānadhamma* and canonical teachings manifests that the symbiotic relationship of the material and spiritual aspects was a strong factor in the historical growth of Buddhism and spiritual evolution of the Buddhists.

Notes

1. '*Dāna* and *Dakṣiṇā* as Forms of Exchange', ed. Romila Thapar, *Ancient Indian Social History*, Delhi: Orient BlackSwan, 2010, p. 94.
2. *Viśuddhimagga*, ed. C.A.F. Rhys Davids, London: Pāli Text Society, 1975, p. 60.
3. *Itivuttaka*, ed. E. Windisch, London: Pāli Text Society, 1889, p. 98.
4. Marcel Mauss, *The Gift: Forms and Functions of Exchange in Archaic Societies*, London: Cohen and West, 1954.
5. P.V. Kane, *History of Dharmashāstras*, vols. I–III, Poona: Bhandarkar Oriental Research Institute, 1930–46; Thapar, *Dāna* and *Dakṣiṇā*.
6. R.S. Sharma, 'Land Grants in Early India', in *Proceedings of First All India Seminar of Indian Economics*, ed. B.L. Ganguly, Delhi, 1961; Vibha Upadhyaya, *Prācheen Bhārata me Bhoomidāna*, Jaipur, 1992.
7. D.D. Kosambi, *An Introduction to the Study of Indian History*, Bombay, 1956; *Myth and Reality*, Bombay: Popular Prakashan, 1962; Narendra Wagle, *Society at the Time of the Buddha*, Bombay: Popular Prakashan, 1966.
8. Ellison Bank Findly, *Dāna—Giving and Getting in Pāli Buddhism*, Delhi: Motilal Banarsidass, 2003; Archana Sharma, *Dāna se Dānapāramitā tak—Bauddha Paramparā me Dāna ke Vividh Ayām*, Vārānasī: Vishwavidyalaya Prakashan, 2010.
9. Findly, *Dāna—Giving and Getting*, Preface, p. 14.
10. Lama Anagarika Govinda, *Living Buddhism for the West*, Boston: Shambhala Publications, 1990.

11. *Mahāparinibbāna Sutta*, II.33, tr. Sister Vajira, http://www.accesstoinsight.org/tipitaka/dn/dn.16.1-6.vaji.html, accessed on 24 August 2015.
12. Ibid., II.34.
13. I.B. Horner, *The Book of the Discipline*, London: Pāli Text Society, repr, 1949, vol. I, Introduction, p. 4.
14. For example, *Agañña Suttānta, Dīgha Nikāya*, III, ed. T.W. Rhys Davids and J.E. Carpenter, Pāli Text Society, 1911, pp. 80ff; *Vasala Sutta, Suttanipāta*, ed. D. Anderson and H. Smith, Pāli Text Society, 1913, pp. 21ff, *Vāseṭṭha Sutta, Suttanipāta*, pp. 115ff.
15. *Majjhima Nikāya*, I.341.
16. Findly, *Dāna—Giving and Getting*, p. 14.
17. *Vessantara Jātaka*, no. 547.
18. Ibid., *Akiti Jātaka*, no. 480; *Śivi Jātaka*, vol. 499; *Sasa Jātaka*, no. 316 are other tales that record such acts of unhesitant generosity. Reiko Ohnuma deals extensively with bodily self-sacrifice in *Head, Eyes, Flesh, Blood—Giving Away the Body in Indian Buddhist Literature*, Delhi: Motilal Banarsidass, 2009.
19. *Viśuddhimagga*, p. 325.
20. *Suttanipāta*, I.12.221, translated as *Buddha's Teachings, Being the Suttanipāta or Discourse Collection* by Lord Chalmers, Harvard Oriental Series, vol. 37, Cambridge: Harvard University Press, 1932, p. 53.
21. Mohan Wijayaratne, *Buddhist Monastic Life—According to the Texts of the Theravāda Tradition*, tr. Claude Grangier and Steven Collins, Cambridge: Cambridge University Press, 1990, p. 1.
22. *Suttanipāta*, I. 3. 71, p. 11; *Saṁyutta Nikāya*, translated as *Book of Kindred Sayings* by C.A.F. Rhys Davids and F.L. Woodward, 5 vols., London: Pāli Text Society, 1917–30, III, p. 118.
23. Cf. *Vinaya*, I. 94, ed. H. Oldenberg, vols. 1–7, London: Pāli Text Society, 1879–83; *Udāna*, 57, ed. P. Steinthal, London: Pāli Text Society, 1885.
24. For a discussion on the evolution of Buddhist monasticism in this framework, see Neekee Chaturvedi, 'Gleanings of Monastic Buddhism in the *Suttanipāta*', in *Bharati*, Banaras Hindu University, vol. 36, 2012, pp. 76–82; Wijayaratne, *Buddhist Monastic Life*, 1990, pp. 18–30.
25. *Vinaya*, I. 20–1.
26. For example, *Kasibhāradvājasutta Suttanipāta*, I.4; ibid., *Sundarīkabhāradvājasutta*, III.4; ibid., *Selasutta*, III.7.
27. Some *Suttas* also record resentment on their entry in the villages, e.g., A brāhmaṇa admonishes the Buddha in the *Vasala Sutta*, I.7; ibid., with the words, '*Tatr'eva muṇḍaka, tatr'eva samaṇaka, tatr'eva vasalaka titthāhi'iti'*.
28. *Dhammapada*, IV.49, tr. S. Radhakrishnan, Oxford University Press, 1966, p. 75.
29. *Vinaya*, IV.90; cf. Nuns, *Pācittiya* 122.
30. Cf. *Vinaya*, II.97, where a monk is permitted to ask for clothes, wood, transportation, etc., but never money; *Nissagiya Pācittiya*, rule 20, *Bhikkhuni Pāttimokkha*, where accepting money for robes is regarded as an offence.
31. *Majjhima Nikāya*, I–IV, ed. V. Trenckener, R. Chalmers, Rhys Davids, Pāli Text Society, 1888–1925, III.81; *Aṅguttara Nikāya*, I–VI, ed. R. Morris, E. Hardy, C.A.F. Rhys Davids, Pāli Text Society, 1885–1910, IV.406.
32. *Dhammapada*, 223.
33. Lily De Silva, 'Giving in the Pāli Canon', in *Dāna: The Practice of Giving, Selected Essays, Access to Insight* (*Legacy Edition*), ed. Bhikkhu Bodhi, 30 November 2013, http://www.accesstoinsight.org/lib/authors/various/wheel367.html, accessed on 26 August 2015.

34. *Dīgha Nikāya*, I., p. 63.
35. Jotiya Dheerasekara, ed., *Encyclopaedia of Buddhism*, vol. IV, Colombo: Government of Sri Lanka, 1979, p. 307.
36. Ibid.
37. *Viśuddhimagga*, p. 184.
38. *Saṁyutta Nikāya*, V., pp. 369–70.
39. *Saṁyutta Nikāya*, V., p. 30.
40. *Dhammapada*, 241.
41. *Saṁyutta Nikāya*, I, p. 18.
42. *Majjhima Nikāya*, III, pp. 255–6.
43. Wijayaratne, *Buddhist Monastic Life*, 1990, p. 128.
44. *Dhammapada*, 308, p. 156.
Seyyo ayogulo bhutto tattoo aggisikhūpamo
yaṁ ce bhuñjeyya dussīlo raṭṭhapiṇḍam asaññato.
45. Ibid., p. 129; cf. *Vinaya Pitaka*, II.124ff.
46. *Vinaya Pitaka*, II, pp. 124–7.
47. *Dīgha Nikāya*, III, p. 218.
48. E.W. Burlingame, tr., *Buddhist Legends: Dhammapada Origin Stories*, London: Pāli Text Society, 1969, II, *Jātaka*, no. 424, pp. 67–8; See also *Dakkhiṇāvibhaṅga Sutta, Majjhima Nikāya*, vol. III, pp. 254–5.
49. *Dīgha Nikāya*, III, 5, 227; *Saṁyutta Nikāya*, I.233.
50. *Jātaka*, no. 547.
51. *Aṅguttara Nikāya*, IV, *Dānavaggo*, 8.4.4.
52. *Cariyapiṭakaṭṭhakathā* (*Paramatthidipani*), ed. D.L. Barua, London: Pāli Text Society, 1939, pp. 226–7.
53. *Dhammapada*, V.354, p. 169.
54. *Itivuttaka*, ed. E. Windisch, London: Pāli Text Society, 1889, p. 98.
55. *Cariyapiṭakaṭṭhakathā.*
56. Based on the rendering of *Cariyapiṭakaṭṭhakathā*, translated by Bhikkhu Bodhi in *The Discourse on the All-Embracing Net of Views: The Brahmajāla Sutta and Its Commentaries* by Acariya Dhammapala as 'The Perfection of Giving' in Silva, *Dāna—The Practice of Giving.*
57. *Suttanipāta, Khaggavisāṇa Sutta*, I.3.38.
vaṁso visālo va yatahā vissato
puttesu dāresu ca ya apekhā
vamsākalīro va assajamāno
eko care khaggavisāṇakappo.

See also ibid., *Pabbajjā Sutta*, III.1.405, *Dhammacariya Sutta*, II.6.274; *Muni Sutta*, I.12.221; *Aṅguttara Nikāya*, I.80; *Majjhima Nikāya, Ariyapariyasena Sutta*, I.162.
58. '*Abbhāmuttovacandimā*', *Dhammapada*, V.382, p. 176.
59. *Suttanipāta, Dhaniya Sutta*, I.2, *Kasibhāradvāja Sutta*, I.4, *Vasala Sutta*, I.7, etc.; *Saṁyutta Nikāya*, I.165, 167, 171 ff.
60. *Saṁyutta Nikāya*, II.236; *Aṅguttara Nikāya*, I. 88, II.164, 347.
61. *Saṁyutta Nikāya*, III.474; *Aṅguttara Nikāya*, I.25.
62. *Aṅguttara Nikāya*, I.26; *Majjhima Nikāya*, I.304.
63. *Aṅguttara Nikāya*, V.54–6.
64. C. Sivaramamurti. 'Amaravati Sculptures in the Madras Government Museum', *Bulletin of the Madras Government Museum*, n.s., vol. IV, repr., Madras, 1977, pp. 283–98.
65. Janert Klause, ed., *Mathura Inscriptions*, Gottingen: Vanehoeck and Ruprect, 1961.

66. John Marshall, *The Monument of Sanchi*, repr., Delhi: Swati Publications, 1983; Upinder Singh, 'Sanchi: The History of the Patronage of an Ancient Buddhist establishment', *The Indian Economic and Social History Review*, vol. 33, no. 1, 1996, pp. 15–16.
67. Alexander Cunningham, *The Stupa of Bharhut: A Buddhist Monument Ornamented with Numerous Sculptures*, Varanasi: Indological Bookhouse, 1962; Luders, ed., *Bharhuta Inscriptions, Corpus Inscriptionum Indiacarum*, vol. II, pt. 2, Ootacamund: Government Epigraphist for India, 1963.
68. Mohini Chaturvedi, *Bauddha Upasaka—Ek Adhyayana*, Varanasi: Kala Prakashan, 2013, pp. 177–8; Barnes Nancy, 'The Nuns at the Stupa: Inscriptional Evidence for the Lives and Activities of Early Buddhist Nuns in India', ed. Ellison Bank Findly, *Women's Buddhism, Buddhism's Women: Tradition, Revision and Renewal*, Boston: Wisdom Publication, 2000; Gregory Schopen, *Bones, Stones and Buddhist Monks: Collected Papers on the Archaeology, Epigraphy and Texts of Buddhist Monuments in India*, University of Hawaii Press, 1997; Rupali Mokashi, 'Unveiling *Bhikkuṇīs* in Oblivion: What Deccan Cave Inscriptions Reveal about the Ancient *Bhikkuṇī Sangha*', in The *Voices and Activities of Theravada Buddhist Women*, Winter, 2012.

14

The Practice of *Dāna* in Ancient Indian Buddhism

K.T.S. SARAO

THE WORD '*DĀNA*' may be defined as 'giving' or 'offering' to another person, something of value that one owns for the benefit of the person on whom that particular thing is bestowed. As the practice of *dāna* was crucial to the survival of the *saṃgha* and was also a means of generating religious merit, it is considered of primary ethical value in ancient Indian Buddhism.[1] As the *saṃgha* subsisted primarily on the generosity and support of its lay supporters and well-wishers, the practice of *dāna* became central to its survival and had significant social and economic implications. In other words, *dāna* ought to be understood within the context of the relationship of complete economic dependence of the *saṃgha* on the support of the laity, who made to the *saṃgha* an offer of food and other material things (*āmisadāna*). In return, the donors earned social status and merit (*puñña*) leading to better rebirth or even liberation from the *samsara*. The *saṃgha* also offered to its supporters a gift of spirituality (*dhammadāna*) which is exalted as the highest gift.[2] Noticeably, the relative impurity of cooked food amongst the caste-ridden brahmanical Hindus was in sharp contrast to the practice of the Buddhists who considered cooked food as the most acceptable form of *dāna*.

The importance of *dāna* in the ethical life of an individual can be judged from the fact that it occupies the first place in several ethical categories. It is the first among the three ways of earning merit (*punnakiriyavatthu*): giving (*dāna*), moral discipline (*sīlamayapuñña*), and meditative cultivation (*bhāvanāmayapuñña*).[3] Among the four characteristics of sympathy (*sangahavatthūni*), *dāna* is the first, the other three being *peyyavajja* (kindly speech), *atthacariyā* (sagacious conduct), and *samānattatā* (impartiality).[4] It is the first of the ten perfections (*pāramita*) of a *Bodhisattva*.[5] For a long period in *saṁsāra*, the *Bodhisattva* in the *Jātaka* tales is shown practicing the virtue of *dāna*. The *Vessantara Jātaka* describes how he, once born as a king, voluntarily gave away everything including his family members.[6] In another *Jātaka*, as a hare, he willingly offered his own flesh to save a fatigued and hungry wayfarer from imminent death.[7]

In the Buddhist method of graduated teaching (*ānupubbikathā*), a sermon on *dāna* (*dānakathā*) is the first step.[8] Ordinary people who went to the Buddha for the first time were admonished about the virtue of engaging in different *dāna* related activities. The *dhamma* talks given to householders at the end of the invited meals were gifts in return, a *dhammadāna.*[9] In this regard, the Buddha says that the teaching is not done for the sake of any of the four requisites, but instead only out of compassion (*anukampā*) and for the welfare of others.[10] The *mahādāna* (great *dāna*), a special offering of food and presents to the *saṃgha* by the laity that usually extended over a week or more was particularly viewed as a meritorious deed.[11] While texts on lay morality put emphasis on *dāna* by the lay supporters, donative inscriptions refer to donations made by the monks and nuns for the purposes of building and supporting Buddhist institutions. Support by kings such as Aśoka shows the significance of royal patronage when Buddhism was in its infancy. In fact, *dāna* is considered as the first of the ten duties of a king (*dasarājadhammā*).[12]

Transfer of merit earned through *dāna* related activities was an important activity in early Buddhism. Since the transfer took place through a formal ritual in which the monks and nuns acted as channels of transference, they received *dāna* for their role in the ritual. Economic support that accrued as a result of this activity was an integral part of the institutional life of Buddhism. However, it may be pointed out here, that the practice of merit transference is completely at variance with the Buddhist theory of *kamma*, according to which, an individual is entirely accountable for all his actions and must face their consequences all by himself. According to the Pāli *Tipitika*, retribution of *kamma* is irreversible and one's fate after death cannot be influenced by others. According to Gombrich, the practice of merit transference originated out of emotional needs to escape the responsibility of orthodox *kamma* doctrine. By transferring merit, one could improve the situation of dead relatives, and one's own state after death could be influenced in the same way.[13]

Cāga which is closely allied to *dāna*, is listed in the Pāli texts as a wholesome force (*kuśala-saṁkhāra*), i.e. non-greed (*alobha*), as satisfaction (*saṃtuṭṭhi*) with minimum is central to Buddhism. The opposite of *cāga* is avarice (*macchariya/macchera*), an unwholesome force (*akuśala-saṁkhāra*) whose characteristic is 'holding on to one's own possessions', i.e. being averse to sharing one's own possessions with others and, withholding a *dāna*, i.e. stinginess (*adāna*) as a mental malady which must be renounced through the power of wisdom.[14] Thus, *cāga* is a morally wholesome quality which makes one well-disposed towards giving away or sharing one's possessions with others. In its practical application, *cāga* refers to continuous habit of giving and sharing according to one's means and ability. *Cāga* is a charitable action done to promote the happiness of others, mainly through the offer of various necessities like food, drink, and shelter.[15]

Abhayadāna (*dāna* of fearlessness) is another important feature of the Buddhist institution of *dāna*. It has been pointed out in the Pāli texts that if a person can offer security and freedom from fear to others by his behaviour, this is the highest form of *dāna*.[16] Similarly, the *Sumaṅgalavilāsinī* considers the *dāna* of one's life as the highest level of *dāna*.[17] Since life is regarded as the most precious thing for every being, it is put forward by Buddhism as the fundamental duty of every human being to abstain from causing any harm to a living being, and also to act in such a manner, that one's behaviour leads to the greatest good and happiness of maximum number of beings.[18] Talking about the ethical life of an individual, the *Sāmaññaphala Sutta* has pointed out that the first step in the ethical life of a Buddhist should be to avoid causing injury to living beings, to put away those things that are used in inflicting injury to life, to shrink at the thought of causing injury to living beings, be compassionate to all forms of life, and behave in such a manner as to bring about the welfare of all beings.[19] From a Buddhist perspective, generosity and mutual cooperation are fundamental to the building of a healthy society. If an individual covets too much, is interested only in his own welfare, and is unwilling to share some of his things for the good of others when a need for them arises, such an individual earns the hatred of the society.[20] Thus, it is said: 'One who gives makes many friends' (*dadaṃmāttiniganthati*).[21] The *Aṅguttara Nikāya*[22] lists five benefits that accrue to a donor: (1) a donor becomes acceptable to many people, (2) peace-loving good people like to associate themselves with him, (3) a good reputation spreads about him, (4) he can feel happy that he is doing his duty as a layman, and (5) after death, he is reborn in a good stage, in heaven. A person who gives another a gift of food thereby, gives the recipient the following five things with which the donor also becomes endowed in the future: long life, complexion, happiness, strength, and promptitude.[23]

According to the *Aṅguttara Nikāya*,[24] five appropriate *dānas* (*kāladāna*) are *dāna* of food given to a guest, *dāna* given to a departing person, *dāna* given to an ailing person, *dāna* made to a deserving person during a famine, and *dāna* made from the grains of the new harvest. Eight material objects suitable for *dāna* (*dānopapatti*/*dānoppatti*) mentioned in the Pāli texts are: *anna* (bread), *pāna* (water), *vattha* (clothes), *yāna* (vehicle), *mālā* (garlands), *gandha-vilepana* (scented ointment), *seyyāvasatha* (conveniences for lying down and dwelling), and *padīpeyya* (lighting material).[25] Five treasures worthy of the best *dāna* are: *khettaggadāna* (gift of thc best of standing crop), *rāsaggadāna* (gift of the best of thrashing floor), *koṭṭhaggadāna* (gift of the best of granary), *kumbhiaggadāna* (gift of the best of pottery), and *bhojanaggadāna* (gift of the best of food).[26] That which constitutes a *dāna* (*dānavatthu*)[27] or materials for a gift (*dānopakaraṇa*)[28] that drew the attention of early Indian Buddhism includes as varied things as *dinnadāna* (*dāna* of alms),[29] *pupphadāna* (*dāna* of flowers),[30] *phaladāna* (*dāna* of fruit),[31] *bhattadāna* (*dāna* of a meal),[32] *kaññādāna* (*dāna* of a girl in marriage),[33] *veḷudāna* (*dāna* of bamboo),[34] and *jīvitadāna* (*dāna* of life, i.e. to save or spare a life).[35]

Miserliness is described as a stain in a giver (*macheraṃdadatomalaṃ*).[36] In a passage in the *Saṁyutta Nikāya,* it has been pointed out that a person 'who desires merit has to overcome miserliness and be free from the stain of miserliness in giving *dāna* for, one must have merit as a good foundation for the next life'.[37] In the same text, it is further mentioned that 'A little gift given by an innocent man who looks after wife and children well and leads a virtuous life, is worth many times of the grand sacrifice made by a corrupt man who is a source of irritation to many others'.[38] In a *Sutta* in the *Majjhima Nikāya*, discussing the worth and purity of a gift, the Buddha says:

> A gift may be clean and pure from the side of the donor, but not so from the side of the recipient. This happens when the donor is virtuous, but the recipient is corrupt and given to vices. Again, a gift may be clean and pure from the side of the recipient, but not so from the side of the donor. It happens when the recipient is virtuous and the donor not so. Again, a gift may be unclean and impure from the side of the donor as well as from the side of the recipient. It happens when both donor and recipient are corrupt and given to vices. Lastly, a gift may be clean and pure from the side of the donor as well as the recipient. It happens when both of them are virtuous and pure.[39]
>
> The act of sharing one's good fortune is a deed of compassion and friendliness and, as such, very praiseworthy and meritorious.[40] In other words, *dāna* is ethically productive because it is rooted in a selfless disposition of compassion directed towards assuaging the suffering of another. Further, emphasizing the importance of mind's condition, Malalasekera points out that 'in order to share in the good deed done by another, there must be approval of it and joy in the beneficiary's heart . . . it is the thought which . . . really matters'.[41]

Occasions which marked some important event or happening in the life of a donor, such as marriage, childbirth, death, coronation, and starting a new business, etc.,[42] on which donation took place, hint at the motives behind *dāna* giving. For instance, according to the *Pañcavudha Jātaka,* on the occasion of the naming ceremony of their son, the parents offered many gifts to 800 brāhmaṇas.[43] Similarly, in the *Mahāpukkusa Jātaka* it has been mentioned that a recently married couple invited the Buddha and bestowed great gifts on him and the accompanying monks.[44] In the same way, it is pointed out in the *Kassapamaṇḍiya Jātaka* that a householder gave away in alms all his money after performing the funeral rites of his mother.[45] The *Dīgha Nikāya* and the *Aṅguttara Nikāya* offer eight motives for *dāna*-making.[46]

1. Some give spontaneously (*āsajja*).
2. Some give through fear (*bhaya*).

3. Some give because they had received things from those to whom they are giving now (*adāsimetidānaṃditi*).
4. Some give, expecting a better return in future from the recipients (*dassatimetidānaṃditi*). When one gives *dāna* to the *saṃgha*, the *dāna*-giver is sure to get a manifold return in future lives.
5. Some give because they consider it a good thing to give.
6. Some give thinking: 'I am cooking, they do not. So it behaves of me to give something to them.'
7. Some give just to get a good reputation.
8. Some give for psychological satisfaction.

Perhaps, the most important reason as to why people give *dāna* is the desire of temporal gain and spiritual merit. It has been pointed out in the *Dīgha Nikāya*, 'That which he gives he hopes to receive in his turn'.[47] The Pāli texts actually offer instances of specific gifts which brought abundant returns to the donors. Hence, in the *Milindapañha*, one comes across the story of a slave called Punnaka, who, on giving a meal to Sāriputta became a treasurer.[48] Thus, an ordinary man on seeing a wealthy man gives *dāna*, expecting to be rewarded in the next life (*dānaṃhotiparamhiloke*).[49]

The concept of sin (*pāpa, aparādha*) and the need for its expiation was widely prevalent at the time of the Buddha.[50] It has been suggested that among the *dāna*-making communities, the overwhelming majority came from the well-heeled mercantile and ruling classes, 'it was perhaps a sense of guilt produced by the exploitative nature of their economic pursuits as well as the increasingly impersonal and unscrupulous manner of their social dealings which induced them to make *dāna*'.[51] Same type of motive may be seen in the case of *dāna* made by the members of professional groups such as the courtesans and moneylenders who were looked upon with disapproval.[52] However, it has been pointed out in the Pāli texts that 'people who are up to many vices give in charity having caused lot of misery to others. That charity given after causing a lot of hardship and bewilderment to others is not worth even a fraction of a little gift made in a humble innocent way'.[53] Intention and moral character of the donor as well as *dāna* receiver appear to be crucial for the purposes of earning merit. The Pāli texts indicate that the *saṃgha* is a field of merit (*puññakkhetta*) and hence *dāna*-making to the *saṃgha* is the best way to earn merit.[54] Though, perhaps, the most powerful motive for *dāna* making in ancient Indian Buddhism was the desire for personal welfare and gain, *dāna*-making appears to have also been central to selfish considerations such as to gain happiness, to keep up 'outward appearance' for diplomacy or for the sake of a gift given in return.[55] The *Vinaya Pitaka* refers to 'wishing-gift' (*abhisaṃkhārikaṃ*) which, according to Rhys Davids and Oldenberg, is 'a gift by the giving of which the donor expressly wished that a particular result should be brought about by the normal effect of that good act in a future birth'.

Further, fear and concern for personal safety were also important motives for *dāna*-making by those engaged in perilous undertakings. The *Vimānavatthu* and the *Jātakas* give examples of merchants making gifts before setting out on hazardous journeys to foreign lands.[56]

As the practice of *dāna* giving became intimately linked to the Buddhist doctrines of *kamma* and rebirth, self-interest became fundamental to the making of the ritual of *dāna*. It has been suggested that such a development highlights not only the increasing preoccupation of an individual with his own self and his deep anxiety for personal welfare both in this world and in the next, but also his declining interest in the welfare of the community. 'Widespread practice of gift-making for the sake of gaining better station in next life would therefore bespeak growing individualism, which was fast superseding collective identity'.[57] Gombrich has categorized *dāna*-making into two parts, on the basis of motives: 'that with thought of worship (*pūjābuddhīya*) which is motivated by respect, and that with thought of favour which is motivated by pity'.[58] An example of the first one is a gift to the *saṃgha*, and the example of the second one is a gift to a beggar. Thus, in Gombrich's view, *dāna* to religious beneficiaries is made more out of respect for one's religion than pity or any material reasons. But this does not appear to be exactly correct as 'even gift to the *saṃgha* would be found to be inspired as much by the desire to earn spiritual merit or even fame for oneself as by respect for one's religious order'.[59] Interestingly, Malinowski has suggested that 'most if not all economic acts are found to belong to some chain of reciprocal gifts and counter-gifts, which in the long run balance, benefitting both sides equally'.[60] In other words, Malinowski does not consider gift giving as central or for that matter of much significance in a class-stratified society.

It has also been suggested that the 'recipient puts himself in a position of dependence vis-á-vis the donor'.[61] Pāli literature is full of examples, whereby the laity was able to influence not only individual decisions of the monks, but the whole structure of the *saṃgha*. This power derives from the monks' dependency on the support of the laity. The case of a monk from Kauśambī is a good example of this, whereby the laity was able to reverse the decision of the *saṃgha* to get the monk rehabilitated.[62] There is a constant need to maintain the fiction that the monk is not dependent upon the householder and that the asymmetry in the relationship between the giver and recipient is the natural thing. The recipient reluctantly accepts what is offered, as a favour to the giver. All of the *dāna* theorists insist that *dāna* be unreciprocated, that is, given without expectation of return from the recipient. This is one of the notable features of South Asian gift ideology since it violates what one sociologist has called the 'moral norm of reciprocity'.[63] Gifts to monks, nuns, and brāhmaṇas are conceived to flow only in one direction, and the texts play down any notion that the religions are required to make returns of any sort for their support. In practice, of course, the religious recipients of *dāna* may, to different degrees, feel obliged to preach or give *dhammadāna* in return for their material support. However, it must be noted that unless on a special lunch invitation, where *dhammadāna* may have been offered in return for a hearty meal, the monks, and the nuns did not reciprocate by giving *dhammadāna* while on begging rounds.

In conclusion, it may be said as suggested by Maria Heim, pious and devout people enjoy 'supporting the symbols and institutions of their religion, from genuine religious feeling to enhancing one's social standing through gifts'.[64] Thus, 'while self-interest in future heavenly or soteriological rewards may comprise part of the gift's value, it does not necessarily exhaust it. *Dāna* is a coincidence of interests . . . simultaneously interested and other-regarding'.[65] In fact, it 'can be messy, and contain both prudence and benevolence, duty and pleasure, freedom and obligation'.[66] Above all:

> *dāna* has allowed the theorists the opportunity to consider the value of a one-way, unreciprocated gift, not because such an act is entirely selfless and pure, but because it makes possible valued human relationships based on esteem and admiration. The presence of indigenous scholastic literatures in which pre-modern South Asians have theorized their own gift giving practices should temper some of the stronger claims voiced by anthropologists about the logic of the gift, the universality of reciprocity, and the axiomatic superiority of the donor.[67]

The exalted status of the recipient is the very condition for esteem and respect to occur in the donor. Admiration requires a textured social world, where certain figures look apart because of their moral excellence or religious virtuosity. The hierarchical values of recognition and esteem for religious distinction were viewed as some of the foundational elements of the moral and religious life. Indeed, a significant part of what it may mean to be moral or religious in South Asian religions is esteem to certain types of others. That such systems are very susceptible to ambivalence, tension, and corruption, especially when they lose sight of their moral underpinnings through institutionalization (as recognized by some of the texts), do not make them inherently corrupt.

Notes

1. *Vinaya Pitaka*, I.236; *Dīgha Nikāya*, I.53.
2. *Itivuttaka*, 98.
3. *Dīgha Nikāya*, III.218.
4. *Suttanipāta*, VV.262, 263; *Aṅguttara Nikāya*, I.92; *Jātaka*, I.86; III.471; VI.574; *Sumaṅgalavilāsinī*, I.318.
5. *Jātaka*, I.73.
6. Ibid., no. 547; see also, M. Cone and R.F. Gombrich, tr., *The Perfect Generosity of Prince Vessantara: A Buddhist Epic*, Oxford: Clarendon Press, 1977.
7. Ibid., no. 316.

8. *Dīgha Nikāya*, I.110; II.41.
9. *Vinaya Pitaka*, I.247.
10. *Majjhima Nikāya*, II.239.
11. *Petavatthu*, 111, 112.
12. *Jātaka*, III.274.
13. R.F. Gombrich, 'Merit Transference in Sinhalese Buddhism: A Case Study the Interaction between Doctrine and Practice', in *History of Religions*, 1972, vol. II, pp. 203–19.
14. *Aṅguttara Nikāya*, V.40, 209; *Milindapanho*, 279.
15. S. Tachibana, *Ethics of Buddhism*, new edition, London: Routledge, 1995, p. 200.
16. *Jātaka*. I.21, 535; V.232.
17. *Sumaṅgalavilāsinī*, 427.
18. *Saṁyutta Nikāya*, V.352–5.
19. *Dīgha Nikāya*, I.63.
20. *Suttanipāta*, VV.98, 102, 124.
21. Ibid., VV.187.
22. *Aṅguttara Nikāya*, III.41–2.
23. Ibid., III.41–2.
24. Ibid., III.41.
25. Ibid., IV.239; *Dīgha Nikāya*, III. 258.
26. *Suttanipāta Commentary*, V.270.
27. *Dīgha Nikāya*, III.258.
28. *Petavatthu Commentary*, 105.
29. *Jātaka*, III.52; *Dhammapada Atthakathā*, I.396.
30. *Sammoha-Vinodanī*, 336.
31. Ibid., 337.
32. *Petavatthu Commentary*, 54.
33. *Pañcagatidīpana*, 85.
34. *Milindapānho*, 369.
35. *Jātaka*, I.167; II.154.
36. *Dhammapada*, V.241.
37. *Saṁyutta Nikāya*, I.18.
38. Ibid.
39. *Majjhima Nikāya*, III.225–6.
40. G.P. Malalasekera, 'Transference of Merit in Ceylonese Buddhism', in *Philosophy East and West*, 1967, pp. 85–90.
41. Ibid., p. 86.
42. *Jātaka*, II.205; IV.183.
43. *Jātaka*, I.137.
44. Ibid., IV.183.
45. Ibid., III.24.
46. *Dīgha Nikāya*, III.258; *Aṅguttara Nikāya*, IV.236.
47. *Dīgha Nikāya*, III.259.
48. *Milindapanho*, IV.8.25.
49. *Itivuttaka*, 19.
50. *Suttanipāta*, VV.23, 552; *Vinaya Pitaka*, I.98, 164.
51. Vijay Nath, *Dāna: Gift System in Ancient India (c.600 BC– c.AD 300)*, New Delhi: Munshiram Manoharlal, 1987, p. 29.
52. *Dīgha Nikāya*, II.98.

53. Ibid., III.256.
54. Ibid., I.16, 11.
55. *Milindapanho*, IV.8.10.
56. *Jātaka*, IV.493.
57. Nath, *Dāna: Gift System*, p. 32.
58. R.F. Gombrich, *Buddhist Precept and Practice: Traditional Buddhism in the Rural Highlands of Ceylon*, Oxford: Clarendon Press, 1971, p. 247.
59. Nath, *Dāna: Gift System*, p. 40.
60. B. Malinowski, *Crime and Custom in Savage Society*, Totowa, NJ: Littlefield, Adams & Co., 1972, p. 40.
61. Marcel Mauss, *The Gift*, tr. W.D. Halls, London: Routledge, 1993, p. 59.
62. *Mahāvagga*, X.
63. A. Gouldner, 'The Norm of Reciprocity: A Preliminary Statement', in *American Sociological Review*, vol. 25, no. 2, 1960, pp. 162–78.
64. Maria Heim, *Theories of the Gift in South Asia: Hindu, Buddhist, and Jain Reflections on Dāna*, New York: Routledge, 2004, pp. 141–2.
65. Ibid., p. 141.
66. Ibid., p. 144.
67. Ibid., pp. 144–5.

15

Dāna: Gifts and Grants in the Name of the Buddha Bhaṭṭāraka in the Vrata System of Brahmanical Religion during Early Medieval India

A New Perspective

R.M. BHARADWAJ

THE SUBJECT-MATTER OF *dāna* is a topic of major concern in all the religious systems in India—Brahmanism, Buddhism, and Jainism, as it was through this that their existence, maintenance and growth, with the support of the laity and the political elites, were envisaged. Hundreds and thousands of verses have been solely devoted to this institution in the respective scriptures and the commentaries thereon, in which the different motives, occasions, nature, and kinds of gifts and grants, the benefactors and the beneficiaries, with their various socio-economic ramifications, have been discussed.[1] Our only concern here is to add a new perspective and new information about the occasions and the beneficiaries of the gifts and grants made in the name of the Buddha in the *vrata* system of brahmanical religious tradition, as found in the brahmanical religious texts, stone and copperplate land grant inscriptions belonging to the early medieval period, and which have remained unnoticed so far, to make the subject a little more comprehensive. It would be interesting to note that despite several instances of bitterness about the heterodox sects, more particularly the Buddhists, in the *vrata*-related verses in the brahmanical texts, we do notice attempts at inclusiveness through several *vratas* serving as the occasions for the celebration of the sacred days, auspicious for the Buddhists and giving gifts and grants, mostly to the brāhmaṇa priests but also to the Buddhists and the poor people.

A little history of the origin and development of the *vrata* culture in the brahmanical texts will help to understand its nature and functioning and its use as an occasion to accommodate Buddhism during early India. Originating from the *Ṛigveda*, *vrata* emerged as a popular religious institution in the *Smṛtis, Dharmaśāstra, Purāṇas, Mahābhārata, Jyotiṣ*, and *Nibandha* texts and the inscriptions during early India. The principal meaning of the word *vrata*, from about at least the first century CE onwards has been that of a religious undertaking or vow, observed on a certain *tithi* (lunar day), *vāra* (solar day), weekday, *nakṣatra* (planetary constellation), *māsa* (month) or other period, for securing some desired object by the worship of a deity, usually accompanied by restrictions to food and behaviour.[2] P.V. Kane in his *History of Dharmaśāstra* says that a *vrata* comprehends several items such as *snāna* (bath), *Prātah-Sandhyā* (the morning prayer), *Saṁkalpa* (resolve or vow to undertake a *vrata*-rite), *homa* (offering into the fire), *pūjā* (worship) of the deity or deities in whose honour the *vrata* is undertaken, *upavāsa* (fasting), feeding the brāhmaṇas, maidens or married women or the poor and *dāna* (gifts such as cows, money, garments and sweetmeats, etc.) and the observance of certain rules of conduct during the course of the *vrata*.[3]

Here, one point which is to be noted is that the once simple looking *vrata* became one of the foremost topics of discussion of the *Purāṇas, Smṛtis,* and *Jyotiṣ* texts of the Gupta and the post-Gupta period and its number appears to be increasing during this period. Kane says that the number of *vrata*s in the first century of the Christian era was not large but gradually, their number increased and reached up to the region of 1000.[4] Some of the *Purāṇas* which belong to this period have devoted thousands of verses to them, like the *Bhaviṣya Purāṇa* contains about 12,500 verses on *vratas*, *Matsya Purāṇa* (chaps. 54–92 and 95–101) has about 1,230 verses (most of which occur in the *Padma Purāṇa*), the *Varāha Purāṇa* (chaps. 39–65) has about 700 verses and the *Viṣṇudharmottara Upapurāṇa* about 1,600 verses on them. There is no topic of *Dharmaśāstra* except, probably, that of *Tīrthayātrā* (pilgrimage) and *Śraddha* (funeral rites) on which *Purāṇas* wax so eloquent as on *vratas* and on a modest calculation, the *Purāṇas* contain about 25,000 verses at least on *vratas*.[5] The *Krityakalpataru*, an important extant published work of *Nibandha* form of early twelfth century CE by Lakṣhmīdhara, mentions about 244 *vratas*[6] and only a century and quarter later, the *Caturvarga-cintāmaṇi* of Hemādri, another *Nibandha* text, mentions about 700 of them.[7]

R.S. Sharma writes that, in many ways the medieval period (including the early medieval period starting from about the sixth century CE) was an age of elaboration and proliferation and this is true not only for castes (*Jātis*) and *gotras* (belonging to one common ancestor) but also for *tīrthas* and *vratas*.[8] What might have been the reasons behind the coming into being of such a large number of *vrata*? Sharma further says that this must have been partly due to the result of the liberal attitude adopted by the *Smārta* (authors of the *Smṛti* texts on religious, social and legal matters) and the *Purāṇic* writers to widen the social base of religions in place of the narrow (caste-based) religions of the *Vedas* and that of *vratas,* which may have multiplied because they were thrown open to all.[9] Kane quotes Devala, an eighth to ninth century CE *Smṛti* writer according to whom, women and members of all *varṇas* (castes) were allowed to perform *vratas* and were supposed to be released from sin.[10] The *Matsya Purāṇa* (Matsya, 7032) says that the *vratas* may be observed by all, without discrimination '*Avicåreṇa . . . Anuṣṭheyam*'.[11]

The moot point here is, what were the compelling forces behind this apparent religious liberality of the *Purāṇic* writers? Under considerable social, religious and political pressure, the brahmanical social and religious ideologues had to adopt liberality and relax the rules of the religious rituals. The pre-eminent social and religious position of the brāhmaṇas, the authority of the *Vedas* and the *Varṇāśramadharma* (the duties of the castes and the four stages of life), which served their interests well came under attack from the heterodox sects, the early character of Vaiṣṇavism and Śaivism, the coming of the foreigners and the emergence of *Tantrism*, among others.

The brahmanical religion, rooted in the *Vedas* allowed the highest place to the brāhmaṇas in the society. They formed the intellectual class among the *Āryans* and commanded the highest respect. Their duties were the performance of sacrifices, the study of the *Vedas* and making gifts and they depended for maintenance, upon the liberality of kinds and others received, mainly, in the forms of priestly fees and gifts. They enjoyed allowances and preferences, even in the courts of justice. The śūdras were to serve the twice born who claimed absolute rights over the earning of their respective slaves (*Tadartho 'sya nicayaḥ Syāt-Gautam Dharmasūtra*).[12] Such a state of Brahmanism continued more or less smoothly for a time until there arose many new religious systems, some of which were clear protests against the position of the brāhmaṇas and the authority of the *Vedas*, while others were not favourable to the *Varṇāśramadharma*. The rise and propagation of these rival faiths proved very fatal to the sacrificial religion of the Vedic brāhmaṇas, which was already on the decline.[13]

The religion of the Buddha, like Mahāvīra and Maṅkhaliputta, was in every way, detrimental to the interests of Brahmanism. The Buddhists, especially those who entered the *saṃgha*, practised *ahiṁsā* (non-violence), did not regard the *Vedas* the Vedic gods and goddesses, and the brāhmaṇas did not recognize caste distinctions and cared little for the *Varṅāśramadharma*. In their opinion, '*śraddha*' was a mere policy of the brāhmaṇas. These and similar other ideas and practices of the Buddhists made them the bitterest enemies of Brahmanism.[14]

An account of this social disorder can be gathered from the early Buddhist literature and *Purāṇas*. In the latter treatises, there are chapters on the descriptions of the Kali-age (*Kaliyuga*) which can reasonably be taken into account on the Hindu society during the period ranging from the time of the prevalence of the Buddhism and Jainism, i.e. from the reign of the Nandas (of Magadha) to the end of the Andhra rule (till *c.*230 CE) in western India. As these chapters (*Matsya Purāṇa*, 144, 40 and 43; *Vāyu*, 58, 40; *Kūrma*, I 29, 7; and so on) speak of many śūdra kings who ruled in the Kali-age and encouraged the spread of Buddhism and Jainism and as in the *Purāṇas,* Mahāpadmananda is called the first śūdra king.[15]

Some of the chapters of the *Purāṇas* which come from comparatively early dates (like the chap. 44 of the *Matsya*, chap. 58 of *Vāyu* and other chaps. of the *Bhāgavata*, *Kūrma, Brahmāṇḍa*, and *Visṇu Purāṇas*) give the picture of a society in which the people often neglected the caste and *Āshrama* rules and were influenced by the non-brahmanic and anti-brahmanic ideas as they spoke ill of the brāhmaṇas, the *Vedas*, the *Dharmaśāstra* and the *Purāṇas* on account of the spread of Buddhism and Jainism, and defied the supremacy of the brāhmaṇas. This was the state of society during the fourth century BCE to third–fourth century CE as described in the verses common to the chapters on the description on the Kali-age. Thus, the *Purāṇas* give a dismal picture of the troubles of the Kali-age.[16]

Kane maintains that in order to wean away the common people from these two schisms (Buddhism and Jainism), it is probable that the learned followers of the Vedic system hit upon the idea of glorification of the *vratas* and promised heaven and other worldly and spiritual rewards to those who performed them and that were comparatively easy and within the reach of all, instead of sacrifices which were costly.[17] Hazra also says that apart from other measures, the authors of the *Purāṇas* and *Nibandhas* are found to have attempted to re-establish the *Varṇāśramadharma* (among the śūdras and women) through the *Purāṇic vratas* and *pūjas* (worship).[18]

It is against this background that we shall be analysing the references to the gifts and grants in the name of the divine Buddha and *saṃgha* in brahmanical literature. For this purpose, among the literary sources, we have scanned, for references to the Buddha, three *Smṛtis* work—the *Visṇu Smṛti*, *Nārada Smṛti* and *Devala Smṛti*, five *Purāṇas*—the *Bhāgavata*, *Matsya*, *Nīlamata, Agni,* and *Vāmana* and the two *Jyotiṣ* texts—the *Bṛhatsaṃhitā* of Vārāhamihira and *Rājamārtaṇḍa* of King Bhoja, and also the *History of Dharmaśāstra* by P.V. Kane and the inscriptions of the period of our study. Here also, at various places, we do find that the *Smṛtis* and *Purāṇas* do exhibit some enmity and bitterness towards the heterodox sects when the performers have been warned not to talk and give gifts to the atheists and monks. Kane quotes the *Bhaviṣya Purāṇa* (*Brahma Parva*, chap. 104, verses 2–24) where the *Trigati Saptamī Vrata*[19] warns its performers not to talk to an atheist. *Bhaviṣya Purāṇa* (*Brahma Parva*, chap. 1, verses 1–12) where the *Sarvāpti Saptamī Vrata*[20] also warns its performers not to talk to an atheist; in the *Bhaviṣya Purāṇa*, the *Putrasaptamī Vrata*[21] also warns its performers not to talk to an atheist in the course of a *vrata*; *Matsya Purāṇa* (chap. 69, verses

19–65), where the *Bhīmadvādaśī Vrata*[22] warns its performers not to talk to an atheist; the same *Purāṇa* in the *Vibhūtidvādaśī Vrata*[23] warns its performers not to indulge in talks with the *Pāṣaṇḍins*, i.e. atheists, in the course of the *vrata*. The *Brhamakṛchhra Vrata*[24] of the *Devala Smṛti* (verses 2134–47) which prescribes that the performer should perform this *vrata* by giving eight milk cows, with their horns adorned with gold to the *Veda*-knowing brāhmaṇas and that its performers will destroy sins like, giving food to the chief of the monks' church, which seems to include the Buddhist monks, among others. Apart from these references, there are various other references in the *Purāṇas* and *Nibandhas*, where the performers of the *vratas* have been expressly warned not to indulge in talks with the atheists along with other forbidden categories of people in course, during a *vrata.*

But despite such anti-atheist references in the *Smṛti* and *Purāṇas*, the references to at least six *vratas* in the *Purāṇa*, *Nibandhas*, and *Jyotiṣ* text and three *vratas* in the inscriptions about the Buddha and Buddhist establishment come to us as a pleasant surprise. The honourable place where Lord Buddha and the Buddhist establishment have been accorded in the ever-widening sphere of *vrata*-culture during the period of our study hints at striking a rapport with the powerful and the popular religious personality with a very powerful religious philosophy and mass following on the part of the *Smārta* and *Purāṇic* religious teachers. The latter have accorded the same religious status to Lord Buddha, as has been accorded to other Vedic and *Purāṇic* deities and given birth to the same set of traditional rituals for worshipping the Buddha which was obtained for other deities in the *Smṛtis*, *Purāṇas* and *Nibandhas*, and this way the *Smārta-Purāṅic* religious ideologues absorbed an influential religious ideological fold by turning the latter into one of their deities through the concept of *avatāra* (theory of incarnation). Let us have a look at these *vratas*.

1. *Buddhajanmamahaḥ* (the festival of the birth of Lord Buddha): The seventh–eight century CE *Nīlamata Purāṇa* of Kashmir mentions this *vrata* and says that the birthday of lord Buddha should be celebrated in the bright half of the month of *Vaiśākha*, when the moon is the *Puṣya nakṣatra*. The image of the Buddha should be bathed with holy water and established with the texts uttered by the Śakya. The *vihāras* (dwellings of the Śakyas) and *caityas* (abodes of the god) should be whitewashed, decorated and the monks be given *cīvara* (saffron-coloured robes worn by the Buddhist monks) food and books and *naivedya* (remains of the food-offering to the lord) and gifts be given to the poor people. All this celebration should go on for three days and singing and dancing should also take place. It should also be noted that in the *Nīlamata Purāṇa* also, the Buddha is declared to be an *avatāra* of god

Visṇu in *Kaliyuga*.[25] The Buddha's *Parinirvāṇa* (final emancipation from the cycle of birth and death) took place in the lunar month of Kārttika, according to the *Sarvāstivādins* and, in Vaiśākha according to the Ceylonese tradition vide Bajaur casket inscription of Menander's reign in Epigraphia Indica (vol. 24, p. 6).[26]

2. *Jyaiṭha Śukla Dvitīya*: Kane quotes this *vrata* from Hemādri's *Caturvarga-cintāmaṇi* (*Vrata Khaṇḍa*, pt. I, p. 1039), who in turn has borrowed it from the *Varāha Purāṇa* (48.20–2) of about *c*.800 CE talks about which *avatāra* (incarnation) out of the well-known ten (including the Buddha and the Kalkin as separate) is worshipped for which purpose and motive.[27]
3. *Buddha-dvādaśī*: The early twelfth century the *Nibandha Krityakalpataru* quotes this *vrata* from the *Varāha Purāṇa*, which prescribes that on the twelfth of the bright half of the month of Śrāvaṇa, the performer should worship the god Buddha representing the god Visṇu and establish a pot and place a golden image of the Buddha on it and after worshipping him, donate it to a brāhmaṇa. The king Śuddhodana observed this *vrata* and the god Visṇu himself was born to him as his son, in the form of the Buddha. The sage *Durvāsā* says in the *Varāha Purāṇa* that by performing this *vrata*, the performer will get wealth, sons and grandsons like the King Śuddhodana.[28] Kane says that the *Varāha Purāṇa* (55.37) refers to the *avatāras* from *Nṛsiṃha* to *Rāma* and it proceeds to '*namostu te Buddha Kalkin Vareṣa*' ('Salutations to the Buddha who is a revered god in the Kali-age'). The fifth–sixth century CE *Jyotiṣ* text, *Bṛhatsaṃhitā* by Vārāhamihira (57.44) provides directions for making the image of the Buddha.[29]
4. *Buddhavrata*: Kane has taken this *vrata* from Hemādri's *Caturvarga-cintāmaṇi* (on *Vrata*, pt. II, p. 578), who, in turn has taken it from the *Bhaviṣyottara (Upa)-Purāṇa* which says that when the planet Buddha (mercury) comes to the *Vaiśākha nakṣatra*, one should observe this *vrata* for seven days by keeping fast during the day and eating only at night and place a golden image of Buddha in a bell metal vessel and worship him with white garlands and *gandha* and donate it to a brāhmaṇa. The Buddha sharpens intellect and conveys real knowledge.[30]
5. *Buddhāṣṭamī*: Kane has taken this *vrata* from the eleventh century *Jyotiṣ* and *Dharmaśāstric* texts of *Nibandha* form, the *Rājamārtaṇḍa* by King Bhoja Paramara and the *Caturvarga-cintāmaṇi* of Hemādri (on *Vrata*, pt. I, pp. 866–73) who has taken it from the *Bhaviśyottara* (541.59) which says that when the bright eight days fall on the *Buddha tithi*, i.e. Wednesday, the performer (*vratin*) should eat only once a day and donate on eight *astamis* (eighths), respectively, eight jars full of

water, with a piece of gold inside and with different edibles on each *astami*, and at the end, donate a golden image of the Buddha.[31]

6. *Buddhāṣṭamī*: The ninth century CE work *Agni Purāṇa* (chap. 184, verse 920) says that this *vrata* is performed on the eighth lunar day of a month, the effect of which sets the manes free from hell and leads them to heaven.[32]
7. *Śrāvaṇa Śukla Pañcamī*: The Bodhgayā stone inscription of King Tunga Dharmāvaloka, of the Rasasktrakuta dynasty mentions this *vrata* which states that King Tunga Dharmāvaloka dedicated a well-scented temple (*gandhakutī*) for the service of Lord Buddha at Bodhgayā on the sacred *vrata* day of *Śrāvaṇa Śuka Pañcamī* in the tenth or the early eleventh century CE.[33]
8. *Viṣuva Saṅkrānti*: A copperplate inscription of King Vigrahapala III of the year *c.*1066 CE records the grant of land, in the provenance of Bengal, by the king after a ceremonial bath in the Ganges, on the pious occasion of *Viṣuva Saṅkrānti* (vernal equinox). The land was granted in the name of the Buddha *Bhaṭṭāraka* (the venerable one) for the religious merit and fame, in favour of a brāhmaṇa with the request to the cultivators to pay all due, payable to the king (*rājā pratyādāya*) to the (brāhmaṇa) donee.[34]
9. *Candroparāge*, i.e. Lunar Eclipse: The Āmgāchī grant of King Vigrahapala III of the Pāla dynasty, of the year *c.*1067 CE, records the grant of a village to a brāhmaṇa by the king, in honour of the Buddha *Bhaṭṭāraka*, after bathing in the Ganges on the sacred *vrata* day of a lunar eclipse, which fell on the ninth day of the bright half of *Caitra*, i.e. *Caitra navami*. The grant was given along with the rights of *daśaparādhadaṇḍa* (fines from the ten offences), *cauroddharaṇa* (catching thieves), *acāṭabhaṭa praveśa* (free from the entry of the regular and the irregular army of the king) and *samasta bhāga-bhoga-kara-hiraṇyādi* (with all shares, taxes and mining of gold, etc.) to the brāhmaṇa donee.[35]

This way, we see that at least nine *vratas* have emerged before us in some of the *Purāṇas*, *Nibandhas* and *Jyotiṣ* texts (like the *Rājamārtaṇḍa*) and the inscriptions which prescribe the worship of the image of the Buddha along the traditional line of worship of other *Purāṇic* and *Smārta* deities, giving gifts to the Buddhist monks and the Buddhist establishment, and the giving away of the golden image of the Buddha, the land and the village and other things to the brāhmaṇa priests and other poor people on the religious occasion of the *vratas* dedicated to the Buddha, suggests that the *Smārta* and *Purāṇic* writers were coming to terms with Buddhism and were broadening up the base of their religion by absorbing a powerful and popular religious personality, his religion and his followers. Where, on the one hand, this absorption of Buddhism helped strengthen the brahmanical religion and broaden up its social and religions base, it also seemed to have marginally shrunken the exclusiveness of the Buddhist religion which, in turn, would have led to the shrinking of the mass following, which it once enjoyed.

But, our hunch in presenting this paper is also to show a new perspective in the sense that an entirely new kind of occasion in the form of the sacred *vrata* days is discernible in some of the brahmanical texts. In the seventh to the eighth century CE the *Nīlamata Purāṇa* of Kashmir, Lord Buddha's birth ceremony has been asked to be celebrated with much fanfare by the writer. The image of the Buddha is bathed with holy water and established with the texts uttered by the Śakya Buddha himself. The *vihāras* and the *Caityas* are white-washed, decorated and the monks are given *civara*, food and books, and gifts and *naivedya* are distributed amongst the poor. It has been asked to celebrate this for three days with singing and dancing. In the supposedly tenth–eleventh century, a Rashtrakuta King Tung Dharmāvaloka dedicates a *gandhakutī* for the service of the Lord Buddha at Bodhgayā on the sacred *vrata* day of Śrāvaṇa Śukla Pañcamī. In other *vratas* named after the Buddha, the golden image of the lord is worshipped but is donated to the persons of the priestly class, the brāhmaṇas, who have no objection in accepting gifts of gold in the name of a god whose position is still tenuous amongst this class, despite his inclusion in the list of the *avatāras* of Visṇu. During the eleventh century CE in Bengal, the famous Pāla king celebrates two brahmanical, religiously meritorious *vrata* days of *Viṣuva Saṅkrānti* (vernal equinox) and *Candroparāge* (lunar eclipse), takes ritual bath in the river Ganges and grants land and village in the name of the Buddha *Bhaṭṭāraka*, but to the persons of the priestly class of brāhmaṇas. In the last two cases, only the name of the Buddha has been used but the occasions are the brahmanical *vrata* days and the grantees are also not the Buddhist monks, but the brāhmaṇa priests. This is a beautiful example of an attempt of diplomacy as well as syncretism on the part of the Pāla ruler. The brāhmaṇas also have no objection in receiving grants in the name of the Buddha. It also speaks about the fact that the religion of the Buddha had become too prevalent amongst the populace, which the priestly brāhmaṇas just could not ignore. The *Bhaviṣyottara* (*Upa)-Purāṇa* and the *Caturvarga-cintāmaṇi* by Hemādri betray a strong and rare statement on the part of the priestly ideologues when, the reward of the celebration of the *Buddvhavrata* is that 'the Buddha will sharpen intellect and convey real knowledge'. The use of *vrata* occasions and the gifts and grants made on such occasions may be analysed differently by different scholars in future studies on the subject, but the above-mentioned points, I hope, may be seen as adding a new perspective to the subject of occasion, motive, and the nature of gifts and grants in the brahmanical religious texts and inscriptions during the early medieval period in India.

Notes

1. Radha Madhav Bharadwaj, *Vratas* and *Utsavas* in north and central India: A Study of the Literary, and Epigraphic Sources Between the Fifth and Twelfth Centuries AD, unpublished Ph.D. Thesis of the University of Delhi, 2007, pp. 37–359. In these pages, a number of the *Smṛtis*, *Purāṇas*, *Jyotiṣ* texts, *Nibandhas* (religious treatises) and the inscriptions belonging to north-central India between the fifth and twelfth centuries have been thoroughly scanned to shed light on the original and relevant information regarding the occasions, motives, donors, and donees, and the nature of gifts and grants have been recorded and analysed. For more information, also see, V. Nath, *Dāna: Gift System in Ancient India* (*c.*600 CE–*c.*300 AD), New Delhi: Munshiram Manoharlal, New Delhi, 1987, p. 29; For gifts in the Buddhist scriptures, see various sutras in the texts like the *Vinay Pitaka*, *Dīgha Nikāya,* and *Aṅguttara Nikāya*; Richard F. Gombrich, *Buddhist Precept and Practice: Traditional Buddhism in the Rural Highlands of Ceylonese Tradition*, Clarendon Press, Oxford, 1971, p. 247 (to name just a few original and some secondary works).
2. Bharadwaj, '*Vratas* and *Utsavas*', pp. 26–33, 36–101, 130–246, 278–359; also see, P.V. Kane, *History of Dharmasāstra*, vol. V, pt. I, Poona: Bhandarkar Oriental Research Institute, 1958, p. 28.
3. Ibid., p. 31.
4. Ibid., p. 46.
5. Ibid., p. 57.
6. K.V. Rangaswami Aiyangar, ed., *The Kṛtyakalpataru of Bhaṭṭ Lakṣmīdhara*, Baroda: Baroda Oriental Institute, 1953, pp. 1–469.
7. Saratchandra Siromani, ed., *The Caturvarga-Cintāmaṅi of Hemādri*, Varanasi: Choukhambha Sanskrit Santhan, 1985.
8. R.S. Sharma, *Perspectives in Social and Economic History of Early India*, New Delhi, 1983, p. 229.
9. Ibid.
10. Kane, '*Dharmaśāstra*', p. 51.
11. R.C. Hazra, *Studies in the Purāṅic Records on Hindu Rites and Customs*, 2nd edn., Delhi: Motilal Banarsidass, 1975, p. 256.
12. Ibid., pp. 193–4.
13. Ibid., p. 194.
14. Hazra, '*Purāṅic Studies*', p. 197.
15. Ibid., p. 206; *Matsya Purāṇa*, pp. 176–88, 272; *Vāyu*, pp. 326–27a.
16. Ibid., pp. 208–10.
17. Kane, '*Dharmaśāstra*', p. 43.
18. Hazra, '*Purāṅic Studies*', p. 238.
19. Kane, '*Dharmaśāstra*', pp. 141–5.
20. Ibid., pp. 168–9.
21. Ibid., pp. 166–7.
22. Ibid., pp. 354–9.
23. Ibid.
24. M.L. Wadekar, *Devala Smṛti: Reconstruction and a Critical Study*, vol. I (Introduction and Text), Delhi: Koshal Book Depot, 1996, pp. 259–61.
25. Ved Kumari, ed., *The Nīlamata Purāṇa*, vol. I, Jammu and Kashmir: Jammu and Kashmir Academy of Arts, Culture and Languages, 1968, p. 2002.

26. Kane, '*Dharmaśāstra*', p. 257.
27. Ibid., pp. 262–3; for the period of the verses in *Varāha Purāṇa*, Ch. 48; see Hazra, '*Purāṇic Studies*', p. 180.
28. Aiyangar, '*Kṛtyalkalpataru*', pp. 331–2.
29. Kane, '*Dharmaśāstra*', p. 357.
30. Ibid.
31. Ibid.
32. M.N. Dutta Shastra, *Agni Purāṇa*, vol. II, Varanasi, 1967, pp. 675-6.
33. Bhagwant Sahai, *The Inscriptions of Bihar*, New Delhi, 1983, p. 127.
34. D.C. Sircar, *Two Pāla Plates from Belwa: Plate of Vigrahapala III; Regnal Year 11*, Epigraphia Indica, vol. XXIX, Delhi, 1957, pp. 9–13.
35. R.D. Banerjee, *The Āmagāchī Grant of Vigrahapala III; The 12th Year*, Epigraphia Indica, vol. XV, repr., New Delhi, 1982, pp. 293–301.

Bibliography

Original Sources

Advayavajrasaṁgraha, tr. Haraprasad Sastri, Baroda: GOS, no. XL, 1927.

Ain-i-Akbari (Abul Fazl), 2 vols., tr. H.S. Jarrett, New Delhi: Low Price Publications, repr. 2011.

Amarakosha of Amarasimha, ed. T. Ganapati Sastri, 4 vols., Trivandrum, 1914–17.

Aṅguttara Nikāya, tr. E.M. Hare, *The Book of Gradual Sayings*, 5 vols., Indian edn., New Delhi: MLBD, 2006.

Arthasastra of Kautilya, tr. R. Shamasastri, Mysore: Banglore Government Press, 1915.

Aśokavadana, tr. J.S. Strong, *The Legend of King Aśoka: A Study and Translation of the Aśokavadana*, New Delhi: MLBD, repr. 2002.

Avadānasarasammuccaya, tr. Michael Hahn, *Der grosse Legendenkranz (Mahājātakamala): Eine Mittelalteriliche buddistischu legendensammlung aus Nepal*, Wiesbaden: O. Harrassowitz, 1985.

Avādānaśataka, tr. J.S. Speyer, *Avadanacataka: A Century of Edifying Tales Belonging to Hinayana*, 2 vols. in one, The Hague: Mouton and Co. 1958.

Caturvarga-Cintāmaṅi of Hemādri, ed. Śaratchandra Śirōmaṇi, Vārānasī: Choukhambha Sanskrit Santhan, 1985.

Cullavagga, tr. T.W. Rhys Davids and Herman Oldenberg, *Vinaya Text*, Sacred Books of the East, vols. XVII, XX, New Delhi: Low Price Publications, repr. 1996.

Dhammapada, tr. F. Max Müller, Sacred Books of the East, vol. X, New Delhi: Low Price Publications, repr. 2006.

Dhammapadaatthakatha, ed. C.S. Upasaka, Nalanda: Nav Nalanda Vihara, 1973.

Dīgha Nikāya, tr. Maurice Walshe, *The Long Discourses of the Buddha* (A Translation of *Dīgha Nikāya*), Boston: Wisdom Publication, 2012.

Divyāvadana, ed. Edward B. Cowell and Robert A. Neil, *The Divyavadana: A Collection of Early Buddhist Legends*, Amsterdam: Oriental Press, 1970.

Gautama-Dharmasūtra, tr. L. Srinivasacharya, Mysore: The Government Branch Press, 1917.

Itivuttaka, ed., E. Windish, London: Pali Text Society, 1889.

Jātaka, E.B. Cowell, *The Jātaka or the Stories of Buddha's Former Births*, vols. I–V, New Delhi: Munshiram Manoharlal, 1990, repr., V. Fausball, London: Freebner and Co., 1872.

Jātakamālā, ed. J.S. Speyer, *The Gātakamala or Gārland of Birth Stories by Aryasura: Sacred Books of Buddhists*, New Delhi: MLBD, repr. 1990.

Kṛtyakalpataru of Bhaṭṭ, ed. *Lakṣmīdhara*, K.V. Rangaswami Aiyangar, Baroda Oriental Institute, 1953.

Mahāprajñāpāramitāśāstra, tr. Lamotte, Étienne, Treatise on the Great Virtue of Wisdom of Nāgārjuna, Leuven, 1980.

Mahāvagga, I.B. Horner, *The Book of the Discipline* (*Vinaya-Pitaka*), vol. 3 (*Mahāvagga*), London: The Pali Text Society (first published in 1951), 1982.

Mahāvastu, tr. J.J. Jones, London: Luzac and Company, 1949.

Majjhima Nikāya, I.B. Horner, *The Collection of the Middle Length Sayings* (*Majjhima Nikāya*), vol. I, Pali Text Society, Oxford (first printed in 1954), repr. 1995.

Manusmriti, 'With Medhatitithi's Commentary', ed. J.R. Gharpure, Bombay, 1920.

Milindapanho, ed., V. Trenckner, London: Williams and Norgate, 1880.

Mūlasarvāstivāda Vinaya, ed. G. Bagachi, *Mulsavastivdvinoyavastu*, vol. I, Darbhanga: Mithila Vidyapeeth, 1967.

Nīlamata Purāṇa, ed. Ved Kumari, vol. I, Jammu and Kashmir: Academy of Arts, Culture and Languages, 1968.

Rehla of Ibn Battuta, ed. Mahdi Husain, Baroda: Oriental Institute, 1976.

Saddharma Pundarika, ed. P.L. Vaidya, Darbhanga: Mithila Institutes, 1960.

Sammoha-Vinodanī: Abhidhamma-Piṭakake Vibhaṅgh Aṭṭhakathā, ed. A.P. Buddhadatta, London: Pali Text Society, 1923.

Saṁyutta Nikāya, F.L. Woodword, *The Book of the Kindred Sayings* (*Saṁyutta-Nikāya*) *or Grouped Sutta*, Oxford: The Pali Text Society (first published in 1927), repr. 1996.

Siksasamuccya (Shantideva), tr. Cecil Bendall, *A Compendium of Buddhist Doctrine*, New Delhi: MLBD, 1990.

Sumaṅgalavilāsinī: Buddhaghosa's Commentary on the Dīgha Nikāya, ed. T.W. Rhys Davids, J.E. Carpentier and W. Stede, 3 vols., London: Pali Text Society, 1886–1932.

Suttanipāta, ed. K.R. Norman, Oxford: Pali Text Society, 2001.

Theragātha, tr. K.R. Norman, Oxford: Pali Text Society, 1969.

Therīgātha, tr. C.A.F. Rhys David and K.R. Norman, Oxford: Pali Text Society, 1989.

Vimānavatthu, ed. N.A. Jayawickrama, London: Pali Text Society, 1977.

Vinaya Pitaka, ed. H. Oldenberg, London: PTS, 1879–83, tr. T.W. Rhys Davids and Herman Oldenberg, *Vinaya Texts*, 3 vols., Sacred Books of the East, New Delhi: Low Price Publications, repr. 1996.

Viśuddhimagga, tr. Bhikkhu Nynmoli, *The Path of Purification*, London: Shambhala, 1976.

Yajñavalkya Smriti, with the commentary of Vijanesvara, ed. Vasudev Lakshman Shastri, Bombay: Nirnayasagar Press, 1913.

Chinese Sources

Beal, S., *Si-yu-ki, Buddhist Records of the Western World*, tran. from the Chinese of Hiuen-Tsang, 2 vols., London, 1906, New Delhi: Low Price Publications, repr. 1995.

Giles, H.A., *The Travels of Fa-hien or Record of Buddhist Kingdom*, Cambridge, 1923.

Julien, S., *Memoires sur les Contrees Occidentales*, trans. of Hiuen-Tsang, Paris, 1857–8.

Legge, J.H., *Record of the Buddhist Kingdoms, being an Account of the Chinese Monk Fa-hien's*, New Delhi: Oriental Publication, repr. 1972.

Takakusu, J.A.I.-Tsingh, *A Record of the Buddhistic Religion as Practiced in India and Malay Archipelago* (*AD 671–695*), New Delhi: Munshiram Manoharlal, repr. 2001.

Watters, Thomas, *On Yuan Chwang's Travels in India*, AD 629–645, ed. T.W. Rhys Davids and S.W. Bushell, 2 vols., London, repr. 1904, New Delhi: Low Price Publications, 2000.

Tibetan Sources

Dhammasvamı, *Biography of Dhammasvamı* (*Chag lo tsa-ba Chos rje-dpal*): *A Tibetan Monk Pilgrim*, tr. George Roerich, Patna: K.P. Jayaswal Research Institute, 1959.

Sumpa, Khan, *Pag Sam Jon Zang*, by po yece pal jor, ed. Sarat Chandra Das, *History of Rise, Progress and Downfall of Buddhism in India*, Calcutta: Princeton Jail Press, 1908.

Tārānāth, tr. Lama Chimpa and A. Chattopadhyaya, *Taranatha's History of Buddhism in India*, Shimla: Indian Institute of Advanced Studies, 1970.

Bo-ston, tr. E. Obermiller, *Bo-ston's History of Buddhism*, Wisdom Publication, Boston, 2001.

Secondary Sources

Adhya, G.L., *Early Indian Economics*, Bombay: Asia Publishing House, 1966.

Agrawala, Vasudeva Sharan, *Sārnāth*, Delhi: ASI, 1980

Aiyangar, S. Krishnaswami, *Manimegalai and its Historical Setting*, London: Luzac, 1927.

Aiyanger, K.V.R., *Aspects of Ancient Indian Economic Thought*, Vārānasī: Banaras Hindu University, 1965.

Akira, Hirakawa, *A History of Early Buddhism: From Sakyamuni to Early Mahāyāna*, Hawaii: University of Hawaii Press, 1990.

Altekar, A.S. and V. Mishra, *Report of Kkumrahar Excavation 1951–55*, Patna: K.P. Jayaswal Institute, 1959.

Amore, R.C., *The Concept and Practice of Doing Merit in Early Theravāda Buddhism*, Ph.D. Dissertation, Columbia University, 1971.

Aronson, Harvey B., *Love and Sympathy in Theravāda Buddhism*, Delhi: Motilal Banarsidass, 1980.

Bahadur, Rai Ram Anugarah Narayan Singh, *A Brief History of Bodh Gaya Math*, Calcutta: Bengal Secretariat Press, 1892.

Banerjee, R.D., *The Āmagāchī Grant of Vigrahapala III: The 12th Year, Epigraphia Indica*, vol. XV, repr., New Delhi: ASI, 1982.

Barua, B.M., *Aśoka and his Inscriptions*, Calcutta: New Age Publishers, 1946.

Basham, A.L., 'Emperor Aśoka', in *Indological Studies: D.C. Sircar Commemoration Volume*, ed. S.K Maity and Upendra Thakur, New Delhi, 1987, pp. 64–70.

Bhandarkar, D.R., *Carmichael Lectures on Ancient Indian Numismatics*, New Delhi: Asian Educational Services, 1921; repr. 1990.

Bhandarkar, D.R., *Aśoka*, Calcutta: Calcutta University, 1955.

Bailey, F.G., ed., *Gifts and Poison: The Politics of Reputation*, New York: Schocken Books, 1971.

Bharadwaj, Radha Madhav, *Vratas* and *Utasavas*, in North and Central India: A Study of the Literary, and Epigraphic Sources Between the Fifth and Twelfth Centuries AD, unpublished Ph.D. Thesis of the University of Delhi, 2007.

Bhattacharya, Binoytosh, *Indian Buddhist Iconography*, Calcutta: K.L. Mukhopadhyaya, 1968.

Bhattacharya, G., 'Dāna-Deyadharma: Donation in Early Buddhist Records (in Brāhmī)', in *Investigating Indian Art: Proceedings of a Symposium on the Development of Early Buddhist and Hindu Iconography*, ed. M. Yaldiz and W. Lobo, Berlin: Museum fur Indische Kunst, 1987.

Biswas, T.K. and B. Jha, *Gupta Scultpures*, Vārānasī: Bharat Kala Bhavan, 1985.

Bodhi, Bhikkhu, ed., *Dāna: The Practice of Giving*, The Wheel Publication No. 367/369, Kandy: Buddhist Publication Society, 1990.

Boulding, Kenneth, *The Economy of Love and Fear: A Preface to Grants Economics*, California: Woodsworth Publishing Company, 1973.

Brekke, Torkel, 'The Early Sanmgha and the Laity', *Journal of the International Association of Buddhist Studies*, 1997.

———, 'Contradiction and the Merit of Giving in Indian Religions', *Numen*, 1998, vol. 45, no. 3, 1998, pp. 287–320.

Bremner, R.H., *Giving: Charity and Philanthropy in History*, London: Transaction Publishers, 1994.

Bühler, G., 'Votive Inscriptions of Sanchi', *Epigraphia Indica*, New Delhi: ASI, 1894.

Burr, Angela, 'Merit-Making and Ritual Reciprocity: Tambiah's Theory Examined', *Journal of the Siam Society*, vol. 66, pt. I, 1978, pp. 102–8.

Chakraborty, S.K., *A Study of Ancient Indian Numismatics (Indigenous System) from the Earliest Times to the Rise of the Imperial Guptas*, Mymensingh, 1931.

Chakravarti, Uma, *The Social Dimensions of Early Buddhism*, New Delhi: Oxford University Press, 1987.

Chandra, Moti, *The World of Courtesan*, New Delhi: Vikas Publishing House, 1973.

Chattopadhyaya, Debiprasad, *Studies in the History of Science in India*, New Delhi: Ashajyoti Press, 1992.

Clark, Mathew, *The Dashnami-Samnyasis: The Integration of Ascetic Lineages into an Order*, Netherlands: Brill Leiden, 2006.

Cone, Margaret and Richard Gombrich, *The Perfect Generosity of Prince Vessantara*, Oxford: Clarendon Press, 1977.

Cone, M. and Gombrich, R.F., tr., *The Perfect Generosity of Prince Vessantara: A Buddhist Epic*, Oxford: Clarendon Press, 1977.

Cumming, Mary, *The Lives of Buddha in the Art and Literature of Asia*, Ann Arbor: Centre for South and South-East Asian Studies, University of Michigan, 1982.

Cunnigham, Alexander, *The Bhilsa Topes or Buddhist Monuments of Central India*, Vārānasī: Indological Book House (Indian Edn.), 1966.

———, *Mahabodhi or the Great Buddhist Temple under the Bodhi Tree at Buddha Gaya*, London: W.H. Allen and Co. Publisher to India Office, 1892.

———, *Archaeological Survey of India Report*, vol. I, New Delhi: Indological Book House, 1972.

Dasgupta, Sashibhusan, *Obscure Religious Cults*, Calcutta: K.L. Mukhopadhyaya, 1962.

Davids, Rhys, T.W., *Buddhist India*, London: Putnam, 1903.

Dayal, Har, *The Bodhisattva Doctrine in Buddhist Sanskrit Literature*, New Delhi: MLBD, 1970.

de Silva, Lily, 'Giving in the Pali Canon', in *The Practice of Giving*, ed. Bodhi Bhikkhu, Kandy: BPS, 1995.

de Silva Padmasiri, 'The Pathological Facets of the Culture of Economics: Does Ethics Offer a Path to Recovery and Strategies for Social Welfare', *East-West Philosophy Conference*, Honolulu, 2011.

———, *Buddhism, Ethics and Society*, Clayton: Monash Asia Institute, 2002.

———, *Environmental Philosophy and Ethics in Buddhism*, London: St. Matins Press, New York, Flanagan, 1998.

Deepak, Lal, *Hindu Equilibrium*, Oxford: Clarendon Press, 1988.

Dey, Nandulal, *Vikramaśila Monastery*, *JASB*, new series, vol. V, 1909.

Dhammika, S., 'A History of Bodh Gaya', http://www.buddhanet.net/e-learning/pilgrim/pg_histbg.htm, accessed on 6 January 2010.

Dharmadhikari, T.N., *Yajnayudhani* (*An Album Of Sacrificial Utensils With Descriptive Notes*), Poona: Tilaka—Maharashtra—Vidyapitha, Vaidika Samsodhana Mandala, 1989.

Dutt, Nalinaksh, ed., *Gilgit Manuscripts*, vol. III, pt. 1, *Mlasarvastivda Vinayvastu*, Calcutta: Calcutta University Press, 1947.

Dutt, Sukumar, *Buddhist Monks and Monasteries of India*, New Delhi: MLBD, 2000.

———, *Early Buddhist Monachism*, New Delhi: MLBD, 1996.

Egge, James, *Religious Giving and the Intervention of Karma in Theravāda Buddhism*, Surrey: Curzon Press, 2002.

Ekman, Paul, ed., *A Conversation between the Dalai Lama and Paul Ekman: Emotional Awareness*, New York: Henry Holt and Company, 2008.

Endo, Toshiichi, *Dāna: The Development of its Concept and Practice*, Colombo: Gunasena, 1987.

Falk, Nancy A., 'Exemplary Donors of the Pāli Tradition', in *Ethics, Wealth, and Salvation: A Study in Buddhist Social Ethics*, ed. R. Sizemore and D. Swearer, Columbia: University of South Carolina Press, 1990, pp. 124–43.

Findly, E.B., *Dāna: Giving and Getting in Pali Buddhism*, New Delhi: MLBD, 2003.

Foucher, A., *The Beginning of Buddhist Art and other Essays in Indian and Central Asian Archaeology*, New Delhi: Asian Educational Services, repr. 1994.

Fromm, Erich, *To have or to Be?* London: Abacus, 2001.

Ganguly, D.C., 'The North India during the Eleventh and Twelfth Centuries', *The Struggle for Empire*, Ch. II, Bharatiya Vidya Bhavan's History and Culture of Indian People, vol. III, Bombay: Bharatiya Vidya Bhavan, 1957.

Ghosh, A., *A Guide to Nālandā*, New Delhi: ASI, 1950.

Gombrich, R.F., 'Merit Transference in Sinhalese Buddhism: A Case Study the Interaction between Doctrine and Practice', *History of Religions*, 1972, pp. 203–19.

———, *Buddhist Precept and Practice: Traditional Buddhism in the Rural Highlands of Ceylon*, Oxford: Clarendon Press, 1971.

———, 'The Ethics of Intention', in *Buddhist Ethics: A Cross Cultural Approach*, ed. Charles S. Prebish, Dubuque, Iowa: Kendall Hunt Publishing House, 1992, pp. 92–111.

Gonda, Jan, 'Gift', in *Change and Continuity in Indian Religion*, The Hague: Mouton, 1965.

Gopinath Rao, T.A., *Elements of Hindu Iconography*, vol. I, pt. II, New Delhi: MLBD, repr. 1968.

Gouldner, A., 'The Norm of Reciprocity: A Preliminary Statement', *American Sociological Review*, vol. 25, no. 2, 1960, pp. 162–78.

Granoff, Phyllis, 'The Sacrifice of Manicuda: The Context of Narrative Action as a Guide to Introspection', in *Kalyanmitra*, ed. V.N. Jha, Poona: Poona University, 1990.

Grey, Leslie, *A Concordance of Buddhist Birth Stories*, London: PTS, 1994.

Grierson, George A., I.C.S., *Notes on the District of Gaya*, Calcutta: Bengal Secretariat Press, 1893.

Gringold, Elsa, 'Compassion Fatigue and How to Avoid It', in *The Power of Compassion*, ed. Marion Kostanski, Melbourne: Victoria University, 2005.

Hanh, Michael, *Haribhatta and Gopadatta, Two Authors in Succession of Āryasūra: On the Rediscovery of Parts of Their Jatakamalas*, 2nd edn., Studia Philologica Buddhica Occasional Paper I, Tokyo: International Institute of Buddhist Studies, 1992.

Hasting, James, *Encyclopaedia of Religion and Ethics*, Edinburg: T and T Clark, 1908–27.

Hazra, R.C., *Studies in the Purāṇic Records on Hindu Rites and Customs*, New Delhi: MLBD, 1975.

Heesterman, J.C., *The Ancient Indian Royal Consecration: The Rājasūya Described According to the Yajus Texts and Annoted*, S' Gravenhage: Mouton and Co., 1957.

———, 'Reflections on the Significance of the Dakṣiṇā', *Indo-Iranian Journal*, vol. 3, 1959, pp. 241–58.

Heim, Maria, 'Dāna', *Encyclopedia of Buddhism*, R.E. Buswell (editor-in-chief), New York: Macmillan, vol. I, 2003, p. 196.

Heim, Maria, *Theories of the Gift in South Asia: Hindu, Buddhist, and Jain Reflections on Dāna*, New York: Routledge, 2004.

Held, Virginia, *The Ethics of Care, Personal, Political and Global*, Oxford: Oxford University Press, 2012.

Hibbets, Maria, 'Saving Them from Yourself: An Enquiry into the South Asian Gift of Fearlessness', *Journal of Religious Ethics*, vol. 27, no. 3, 1999, pp. 437–62.

Holt, J.C., 'Assisting the Dead by Venerating the Living: Merit Transfer in the Early Buddhist Tradition', *Numen*, vol. 28, fasc. 1, 1981, pp. 1–28.

Hultzsch, E., *Corpus Inscriptionum Indicarum*, 1, Inscriptions of Asoka, New Delhi: ASI, repr. 1969.

Imam, Abu, *Sir Alexander Cunningham and the Beginning of Indian Archaeology*, Dacca: Asiatic Society of Pakistan, 1966.

Inden, Ronald, 'The Ceremony of the Great Gift (*Mahādāna*): Structure and Historical Context in Indian Ritual and Society', in *Asie du Sud, Traditions et Changements*, Paris: Etudes du Centre National de la Recherche Scientifique, 1979, pp. 131–6.

Jafri, S.Z.H., 'Madrasa and Khanqah, or Madrasa in Khanqah? Education and Sufi Establishments in Northern India', in *Islamic Education, Diversity, and National Identity: Dini Madaris in India Post 9/11*, ed. Jan-Peter Hartung and Helmut Reifeld, New Delhi: Sage Publications, 2006.

Jafri, S.Z.H. and Helmut Reifeld, eds., *The Islamic Path: Sufism, Politics and Society in India*, Delhi: Rainbow Publication, 2006.

Jayaswal, Vidula, 'Antiquity to Vārānasī as Revealed by the Excavation at Aktha (2008–9)', *Puratattva*, Bulletin of Indian Archaeological Society, no. 39, 2009, pp. 141–6.

———, *From Stone Quarry to Sculpturing Workshop: A Report on the Archaeological Investigations around Chunar, Varanasi and Sarnath*, New Delhi: Agam Kala Prakashan, 1998.

———, *Ancient Varanasi: An Archaeological Perspectives* (*Excavations at Aktha*), New Delhi: Aryan Books International, 2009.

Jayaswal, Vidula and I. Singh, 'Sculpturing Process: A Study of Past and Present', *From Stone Quarry to Sculpturing Workshop: A Report on the Archaeological Investigations around Chunar, Varanasi and Sarnath*, New Delhi: Agam Kala Prakashan, 1998, pp. 232–7.

———, 'Aktha: A Satellite Settlement of Sarnath, Vārānasī (Report of Excavations Conducted in the Year 2002)', *Bharati*, Bulletin of the Department of Ancient Indian Hisotry, Culture and Archaeology, Banaras Hindu University, 2003, vol. 26, pp. 61–180.

———, *From Stone Quarry to Sculpturing Workshop: A Report on the Archaeological Investigations around Chunar, Varanasi and Sarnath*, New Delhi: Agam Kala Prakashan, 1998.

Joel, Kupperman, 'The Emotions of Altruism, East and West', in *Emotions in Asian Thought*, ed. Marks Joel and Ames Roger, Albany: Suny Press, 1995.

Kane, P.V., *History of Dharmasåstra*, vol. V, pt. I, Bhandarkar Oriental Research Institute, Poona, 1958.

Kapoor, Rakesh and Amit Kumar Sharma, *Religious Philanthropy and Organized Social Development Effort in India*, Delhi: Indian Centre for Philanthropy, 2000.

Katz, Nathan, *Buddhist Images of Human Perfection*, New Delhi: MLBD, 2010.

Kern, H., 'The Inscriptions of Junnar', *Indian Antiquary*, vol. 6, 1877, pp. 39–41.

Keyes, C.F., 'Merit-Transference in the Kammic Theory of Popular Theravāda Buddhism', in *Karma: An Anthropological Enquiry*, ed. C.F. Keyes and E.V. Daniel, Berkeley: University of California Press, 1983, pp. 261–86.

Konow, Sten, *Corpus Inscriptionum Indicarum*, Kharoshṭhî Inscriptions with the Exception of those of Aśoka, Calcutta: ASI, 1929.

Kramrisch, Stella, *Indian Sculpture*, New Delhi: MLBD, 1933.

Kyaw, U. Ba, tr., *Elucidation of the Intrinsic Meaning, So Named the Commentary on the Peta-Stories* (ed. and Annotated by P. Masefield), London: Pali Text Society, 1980.

Laidlaw, James, 'A Free Gift makes no Friends', *Journal of the Royal Anthropological Institute*, vol. 6, 2000, pp. 617–34.

Lamotte, Etienne, *Le traité de la grande vertu de sagesse de Nāgārjuna*, 5 vols., Bibliothique du Muśeon 18. Louvain: Bureaue du Museon, 1944–1980.

Law, Bimala Charan, *Heaven and Hell in Buddhist Perspective*, Singapore: Buddhist Meditation Centre, 2010.

Lebra, Takie Sugiama, 'An Alternative Approach to Reciprocity', *American Anthropologist*, vol. 77, issue 3, September 1975, pp. 550–65.

Levbin, G. Bangard and A. Vigasin, *The Image of India*, Moscow: Progress Publications, 1984.

Levi Strauss, Claude, *The Elementary Structure of Kinship*, London: Eyre and Spottis Woode, 1989.

Lin-Bodien, C.G., 'An Early Yaksha from Aktha near Sarnath (Vārānasī, UP)', in *Chahavi* (*Rai Krishnadas Felicitation Volume*), ed. Anand Krishan, 2 vols., Vārānasī: Bharat Kala Bhavan, 1981, pp. 294–7.

Luder, H., *A List of Brahmi Inscriptions from Early Times to about* AD *400*, Berlin 1912; Vārānasī: Indological Book House, repr. 1973.

Majumdar, R.C., *Corporate Life in Ancient India*, Calcutta: K.L Mukhopadhyaya, 1969.

Majumdar, B., *A Guide to Sārnāth*, New Delhi: Government Press, 1947.

Majumdar, N.G., 'A List of Kharošṭhî Inscriptions', *Journal and Proceedings of the Asiatic Society of Bengal*, vol. 20, 1924.

Malalasekera, G.P., *Dictionary of Pali Proper Names*, New Delhi: Munshiram Manoharlal, 1937; repr. 1995.

———, '"Transference of Merit" in Ceylonese Buddhism', *Philosophy East and West*, 17 January 1967, pp. 85–90.

Malinoswki, Bronislaw, *Argonauts of The Western Pacific: An Account of Native Enterprises and Adventure in the Archipelago of Melanesian New Guinea*, London: George Routledge and Sons, 1932.

———, *Crime and Custom in Savage Society,* Totowa, NJ: Littlefield, Adams and Co., 1972.

Marshall, John, *Taxila*, 3 vols., New Delhi: MLBD, repr. 1975.

Marshall John and S. Know, 'Sārnāth', New Delhi: Archaeological Survey of India, repr. 1990.

Marshall, John, 'Excavations at Sārnāth', *Archaeological Survey of India Annual Report 1904–5*, New Delhi: Swati Publications, repr. 1990.

Marshall, John and Alfred Foucher, *The Monuments of Sānchī*, New Delhi: Swati Publications, 1982.

Mauss, Marshal, 'A Category of Human Mind: The Notion of Person; The Notion of Self', in *The Category of the Person: Anthropology, Philosophy, History*, ed. Michael Carsithars et al., tr. W.D. Halls, Cambridge: Cambridge University Press, 1985.

———, *The Gift: The Form and Reason for Exchange in Archaic Societies*, tr. W.D. Halls, New York: Norton, 1990.

Misra, V.D., J.N. Pal, M.C. Gupta and P.P. Joglekar, *Excavations at Jhusi (Pratishthanapur): A fresh light on the Archaeological Profile of the Middle Gangatic Plain*, Special Report no. 3, New Delhi: Indian Archaeological Society, 2009.

Mitra, Debal, *Ratnagiri*, vols. I and II, New Delhi: ASI, 1983.

Mookerji, R.K., *Aśoka*, New Delhi: MLBD, repr. 2002.

———, *Local Government in Ancient India*, Oxford: Clarendon Press, 1920.

Ñāṇamoli, Bhikkhu, *Path of Purification*, Taiwan: The Corporate Body of the Buddha Educational Foundation, 1996.

Nance, Richard F., *Speaking for Buddhas: Scriptural Commentary in Indian Buddhism*, New York: Columbia University Press, 2011.

Nath, Vijay, *Dana: Gift System in Ancient India: A Socio-Economic Perspective*, New Delhi: Munshiram Manoharlal, 1987.

Nath, Vishwambara, *The Universal Message in the Bhagavadgītā*, New Delhi, 1998.

Nedumpara, Jose J., *Political Economy and Class Contradictions*, New Delhi: Anmol Publications, 2004.

Newman, W., *The Bodh Gaya Temple Case: H. Dharampala vs Jaipal Gir and Others*, Proceedings of the Gaya District Court and Judgement of the High Court, Calcutta: Caxton Press, 1895.

Niyogi, Pushpa, 'Organization of Buddhist Monasteries in Ancient Bengal and Bihar', *Journal of Indian History*, vol. 54, 1976, pp. 273–98.

Norman, K.R., *The Group of Discourses*, Oxford: Pali Text Society, 1992.

———, *The Word of the Doctrine* (*Dhammapada*), Oxford: Pali Text Society, 2000.

Oertel, F.O., *Annual Report 1904–5*, Archaeological Survey of India, Delhi: Swati Publications, repr. 1990.

Ohnuma, Reiko, *Bodily Self-Sacrifice in Indian Buddhist Literature*, Delhi: MLBD, 2009.

Olivelle, Patrick, *The Origin and Early Development of Buddhist Monachism*, Colombo: M.D. Gunasena, 1974.

Pachow, W., *The Comparative Study of the Pratimoksha*, Santiniketan: Sino Indian Cultural Society, 1955.

Pande, G.C., *Vedic Samskriti* (in Hindi), Allahabad: Lokbharati, 2001.

Parry, Jonathan, 'The Gift, the Indian Gift and the "Indian Gift"', *Man*, n.s., vol. 21, no. 3, 1986, pp. 453–73.

Pathak, V.S., 'Date of Buddha's Mahaparinibbana and Inscriptions of Asoka', *Bharati* (The Bulletin of the Department of Anceint Indian History, Culture and Archaeology), ed. V. Jayaswal, vol. 26, 2002, pp. 5–28.

Pinch, William R., *Warrior Ascetic and Indian Empires*, Cambridge: Cambridge University Press, 2006.

Prebish, Charles S., 'Vinaya and Prtimoksha: The Foundation of Buddhist Ethics', in *Studies in the History of Buddhism*, ed. A.K. Narain, New Delhi: B.R. Publishing Corporation, 1980.

Rachels, J.,'Naturalism', in *Blackwell Guide to Ethical Theory*, ed. La Folette, Oxford: Blackwell, 2000.

Rahula, Walapola, *History of Buddhism in Ceylon: The Anuradhapura Period, 3rd Century BC–10th Century AD*, Colombo: M.D. Gunasena, 1966.

Rapson, E.J., *Catalogue of the Coins of the Andhra Dynasty, the Western Kshatrapas, the Traikutaka Dynasty and the 'Bodhi' Dynasty, in the British Museum*, London: British Museum, 1908.

Ray, H.P., *Monastery and Guild—Commerce under the Satavahanas*, New Delhi: Oxford University Press, 1986.

———, *The Winds of Change*, New Delhi: Oxford University Press, 1994.

Ray, Reginald A., *Buddhist Saints in India: A Study in Buddhist Values and Orientation*, Oxford: OUP, 1994.

Renfrew, Colin, *Archaeology*, London: Paul Bahn, 1991.

Roerich, George, *Biography of Dharmasvamin: A Tibetan Monk Pilgrim*, Patna: K.P. Jayaswal Institute, 1959.

Sahai, Bhagwant, *The Inscriptions of Bihar: from Earliest Times to the Middle of the 13th Century*, New Delhi: Ramanand Vidya Bhavan, 1983.

Sahlin, Marshal, *Stone Age Economics*, Chicago: Aldine Atherton, 1972.

Sahni, D.R. and Jean Philippe Vogel, *Catalogue of the Museum of Archeology at Sārnāth*, New Delhi: Indological Books, repr. 1972.

Salomon, Richard, *Indian Epigraphy—A Guide to the Study of Inscriptions in Sanskrit, Prakrit, and Other Indo-Aryan Languages*, New Delhi: Munshiram Manoharlal, 1998.

Sarao, K.T.S., *Decline of Buddhism in India: A Fresh Perspective*, Delhi: Munshiram Manoharlal, 2013.

Sarkar, Sir Jadunath, *A History of Dashnami Naga Sanyasi*, Allahabad: Sri Panchayti Akhara Mahanirvani, 1959.

Sastri, Hirananda, *Nālandā and its Epigraphic Material*, New Delhi: ASI, 1999.

Sastri, S. Sitarama, *Aitareya and Taittirīya Upaniśads and Sri Shankara's Commentary*, Madras, 1923.

Schopen, Gregory, 'Two Problems in the History of Indian Buddhism: The Layman/

Monk Distinction and the Doctrines of the Transference of Merit', *Studien Zur Indologie und Iranistik*, vol. 10, 1985, pp. 9–47.

———, *Bones, Stones, and Buddhist Monks: Collected Papers on the Archaeology, Epigraphy, and Texts of Monastic Buddhism in India*, Honolulu: University of Hawaii Press, 1997.

———, *Indian Monastic Buddhism: Collected Papers on Textual, Inscriptional and Archaeological Evidence*, New Delhi: MLBD, 2010.

Schroeder, William, 'Continental Ethics', in *Blackwell Guide to Ethical Theory*, ed. La Fotell, Oxford: Blackwell, 2000.

Seligman, Martin, *Florourish*, North Sydney: William Heinman, 2012.

Sharma, R.S., *Indian Feudalism* (*c.*AD 300–1200), New Delhi: Macmillan, 1998.

———, *Perspectives in Social and Economic History of Early India*, New Delhi: Macmillan, 1983.

Shrimali, K.M., 'Religions in Complex Societies: The Myth of "Dark Age"', in *Religion in Indian Society*, ed. Irfan Habib, New Delhi: Tulika Books, 2017, pp. 36–70.

Singer, Peter, *The Life You Can Serve*, Melbourne: Text Publishing, 2009.

———, ed., *A Companion to Ethics*, Cambridge: Blackwell, 1991.

Singh, Anand, 'Early Buddhist Order and the Lay World', in *Transformation in Indian History*, ed. S.Z.H. Jafri, New Delhi: Anamika Publications, 2009, pp. 116–26.

———, *Buddhism at Sārnāth*, Delhi: Primus, 2014.

Sircar, D.C., *Two Pāla Plates from Belwa: Plate of Vigrahapåla III*; *Regnal Year 11*, *Epigraphia Indica*, vol. XXIX, New Delhi: ASI, 1957.

———, *Select Inscriptions bearing on Indian History and Civilization, from 6th Century BC to 6th Century AD*, New Delhi: Asian Humanities Press, repr. 1986.

Sizemore, R.F. and D.H. Swearer, eds., *Ethics, Wealth, and Salvation: A Study in Buddhist Social Ethics*, Columbia: University of South Carolina Press, 1990.

Spiro, Melford, *Buddhism and Society: A Great Tradition and Its Burmese Vicissitudes*, Berkeley: University of California Press, 1970.

Srivastava, Prashant, *The Apracharajas: A History based on Coins and Inscriptions*, New Delhi: Agam Kala Prakashan, 2007.

Strong, John S., *Relics of the Buddha*, Delhi: MLBD, 2007.

Sujato, Bhikkhu Bhikkhuni, *Vinaya Studies: Research and Reflections on Monastic Disciplines for Buddhist Nuns*, Australia: Santipada Publications, 2011.

Swaris, Nalin, *The Buddha's Way to Human Liberation: A Socio-Historical Approach*, New Delhi: Sarasavi Publishers, 2009.

Tachibana, S., *Ethics of Buddhism*, London: Routledge, 1995.

Thapar, Romila, 'Dāna and Daksina in Forms of Exchange', in *Cultural Pasts: Essays in Early Indian History*, ed. Romila Thapar, New Delhi: OUP, 2000.

———, 'Patronage and Community', in *Cultural Past: Essays in Early Indian History*, New Delhi: OUP, 2000.

Thaplyal, K.K., *Aśoka: The King and the Man*, New Delhi: Aryan International Publication, 2012.

———, *Guilds in Ancient India*, New Delh: Agam Kala Prakashan, 1966.

———, *Studies in Ancient Indian Seals*, Lucknow: Akhil Bhartiya Sanskrit Parishad, 1972.

Trevithick, Alan, '"British Archaeologists, Hindu Abbots, and Burmese Buddhists: The Mahabodhi Temple at Bodh Gaya", 1811–1877', *Modern Asian Studies*, vol. 33, Cambridge University Press, 1999, pp. 635–56.

———, *The Revival of Buddhist Pilgrimage at Bodh Gayā: 1811–1949*, Das, New Delhi: MLBD, 2006.

Vogel, J.Ph., 'Buddhist Sculpture from Benāres', *Annual Report 1902–4*, New Delhi: Archaeological Survey of India, 1906, pp. 212–26.

Wadekar, M.L., *Devala Smṛti: Reconstruction and a Critical Study*, vol. I (Introduction and Text), New Delhi: Koshal Book Depot, 1996.

Wagle, Narendra, *Society at the Time of the Buddha*, Bombay: Popular Prakashan, 1966.

Ward, Glenn, *Post Modernism*, Chicago: McGraw Hill Company, 2003.

Warder, A.K., *Indian Buddhism*, Delhi: MLBD, 2008.

Weber, Max, *The Religion of India*, Glencoe: Free Press, 1958.

Wijayratna, Mohan, *Buddhist Monastic Life: According to Texts of Theravada Tradition*, tr. Claude Grangier and Stevan Collins, Cambridge: Cambridge University Press, 1990.

Wilson, H.H., *Glossary of Judicial and Revenue Terms*, London: W.H. Allen and Co., 1855.

———, *Ariana Antiqua: A Descriptive Account of the Antiquities and Coins of Afghanistan*, New Delhi: Oriental Publishers, 1971.

Winternitz, M., *A History of Indian Literature*, New Delhi: Munshiram Manoharlal, 1981; repr. 1987.

Woodward, F.L., *As It Was Said*, Oxford: Pali Text Society, 1996.

———, *Udāna: Verses of Uplift and Ittivuttaka as it was Said*, Oxford: Pali Text Society, 1996.

Yule, George, *Pragmatics*, Oxford: Oxford University Press, 1996.

Lexical Works

DPI Dictionary of Pali Idioms, Kākkāpalliye Anuruddha Thero, Hong Kong, 2004.

DPL Dictionary of Pāli Language, R.C. Childers, New Delhi, 1993.

PED Pāli English Dictionary, Rhys Davids, William Stead, London, 1959.

PSED Practical Sanskrit English Dictionary, Vaman Shivram Apte, Delhi, 1995.

SED Sanskrit-English Dictionary, M. Monier Williams, Hong Kong, 1990.

ŚSN Śabdastomamahānidhi, Sri TārānāthaTarkavācaspati, Calcutta, 1814.

Reports and Journals

Asiatic Researches (*AR*)

Bengal Regulation XXXVII of 1793 dated 1 May 1793 in Bengal Code, 5th edn., vol. 1, Bengal Government Press, Alipore, 1939.

Catalogue of Nālandā Museum
Corpus Inscriptionum Indicarum (*CII*)
Epigraphia Indica (*EI*)
Indian Antiquary (*IA*)
Indian Historical Quarterly (*IHQ*)
Journal of Numismatic Society of India (*JNSI*)
Journal of Royal Asiatic Society of Bengal (*JRASB*/*JASB*)
Reports of Archaeological Survey of India (*ASIAR*)

Index